About This Book

Why is this topic important?

Corporations, nonprofit groups, government agencies, and international organizations conduct count-less thousands of retreats every year, requiring a significant investment of time and money, for exec-utives, staff members, and board members.

Many participants are dissatisfied with the results because the retreats don't work. That is, the outcomes don't lead often enough to positive, sustainable change.

But retreats *can* work, and many do, when carefully tailored to fit the organization, designed to meet its needs, and skillfully facilitated. This book can help executives and internal and external facilitators ensure that their retreats *will* work.

Retreats are not the same as meetings. Because retreats are relatively long, delve deeply into key issues, and are fluid in structure, they require much more expertise in design and skill and nuance in facilitation than the typical meeting or conference.

And because they are costly in terms of facilities, professional facilitation fees, and staff time, they must represent a solid business investment.

Many retreats are facilitated by outside consultants, but it's also common for organizations to have managers or other staff members lead retreats. Many people who facilitate retreats infrequently may lack the experience, the confidence, or the skills needed to create the climate of trust and to deal effectively with the unexpected that are essential for a retreat's success.

Many readers of the first edition of our book told us that they found it of great help to them in designing and leading successful retreats. We received many requests from colleagues and from students in our facilitation institutes to write a follow-up volume that would contain even more guidance and exercises they could use to accomplish their goals.

This new and greatly expanded edition is our answer to those requests. It spells out in greater detail than the earlier volume how to plan and lead a retreat that gets results, from its inception through follow-up back in the workplace, and provides more than twice the number of exercises. Moreover, it contains a CD with support materials that facilitators can print out, including templates for the exercises and guidance for executives.

What can you achieve with this book?

Retreats That Work: Everything You Need to Know About Planning and Leading Great Offsites, Expanded Edition, with CD, gives you, the retreat planner, every tool you need to design and lead successful offsite retreats. This book contains eighty-one creative retreat exercises, hundreds of tips to avoid pitfalls in your retreat design and facilitation, and advanced facilitation techniques to help ensure a successful outcome.

You will learn

- How to plan a retreat that leads to positive change
- The eleven "Sins of Omission"—the biggest mistakes retreat planners and facilitators commonly make (and how to avoid them)
- How to keep participants energized and on task
- What you can do to correct course if things go wrong, even horribly wrong, at the retreat
- How to use tested exercises in a variety of retreat formats

How is this book organized?

Section One includes information and materials for the retreat designer and facilitator on such subjects as how to negotiate a successful relationship with your client (and when to advise him or her *not* to hold a retreat), how to plan and facilitate a retreat (including what to do when things go wrong), and how to incorporate innovative exercises into retreats for specific purposes such as strategic planning or team building.

Section Two contains advice for your client (which is reproducible from the CD) on how to partner successfully with the facilitator; how to determine the retreat's goals; the logistical details he or she must attend to; and his or her role before, during, and after the retreat to help ensure its success.

In addition to the guidance you can print out for your client, the CD contains templates, handouts, checklists, and other materials you can reproduce for retreat participants.

About Pfeiffer

Pfeiffer serves the professional development and hands-on resource needs of training and human resource practitioners and gives them products to do their jobs better. We deliver proven ideas and solutions from experts in HR development and HR management, and we offer effective and customizable tools to improve workplace performance. From novice to seasoned professional, Pfeiffer is the source you can trust to make yourself and your organization more successful.

Essential Knowledge Pfeiffer produces insightful, practical, and comprehensive materials on topics that matter the most to training and HR professionals. Our Essential Knowledge resources translate the expertise of seasoned professionals into practical, how-to guidance on critical workplace issues and problems. These resources are supported by case studies, worksheets, and job aids and are frequently supplemented with CD-ROMs, websites, and other means of making the content easier to read, understand, and use.

Essential Tools Pfeiffer's Essential Tools resources save time and expense by offering proven, ready-to-use materials—including exercises, activities, games, instruments, and assessments—for use during a training or team-learning event. These resources are frequently offered in looseleaf or CD-ROM format to facilitate copying and customization of the material.

Pfeiffer also recognizes the remarkable power of new technologies in expanding the reach and effectiveness of training. While e-hype has often created whizbang solutions in search of a problem, we are dedicated to bringing convenience and enhancements to proven training solutions. All our e-tools comply with rigorous functionality standards. The most appropriate technology wrapped around essential content yields the perfect solution for today's on-the-go trainers and human resource professionals.

Pfeiffer
www.pfeiffer.com   *Essential resources for training and HR professionals*

RETREATS THAT WORK

Everything You Need to Know About
Planning and Leading Great Offsites

EXPANDED EDITION

Merianne Liteman, Sheila Campbell,
and Jeff Liteman

Pfeiffer
A Wiley Imprint
www.pfeiffer.com

Library of Congress Cataloging-in-Publication Data

Liteman, Merianne.
  Retreats that work : everything you need to know about planning and leading great offsites / Merianne Liteman, Sheila Campbell, and Jeffrey Liteman. — Expanded ed.
      p. cm.
  Prev. ed. entered under Campbell.
  Includes bibliographical references and index.
  ISBN-13: 978-0-7879-8275-1 (pbk.)
  ISBN-10: 0-7879-8275-X (pbk.)
  1. Management retreats—Handbooks, manuals, etc. I. Campbell, Sheila. II. Liteman, Jeffrey. III. Campbell, Sheila.
Retreats that work. IV. Title.
  HD30.4.C355 2006
  658.4'56—dc22
                                                                                2006011519

Acquiring Editor: Matthew Davis   Manufacturing Supervisor: Becky Carreño
Director of Development: Kathleen Dolan Davies   Editorial Assistant: Leota Higgins
Production Editor: Nina Kreiden   Illustrations: Arlyne Glickman
Editor: Elspeth MacHattie

Printed in the United States of America

Printing   10   9   8

Contents

CD Contents

Acknowledgments

This book would not have been possible without the care and support of our families, friends, and colleagues. In particular, we would like to thank

- Our families and friends, whose love and encouragement sustained us throughout the challenging process of writing and editing this book.
- Our wonderful team at Jossey-Bass/Pfeiffer, including Matthew Davis, senior acquisitions editor, for his enthusiastic and deep commitment to this book; Kathleen Dolan Davies, director of development; Susan Rachmeler, senior development editor, and Samya Sattar, developmental editor, who were so helpful in the organization of this book; and Nina Kreiden, production editor, who was a joy to collaborate with and a master of flexibility reconciling our crazy work schedules with the demands of getting this book out on time; as well as Elspeth MacHattie, copyeditor extraordinaire, who helped us ensure that we were as clear and consistent as possible.
- Arlyne Glickman, who created most of the graphics for this edition.
- Our clients, who invite us into their organizations and openly share their issues and insights. They challenge us, stretch us, inspire us, and teach us.
- The students in our retreat facilitation institutes, who have helped us refine our thinking about retreats with their stimulating questions and thorny dilemmas.
- The Center for Creative Leadership's Leading Creatively program and Airlie conferences, which nourish our creative spirits and keep us learning.

- Our classmates and professors in American University's AU/NTL and Georgetown University's OD programs, who years ago gave us labs in which to try out many of our ideas.
- One another, for making co-facilitating, co-teaching, and partnering on writing this book such a joy.

Merianne, Sheila, and Jeff

Introduction

This book is for anyone who has to plan or lead an offsite retreat, whether for the first time or the umpteenth time.

This book is for anyone who wonders, "Where do I start?" It's for anyone who is concerned about keeping the discussion focused. It's for anyone who has ever facilitated a retreat and watched, stunned, as it careened off in unforeseen directions and who wants to make sure that doesn't happen again (or at least know what to do if it does).

And it's for anyone—facilitator, planner, convener, or participant—who wants to ensure that the next retreat he or she takes part in is a success, a worthwhile investment of everyone's time and energy.

Why We Wrote This Book

This book is a guide, a resource, a reference, a collection of stories and cautionary tales. It contains scores of exercises and activities—indexed and annotated by title, purpose, and type of retreat at which they work best—to make them easy to find and use.

The enclosed CD-ROM allows users to print out certain chapters in their entirety to give to their clients (or bosses) and to duplicate templates and handouts for specific exercises.

The Table of Contents provides detailed information about what is found in each chapter.

We also use three icons in the text to identify certain helpful materials.

 This icon tells you that material mentioned in the text, such as a handout, is available on the CD. It also identifies text that is duplicated on the CD and that you can print out.

 This icon identifies a *recommended resource*—a publication, Web site, or tool that may be especially useful to you.

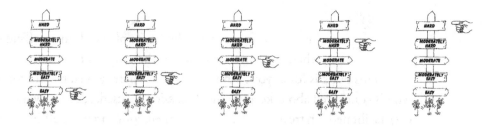

One of these icons appears at the beginning of each activity to indicate its level of difficulty to facilitate (Easy, Moderately Easy, Moderate, Moderately Hard, and Hard). Higher levels of difficulty relate to an activity's potential to raise sensitive issues that will require skillful facilitation or the need for some particular skill on the part of the facilitator, such as the ability to generate unusual idea associations quickly. When we have rated an activity as Moderately Hard or Hard, we explain the reasons in our Facilitator Notes section.

Finally, we have provided an extensive bibliography and a list of our recommended resources so experienced and novice facilitators alike can find additional information to help them do their best work.

At their best, retreats are a powerful means to bring about positive change. They provide a space where people are freed from their day-to-day flurry of activities so they can think in fresh ways. The casual dress and informal structures of a retreat create an environment where participants can get to know and learn to trust one another, explore issues more openly, and generate new ideas more creatively.

Retreats give people time to dig deeply into their organization's issues and develop appropriate strategies to address them. As a result, key decisions and plans made at retreats often have more solid and lasting support and greater impact than those made in more hierarchical meetings.

We've written this book because we love retreats that work—designing and leading them and also taking part in them—and because we've seen retreats fail when they might have succeeded.

Too many retreats have had no effect when people get back to their everyday work. People only have to experience one or two of these time-wasting offsites to flinch the next time they hear, "We're going to have a retreat."

We want to help experienced professionals and first-time facilitators alike lead retreats that will make a difference long after the participants have returned to their workplaces, so that the next time people hear, "We're going to have a retreat," they will say, "Great! I only hope it's as good as the last one."

What You'll Find in This Book

This book is full of information about retreats, gleaned from our experience (including the mistakes we have made) as designers and leaders of hundreds of offsites, from the questions we have received from the internal facilitators we train in retreat design and facilitation, from the stories related to us by our colleagues in the field, and from readers of the first edition of our book.

Whether you are an experienced internal or external consultant, professional facilitator, or human resource manager, or are facilitating a retreat for the first time, you will find all the elements you need to plan and design a retreat that works in Chapters 1 through 14. The detailed Table of Contents should help you navigate through this book easily.

We don't expect that you will read this book straight through but rather that you will pick and choose from its offerings according to your needs. Here are some examples of how you might use it.

If you are particularly concerned about *establishing an effective working relationship with your client,* we'd urge you to focus on Chapters 1, 15, 16, and 17.

If difficulty with *managing conflict or encouraging reticent participants to speak up* has been an issue in the past, you might want to read especially carefully Chapters 3, 5, 6, 7, 10, 11, and 13.

If your group has had difficulty *doing planning or making decisions during a retreat or implementing what comes out of a retreat,* we call your attention to Chapters 8, 9, 14, and 17.

If you are looking to *expand the repertoire of what you include in your retreat designs,* we'd direct you to Chapters 7 through 14, which contain eighty-one practical, tested retreat activities.

Although each activity appears in a chapter about leading a specific kind of retreat, most are suitable for almost any offsite. Please be sure to look at the various activities indexes in Chapter 18 to find the best activities for your needs. You will also find ready-to-reproduce templates and handouts for these activities on the CD that accompanies this book.

All the materials in Chapters 15 through 18 are also available on the CD so that you can give them to your client to help him or her establish the conditions to make the retreat and its follow-up a success. The Appendix to this book contains checklists and other supportive tools, which you can also duplicate from the CD for your client to use.

We wrote the first edition of *Retreats That Work* because there was no manual for us when we started leading retreats many years ago.

With the feedback we have received from readers of the first edition and from our retreat facilitation institute students, we have now greatly expanded that first book with forty-seven new activities and more information about how to design and lead retreats and also how to recover when things go wrong.

We hope this new edition will be a useful reference tool that you and your clients will come back to again and again as you design and facilitate your own retreats that work!

We welcome your feedback, suggestions, and stories of your own experiences—what worked and what didn't—with designing, leading, or taking part in offsite retreats. You can reach us through our Web site: http://www.retreatsthatwork.com

We look forward to hearing from you.

SECTION ONE

Materials for the Facilitator

Chapter 1

Working with the Client

If you earn your living facilitating retreats, you've probably noticed that not everyone thinks a retreat is the greatest thing since microwave popcorn.

When your client announces, "We're going to have a retreat," you can't expect universally positive responses. Some people will love the idea of dedicating time to talking about new ideas and maybe hanging out with more senior leaders. Others will dread the very same things. Some will recall successful retreats they've attended. Others will remember bad experiences they've had or heard about.

Retreats can make people feel vulnerable. Your client may say, "We want to hear the truth," but not every participant will believe that. Some may remember the time Sali Ann spoke out at a retreat and shortly afterward was abruptly dismissed for reasons that were never disclosed.

And many might recall that after the last retreat they attended, nothing changed—except they had more work waiting on their desks when they returned to the office.

Emotions can be exposed and expectations can be dashed at retreats. "Just let me get through these two days without getting angry," a reluctant participant might think. Another—eager but perhaps naïve—might believe, "At last I'm going to convince people to do what I've been proposing for the last six months."

Retreats often require an overnight stay; managing the logistics of being away from home can be difficult for some people.

Retreats are expensive. In addition to the costs of a site, meals and lodging, and transportation (and your fees, if you're external), organizations must tap their most valuable asset, staff time.

Moreover, retreats require a commitment to follow through after the participants return to work. The seeds planted at a retreat must be nurtured before the fruit can be harvested. If there is no follow-through, people will have spent many hours behind the plow for nothing.

Finally, retreats are risky. An ill-conceived, poorly timed, or ineptly led retreat can make ongoing problems worse and take your client's organization backward. Think of everything that can go wrong in a meeting, magnify it in intensity and duration, and that merely scratches the surface of what can go wrong at a retreat.

So why should your client incur the costs and take the risks? And why on earth would you want to get involved?

As we like to explain to our clients, retreats are investments in an organization's future. Unlike meetings, which typically focus on current issues and con-

The Terms We Use

- For the sake of simplicity, clarity, and grammar, we will use *he* and *she* interchangeably when referring to the client, facilitator, and others. Our use of these personal pronouns is completely arbitrary; both men and women play all roles in retreats.

- We use the terms *retreat*, *offsite*, and *offsite retreat* interchangeably.

- We use the word *client* to refer to the person who is convening the retreat and who has the power to approve the participants' recommendations. He or she may be a team leader, division chief, CEO, executive director, board chair . . . you get the idea.

All the stories in this book are real, though names and other identifying data of individuals and companies have been changed to preserve our clients' confidentiality.

"Retreats" That Aren't Really Retreats

Many executives think that having a retreat with no other purpose than bringing people together on a regular basis is a good practice at best and harmless at worst. It is neither. A retreat is not a company picnic, a party, a "town hall" meeting, or an executive briefing session. Referring to such events as retreats gives retreats a bad name. Participants in a retreat without a clear business-related purpose may see the offsite as a waste of valuable time that might otherwise have been spent doing "real" work.

cerns, retreats take a longer view and focus on deeper, longer-term issues. Thus, although some up-front investment is required and there are various risks, the potential payoff of retreats is considerable.

And it's a wonderful feeling knowing that you have helped an organization get back on track and have contributed to a more rewarding and productive workplace for its employees.

Differences Between Retreats and Meetings.

	Meetings	Retreats
Setting	Usually conducted onsite	Conducted offsite
Attendance	Often participants do not work together closely	Generally participants are from the same department, work group, or management level
Dress	Business or business casual	Casual
Length	Less than a day; often only an hour or so	Daylong or longer; often includes downtime for participants
Discussion size	Whole group discussion	Mix of whole and small group discussions
Purpose	Convey or exchange information or make a specific decision	Explore issues or ideas and plan for the future
Structure	Hierarchical by nature; led by one person	Participative by nature; participants talk with one another
Outcomes	Generally predictable	Generally unpredictable
Risk	Low	Potentially high
Capacity to drive change	Generally low	Potentially high
Emotional involvement	Emotions not usually in open play	Can be emotionally intense

Nine Reasons to Hold a Retreat

1. To Explore Fundamental Concerns

Suppose turnover in your client's organization is exceptionally high or staff morale low. Or the organization has seen a significant drop-off in customers or an increase in their complaints. A retreat can be the ideal forum to explore and address the underlying causes.

2. To Harness the Collective Creativity of the Group

When it is important to generate ideas for new products, services, or work processes, typical brainstorming sessions often fail to produce significant results. Retreats, free of routine workplace demands, have fewer barriers to imagination and creative thinking. The offsite setting can help innovative solutions emerge.

3. To Foster Change

A retreat can promote new approaches to strategic planning, product design, service delivery, or marketing. The open discussion that characterizes well-run retreats fosters understanding of and commitment to new directions.

4. To Change Perceptions, Attitudes, and Behavior

In every organization, people make up stories to account for things they don't understand. These stories lead to attitudes and actions that can be harmful to the organization. A retreat can be an ideal setting for participants to raise concerns and ask questions. Participants can share information, clear up misunderstandings, discuss the impact of past decisions, and modify those decisions if priorities have changed or if prior decisions failed to achieve their purpose.

5. To Correct Course When Things Are Going Wrong

Executives cannot turn organizations around by fiat. People will change only when they see that it is important to do so. Retreats provide a forum for discussions about the reasons for and the urgency of a desired change. When people play a role in deciding what should be improved, they are more committed to ensuring that the change effort succeeds.

6. To Transform the Organization's Culture or Improve Relationships Hindering Its Effectiveness

Suppose members of a team or division are having difficulty communicating effectively with one another. Or two departments seem unable to work together. Or people are afraid to tell your client what they think she might not want to hear. Retreats can help people open up to one another and can create a climate of trust.

7. To Create a Collective Vision for the Organization

Much of the tension that exists in organizations stems not from inherent personality conflicts but rather from individuals pursuing their own (and sometimes conflicting) visions of what is best for the organization. These visions often clash with one another because none of them necessarily represents the complete picture of an organization's circumstances. Retreats can foster alignment by helping participants understand and build commitment to the organization's overall priorities. Greater understanding and commitment encourages individuals to hold themselves accountable for the organization's success, not just the interests of their own work groups.

8. To Accomplish Something That Cannot Be Done by the Leader Alone

No matter how experienced and competent leaders are, they can't do everything on their own. Retreats provide an environment in which everyone can contribute knowledge, expertise, and skills to address issues that often plague and confound busy executives.

9. To Make Tough Decisions

Leaders often confront very tough decisions: Should they eliminate a signature product or service? Close down a particular operation? Reduce staff? Change the nature of a long-standing alliance? There will be greater commitment to the eventual course of action if many people from different levels in the organization have participated in

CD A1, "Is a Retreat Right for Your Organization?" lists reasons to hold and not to hold a retreat in a format that you can reproduce for your client.

deciding what to eliminate or change and how to go about doing so, rather than simply being told by the leaders what to do. At a well-led retreat, leaders receive the benefit not only of broad participation in idea generation but also of better decisions, because the group collectively will have a wider perspective and a greater number of ideas than the leader does alone.

Ten Reasons Not to Hold a Retreat

A retreat is not the best means of responding to every situation and addressing every concern a client might have.

We believe the potential for more harm than good exists if the client isn't willing to allow the kind of open and passionate discussion that is a hallmark of a good retreat. If he has a secret agenda, isn't willing to be influenced, or sees the

What Can a Retreat Achieve?

A well-conceived, well-designed, well-run retreat can

- Help change an organization's strategic direction

- Generate new solutions for old problems

- Get everyone pulling in the same direction

- Help people feel heard about issues that matter to them

- Deal with sources of overt or buried conflict

- Allow colleagues to get to know and come to trust one another

- Foster new ways of working together

- Help people see things in new ways and envision new possibilities for themselves and the organization

- Create a common frame of reference for past events and future expectations

- Contribute to creating a new and healthier culture for the organization

- Encourage people to take risks that are necessary for the organization to thrive

How many retreat facilitators does it take to change a light bulb? Just one, but the light bulb has to really want to change.

retreat as a panacea, a reward for the staff, or a ritual to endure before moving ahead with his own predetermined plans, the retreat is not likely to be a success. We recommend that you not agree to facilitate a retreat if you believe your potential client has any of these aims:

1. To Improve Morale Through the Retreat Alone

Although taking positive action based on the recommendations made at a retreat can increase participants' commitment to the organization, the client shouldn't expect that simply holding a retreat will improve morale. In fact just the opposite can happen. A retreat can have a negative impact if the issues that come up aren't dealt with appropriately, if people feel that they are not heard and their concerns are not taken seriously, if conflict is not managed successfully, if trust is violated, or if participants feel the retreat was a waste of their time.

2. To Use the Retreat to Reward People for Their Hard Work

Participants rarely see retreats as rewards for doing their jobs well. They're likely to have even more work waiting for them when they return from a retreat, juggling family needs can be difficult, and many would find time off with family and friends more rewarding than attending an offsite.

3. To Discover and Punish Non-Team Players

This is a terrible reason to have a retreat. If people sense that the leader's purpose in bringing them together is to find out who is loyal and who is not, it will erode trust and do great—if not irreparable—harm to the organization's culture.

4. To Advance a Covert Agenda

If your client tries to pursue an agenda that is different from the retreat's stated purpose, she will undermine trust in herself personally as well as in the organization. It is far better for the leader to tell participants that she has decided, for example, to cut a department's head count and to ask for their help in determining the best way to handle layoffs than for her to try to manipulate them during the retreat into endorsing her idea. When people figure out what their boss is up to (and they will!), it will foster resentment and engender much more resistance to her ideas than she would encounter if she had been truthful all along.

5. To Control the Conversation

It's counterproductive for your client to try to control what is said or who is authorized to say what. Your client must understand that just because something isn't said out loud doesn't mean that people aren't thinking it. Trying to direct what participants talk about deprives your client of strategic information he needs to make informed decisions. Putting everything out on the table and having a candid dialogue about participants' perceptions and misperceptions is better for your client and for the organization as a whole than trying to stop people from saying what's on their minds.

6. To Squelch Conflict

Some people relish conflict, but most dread it. Typically, the more people care about each other, the more averse they are to confronting conflict openly. But aiming to avoid conflict at all costs will practically guarantee that it will crop up in some form or another and that it won't be managed effectively. Successful retreats almost always involve surfacing and dealing with disagreements, disputes, or differences of opinion. If no conflict emerges, chances are participants are not being honest with themselves or with others or that the retreat is not focused on issues that are of great concern to them. Conflict is inevitable (and actually healthy) when people care about something. Your client should understand that it's key not to ignore or dismiss it. Instead, she should take advantage of your expertise to find ways of managing conflict so that its underlying causes can be explored openly.

7. To Create a Platform for the Client's Own Ideas

Retreats provide a valuable opportunity for leaders to hear from others. Coach your clients not to squander it by doing too much of the talking themselves. It is best for leaders mostly to listen to what others have to say, and to repress their inclination to lead discussions, persuade others, and resolve disputes.

8. To Disregard What Participants Recommend

There is nothing more demoralizing to participants than being led to believe that they have a role in the decision-making process, only to learn that key decisions were preordained. Participants will naturally expect that their leader will take their advice into consideration before reaching a decision, and that if he doesn't accept their recommendations he will explain why. If an executive asks participants to rubber-stamp decisions that he has already made, or if after the retreat he announces and attributes to the participants decisions they didn't make or ideas they didn't generate, the effect is likely to be very destructive.

9. To Defend the Client's Point of View, Promote the Client's Position, or Maintain the Status Quo

Retreats are associated with change in most people's minds. If your client wants things to stay the same, she should have a meeting to encourage everyone to keep up the good work or throw a party to thank everybody for a job well done. We advise our clients to reserve retreats for times when they'd like things to be different. And remember, the first person who is likely to have to change is your client. If you detect no willingness to explore more productive leadership practices on her part, discourage her from holding a retreat.

10. To Merely Keep Up the Tradition of Having Annual Retreats

Many clients think that having a retreat with no other purpose than to bring everyone together on some regular basis is a good practice at best and harmless at worst. It is neither. A retreat is not a company picnic. Frivolous offsites give retreats a bad name. We urge our clients not to plan retreats unless they have serious purpose in mind.

And, for us, a retreat is not a conference. A parade of presentations by in-house or outside experts can provide valuable information or training, but it doesn't constitute a retreat. It's certainly important that people be well informed, but a retreat—at least as we use the term in this book—is about sparking change, not just absorbing or exchanging information.

This isn't to say that we're against an "annual" retreat if it serves a serious purpose. Your client might be able to take advantage of a tradition of holding regular retreats to accomplish some important things. No matter how retreats may have been conducted in the past, you can work with your client to structure the next one to address key issues that are of genuine concern to him and to the participants.

We believe you can't be successful as a retreat facilitator unless you are willing to walk away from a client, no matter how potentially lucrative, if a retreat is not the right tool for the organization at the time.

When Is a Retreat Not the Right Tool?

Don't agree to facilitate a retreat if your client intends to

- Use the offsite just to improve morale

- Reward people for their hard work

- Punish non-team players

- Advance a covert agenda

- Control the conversation

- Avoid conflict

- Create a platform for her own ideas

- Disregard what participants recommend

- Defend his point of view, promote his position, or maintain the status quo

- Merely keep up the tradition of having annual retreats

What If the Client Is Your Boss?

We recommend, if at all possible, that you avoid facilitating a retreat for your supervisor. It is almost impossible to be perceived as neutral under these circumstances, and few internal facilitators feel comfortable standing up forcefully to their boss when the boss's behavior is hampering the group's effectiveness.

It is far better to ask an internal facilitator who does not report to your boss to lead the retreat, to partner with an external facilitator who won't have the same credibility issues vis-à-vis your supervisor or the group, or to leave the facilitation entirely to an external facilitator.

> For guidelines on how internal facilitators can contract with their supervisors, see *The Skilled Facilitator*, by R. M. Schwarz (1994, pp. 289–293).

Aligning Yourself with the Client

Although it is your responsibility to design and lead the retreat, you must be fully aligned with your client—the person who has called for the retreat to take place. Otherwise you may end up with a design that's elegant but inappropriate. No matter how well or how often you design and lead retreats, you cannot afford to plunge ahead with your vision at the expense of your client's. Keep in mind that you have never designed this particular retreat before. However many successes you have enjoyed in the past, each retreat is an adventure into uncharted territory.

But what if your client isn't sure what he wants? Beware of trying to design and lead a retreat with no explicit change goal.

In some situations the client will be your primary contact; in others he will delegate that responsibility to someone else, such as the director of human resources. Even if the client wants you to work closely with another person when you are planning the retreat, however, you must have sufficient access to the client throughout the process so you can be sure that you are working to meet his expectations, not someone else's understanding or interpretation of his wishes.

It is equally important that you and the client agree that you will plan and facilitate the retreat with the organization's and the participants' overall interests in mind, not just the client's. The client should be willing to have you inform the participants that you are working on everyone's behalf. He should understand that the offsite will fail if it is seen merely as a tool to advance his own agenda.

You and the client must be clear about what you expect of one another. The client, for instance, has the right to expect that your retreat plan will

The terms *agreed-on outcomes* and *desired outcomes* refer in general to what the client and the participants want to be different as a result of the work done at the retreat and to why the client wants to hold a retreat. They do not suggest any specific decisions or recommendations the client might have in mind.

- Be suitable for the participants, taking into consideration their level of experience and expertise and their comfort level with certain types of activities
- Focus sharply on delivering the agreed-on outcomes (based on the client's goals and what you learn from your pre-retreat interviews or surveys)
- Engage the participants, so they are strongly committed to the decisions or recommendations they make
- Use participants' time wisely
- Allow for changes if something unexpected happens, but still move the group toward the desired outcomes
- Include time to discuss how decisions reached or recommendations made at the retreat will be implemented and integrated into the organization's work

You also need commitments from the client, particularly that

- He has no hidden agenda. If he hopes certain decisions will come from the participants, he has to let go and see if his hopes are realized—and be willing to proceed even if they are not.
- You will have access to him and other retreat participants in advance to solicit their input.
- He will make available to you all relevant documents (such as staffing patterns, organization charts, previous studies, internal and external surveys, reports from other retreats, and the like) that you might need.
- He intends to implement the action plans agreed to.
- Participants will not be punished (by him or anyone else in the organization) for expressing their opinions.
- You will have the freedom to "design in the moment" to ensure that the retreat stays on track toward meeting its goals.

- You will not be asked to violate participants' confidentiality or make an assessment of any individual's loyalty, competence, potential, or behavior.

Urge your client to express his desired outcomes for the retreat in observable terms so that both you and he will be able to tell whether these outcomes have been achieved. Desired outcomes shouldn't be a hidden agenda. Your client should be willing to disclose his overall goals for the retreat to the participants.

You may need to ask him some pointed questions to make sure you'll be helping the group address core issues, not merely symptoms of the problems they're experiencing. Facilitators are often presented with issues that appear to be process problems ("Wayne and Andrés don't get along with each other") when what is underneath may be a much more basic problem ("Wayne and Andrés don't agree on the priorities for our business").

You will need an explicit understanding from the client about the kinds of decisions that can be made at the retreat. Participants are often asked to come up with new ideas without being given the authority to make final decisions about what will be implemented. If this is the case the client will have to make the boundaries clear to the participants up front, saying, for instance, "At this retreat we're going to explore issues and come up with alternatives to resolve them, but we won't make the final decisions about how to proceed. Our recommendations will go to Stan and the rest of the management team for their consideration."

It's very important that you and the client understand one another's roles and that you trust each other. It's critical, for example, that the client accept that you will be leading the retreat and that he will be a participant. You don't want to find yourself in a situation where you are engaged in a tug-of-war with the client in front of the group. Discuss this thoroughly in advance with your client. How and when will you give your client feedback if you see him doing something that could endanger the retreat's success? (We encourage you to print out Chapter 16, "Your Role at the Retreat," from the CD, and ask your client to look it over; it can focus this dialogue.)

Make sure the client knows how you plan to lead the retreat. He may not like surprises. Discuss with him the extent of your participation.

For instance, because we conduct many creative thinking retreats, we have sharpened our own skills at generating innovative, even off-the-wall ideas that in turn often spark even better ideas from the participants. We need to know whether the client would like us to contribute ideas or just facilitate the participants' idea-generating process.

When we take an active part, the organization often ends up with more diverse ideas, but sometimes the client (or the group) does not want the facilitator involved with the issues. If we think we have content expertise to offer in a given situation, we discuss in advance with the client and, if possible, the group what role they want us to play, instead of simply jumping in and offering our expertise.

You cannot forecast every situation that will occur at a retreat, so it is critical that you and your client talk about anything that either of you is concerned about. You must understand one another, and both you and your client must feel comfortable with how you will handle unexpected situations that might occur. Know your client's hot-button issues. What are the sensitive topics on which you will need his guidance? How will he respond to negative feedback from participants? How will you and he check in with one another during the retreat to make sure you are on track with his expectations? There will often be little time to confer with your client if a discussion suddenly takes a turn he does not like, so you should know in advance how you will handle such situations.

Checklist for Partnering Effectively with Your Client

Here are some questions we keep in mind to ensure that our relationship with the client is on track:

☐ Are we clear on exactly who our client is within the organization?

☐ Are the client's expectations of us clear? Do we know what specifically the client wants from us?

☐ Do we and the client agree on the outcomes for the retreat?

☐ Are we and the client in alignment about the balance between the business concerns and the interpersonal issues that will be addressed at the retreat?

- [ ] Will the client respect our need to protect the confidentiality of the people we interview?

- [ ] Do we and the client concur on whose desires and needs should be taken into account in planning the retreat?

- [ ] Does what the client want or need from a facilitator match our skills? Can we deliver the results the organization requires?

- [ ] Can we be open with this client? (Or do we feel the need to impress him or her or to hide our concerns?)

- [ ] Are we neutral about the culture (rather than being staked in particular outcomes)?

- [ ] Do our personalities fit well with the client's? (Do we and the client like one another? Do we and the client trust one another? Are we and the client candid with one another? Do we want the client to succeed?)

- [ ] Do both we and the client feel free to walk away from this relationship if it's not productive? (Or are we financially overdependent on the client? Or is the client overdependent on our expertise and unwilling to do the hard work himself or herself?)

- [ ] Does the client seem to value our perspective and expertise?

- [ ] Does the client seem interested in his or her potential contribution to issues the organization is facing?

- [ ] Is the client willing to listen to our questions and concerns?

- [ ] Does the client have realistic expectations of us (and of the retreat) in terms of our ability to "fix" the organization?

- [ ] Do we and the client see one another as partners? (Or is there a hierarchical relationship?)

- [ ] Is the client willing and able to give us access to people (including key decision makers) and information so we can understand the full picture?

- [ ] Does the retreat seem more important to us (or to others in the organization) than it is to the client?

- [ ] Are the budget and the time allocated for the retreat sufficient for the agenda the client has in mind?

- [ ] Do we have enough access to the client to get our needs met and our questions answered?

- [ ] Is the client willing to take prudent risks for the good of the organization?

- [ ] Is the client willing to change?

- [ ] Is the client committed to implementing what is agreed to at the retreat?

We know of no better resource to guide you in contracting with your client than Peter Block's classic text, *The Flawless Consulting Fieldbook & Companion* (2001).

Kinds of Retreats

You will need to ascertain from your client the kind of retreat he or she is planning to convene. There are many kinds of retreats, each with its own characteristics and special planning concerns that you will have to take into account as you develop your retreat design. Some of the most common are described in the following section.

Executive

In an executive retreat top managers get together without other employees, usually to chart strategic direction, measure progress against goals, foster teamwork within their group, establish new priorities, or make key decisions. The CEO frequently takes the lead in setting the retreat agenda.

Board or Board and Staff

Board retreats typically are used to align the actions of the staff with the priorities set by the board or to help the board members understand strategic and operational issues faced by the staff. Because of this board-staff interrelationship, such retreats usually include some or all of the organization's senior staff in addition to the board members. Occasionally a board will want to hold a retreat without any staff members present. That might occur if the board is focusing on sensitive topics such as its own dynamics or effectiveness, its relationship with the senior staff, or the need for succession planning in a founder-run organization.

Single Department

Retreats for a single department are often scheduled when a new department head arrives, when the organization's leaders have mandated performance improvements, or when the department needs to measure progress against goals and establish a strategy and priorities for the coming year. Such retreats can be very helpful in focusing everyone on the new goals and involving the whole department in determining the best ways to meet them.

Interdepartmental

Occasionally people from two or more departments in the same organization jointly convene a retreat to devise better ways of working together. Because there's no hierarchical relationship between the departments, one challenge for participants in such retreats is to maintain the course decided on when everyone goes back to the pressures of the everyday work environment.

Teamwork

Managers frequently want to convene retreats to improve teamwork. The casual nature of retreats encourages people to get to know and understand each other better. We believe that the best way to build teamwork at the retreat is not through formal team-building exercises but by having participants work together to solve real workplace dilemmas and enhancing skills that transfer back to the office.

Associations and Membership Organizations

Because people in key positions in nonprofit associations and membership organizations are often volunteers who don't work together every day, retreats can be a highly effective way of gathering the paid and unpaid leadership in one place to address broad issues.

Customer or Vendor

Organizations sometimes wish to bring together important shareholders, customers, vendors, or clients. Such retreats can help a new partnership start on the right foot or can strengthen an existing relationship.

Whole System

At times organizations want to bring their entire workforce or even all their stakeholders, including customers, vendors, regulators, or community activists, together at an offsite. The goal of such a retreat is usually to reach a common understanding of key issues and foster better working relationships.

Creativity

Organizations are increasingly using retreats to spark creative thinking about their products, services, and processes. Specialists in creativity often lead these retreats, sometimes at facilities designed for that purpose. A creativity segment may also be a component of another kind, such as a strategic planning retreat in which participants learn creative thinking techniques and then immediately apply them to solve real problems.

Fixed Format

Certain retreats follow a fixed format that serves specific purposes. These formats include large systems interventions, such as Future Search® and Open Space®; real-time simulations; and General Electric's Work-Out™ program, which has been used by many organizations to focus their managers on performance and change issues.

Using a Specialized Retreat Format

Some clients will have a particular specialized retreat format in mind. They may propose that you facilitate a prepackaged methodology designed to address issues that are common to most organizations. Typically, such a specialized format can be used either by itself or in conjunction with custom-designed segments.

We believe that the best retreats are tailor-made to fit an organization's specific needs, and in Chapters 3 and 4 we'll walk you step-by-step through the process of planning and custom designing a retreat that will get results.

We have, however, successfully integrated specialized retreat formats into longer retreats when we felt that this would be the best means of addressing the organization's concerns.

Certain specialized retreat formats require that the facilitator be trained and certified in their methodology. Thus, if a client requests one of these specialized formats or if you are interested in using one, you will have to become certified or work with another facilitator who is certified to lead it.

What follows is not a comprehensive list of specialized formats, but it will give you an idea of the choices available for you to consider.

Specialized Retreat Formats

Large system interventions. A large group of participants (perhaps 100 or more), representing a broad range of stakeholders, work through a predesigned methodology.

Open Space Technology. Participants design their own agenda at the retreat itself.

World Café. Participants engage in a series of rotating conversations about topics of significant interest to them.

Simulations. Participants engage in highly realistic exercises that provide a springboard for assessing organizational issues.

Appreciative inquiry. Participants build on past successes to create plans for the future.

Outdoor experiences. Participants engage in exercises that require them to work as a team.

Work-Out. A structured process guides participants to suggest performance improvements.

Large System Interventions

Large system interventions are sessions in which many people—often more than a hundred—representing many different segments of an organizational system (and sometimes the entire organization) gather to explore and plan for change.

One of the best-known large system interventions is the three-day Future Search. Although the originators describe Future Search as a conference or meeting, its highly experiential approach makes it very similar to a retreat.

What is unusual about a Future Search conference is that stakeholders from all groups affected by the organization participate. For a nonprofit health clinic, for instance, participants might include not only the clinic's leaders, but also board members, employees, patients (including former patients and potential patients), referral sources, government health officials, volunteers, individual donors, clinic neighbors, representatives of charitable foundations, complementary services such as food banks and housing agencies, media, vendors, churches, and other organizations that serve the same constituency.

If you want to learn more about Future Search, we recommend *Future Search: An Action Guide to Finding Common Ground in Organizations and Communities,* by Marvin R. Weisbord and Sandra Janoff (1995). If you are considering using this technology, however, we strongly advise you to get trained by one of the founders. See also www.futuresearch.net.

Having all these voices in one room for a concentrated focus can have a major impact on the organizations involved, helping them find common ground and new ways to support one another's work.

Open Space Technology

Open Space is a method developed by organization consultant Harrison Owen. In Open Space participants design and conduct their own retreat sessions. Open Space is particularly appropriate for retreats where, as Owen says in his book *Open Space Technology* (1997b, p. 15), "A diverse group of people must deal with complex and potentially conflicting material in innovative and productive ways. It is particularly powerful when nobody knows the answer and the ongoing participation of a number of people is required to deal with the questions."

Harrison Owen does not certify facilitators. He offers his methodology for anyone who cares to learn it by reading his books *Open Space Technology: A User's Guide* (1997) and *Expanding Our Now: The Story of Open Space Technology* (1997). Nevertheless, Open Space requires a specific set of conditions for success and expert, confident facilitation.

At the beginning of an Open Space session the participants themselves determine the topics they would like to address and the individuals who will convene various subgroups to discuss each topic. Then participants decide which subgroups they will take part in to discuss the issues that are most important to them. This sounds (and sometimes seems) chaotic, but it takes place in a well-structured environment. There is a formal process for involving the entire group in the work that has taken place in the individual sessions, so all participants have the opportunity to discuss any topic.

Open Space is not suitable for every situation. It will not work in an organization where the leader wants to maintain tight control. It yields a different result than tightly structured retreats do, one that often can't be foreseen but that does very accurately reflect the group's concerns.

World Café

World Café is a method developed by Juanita Brown and David Isaacs for creating collaborative dialogue.

The format is flexible and can be used for groups of any size as long as there are at least twelve participants. There are seven guiding principles for facilitating an effective World Café:

- Clarify the context.
- Create a hospitable environment.
- Explore questions that matter.
- Encourage everyone's contribution.
- Connect diverse perspectives.
- Listen together for insights and deeper questions.
- Harvest and share collective discoveries.

The World Café conversations take place in small groups of four to five participants. Participants talk about issues that matter to them and to the organization and they draw their key ideas on paper tablecloths. In the course of several rounds of conversation, people move from table to table, carrying themes from their previous conversations with them. In a whole group conversation at the end, participants share key themes and insights.

Much like Open Space, World Café is not suitable for environments where there is a predetermined answer, where detailed information gathering and action planning is the goal, or where the time for conducting the conversations is very limited. It works very well, however, when the group wants to explore a topic in depth and increase buy-in for the outcomes.

For more information on this methodology consult *The World Café: A Resource Guide for Hosting Conversations That Matter,* by Juanita Brown and The World Café Community (2002), and also visit www.theworld cafe.com.

Simulations

A simulation is a structured activity in which participants must confront problems and work to find solutions. Simulations are usually built around a realistic narrative that challenges participants to respond to changing circumstances or new information. The best are interactive and engaging and can be adapted to address multiple issues of the sort that arise in most organizations.

Simulations are most commonly employed as training tools, but some can be used to great effect to help participants recognize patterns that characterize their workplace interactions. In addition, they can help participants gain specific insights or skills they need to achieve their goals for the retreat. Be aware, however, that most simulations take several hours to run and debrief, so you will

Barry Oshry's perspectives on organizations are outlined in *Seeing Systems: Unlocking the Mysteries of Organizational Life* (1996) and *Leading Systems: Lessons from The Power Lab* (1999), books that come out of his experience leading an intense six-day residential program called The Power Lab. We highly recommend Power & Systems' certification program, which is a prerequisite for leading an Organization Workshop. For more information on the Organization Workshop, go to www.powerandsystems.com.

want to use them only in retreats that last longer than a day. And some can come across as "games," which participants may resent "playing."

A number of companies produce off-the-shelf simulations that can provide a framework around which to build an offsite retreat. One of our favorites is the Organization Workshop: Creating Partnership®, developed by Barry Oshry, cofounder of Power & Systems. The Organization Workshop takes a minimum of half a day to facilitate and debrief but can establish an extremely useful framework for addressing communications, cooperation, and teamwork issues in an experiential way. We are certified to present this workshop and have found it particularly useful as a part of retreats for organizations that are struggling with turf battles or lack of cooperation and coordination between departments.

This highly engaging simulation centers on an organization exercise in which participants are randomly selected to be top executives, middle managers, workers, or customers who must then interact in a rapidly changing, high-pressure environment. The simulation is interrupted at key points to provide participants with practical strategic frameworks that help them understand what they are experiencing and how they can apply what they have learned to what happens in their own organizations. Some of our clients have told us that they found this experience transformational.

The Center for Creative Leadership and Discovery Learning have co-created an excellent and highly flexible simulation called EdgeWork®, which can be run in four to six hours. Participants start the simulation "day" with an in-basket of internal memos, newspaper articles, and reports but are quickly drawn into a breaking crisis. EdgeWork can help an organization examine its habitual ways of managing both its everyday work and the critical problems that it must address.

One interesting dimension of the EdgeWork scenario is that it explores not only internal issues but also the relationship between two companies, one a manufacturer of a high-tech product and the other a service company that uses the manufactured product. When used by an organization engaged in strategic alliances, EdgeWork can draw attention to how these critical relationships work.

For more information about EdgeWork go to www.ccl.org.

Another often-used simulation for fostering teamwork and rethinking processes is Paper Planes, Inc.® Participants work together to manufacture paper planes; as the simulation runs, people observe the impact of how they choose to organize their work and cooperate with each other.

And Pfeiffer (our publisher) offers several one- and two-hour survival simulations in which groups must make individual and joint choices about items they will need to survive in dramatic situations such as being stranded in the Himalayas or the Amazon or lost at sea. These simulations emphasize the synergy obtained through joint effort. In addition, you can use these simulations to help groups explore organization issues such as communication, leadership, power and authority, decision making, and conflict management.

You can find out more about Paper Planes, Inc., at www.discovery learning.com.

You can find out more about these simulations at www.pfeiffer .com/Wiley/CDA (enter the keywords "survival simulation").

Appreciative Inquiry

Appreciative Inquiry (AI) is a methodology that in the words of its primary originator, David L. Cooperrider (1995), uses "the best of the past and present" to "ignite the collective imagination of what might be."

Appreciative Inquiry flips traditional problem solving on its head. Rather than focusing on problems—identifying them, finding their causes, deciding on possible solutions, and taking action to overcome them—groups following the AI approach explore what they do well, envision possible scenarios for the future, discuss what they would like to see happen, and come up with innovative solutions that are grounded in current successes. Appreciative Inquiry has been combined very successfully with Future Search conferences when applied to large systems.

When skillfully facilitated, AI works particularly well in organizations that have undergone difficult transitions. We used it to stunning effect in a retreat for an organization that had gone through a poorly managed downsizing. For the first time, employees who were frightened, cynical, and burned out were able to talk about what they did best and what they aspired to for the future. This

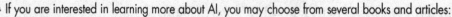

If you are interested in learning more about AI, you may choose from several books and articles:

- *Appreciative Inquiry Handbook: The First in a Series of AI Workbooks for Leaders of Change,* by David L. Cooperrider, Diana L. Whitney, and Jacqueline M. Stavros (2003), contains many AI tools as well as templates, session outlines, and exercises.

- *Appreciative Inquiry: Change at the Speed of Imagination,* by Jane Magruder Watkins and Bernard J. Mohr (2001), provides background on AI theory, case studies, and design help for AI sessions.

- *Lessons from the Field: Applying Appreciative Inquiry,* edited by Sue Annis Hammond and Cathy Royal (1998), offers background on AI, case studies from organizations around the world, models, interview guides, and practical applications, such as using AI for strategic planning.

was the beginning of a process that allowed a healthier organization to emerge, something that had eluded the executives in the postdownsizing problem-solving sessions they had convened.

There is no formal training required to lead an Appreciative Inquiry retreat, but when you're using it for the first time you are more likely to be successful if you work with a co-facilitator who is skilled in this methodology.

Outdoor Experiences

Many companies offer outdoor experience programs that combine a physical experience, such as white-water rafting, ropes courses, rock climbing, horseback riding, obstacle courses, hiking, and so on, with facilitation in teamwork, risk taking, and leadership.

Feeding the Zircon Gorilla and Other Team Building Activities, by Sam Sikes (1995), contains several outdoor activities that can be enjoyed by people of all physical abilities.

For many groups and individuals, an outdoor adventure can be a memorable and exhilarating event. Even so, it may not lead to sustained change in the workplace. Moreover, a physically challenging company-mandated experience could prove embarrassing or very difficult for some participants and actually be counterproductive. We believe in the value of conducting some retreat sessions outdoors to stimulate fresh thinking, but we prefer lower-key activities that are focused on real workplace issues, such as engaging in a creative thinking exercise while taking a stroll in a natural setting. In any case, any outdoor program should be selected carefully, keeping in mind the physical abilities of all who will be there and verifying that the facility you work with is experienced, licensed, bonded, and well insured.

Work-Out

Work-Out sessions, which were developed by Jack Welch when he was CEO of General Electric in the 1980s, provide a mechanism to involve management and employees in open dialogue about an organization's strategies. The aim of a Work-Out is to improve processes by eliminating bureaucracy and non-value-added work.

Typically, a Work-Out is a structured two- or three-day process for multilevel, cross-functional teams of twenty to fifty people. The teams participate in a progressive series of large group and breakout discussions.

One premise of Work-Out, as described in *The GE Way Fieldbook* (Slater, 2000), is that the teams will get quick approval from decision makers about the recommendations they offer. At the end the teams meet with top managers to report their conclusions.

> Work-Out is a rigorous methodology for changing an organization's work processes. It is not typically used for a single retreat but may form the framework for a series of sessions. General Electric uses academics and others trained in its system as facilitators. If you are interested in using Work-Out, we recommend that you partner with another facilitator who is experienced in this process.

The Pitfalls of Fixed-Format Retreats

You aren't likely to buy a sweater that doesn't fit just because you like the color or because someone you know has one just like it. As useful as fixed-format methodologies can be under the right conditions, we can't urge you strongly enough not to use one unless you are confident that it's the best way to address your organization's particular concerns. Here's an example of how a fixed-format retreat can go wrong.

A consultant we know, we'll call him Steve, signed a contract to lead a fixed-format retreat for a company that had just undergone a radical downsizing. The client told Steve that the retreat would be a morale builder for the staff, and Steve took the client at his word.

About two hours into the retreat a participant stood up and confronted Steve: "What the hell does this have to do with our circumstances? I've got twice as much work as I used to have. I don't see how any of what we're doing here is going to make it easier for me to do my job tomorrow."

If the format had been flexible rather than fixed, Steve might have been able to stop the action at that point and acknowledge that person's concerns. He could then have facilitated a candid discussion about what had changed in the company since the downsizing and how the group members might be able to work together to relieve some of the pressure they were experiencing in its wake.

Instead, Steve was trapped in the fixed agenda he had agreed to with the client. He didn't have much information about the company or the option of responding in the moment to what had come up. "I'm sorry," he said. "I don't really know anything about your circumstances. This is the retreat I was hired to lead." Of course he lost the respect of the group, and the retreat just deepened employee cynicism.

To avoid such a disaster at the retreats that you lead, we encourage you to negotiate with your client for the flexibility to custom design a retreat that is tailored to fit her organization's circumstances and to alter it in the moment if necessary to accomplish your client's goals.

Chapter 2

Planning the Retreat

Y ou may be concerned (or perhaps even anxious) about how you will manage issues that arise at the retreat. How will you handle a particularly sensitive topic if it comes up just as you are coming to closure? How will you deal with an uncooperative or disruptive participant (or several)? How will you move the group forward if the boss goes on and on? What if you forget someone's name, or if the room's too small, or if lunch is served at just the wrong time? Thorough planning will help you manage and perhaps head off problems that might arise at the retreat. If you skip any chapter of this book, it shouldn't be this one.

Pre-Retreat Interviews with Participants

Never put on a blindfold to cross a busy highway in the middle of the block. And never—repeat, never—agree to design or lead a retreat without having conducted some independent research to assess what's on participants' minds.

Many years ago, when we first started doing this work, the president of a small Canadian company—let's call it Maple Leaf, Inc.—asked us to design a staff retreat. To save money, the company's president, Jane, suggested that we talk with her—and her alone—about the company's issues and work climate. Foolishly, we agreed.

Jane painted a picture of a happy, harmonious work environment. (Okay, we should have seen through this right away, but we didn't.) Teamwork was great, she reported, morale high, and turnover low.

On the second day of the retreat, we broke the staff into small groups and asked each group to come up with a creative way to illustrate what was positive about the company's culture. All went well until the last group made its presentation. In an amazing show of bravado, this group announced, "The truth must be told." And then each person in turn recounted a story about how the staff felt abused by management. Everyone in the room sat in stunned silence.

Had we interviewed staff members in advance, we would have picked up signals that Jane was out of touch with the staff's perceptions. We then would have designed a retreat that addressed the real problems. Unfortunately, by the time the issues surfaced, it was too late for the group to explore them in any constructive way.

We learned a very important lesson from this horrifying experience: the client does not have all the information you need.

And sometimes the client isn't aware of, isn't forthcoming, or doesn't care about how others in the organization feel about having the retreat. The client might believe that the staff members who report to him are looking forward to discussions of the issues and might not realize that other employees are dreading these discussions because they know the boss will, once again, dominate them.

Or members of a board of directors may think that planning retreats are a waste of busy people's time, whereas the staff of the organization feel it's crucial to have the board's guidance on which projects they should take on and which opportunities are not a good use of the organization's resources. Some participants will be less enthusiastic than others about the retreat, and it's important to find out what is on people's minds to ensure that your retreat design will incorporate their concerns.

There are many viewpoints represented in every organization, and you need to hear lots of them. Before designing the retreat it is critical to talk with all or at least a healthy sample of the people who will take part. Besides keeping you from being blindsided, such interviews will foster greater commitment among participants to the retreat's success. When participants can express their hopes and concerns about the organization and the retreat itself, they are less likely to view the experience as being manipulated by management and more likely to feel they have a stake in a positive outcome.

When a retreat has between ten and twenty participants, you might interview all of them before you begin designing. How many participants you interview is ultimately a judgment call based on perceived need, available time, and cost. You might also speak with people who will be affected by the outcome but who will not be at the retreat, such as participants' subordinates, people in other departments, customers, or other external stakeholders.

The interviews can be conducted in person or over the phone. Somewhat counterintuitively, we have found telephone interviews to be a remarkably effective and efficient means of eliciting information prior to a retreat. It surprised us at first to learn that people are often more comfortable speaking candidly over the phone (if they have privacy) than in person. (We suggest that people who work from cubicles use an unoccupied office or conference room for these calls or speak with us from home.)

Observing the group in action—at a staff meeting, for example—can also provide invaluable data about how group members interact with one another and with their leader and also how they manage conflict and divergent viewpoints. This is a particularly useful additional assessment process when a major purpose for the retreat is to build relationships or improve the workplace climate, though it is not, in our minds, a substitute for interviews.

Although focus groups are popular, they don't usually result in the same degree of candor or wealth of information as one-on-one conversations. If you use focus groups, you'll want to supplement them with at least some individual interviews.

Written surveys can also be helpful in collecting information from a large group, in generating quantifiable data, and in protecting respondents' anonymity, but they don't permit the follow-up questions that a skilled interviewer can ask in the moment to clarify or expand on an interesting point. In some situations you might conduct interviews with a cross section of participants and supplement these with surveys completed by all participants. This is particularly effective when you are dealing with a group that is too large to permit all participants to be interviewed individually yet you know it is important to gather everyone's perspective.

Here are some suggestions for conducting effective pre-retreat interviews:

- Establish with the client in advance that you will not reveal to him, or to anyone else, who tells you what during the interviews. Then stand your ground if pressed.
- To foster the necessary candor, assure everyone you interview that you will be reporting broad themes only and will not disclose what any individual tells you or report something in such a way that others might discern who said what.
- In preparing your interview questions, keep in mind that you are not conducting a scientific survey. Different people have different areas of expertise and interest, so you don't need to ask each person identical questions. Moreover, if you conduct, say, half your interviews and get pretty much the same information from most of the people you talk to (assuming they have been randomly selected), use your time in subsequent interviews to explore new ground.
- Don't be afraid to abandon your carefully prepared list of questions if you hear something intriguing. See whether following that new thread opens new perspectives.
- Listen for common themes. Pay attention to the ideas and concerns that come up repeatedly.
- Don't express your own opinions during the interviews. Don't agree or disagree with what you hear, and don't talk about what you've learned from others, even if you conceal identities. Any of these actions could affect what people tell you and thus skew your conclusions.
- Don't be afraid to ask for an explanation of an unfamiliar event, word or phrase, abbreviation, or acronym. If you don't understand something, ask for clarification.
- Don't ask too many questions or you will be inundated with more information than you can analyze, synthesize, and feed back. And don't allow interviews to drag on for more than an hour if you can help it. You are busy and so are the interviewees.

- Listen to the answers. Really listen. Often you will get better data by following up on something someone says than by simply going on to the next question on your list.
- Take notes as you go; don't rely on your memory and assume you can record the important points after the interview is over. (We usually make a point of telling people up front that we are making notes.)

Particularly in telephone interviews—perhaps because they feel more anonymous—people will often talk openly about their relationships with others in the organization. They may express sharp opinions about the abilities of the company's leaders or about their colleagues ("I can't believe that Barbara doesn't see how uncooperative Glen and Carlyn are"). Don't try to steer people away from these personal comments. Listen, but don't comment on, confirm, or dissent from any negative allegations. Your goal is simply to get a sense of what people think and how they feel.

Some people may see the interview as an opportunity to send a message to management by telling you something they expect you to repeat. Don't allow yourself to be used as a conduit for covert messages. A senior manager once told us in an interview, "If Joe doesn't promote me to vice president by the end of the year, I'm leaving. I already have two job offers for more money than I'm making now." That comment had nothing to do with the retreat, and it wasn't our role to report it. If she wanted Joe to know she was thinking about leaving, it was her responsibility to tell him—not ours.

It's a good idea to interview the client last so that you won't be overly influenced by his comments when you speak with others. Interviewing the client last also allows you to probe him about issues—without disclosing specifics—that emerged in your interviews with other participants. This will give you important information about the extent to which the client's point of view corresponds with the perspectives of others who will participate in the retreat.

In Chapter 4, "Reporting Your Findings," pp. 78–83, we help you organize what you have learned in your interviews to present the information at the retreat.

Sample Interview Questions

Here are some of the interview questions we often ask. This list is far from exhaustive. We encourage you to adapt the questions or substitute others that better suit the needs of the organization you are working in or with and that are most likely to advance the retreat's purpose. Open-ended questions will often yield the most useful information. Order your questions in a logical progression so your interviews will flow naturally, like conversations.

- What do you think is most important to accomplish at this retreat?

- What might impede the group's ability to achieve that outcome?

- [*If this group has held retreats before.*] What did you find most helpful at the last retreat? What, if anything, did you find troubling or frustrating about the last retreat and the actions that resulted from it?

- What words would you use to describe your experience at [your organization]?

- What do you think is going well at [your organization]? What do you like most about it?

- How would you describe relationships among the staff? Between staff and management? [Or between the staff and the board?]

- In every organization there is some conflict, disagreement, or difference of opinion. How is conflict or disagreement handled at [your organization]?

- If you had the power to change anything at [your organization], what would you change?

- Of the changes you said you'd like to see, are there any that you think would not be possible? Why not?

- How do you feel about taking part in this retreat?

- If you have any concerns about what might take place, what are they?

- Is there anything else you think I should know, anything I haven't thought of asking, or anything you'd like to add to something you said before?

Identifying the Scope of Issues and Creating the Retreat Plan

A retreat is limited in time, so it must also be limited in scope. The more sharply focused it is, the more likely it is to be productive.

Many issues will be raised during the interview process. Understanding them will help you guide the group through its decision-making processes and bolster participants' ability to identify and tackle potential obstacles to their action plans. But you will not be able to address all—or even most—of the participants' issues at the retreat itself.

> Chapter 4 describes each segment you will need to consider when creating your retreat plan.

We find it most effective to talk with the client in our initial meeting (and throughout the process, as we gain a better grasp of the issues) about what might be accomplished at the retreat. When we believe we have gained clarity on the client's expectations for the retreat, we always verify our understanding with the client. "Will you consider the time well spent," we might ask a client for a board retreat, "if at the end we have clarified the roles of each committee, agreed on a new reporting structure, and laid out an action plan for putting the new structure into place?"

Once you have identified and reached agreement with the client on the issues the retreat will address, you can begin to create your design. The design spells out exactly what you are planning to do (emphasis on *planning* to do) at the retreat, hour-by-hour, including the start and stop times for each activity and the methods by which you will assign people to each breakout session (see "Assigning Participants to Groups," pp. 52–53 in this chapter). The finished design will include lists of what you will need, such as supplies, flip charts, a laptop and projector, and so forth, and the room setup requirements for each segment.

> One useful method for looking at the whole retreat in the planning stage is to lay out the design elements on a wall or flip chart using Post-it Notes. This will give you maximum flexibility to add, remove, and rearrange exercises before committing the design to paper.

We strongly recommend that you not share the details of your retreat plan with the client. Instead, provide him with an overview of what you intend to do. It's best if everyone (including the client) experiences the activities without advance preparation. Also, you must be prepared to abandon a set plan and go with what is happening in the moment, so you don't want the client to be counting on going through every point in your original agenda or sticking to a set hour-by-hour schedule.

Who's Who in Planning a Retreat

To call a meeting, someone sends out a memo or e-mail, reserves a conference room, distributes an agenda, and perhaps makes arrangements for refreshments. A good meeting takes planning, but the process of organizing one is fairly routine.

A retreat isn't as easy; it often takes weeks or even months to plan and organize. And there are very specific roles different individuals must play. Even people who don't attend have a part in determining whether the retreat will be successful. An individual may assume more than one role, but it is critical to ensure that each role is filled and carried out properly.

Your Client—The Retreat Convener

This is the person who decides to hold the retreat. He or she might be the board chair, the CEO, a department head, or a team leader. Almost always the convener is someone who is senior (or at least equal) in title to most of the people who will participate. In fact this relative position matters. People are more likely to see a retreat as important if the person who initiates it is a senior executive.

Sometimes the convener is a group of people—the board of directors, the membership committee, the new markets task force—who jointly agree they need to hold an offsite.

The convener is not just the initiator of the retreat but must also oversee the action plan that comes out of it. He or she will have to commit to ensuring that the plan that emerges from the retreat is implemented, or the effort and expense that went into the offsite will have been wasted. Just as planning takes some time before the retreat, the implementation process, which we discuss in Chapters 14 and 17, can last for several months or longer.

The Facilitator

As facilitator you design and lead the retreat. You might be an external consultant, an internal consultant from the company's human resource or organization development department, or a staff member from another department. In rare cases the facilitator might be the same person who convened the retreat (although we recommend against this).

You plan the flow of the event. Your design focuses on What will we do? and How will we do it? You consider which activities will most likely guide the group to the desired outcome, and you allocate time for each one. You create a plan for the retreat from beginning to end, as well as for what has to be done in advance, such as surveys, interviews, or pre-retreat reading and other assignments.

Sometimes clients want the design and facilitation functions performed by different people. For instance, if you're an internal consultant, you might hire an external consultant to help you design a retreat and then you would lead it. Or, as an internal facilitator, you might create the agenda, alone or in concert with some of the retreat participants, and hire an external consultant to lead the retreat. Or an ad hoc committee might design a retreat for an outside facilitator to lead. None of these scenarios is ideal in our experience. Carrying out someone else's design isn't like being an actor speaking the playwright's words. It's more like putting on someone else's clothes, which may be a different style and size from yours. The facilitator must understand the designer's vision and intentions, and when these two roles are not carried out by the same person, this is an extraordinarily difficult thing to do.

The Administrator

The administrator is responsible for finding a site for the retreat; determining a date that's convenient for intended participants; arranging rooms and travel; planning meals and breaks; and handling logistics, such as ordering audiovisual (AV) equipment, seeing that the meeting room is set up properly, and so forth. For overnight retreats the administrator may have to assign sleeping rooms, coordinate evening social and recreational activities, and maintain a list of emergency contact numbers. This is a key job.

The administrator must work closely with the facilitator because logistical details contribute greatly to the success or failure of a retreat. The facilitator may have special needs, such as extra breakout rooms, unintrusive morning and afternoon breaks, an overhead projector, or a certain number of flip charts that the administrator will need to know about. And the administrator should advise the facilitator of any unique opportunities or challenges the site might offer.

The administrator should be present during the retreat, if at all possible, to handle any last-minute glitches. This will allow the client to be a full-time participant and will keep the facilitator free from extraneous distractions. The facilitator and the participants have a limited amount of time to accomplish the work of the retreat, and the administrator can keep seemingly minor but important details such as a sudden need for more markers or a misunderstanding about how many chairs are needed in the breakout rooms from stalling progress.

In small organizations an internal facilitator or participant might handle the administrator role but avoid this arrangement if you can. It is very frustrating for the flow of a discussion to be interrupted because the facilitator or a participant has to deal with a mix-up over what time lunch is supposed to be served. And whether you are an internal or external facilitator, it is unlikely that you will have the authority to make decisions that involve expenditures of the client's money.

The Reporter

For action plans to be carried out after the retreat, organization members must have a record of what was discussed and decided and what action steps were agreed on at the retreat. This is important both for participants and for people who were not present at the retreat but who will be affected by the outcome.

For more information on how to collect and report the results of the retreat, see Chapter 3, "Capturing the Work Product," pp. 67–69.

There are several ways to capture what occurs at a retreat. One is to save all relevant flip charts. Most commonly, someone transcribes the charts after the retreat and distributes copies to the participants and others who might be involved in implementing the action plan. Some organizations even take the key charts back to the office and display them in prominent locations.

In addition, some clients like to have someone take notes of the proceedings to distribute after the retreat. Sometimes a nonparticipating employee is assigned to take and distribute the notes, but having a nonparticipant write everything down can be inhibiting to the spirit of the retreat. For that reason we suggest that one or more of the participants take notes of the key discussions, decisions, and action plan elements, if the flip charts are not a sufficient record.

Ideally, reporters should be volunteers. If people must be designated to fill this responsibility, remember that note taking is not a secretarial function and should not routinely be assigned to clerical staff who might be among the participants.

The Participants

In Chapter 15 we discuss how your client might determine who should take part in the retreat. Whoever the participants are, however, they have to understand that despite the casual atmosphere, a retreat is real work and each person is expected to make an active contribution to that work. No one should be present merely as an observer, critic, or judge.

The Uninvited

When your client convenes a retreat and determines whom to invite, she is also making a decision about whom not to invite. Unless all members of an intact work group are invited, someone is going to be left out—and most likely will feel left out. It will be vividly noticeable to those who weren't invited that some people are out of the office and, as one person told us, "The rest of us are stuck here covering their work."

Neither you nor your client can prevent those feelings, but she can minimize them by communicating broadly the goals of the retreat and why she invited the people she did. If appropriate, she might ask you to interview or survey nonparticipants so their concerns can be represented at the retreat even if they are absent.

The Feelings of the Uninvited

Prior to a retreat we facilitated in which senior managers planned to formulate a company's response to a crisis that had been covered broadly in the media, we interviewed participants and a cross section of staff members who were not invited to the offsite. Several staff members expressed resentment that Anita, the CEO, seemed not to value their ideas. We communicated the depth of their concerns to Anita, who had thought that staff members wouldn't want to be involved in formulating the company's crisis response strategy. When she learned that staff did want to contribute their ideas, she expanded the list of participants, and the retreat was more successful as a result.

It's only human nature for the people who aren't present to speculate about what's being discussed. Naturally, they will have questions, so you should work with your client to devise a plan, either in advance or at the retreat itself, to communicate as much as possible as soon as possible after the retreat. Help the client think about how to involve those who didn't attend in refining and carrying out the decisions that were made.

Although the people who are not invited won't be physically present, the retreat participants should still take their interests and concerns into account. For example, are you coming up with more work for people who aren't in the room? An old Southern saying goes, "Don't let your mouth write a check that my body's gotta cash." That may be how the people back at the office will feel if the group returns from the retreat with an action plan . . . for them.

Involving Participants in Retreat Planning

Any change initiative generates some anxiety in an organization, and a retreat is no exception. The leader's actions prior to the offsite will have a good deal of influence on the level of anxiety generated and thus on the success of the retreat.

Your client may decide on her own whether or not to hold a retreat and where and when it will take place. She alone may also determine the retreat's purpose. This approach has the obvious advantage of efficiency, but it isn't a sign of willingness to include others' perspectives.

It is far better if your client consults with others in the organization about these questions. This way she will hear a range of ideas as well as concerns about the retreat or its timing. This more collaborative approach may also help squelch rumors, reduce anxieties, and generate broader support for the retreat's goals. This approach demands busy people's time, however, and because decisions typically take longer when many people contribute to them, requires more advance planning.

No matter how collaborative your client tends to be, coach her to keep everyone in the loop as decisions are made. This helps set the stage for a successful retreat. She should communicate the purpose of the retreat in writing to everyone in the organization (or in the department if she is a department head)—not just to those who will take part—at the earliest possible moment. As a practical matter, she should announce the dates and place of the retreat well in advance so participants can arrange their personal and business commitments. And if people will have to share rooms, that should be made public as well.

Ask the client to send a memo to participants and nonparticipants alike introducing you as the facilitator and describing the retreat planning process. This memo should make it clear that you will be working for the good of the entire organization, not just for the client or the small group of retreat participants. It should outline your role before, during, and possibly after the retreat.

Informing Participants About Decisions That Affect Them

One of our clients, Heather, was hired to head a large department of a nonprofit organization that she knew had a history of fractious relationships. Heather decided it would help build team spirit if the retreat were held at one of the organization's project sites. Because this group rarely traveled to see the projects the organization sponsored, they were very excited about this aspect of the retreat. The only downside was that the project site was so remote there weren't enough sleeping accommodations for participants to have single rooms. Staff members were furious to learn when they arrived at the offsite that Heather had asked her assistant to make sleeping room assignments so that people who didn't get along or didn't know each other well would share rooms. Heather hoped that this arrangement would help people come to know and like one another better. Quite a bit of the goodwill Heather had generated by scheduling the retreat at a project site was diminished by not informing or consulting staff members in advance about the sleeping arrangements.

If you will be conducting interviews or surveys, the memo should emphasize your guarantee of anonymity and a promise from the client (or the head of the organization, as appropriate) that there will be no negative consequences for providing candid responses to the interview and survey questions or for speaking honestly at the retreat itself.

Sample Memo

I am pleased to announce that Virginia Rodriguez of the Theta Group will lead our upcoming retreat for department heads. The purpose of this retreat is to explore ways to make our operations more customer-friendly so we continue to increase our monthly sales.

Virginia will help us perform a purposeful self-examination and make decisions about how best to meet the needs of our customers while improving work processes for ourselves.

This initiative will build on previous studies and efforts to improve our operational effectiveness. In the end, all employees—not just the department heads who will attend the retreat—will be asked to make recommendations for change. Therefore Virginia will be taking everyone's perspective into account as she designs the retreat.

Virginia's work with us will consist of three phases: (1) assessment, (2) a two-day retreat for department heads, and (3) support for staff, as needed, to implement the changes that we decide to make as a result of the retreat. [A post-retreat phase may or may not be included in your initial agreement with your client.]

During the assessment phase Virginia will be interviewing everyone who will be attending the retreat and a cross section of other staff members. If Virginia calls you for an interview, please respond candidly to her questions.

Virginia will respect your confidence and will not disclose any comments that could be attributed to a specific individual. She will share her findings with participants at the retreat, but in summary only and without attribution.

The second phase of this initiative will be a two-day offsite retreat for department heads, which will take place October 6 and 7 at the Berkeley Center, about an hour and a half from here. Retreat participants will receive the logistical details soon.

Everyone's candor and openness are key to the success of this initiative, and there will be no repercussions for anyone speaking his or her mind to Virginia during the interviews or publicly at the retreat itself.

I expect that we will use this retreat to address the most pressing concerns facing our staff as we seek to redesign our customer relationships and operating procedures. I hope everyone will take part in this initiative with open minds and a commitment to making our company the best it can be.

Deciding Whether to Work with a Co-Facilitator

There are advantages and disadvantages to having more than one facilitator in the room.

Is Co-Facilitation Right for You (and for the Client)?

We like working with co-facilitators and believe that when two facilitators collaborate well, clients benefit from an equation in which one plus one equals more than two. It's exhausting for one facilitator to monitor many things at once, and over the course of a multiday retreat even the most seasoned facilitator is likely to become fatigued and may miss something important.

When two facilitators work together effectively, they trade off responsibilities seamlessly. While one is setting up an activity, for example, the other may be scanning the room to make sure everyone understands the directions. Or each can watch for different behaviors that might be interfering with the group's effectiveness. Or one can be working with one breakout group, and the other with another.

Facilitators are human beings. We all have our blind spots and emotional triggers. Working with a colleague can help any facilitator see the whole picture and respond appropriately. And co-facilitators can give each other feedback that will help both of them improve how they interact with the group.

It's disastrous to the group's effectiveness, however, when facilitators are not in sync. To avoid such messiness, co-facilitators must take the time to negotiate how they will work together *before* they agree to lead a retreat. If they find they have values differences or if they don't think they can work collaboratively, they should *not* lead a retreat together.

Sometimes it happens that the client will want you to co-facilitate with someone else of his choosing—an internal facilitator who knows the organization well or another external facilitator with whom the client has had experience. Don't agree to this arrangement until you have had a chance to decide for yourself if your style and the proposed co-facilitator's style are compatible. And don't ignore your gut feelings. If you sense that the person wouldn't be a good match for your skills and temperament, don't allow your client to persuade you to co-facilitate with him or her. It's far better for you to decline to facilitate a retreat than to be forced into a partnership that could be destructive for the organization and damaging to your reputation.

The members of every facilitator team will have to establish their own norms for working together, but the important thing is to have these discussions and reach agreement in advance. Here are some of the things we recommend discussing with any potential co-facilitator:

- If the facilitator who is not leading the retreat at a particular time wants to add a point, how do you prefer that this be done (if at all)?
- How open are you to changing the agenda in response to what is happening in the room?
- When do you believe it's important to intervene and when do you like to leave things up to the group?
- How do you want to handle our differences of opinion if they occur in front of the group?
- What are some of the things you do particularly well as a facilitator? Are there areas of your facilitation skills you would like to develop? Can I help you in some way to sharpen those areas?
- When one facilitator is presenting in front of the room, what do you think the other should be doing?

There is more information on how to co-facilitate successfully in Chapter 6, "Co-Facilitation Challenges," pp. 122–123.

Considerations for Internal Facilitators

An internal facilitator might want to work with an external colleague on occasion. Perhaps, as an internal facilitator, you are interested in strengthening your own facilitation skills by collaborating with someone who has more experience, or you might want to enhance your credibility with the group so you can lead post-retreat sessions successfully. Or the size or complexity of the group might require two facilitators.

Internal facilitators often opt for partnerships with external consultants because an employee of the organization may be perceived (often unfairly) as more biased about outcomes than external consultants. In addition, when an internal facilitator challenges something the boss says, she runs the risk—which an external facilitator does not—of appearing insubordinate or disloyal. By the same token, if an internal consultant agrees with or goes along with something the boss says, she may be seen as currying the boss's favor. And often it's easier for an external consultant to stick to the pledge of confidentiality than it is for someone whose continued employment may depend on doing what the boss wants.

Experienced external consultants can more easily negotiate how they will work with the client and senior management, both behind the scenes and in front of the group. For instance, when we lead retreats, we use our role as objective outsiders to coach executives on what behaviors might foster or hinder the success of the retreat. If the actions of a senior manager seem counterproductive to the work of the retreat, we are able to take that person aside during a break and discuss our concern, something that might be difficult for an internal facilitator to do.

The internal facilitator in such an arrangement can contribute a deeper knowledge of the organization and its culture and a greater acquaintance with the people in the room. The external facilitator contributes expertise in designing and leading retreats as well as a more independent status.

Often the reasons for two internal facilitators to partner with one another are similar to those for an internal and an external facilitator to work together. For example, the retreat might require two facilitators but the organization cannot afford to hire outside expertise. Although two internal facilitators can work effectively together, they should discuss in advance how they will collaborate to overcome this arrangement's potential liabilities. These drawbacks include the perception that one, or both, are biased, that they are not free to stand up to an overbearing executive, or that they may compete with one another for top management's attention.

For individuals preparing for co-facilitation, we recommend these resources:

- *The Skilled Facilitator: Practical Wisdom for Developing Effective Groups*, by Roger M. Schwarz (1994, pp. 286–288), has a comprehensive list of questions for co-facilitators.
- *Masterful Facilitation*, by A. Glenn Kiser (1998, pp. 192–195), outlines effective partnering principles for co-facilitators.

Thinking About Logistics

Because the client will usually decide where to hold the retreat, you and she should discuss your needs and preferences before she chooses a venue. The client will need to know the ideal space size, whether smaller rooms are needed for breakout sessions, the room setup that is most conducive to the desired outcome, and what AV equipment is necessary. You don't want to turn up at the retreat site to discover that the meeting rooms are too small or too few or that the facility doesn't have the equipment you need.

It's also a good idea to discuss how flexible the timing of meals can be, so you won't be in the middle of an important discussion while participants' food is growing cold in the dining room.

Years of leading retreats have led us to observe that there's something about sitting around a big table that inhibits free-flowing communication. When people talk across tables, they perceive the conversation as "official" and are more cautious in offering opinions. The most effective setup is often chairs arranged in a circle or—for small groups—living-room-like settings where participants sit in comfortable sofas and chairs. It's all right if participants don't feel quite comfortable without a table in front of them. Retreats should push participants at least a little beyond their comfort zones.

A retreat is not a place for Robert's Rules of Order. The group's own ground rules will be enough.

Tables without tablecloths (called *hard surface tables* by conference centers) are more easily rearranged than covered tables are and provide a better surface for writing and drawing.

When a particular activity demands that people be seated around tables, the most conversation-friendly arrangement is to have six to eight people at small round or rectangular tables. Then you can move people around to different tables for various segments of the work. Avoid long board-style tables or U-shaped table arrangements. Those setups encourage formality, and people tend to settle into "their" places and may be reluctant to change seats.

Virtually all retreats have some small group breakout sessions. Although the facility may be able to provide separate rooms for such sessions, we suggest you keep all the action in one large room if possible, so you can monitor what's going on. A very large room will accommodate people pulling their chairs together to work in various groupings without interfering with one another. They may also be able to spill into a wide hall or sitting area if the main room is too small to accommodate all the breakout groups, or they may be able to work outdoors (weather permitting).

Using Nametags

We recommend using nametags, even when the participants know each other (and sometimes you can't be sure of this anyway). Tags foster the use of first names and will help you keep participants' identities straight. (You should wear one as well.) The type of tag doesn't matter all that much, but keep in mind that stick-on tags are hard to reuse after lunch or on the second day. We recommend tags that slip inside plastic cases that pin or clip on. (The ones that hang around the neck inevitably seem to twist so the back faces out and then they can't be read.)

Managing Flip Charts and Markers

It's helpful for each breakout area to have its own flip chart and markers, although many facilities charge for each easel and flip chart pad so the client may prefer to request as few as possible. In that case give each group a pad or just a few loose sheets of flip chart paper to tape to the wall and write on.

Here are some points to keep in mind about flip charts:

- No matter how much flip chart paper you think you will use, ask the client to order two or even three times as much. It is easy to return if you don't use it, but nothing stops a retreat faster than running out of paper.
- Use nonadhesive flip chart paper and old-fashioned masking tape. Although the sticky-backed 3M flip chart pages are convenient to put up on the walls, they stick to each other very inconveniently when you take them down to prepare the retreat report. Moreover, Post-it Notes don't adhere well to the self-stick 3M paper.
- Make sure easels have a solid back. Easels made for displaying signs and artwork are very difficult to write on.

Preparing Flip Charts in Advance

Good-looking, easy-to-read flip charts communicate volumes about the care and thought you put into preparing the retreat. If you are not naturally gifted at creating eye-catching flip charts, there are resources to help you. PowerPoint slides may be easier for the artistically challenged to create, but you can't hang them on a wall for reference. We find that in the technically advanced world many of us work in, people are, ironically, more drawn to handmade charts than computer-made slides. And you don't have to depend on equipment that could malfunction.

If you want to learn the principles of effective graphic communication, we recommend the following books:

- *Flip Charts: How to Draw Them and How to Use Them*, by Richard C. Brandt (1986), contains an excellent tutorial on how to print attractively and legibly, use color to best effect, and ensure that the overall effect is balanced and pleasing to the eye.

- *A Picture's Worth 1,000 Words: A Workbook for Visual Communications*, by Jean Westcott and Jennifer Hammond Landau (1997), will teach you lettering, simple drawing techniques, and overall flip chart design.

- *101 Ways to Make Meetings Active: Surefire Ideas to Engage Your Group*, by Mel Silberman (1999, pp. 43–44), offers excellent tips on creating better flip charts.

- Don't depend on the retreat facility to supply flip chart markers. Facilities rarely supply enough markers, and inevitably, some of those few will be dried out. Purchase new markers; a good rule of thumb is to bring one new dark marker for every participant.
- Make sure you have enough dark-colored markers. Boxes containing assorted colors typically include yellow, light green, pale blue, pink, and other colors that can't be seen on a flip chart from more than a foot away. Black, red, dark blue, deep green, and magenta work best.

Assigning Participants to Groups

Determining the breakout group assignments in advance saves time at the retreat and helps ensure that the groupings are varied, though there will be times when it's preferable not to preassign participants to groups (see further discussion on this point in Chapter 5, pp. 90–93). There are many inventive ways to move participants into small groups. Depending on the number of participants and your tolerance for momentary chaos, these are some options you might consider:

Stickers on Nametags. One simple method is to put various stickers on people's nametags that indicate their groups for each activity. (This method requires that you get the nametags in advance from your client or that you make the nametags yourself. It adds to your workload before the retreat, but it can make things much easier onsite. An added advantage of making your own nametags is that you will be able to read them. Sometimes the print on client-generated nametags is tiny!)

When you use stickers to specify which groups participants are assigned to for different exercises, you can move people into subgroups quickly. ("All the tigers go to room A; all the zebras to room B," and so on.) Although you might think retreat participants would find such stickers childish, in our experience they get a kick out of them (and often want to take their nametags back to the office). Stickers with a variety of symbols—animals, fish, birds, objects—can be found in office supply stores, party stores, toy stores, and elsewhere. Or you can steal them from your five-year-old.

Puzzle Pieces. You can give every participant a piece of a puzzle and ask each person to find other participants who have the pieces needed to complete the puzzle. The puzzle might be an actual picture puzzle or cards with word associations, so that one person has a card that reads "France," for example, and others have cards with words associated with France, such as "The Eiffel Tower," "Croissant," "The Louvre," and the like. The puzzle might consist of panels from a multipanel comic strip or lines from a poem, a song, or a limerick. Or the puzzle could be made up of different categories of things, with one group having pieces related to musical instruments, another having pieces related to kitchen utensils, and the like. This takes longer than simply going where the symbol on one's nametag indicates, but it's a great energizer.

Objects. You can give all the participants who are to be in the same group the same object, such as the same kind of Post-it pad, playing card, candy, or Beanie Baby.

Making Sounds. You can hand participants slips of papers with sounds they should make or songs they should sing, and they then find others who are making the same sound or singing the same song.

To find other inventive ways to get people into groups, we recommend

- *Getting Together: Icebreakers and Group Energizers,* by Lorraine L. Ukens (1997).
- *50 Creative Training Openers and Energizers,* by Bob Pike and Lynn Solem (2000).
- *Energize Your Audience: 75 Quick Activities That Get Them Started . . . and Keep Them Going,* by Lorraine L. Ukens (2000).

The Facilitator's Toolkit

Certain basics belong in every facilitator's stock of supplies. No matter how dependable the retreat facility seems, we always bring these things with us:

- Several sets of fresh markers, in black, blue, green, and red.

- Two sizes of Post-it Notes, in multiple colors, one pad of each size for every participant, plus about 20 percent extra.

- Extra nametags; some participants will lose their tags, and someone you were not expecting may turn up at the retreat (it happens!).

- Several rolls of masking tape.

- Colored labeling dots (for "voting" on choices; see Chapter 8, "Types of Retreat Decisions," pp. 169–170).

- Bell, chime, whistle, or whatever you like to use to indicate the beginning and ending of timed exercises or to get the attention of people who are engaged in animated discussions.

- A clock or timer (so you won't have to keep looking at your watch during timed exercises).

Creating the Conditions for Success

No matter how experienced the staff of a retreat facility are and how many conversations we have had about how we'd like the room to be set up, we always arrive at the retreat site very early (at least two hours before the participants are scheduled to arrive) to ensure that everything is in order. Sometimes, when a retreat is scheduled to begin first thing in the morning, we like to get there the afternoon before, before the staff have left for the day.

It's important that we're not fiddling around with room setup or wondering where the bathrooms are when the participants turn up. We want to be focused, centered, calm, and ready to greet participants in a casual and friendly manner, rather than seeming frenzied, preoccupied, distracted, and distant.

You'll develop your own rituals for centering yourself so that you are in a frame of mind to attend appropriately to the group. It might be taking a deep breath, making sure you greet everyone personally, or reminding yourself that you have planned this retreat carefully with the participants' best interest in mind and that you will help them create a conducive environment for accomplishing their work. A good night's sleep the evening before doesn't hurt either. Whatever you choose, make sure that you take a moment to look inward before plunging ahead with the agenda.

The first impression you create will linger with participants, so take time to think about how you (or your client) will get participants' attention, begin to build rapport, and start the session.

Inspecting the Meeting Room

- *Room arrangement.* Are the chairs and tables set up exactly as you planned? If not, move them now.

- *Room ambiance.* Is the temperature comfortable? If not, find out how it can be changed. Is the lighting appropriate? If not, what are your options for creating lighting that is more conducive to your work?

- *Your materials.* Is there a table for your own notes and supplies? Has the facility provided the supplies you requested, such as pads of writing paper, markers, and masking tape?

- *Wall space.* Where will you post flip chart pages as they are filled? Is access to the walls blocked by tables, chairs, or lamps? Will you have to post charts on windows? Where will you put charts as the walls fill up? If the facility has restrictions on posting flip charts on the walls, how will you manage that?

- *Equipment supplied by the facility.* Do you have the right number of easels and pads of flip chart paper? Are the pads full, or do some have only a few sheets left? Are easels placed where they need to be, or are they blocking people's view of one another? Is all the AV equipment you ordered in the room and set up properly? Does it work? (Don't take anyone's word for it; test it yourself.) Do you have extra bulbs for your projector?

- *Markers.* If you haven't brought boxes of new markers, have you tested every marker supplied by the facility and discarded those that are dried out?

- *Facilities.* Do you know where the bathrooms are? Where the snacks will be set up? Where (and when) lunch and dinner will be served?

- *Participant place setups.* Are the supplies—markers, writing pads, and pens or pencils—and handouts that participants need in place? Do you have extras in case they're required?

- *Outdoor space.* Do you have access to outdoor space? If so, how is it set up? How far is it from your meeting room? Will participants be able to use it for small group work without taking too much time moving back and forth?

Using Behavioral Assessments

Behavioral assessments are profiles of personality characteristics, preferences, and habitual behaviors. The best assessments have been thoroughly researched for *validity* (the assessment measures what it claims to measure) and *reliability* (a person taking the assessment repeatedly would tend to score the same way each time).

Assessments of individual personality characteristics can be used in any retreat where the focus is on interpersonal effectiveness and personal growth, such as offsites convened for team building or culture change. Assessments that focus on conditions in the organization may also provide useful data for retreats focused on culture change, creative thinking, and strategic planning.

We occasionally use behavioral assessments during a retreat to spark discussions about individual thinking styles and habits that may be affecting people's ability to work together effectively. Such instruments can help participants identify and resolve communication or conflict issues. For example, you might use an assessment as a springboard to help group members discuss the level of trust, degree of cooperation, appropriateness of leadership styles, or patterns of communication within their organization.

In designing the retreat, keep in mind that the best and most reliable instruments usually take time to administer and skill to debrief. Factor that into your planning, and include assessments only if they are the best means of accomplishing the objectives.

Using Assessments Skillfully

Because assessments collect and draw conclusions from data in what appears to be an objective manner, participants often view the results as highly credible or even definitive. However, even with instruments whose validity and reliability have been thoroughly tested (the only ones you'll want to use), it's important to emphasize that the results are still fundamentally subjective.

Make it clear to participants that assessments are nearly always descriptive, not prescriptive. Depending on how accurately the participants answer the questions, the results might describe how things are in the present, but they don't necessarily project or limit how things might be in the future. Point out that

Examples of Assessment Instruments

If you are interested in using an assessment at a retreat, you might consider one of these instruments:

- *Campbell Leadership Descriptor.* This inventory (Campbell, 2002a) explores nine components of organizational leadership: six task components (*vision, management, empowerment, diplomacy, feedback, entrepreneurialism*) and three personal components (*personal style, personal energy, multicultural awareness*). *The Campbell Leadership Descriptor Facilitator's Guide*, by David Campbell (2002b) (no relation to the coauthor of this book of the same name), includes developmental activities, such as case studies and action planning templates, appropriate for a peers-only or a culture change retreat (see Chapters 10 and 13). A participant workbook is also available (Campbell, 2002c).

- *Communication Skills Profile.* This instrument assesses the elements of skillful expression (*slowing my thought processes, making myself understood, testing my conclusions*). It also explores a person's ability to listen and understand others (*listening constructively, getting to the essence, exploring disagreement*). Those taking this assessment are asked to rate their skills in these six dimensions and then compare their self-analysis with their scores on the instrument. In a retreat focused on building a team or improving the culture of the workplace participants might give one another feedback comparing their self-assessment with a peer assessment of strengths and areas that might improve. (See Chapters 10 and 11 for activities that we recommend in such retreats.) The *Communication Skills Profile*, by Elena Tosca (1997), is available through www.pfeiffer.com.

- *KEYS: Assessing the Climate for Creativity.* Created by Theresa Amabile (1995; also see Amabile, Burnside, & Gryskiewicz, 1997) for the Center for Creative Leadership (CCL), KEYS assesses an organization's climate for creativity. It measures characteristics identified in extensive research as prime determinants of creativity in the workplace, such as the amount of autonomy people have and how supportive their supervisors and work groups are. In our experience, KEYS also provides an outstanding framework for discussing such issues as morale, productivity, and effective work practices. In addition, because KEYS is an organizational rather than an individual assessment, it allows a comparison of the ways in which various departments and hierarchical levels perceive the work environment. KEYS is available to users who have been qualified by the Center for Creative Leadership. The instrument must be completed before the retreat in time for it to be scored by CCL. A full debriefing generally takes at least half a day. For more information on the Center for Creative Leadership and KEYS, go to www.ccl.org.

- *Kirton Adaption-Innovation Inventory (KAI).* The KAI was developed in response to a phenomenon its developer, Michael Kirton (1991), observed in organizations: some people are very effective in persuading others to accept their ideas, and others are not. And the difference does not seem to lie in the quality of the ideas. Kirton developed the KAI to measure the root causes of this phenomenon. The KAI is often used to help people understand their styles of creativity, as well as how their patterns of communication may help or hinder understanding and acceptance of their ideas. It can be used both for individual feedback and as a group assessment. It usually takes about three hours to get full value from using the KAI in a retreat. The KAI is licensed only to certified users and must be completed in advance by the participants and scored by the facilitator. For information on the KAI certification course, go to http://www.kaicentre.com.

- *Leadership Practices Inventory (LPI)*. The LPI is a 360° assessment, developed by James M. Kouzes and Barry Z. Posner (2001), that measures thirty leadership behaviors, which are grouped into the Five Practices of Exemplary Leadership® model. The practices are *model the way, inspire a shared vision, challenge the process, enable others to act,* and *encourage the heart*. It usually takes at least half a day to get full value from using the LPI in a retreat. The LPI is available through www.josseybass.com/Wiley for use without any special training or credentials.

- *Myers-Briggs Type Indicator® (MBTI)*. Developed by Isabel Briggs Myers and Katharine Cook Briggs, the MBTI is the most widely used personality inventory, so widely used in fact that you may encounter "MBTI fatigue." If you plan to use the MBTI be sure to ascertain how familiar the group already is with its core concepts.

  The MBTI is often administered as part of team-building retreats because it can help people who work together understand their own and one another's preferences and perspectives. According to Isabel Briggs Myers, the MBTI's results describe "valuable differences between normal, healthy people." Related to concepts developed by the Swiss psychiatrist Carl Jung (1875–1961), the MBTI assesses an individual's preferred and habitual behavior on four scales (the definitions and meanings of which are not self-evident): *extraversion-introversion* (E-I), *sensing-intuition* (S-N), *thinking-feeling* (T-F), and *judging-perceiving* (J-P).

  There are MBTI look-alikes available for free on the Internet. In fact the Internet has become a rich source of assessment instruments, some of them useful and some of them, frankly, very poor. *Caveat emptor;* buyer beware.

  We have used the MBTI selectively with considerable success, but care must be taken to use it only when it makes sense for the particular group and retreat focus. If you decide to include the MBTI in your retreat plan, we recommend that you devote at least a half day to debriefing it. This will give you enough time to dispel the notion that an individual's Myers-Briggs *type* limits that person's range of behaviors and to focus participants instead on the MBTI's capacity to give participants a freer and fuller choice of behaviors. The most successful applications of MBTI have focused not on theory but how people with different preferred behaviors can learn to work better together. The MBTI can be administered only by persons who have received appropriate training and certification. A self-scoring version is available that typically requires less than forty minutes to fill out and score. If you are a qualified user, you can obtain the self-scoring MBTI assessment at www.mbti.com. For information on organizations authorized to conduct workshops to train facilitators to use the MBTI, go to www.mbti.com/qual/worklist.asp#mbti.

- *Strength Deployment Inventory (SDI)*. The SDI, created by Elias H. Porter (1996), helps people identify how they relate to others when things are going well and what changes when they are in conflict situations. The assessment measures people's *valued relating styles* when things are going well: *altruistic-nurturing, assertive-directing, analytic-autonomizing, flexible-cohering, assertive-nurturing, judicious-competing,* and *cautious-supporting*. It also explores stages of conflict when people face opposition. A particularly useful aspect of this assessment is that it produces a portrait of overdone strengths, which can help people see how their strengths can also be liabilities. The component edition of the instrument includes feedback from others. This assessment provides an excellent framework for discussing conflict when that is a key issue for the organization to address in its retreat. If you plan to use it you should allow at least half a day to debrief it. If you are a qualified user, you may obtain the SDI from Personal Strengths Publishing at www.personalstrengths.com.

- *Thomas-Kilmann Conflict Mode Instrument® (TKI).* The TKI is a self-scoring instrument developed by Kenneth W. Thomas and Ralph H. Kilmann (2002). It assesses an individual's preferred and habitual behavior vis-à-vis five modes for managing conflict: *competing, avoiding, compromising, collaborating,* and *accommodating.* We often use the TKI in combination with activities that help the participants assess their individual conflict management styles and explore how differences are typically handled in their organization or work group. (See the Chapter 11 activity "How Conflict Affects Us," p. 311.) The TKI gives the group a framework for exploring individual as well as organizational behavior. It takes a minimum of two hours to debrief in an interactive way that allows participants to explore the benefits and pitfalls of their various conflict-management preferences. If you include the TKI as part of a fuller exploration of how conflict is dealt with in the organization, you should allow at least half a day for using the instrument and discussing how it applies to the organization's circumstances. The TKI is available through www.mbti.com for use without any special training or credentials.

even though the conclusions drawn from assessments may provide helpful data about the organization or group, they aren't *proof* of anything.

Focus the conversation on helping people understand how their preferred and habitual styles of behavior—based on their choices, conscious and unconscious—may help or hinder them at work. Then encourage participants to develop strategies to respond in a more flexible and thoughtful way to the circumstances they typically encounter.

Don't let participants use an assessment to categorize one another's behavior as defined by each person's *type.* Emphasize that assessments are designed for self-understanding and individual growth, not as tools to analyze, evaluate, assign, promote or demote, or manipulate or justify attempts to change others.

If the instrument you are using can be completed and self-scored relatively quickly, we recommend administering it during the retreat. If you hand out an assessment in advance for participants to fill out and bring with them, there will inevitably be one or two people who haven't completed it. This means you will have to decide whether to proceed without that person's results, send the person out of the room to complete the instrument (and thus miss part

> Take care in choosing assessments; many instruments are copyrighted and licensed for use only by people who have been trained and certified by the developers.

of the retreat), or delay the debriefing exercise so the person can complete the form. None of these alternatives is particularly attractive.

If the instrument you use must be scored in advance, ask the client to distribute it well before the retreat, with a cover letter explaining its purpose and the importance of completing it and turning it back to you on time. Allow several extra days to accommodate stragglers who don't meet the initial deadline.

Chapter 3

Retreat Design Issues

The first question a client must be able to answer is, "What do I want to be different as a result of having this retreat?"

Without a clear answer from the client, you won't be able to proceed with the retreat design. You'd be like a travel agent booking flights without first knowing where your client wants to go. Having a vague purpose for a retreat almost guarantees it will be perceived as a failure, for if a retreat has no objectives, how can it achieve them?

The client's answer to the question of what she wants to be different should be specific—"I want us to increase sales, boost productivity, improve customer relations"—rather than general—"I want us to communicate more effectively, get to know each other better, do some brainstorming."

However, the hoped-for result should not be so specific that it doesn't allow retreat participants room to exercise their judgment, explore options, and take part in decision making. If your client's answer to this question is something like, "I want to cut twelve positions, reorganize into three divisions instead of four, move Human Resources into the office of the CEO, and do away with casual Fridays," the organization doesn't need a retreat. An edict will do (though whether it will accomplish its larger purpose is doubtful).

Sins of Omission: The Top Retreat Design Mistakes

If you design and lead many retreats, you'll quickly find your own style—that unique quality you bring to the work that makes you valuable to your clients. The more creative (and courageous) you are in trying out new ideas, the better results you'll get.

Even though we're always interested in fresh approaches to retreat design, we also believe there are a few principles that should be ignored only at the facilitator's peril. (We've made or observed all these mistakes ourselves, and by listing them here we hope to shorten your learning curve.)

1. Not Coming to a Clear Agreement with the Client About Expectations

See Chapter 1, "Aligning Yourself with the Client," pp. 17–21.

What are your client's expectations for you, and what are yours for your client? Do you and the client agree about what will happen at the retreat and afterward? In addition, unforeseen events occur at almost every retreat. You and the client must be clearly aligned on respective roles and expectations so that when something unforeseen takes place, you and she won't struggle over how to handle it.

2. Not Interviewing Participants in Advance

See Chapter 2, "Pre-Retreat Interviews with Participants," pp. 33–38.

A retreat is for everyone in the room, not only the person who convened it. Participants will cooperate far more enthusiastically when they have had input beforehand and when they can see tangible proof at the retreat that you heard them. Conducting even a few interviews can prepare you for possible hidden agendas, undiscussable issues, and covert attacks.

3. Not Providing Enough Variety

Using the same techniques over and over simply bores people. It's hard to keep people's attention throughout a two-day offsite. Use all your creativity to keep participants fully engaged.

See Chapter 5, "Varying the Methodologies," pp. 93–103, for ideas about introducing variety during a retreat.

4. Not Taking the Big Kahuna Effect into Account

The Big Kahuna Effect takes hold when leaders dominate the discussions or create an environment in which people are afraid to say anything they think the leader might not want to hear. No matter what the leader *says* to you or to the retreat participants about being open to candid feedback, you can be sure that at least some of the participants will be concerned about the negative consequences of speaking out. Failing to coach the leader on how to behave at the retreat to achieve the best results, failing to agree in advance with him on how you will respond if he forgets your advice, and failing to include activities that allow people's opinions on sensitive issues to be expressed with anonymity will almost guarantee that the leader won't get valuable feedback, and he, the participants, and the organization will be the poorer for it.

See Chapter 5, "Varying the Methodologies," pp. 93–103, for techniques that minimize the dominance of leaders, and Chapter 16, "Leadership Behavior During the Retreat," pp. 455–462, for materials to use when briefing the leader on his or her role at the retreat.

5. Not Making Opportunities for People to Think Before They Speak

Before an important discussion, give participants a few minutes of silence to collect their thoughts. You might have them write their ideas down before presenting them or ask them to think about something over lunch or dinner. (You may have to strongly encourage extroverts to refrain from speaking up immediately.) Such pauses in the discussions, even if brief, are likely to foster more thoughtful responses.

See Chapter 5, "Varying the Methodologies," pp. 93–103, for methods of using silence effectively in a retreat.

6. Not Allowing for Spontaneous Changes to the Retreat Plan

See Chapter 6, "Changing the Plan," pp. 135–136.

Sticking too faithfully to your carefully developed sequence of activities and precise timetable can blind you to the dynamics of what's happening in the room. You must be ready to stay with a point that participants become really engaged in or to abandon an activity that isn't contributing to the outcome as you anticipated. You may have to insert an activity you hadn't planned on to take advantage of an unexpected opportunity or eliminate an exercise you intended to include because you don't have time for it or it's no longer appropriate. We often describe a day of facilitating a retreat as "eight hours of improv."

7. Not Being Transparent When Changes Occur

See Chapter 7, addressed in its entirety to "How to Recover When Things Go Awry."

There is no such thing as a perfect retreat. You'll forget something. Participants won't follow instructions correctly. Managers will speak out inappropriately. The biggest mistake you can make when something unexpected occurs is to pretend that nothing happened. Acknowledge that something has gone wrong, and ask the group for help in setting it right. We're all human, and participants will appreciate seeing your humanity too.

8. Not Letting Go of Control During the Unstructured Time

See "Using White Space" later in this chapter, pp. 66–67.

Sometimes the best work in a retreat occurs in informal gatherings when the facilitator isn't managing the discussions. Be sure to build some out-of-session time into your design so those moments can occur naturally. Remember that sometimes your presence can inhibit this sort of spontaneity among participants; be strategic about your place and behavior in such activities. (We tend to leave participants to themselves out of session.)

9. Not Forcing the Hard Choices

See Chapter 8, "Types of Retreat Decisions," pp. 169–184.

Participants will perceive the retreat as a waste of time if the action plan is really a plan to think some more about acting. You may be uncomfortable pressing people to make difficult choices throughout the retreat, but that work is critical if the participants are to create an action plan that will lead to meaningful change.

10. Not Leaving Adequate Time for Action Planning

Facilitators too often leave insufficient time at the end of the retreat for participants to review their decisions and put them into a plan that assigns responsibilities, fixes target dates, and defines ways to measure progress. The time required for such planning will depend on the length of the retreat and the complexity of the challenges, but because the action plan is the end product of the offsite, it should not be hurried. Don't leave this critical activity for the last minute, when people are nervously glancing at their watches, worried that they'll miss their planes or get caught in rush hour traffic.

See Chapter 8, "The Nub: Action Planning," pp. 185–192.

11. Not Providing an Appropriate Close

Retreats can be emotionally intense experiences for many participants. People need some time to reflect on what they have achieved together, appreciate one another's contributions, and plan their reentry into the workplace. A rushed closing can undermine some of the good work the group did over the course of the retreat.

See Chapter 14, titled "Closing the Retreat and Working on Implementation," for ideas on how to close in a meaningful way.

Prework for Retreat Participants

Occasionally, you or your client will want to give the participants reading or work assignments to complete before the retreat. For a strategic planning retreat, for example, participants may need to review organizational progress against last year's plan and year-to-date budget figures. Department heads might be asked to bring preliminary descriptions of any new projects they are contemplating for the next year or an evaluation of this year's initiatives.

(Inevitably, some participants will not complete the required reading or work assignments, but even so, this approach is better than making briefings, reports, and PowerPoint presentations part of the retreat itself. Retreats are limited in time. They are not staff meetings. Taking time at a retreat to share such information is usually not a good use of a precious resource. If it is absolutely necessary to have such informational sessions at a retreat, they should be few and brief.)

Prework assignments should be distributed by the client in plenty of time for people to complete them. But don't overdo it; discuss prework requirements with your client to make sure all of it is absolutely necessary. Assigning prework can save time during the retreat, but expect uneven compliance. Some people will eagerly do all that the boss asks; others will not. In a two-day retreat, we often schedule the activities that rely on prework for the second day, giving the participants who didn't finish the prework time to do so the first evening.

If technical or detailed information will be discussed at the retreat, it can be helpful for the client and administrator to assemble a briefing book to be handed out in advance. Even though some people won't have read it, they will have the book with them to refer to during the offsite. Asking individuals to contribute material for the briefing book may also inspire them to complete their assignments, rather than having an empty section in the book where their contribution should be.

Inevitably, some participants will forget their briefing books. It's a good idea to have one or two extras on hand.

Using White Space

Throughout the retreat there will be times when the group is formally in session and other times when it is out of session. We refer to the time between organized discussions or activities, when there's no formal program and the facilitator isn't managing events, as *white space*.

Some of the most meaningful work of the retreat can occur during the white space—in particular in the evenings after dinner—while people are engaged in purely social interaction or physical activities. And you, the facilitator, might not be there to observe it.

At a retreat we facilitated for a publishing company in the north woods of Minnesota, the executive committee spent much of one afternoon discussing how to reorganize two departments. That night, long after most of us had gone to bed, Chip, the CEO, and Roberto, one of the two department heads, had a few beers out on the dock. The next morning at breakfast we heard people asking, "Did you hear Chip and Roberto yelling last night? What was that all about?" It turned out that Roberto was strongly opposed to most of what he'd agreed to during the afternoon session. He hadn't said anything at the time, feeling it would make him appear defensive. But late at night, out on the dock (and with a couple of beers under his belt), he told Chip the truth about how he felt, and Chip reacted angrily. Awkward as the incident was, it brought forward Roberto's true feelings so the group could address them.

As facilitator, you should work to create a trusting atmosphere so that participants will feel comfortable (or emboldened) enough to share their thoughts and concerns during the formal sessions, where others can benefit from hearing them. But some people may feel compelled (or relaxed enough) to call things as they see them only outside the formal sessions. Offering unstructured space for such candid conversations to take place is one reason we prefer that a retreat include an overnight stay.

A challenge for you as the facilitator is to discover what has happened in the white space and bring it back into the formal process. The easiest way is simply to begin the next morning's session by asking, "Did anybody have any new ideas or second thoughts that we should hear about?" We have been amazed at times by the wealth of new possibilities generated by the answers to that question first thing in the morning.

Sometimes a participant will volunteer something to the facilitator during the white space. Can you use that information when you reconvene? It's a judgment call. We usually encourage the participant who confides in us to share her comments with the whole group at the next session. If she won't do so, we may bring it up on our own, if we can do so without disclosing the source. It depends on how important it is and how sensitive it is.

(What we won't do is surprise the person who confided in us by calling on her unexpectedly in a formal session and asking her publicly to share with the whole group what she told us privately.)

Capturing the Work Product

You'll also need to plan how you will record what was decided at the retreat. This is not something you can leave to the last minute to work out.

Before you walk into the room you should know who will be responsible for converting the voluminous flip chart pages into usable notes and whether the group will need a retreat report that is more formal than simply capturing the data on the flip charts.

Read more about capturing the work of the retreat in Chapter 6, "Recording the Group's Work," pp. 132–134, and about preparing the retreat report in Chapter 14, "Writing the Follow-Up Report," pp. 425–426.

There are at least five possible answers to, "Who will type the charts?"—you, the client, one (or more) of the retreat participants, an administrative assistant (AA) back at the office, or an AA who attends the retreat solely for the purpose of recording its proceedings.

Although we often encourage an organization to choose one or more participants to take responsibility for typing the notes, sometimes it's just easier for the facilitator to produce the report. A facilitator-written report is likely to be a straightforward account of the retreat and its results, with little personal interpretation.

The advantage of having a participant write up the notes is that he or she understands the organization's operations and can clarify items in a way the facilitator might miss.

The fourth option—having someone who did not attend type up the notes—usually doesn't work well. Retreat flip charts, written in haste, are notoriously messy. They're full of acronyms and abbreviations (some of which have been invented on the spot), arrows to link things that are out of sequence, diagrams, colored dots, and sticky notes—and just plain sloppy handwriting. Anyone who types from those charts is going to have a hard time deciphering them, and they're bound to make some misinterpretations. Often, however, you may have no choice but to have someone who wasn't there get the basics into a computer. Then a participant can edit those notes.

We don't believe it's a good idea to have someone attend the retreat only to take notes. That person's presence, no matter how unobtrusive, may cause people to censor their contributions to the group's discussions. And that person might find it frustrating not to make contributions of his own and might become, in effect, another participant either openly at the retreat, or covertly, when typing up the notes.

No matter who will handle the flip chart sheets, there is much you can do to make transcribing them easier. Number and title every flip chart page as it is produced, including pages from breakout groups. They may not all make it into the final document, but you will have an easier time locating the information you need later if they are numbered.

At every long break and at the end of the day, organize the flip charts produced so far. Note on each whether it contains decisions and action points or is merely a record of the thinking process that went into decision making. Take any charts the group no longer needs off the wall, label them, make any necessary numbering corrections needed, and set them aside in a safe place so they won't accidentally be thrown out.

Finally, at the end, take down all the remaining charts (those created at the end are likely to be the most important) and sort them. Although there are usually willing hands to help you in this process, we suggest you take the charts down yourself so that you can organize them as you go.

For flip chart paper covered in Post-it Notes, it's most convenient to remove the notes and stack them into folders or staple them together. (Just be sure to carefully label each folder!) These stacked or stapled notes are much less likely to be lost than if they were left on the flip chart sheets. If, however, the sticky notes are arranged on the paper in a specific way—for instance, in columns under headings—then use clear tape to secure the notes in place and fold the chart with the notes inside. (Not all retreat facilities have such tape readily available. You might want to bring some yourself, just in case.)

If much of the work of the retreat is done in breakout sessions, you might want to have laptop computers and printers available for session leaders to record and distribute their notes on the spot. That way, participants in each separate session get a sense of progress in real time. In addition, having these notes already in the computer speeds up the report-writing process.

Design Issues for a Series of Retreats

A complex change initiative, such as a major restructuring, often requires several retreats held over a period of months. Rather than thinking of these as discrete events, it is best to consider them as parts of one multisession retreat. That way, you can build on what has come before while at the same time remaining alert to the need to bring new participants up to speed.

A series of retreats allows participants time between sessions to reflect on what has taken place, test new ideas, solicit input from colleagues who weren't present, gather new perspectives, and think about how they themselves can best contribute to the next session.

To design a series of retreats you must be prepared to deal with changes in the landscape that will take place over time. New leadership, promotions, transfers, turnover, downsizing, growth, new economic realities, shifts in focus and priorities, and personal concerns can all affect successive retreats. In the time between retreats new people will become involved in the process and others will drop out. People may change their minds about certain issues, and concerns might crop up at one session that could have been explored more fruitfully at an earlier stage. Issues that you thought had been resolved may reemerge. *Retreat fatigue* can set in, and participants who were eager to participate at one retreat might be reluctant at another.

The longer the process the more important it is for participants to communicate between sessions among themselves and with colleagues who weren't at the retreats, to prevent potential misinformation and misunderstandings from undermining the process.

You'll want to stay in regular and frequent contact with the client between retreats to observe events as they unfold, provide advice and coaching, and gather up-to-date information to consider in designing the next retreat in the series. You may need to conduct additional interviews with some of the continuing participants or interview new participants. It almost never happens that what was valid at the beginning of the process remains valid throughout.

Chapter 4

Retreat Design Components

Every retreat is different. That said, there are several elements common to most successful offsites. These are the design components we believe will move the group most reliably toward its goals:

- Introduction
- Ground rules or norms
- Individual check-in
- Reporting your findings
- Content segments
- Decision making
- Action planning
- Closing
- Post-retreat follow-up

Introduction

Every retreat should start with a brief welcoming statement. We emphasize *brief*—five minutes should be more than long enough for the group's leader or another high-ranking person in the organization to greet the participants and call the session to order.

The purpose of this introduction is to establish that it's the client's retreat, not the facilitator's; reinforce participants' understanding of the goals of the retreat; set the tone for the work that will follow; and confirm senior management's commitment to following up on the recommendations and decisions that come out of the offsite.

In the welcoming statement the leader should reiterate her desire for an open and candid dialogue and emphasize that there will be no repercussions for speaking out within the parameters of the ground rules the group agrees on. She should also thank participants for the sacrifices they are making by taking time away from work and home.

People will take their cues about the retreat from the words and tone of the introduction. Encourage the leader to make the introduction friendly and informal. We urge our clients not to use charts or PowerPoint presentations. People won't remember a long list of bulleted items. They will, however, remember a compelling personal story from a senior manager or a sincere explanation of what their leader hopes will be different after the retreat. Then the leader should introduce you.

We suggest you explain your role as facilitator. We typically say that we will

- Focus the participants on accomplishing their goals
- Keep the discussions on track and the sessions moving along
- Encourage participants to bring difficult issues or *undiscussables* to the surface and to devise strategies to deal with them
- Use our outsider status to push, challenge, and guide participants

Then you can give the participants an overview of what's going to happen in the retreat and describe briefly and in general terms what kinds of activities you have planned. We recommend that you do not hand out or post a detailed agenda listing each exercise and its specific time frame, as you might for a meeting agenda.

Think of the detailed agenda you will have prepared for yourself as a game plan, not a script to be followed no matter what. The timing never goes exactly as you think it will, and more important, you'll have to be ready to add some elements and abandon others to take advantage of opportunities that present themselves at the retreat.

If you hand out or post a point-by-point agenda, some participants will invariably worry about sticking to it, even when you know you will achieve a better outcome by taking a detour from your planned route. We typically show retreat participants a flip chart with a very general agenda; it covers the major topics but does not list times other than the start and finish of each day. We stress that this agenda is just a guide and that we will add or subtract activities as necessary to help the group move forward.

The "Expectations and Outcomes" activity in Chapter 14, p. 415, collects participants' expectations for the retreat at the beginning and then at the end allows them to compare the final outcomes with their original expectations.

We also frequently outline what organizational dynamics expert Robert Marshak (1995) calls the *Introvert's Protection Act*. Some people need time to gather their thoughts before they speak, so we let participants know that we've designed activities to allow for that. For example, we intentionally include time for quiet reflection, use silence in several group activities, and often ask people to write down their ideas before voicing them.

Participants will have questions about logistics. Will there be scheduled morning and afternoon breaks? Will breaks be long enough for them to call the office? What time will lunch be served? When will the session end for the day? Hearing your answers to these and similar questions up front allows participants to relax and concentrate on the substance of the retreat.

Ground Rules or Norms

After the introductory remarks, help the participants establish ground rules—the behavioral norms they will follow during the retreat. Ground rules help keep discussions focused on the task and encourage participants to treat one another with respect. They provide a framework for the group in determining what behavior is acceptable and what is not.

Some facilitators like to guide participants in establishing their own ground rules from scratch. Unless you have the luxury of a lot of time, however, we recommend that you suggest a set of ground rules and then invite participants to propose additions, deletions, and language changes that will make these ground rules more relevant to them.

Here's a list of retreat norms we often suggest as a starting point for discussion:

Some participants might object to turning off their phones because they're expecting an urgent call. You may be able to resolve this issue by providing the phone number of the retreat facility and asking that the facility hand deliver callers' urgent messages to participants.

- Speak openly and honestly—and only for yourself.
- Participate fully, but don't monopolize the conversation or repeat what others have said.
- Let one person speak at a time. Don't interrupt or engage in side conversations.
- Listen to understand others, not to judge them. Ask questions to draw others out.
- Safeguard other participants' confidentiality.
- Turn off cell phones and pagers during sessions.
- Be on time.

Consider, too, whether the composition of the group indicates the need for additional ground rules. If participants come from different parts of the organization, for instance, help them discuss whether they are expected to represent their departments (for example, marketing) or functions (for example, engineers or administrative assistants) or just themselves during the sessions. (Whatever the case, all participants should be encouraged to work for the good of the whole organization.)

However you arrive at the list of ground rules that will govern behavior at your retreat, be sure to test for agreement before assuming that the group will accept them. Post the rules where everyone can see them.

The introduction and discussion about ground rules should not take much more than twenty minutes. Then it's time to hear from the retreat participants.

Individual Check-In

Even if they seem likely to know each other, it's a good idea to have participants introduce themselves. It gets them talking early on, and it's not safe to assume, just because people work in the same department or office, that they know each other well.

Introductions can be simple—each participant can give his name, his position, and how long he has worked for the organization or been in his present job—but it is better to use the introduction to get participants accustomed to disclosing something about themselves. If they share their expectations and concerns about the retreat (or the changes that might take place as a result) at the start, they are more likely to remain fully engaged as the retreat progresses. Conversely, if people sit silently for too long at the beginning, they are likely to settle into a pattern of passive listening rather than active participation.

Here are some of the questions that we might ask:

- What do you hope we will achieve in this retreat?
- What can you contribute to the success of this retreat?
- What concerns do you have about this retreat?
- What might you need help with during this retreat?

Notice that the emphasis in these questions is on behavior during this retreat—not behavior back at the workplace. You or the client might start by giving a check-in example—both to show participants the kind of information that is helpful and to model openness and brevity. If the client will check in first, coach her in advance on the kinds of check-in comments most likely to foster a positive environment for the rest of the offsite.

For instance, Pamela, the CEO of a marketing consulting firm, started her management retreat with this personal check-in:

> What I hope to achieve by the end of the day tomorrow is a new strategic direction for our company that will set us apart from our competitors. I hope we'll have some fresh ideas about how we work with our clients—ideas that no one else in our industry has come up with.
>
> What I can contribute to the success of this retreat is my deep appreciation of the talents of each person in this room. I believe that together we are an incredibly creative set of minds. I want to encourage all of us to contribute our unique viewpoints and talents.
>
> But I have to admit that while I'm calling for big new ideas, I'm afraid of change. I'm very comfortable with the company right now,

even though I know intellectually that we must change if we want to grow. So I'd like to ask you all to help me accept the ideas we're going to come up with, and to challenge me if I get stuck in resisting new approaches.

Everyone in the room knew that Pamela was resistant to change, but they were surprised that she acknowledged that tendency in herself. This honest check-in encouraged people to believe that the ideas they generated might actually come to fruition. And it inspired other participants to be equally candid in their check-ins. A check-in can help people appreciate others' abilities and can foster an atmosphere of trust.

This is a good time to invoke the Introvert's Protection Act. Once you have explained the check-in, allow participants to think for a few moments about what they're going to say. Otherwise, some will be thinking about their responses rather than listening as others introduce themselves. Or they may react like deer caught in the headlights when it is their turn to speak.

A check-in can proceed in order around the room, but we have found that it works better when people speak up when they are ready or when each speaker chooses who will check in next.

If you decide to let participants just speak up, you will have to be aware of who hasn't spoken and if necessary call on those people at the end.

If you prefer to have participants choose the next person to speak, you can ask that each speaker simply call on another person to check in or, as we often do, ask that each speaker toss a soft object, such as a Koosh™ ball to indicate who should speak next. (Ask people to toss it gently underhand; even soft objects pitched overhand have been known to upset cups of hot coffee.) Waiting for the ball to come their way keeps people alert, and tossing and catching it energizes the group.

Another check-in method is to lay out a selection of pictures, objects, or cartoons and ask that each participant choose one that represents an aspect of his or her personality, interests, or hopes and concerns for the retreat. Each person then tells the group the significance of what he or she selected.

Remind participants to speak to the group—not to you or to the leader—during their check-ins. When we facilitate a check-in, we often sit out of the obvious line of sight—perhaps at the back of the room or outside the circle of chairs—to avoid people's natural inclination to address their comments to the facilitators.

Unless something comes up that affects the group's ability to proceed, don't allow the check-ins to spark conversation or debate. When you give the instructions, be sure to tell the group that the check-ins should move from one person to the next quickly and without commentary from others.

If your group is so large that individual check-ins would take an inordinate amount of time, have participants break into subgroups to check in; every participant should be heard by others in the room.

When you have a day or less for the retreat, you might want to abbreviate the process. After the basics—name and position—we ask fewer questions and stress the need for speed by calling the process the 30-Second Check-In.

Additional 30-Second Check-In questions we use include the following:

- Give us a metaphor—a visual symbol—for how you feel about being here today. (For example, "I feel like a rose today. I can contribute something beautiful, but I've got my thorns for protection.")
- Tell us one thing you'd like to see come out of this retreat.

Caution: Tennis balls and other semihard objects can cause injury when thrown from one person to another in a small space. That's why we recommend Koosh balls, which are soft, light, and easy to catch. They are available in most toy stores. Can't find a Koosh ball, or forgot to bring it with you? A wadded up piece of paper, though less elegant, will work.

Be careful to ask only one or two questions; otherwise, your 30-Second Check-In will become a marathon.

On a multiday retreat we often will do an *energy check-in* on the second or third morning. One of our favorites is to ask participants to board a metaphorical bus (we set the chairs up in rows as on a bus) and to indicate through sound and gestures how they're feeling that morning. As each person gets on the bus in turn, all the passengers mirror the person who just boarded. In this quick and lively check-in activity, participants can feel in their own bodies the energy that is present (or not) in the room.

We are sometimes asked for our favorite retreat *icebreakers*. We don't have any. Icebreakers tend to be games that are unrelated to the work ahead. They can send the wrong signal right at the start of the retreat—that participants are here only to have fun and play games. A check-in is all we've ever needed to break the ice. Although a good retreat can be fun and often is enjoyable, to our minds retreats that have long-term impact are not about playing games.

That being said, if the main purpose of the retreat is to build a team or change an organization's culture, you will probably want to take more time during the check-in for participants to get to know one another better, particularly if the retreat will last two or more days. If you have the luxury of time, you can, for example, ask participants to include in their introductions something about themselves that others in the room don't know. (At one retreat, a participant stunned his colleagues by giving his name and adding, "and I have a mistress." He paused. "My mistress is the opera," he continued, and explained that he was an amateur opera singer, a fact that no one in the room even imagined.)

See Chapters 10 and 11 for activities that are well suited to team-building and culture change retreats.

Reporting Your Findings

At some point during the retreat, you will need to give the group feedback about the interviews or surveys you conducted. Although sometimes we may have reasons to present this information later in the retreat—if it relates to a specific issue, for instance—we prefer to give the feedback as early as possible on the first day of the retreat, because this often puts things on the table that participants otherwise might not be aware of or would be reluctant to acknowledge or deal with.

Remember that retreat interviews do not provide statistically valid data. Well-crafted and carefully analyzed interviews will give you a sense of people's major concerns. Still, until you hear from the participants themselves about how accurate they believe the feedback is, you won't know whether you have captured the whole picture.

We often introduce the feedback with a statement such as this: "I'd like to describe the impressions I've formed from the interviews I conducted with a number of you. I'll tell you what I believe I heard, and then you can let me know if you think I've drawn an accurate picture of how things work around here." We suggest that participants take notes about anything that strikes them as surprising, puzzling, inaccurate, or especially significant, so that when it's time to respond they can recall what they heard.

There are several reasons to give participants feedback from your interviews:

- The people who gave you information are entitled to hear what was said. The information belongs to them, not to you.
- Participants who were interviewed often talk with one another about the issues they raised. If concerns that they know several people expressed are not included in the feedback, participants may believe you are suppressing this information and may be reluctant to raise these issues at the retreat. The group loses the opportunity to discuss these concerns and may also lose trust in the interview process and thus in you.
- Participants who raised issues in the interviews learn that they are not alone in their thinking when they hear that others feel the same way.
- Once something has been said out loud, even if only by the facilitator providing feedback, it becomes less of a taboo subject and it is easier to talk about openly.
- The feedback will stimulate conversation about what really matters to the participants.

Once we have given the feedback, we take time to debrief it. We typically ask the participants to discuss, in small groups or as a whole group, their reactions to what they've heard. We often ask such questions as these:

- What themes emerged from the feedback?
- What are the implications for [your organization]?
- What surprises you about the feedback?
- What is missing from the feedback?

Another technique we use is to ask the participants to write on individual Post-it Notes what they believe to be the most important issues that emerged from the feedback. Then they attach these Post-its to their upper bodies and walk around the room reading others' Post-its in silence. This technique creates immediate ownership of the key issues (because people see who is wearing which issue) and helps participants understand the concerns of others in the room.

The discussion that ensues is often the richest part of the retreat, as participants learn how much common ground they share and often are energized and encouraged by hearing controversial issues spoken of in public.

Should You Give Feedback to the Client in Advance?

Sharing the feedback with the client in advance, rather than having him hear it along with the other participants, has advantages and disadvantages. Some of the advantages are that

- He will have time to think about the issues before being called on to react to them, rather than having to react in the moment at the retreat.
- You will be able to give him some perspective on the issues that were raised.
- You will have an opportunity to coach him on how to address the issues that were raised without appearing defensive.

Some of the disadvantages are that

- Interviewees may be less frank with you if they know that top management will hear the interview results before they do.
- The client may show up at the retreat prepared to refute the points he doesn't agree with.
- The client may ask you to delete some information or otherwise edit your presentation, even though you and he agreed prior to the interviews that you would report the feedback comprehensively and accurately.

We tend to give our clients a summary of the themes a day or two before the retreat and coach them on how to respond in a manner that will advance the purpose of the retreat. And we tell our clients prior to accepting a contract to facilitate a retreat that we cannot delete any information from a feedback report. Knowing your client, choose your strategy accordingly.

How to Present the Feedback

You will gather much more data than you can possibly report to the participants. So you will have to limit your feedback to the most significant themes and trends that several people raised.

After you finish the interviews, sift through the data to find the key points—not just one or two individuals' pet peeves but the issues that have been raised by several people and have the greatest impact on how the organization does business. Whatever you report back at the retreat will be seen as significant, so use your judgment about what to include. If you get something wrong (if you omit an important issue, for instance, or highlight something that doesn't make sense to the participants), the group will let you know.

When deciding what to report, you may be tempted to leave out particularly thorny issues. The client might even encourage you to do so. But if you censor the feedback to make things more comfortable for you or more palatable to the client, you deprive the organization of an opportunity to face up to and address important concerns. Indeed, you may be colluding with the participants and the client in tiptoeing around the very issues that the group needs to explore. Rather than protecting participants from difficult issues, you want to help them create a climate in which they can discuss such issues openly.

At the same time, don't become so focused on the things that people told you are going wrong that you forget to mention what's going right. Focus first on what's working well. Emphasizing only the negative can be devastating to the group's morale and can lead participants to believe that it is futile to try to change anything. Use the feedback as an opportunity to help people recognize what they're already doing right and to look for ways to build on past successes.

> For more on the power of building on the positive, see Chapter 1, "Appreciative Inquiry," pp. 29–30.

Also pay attention to the effects of language: even if the people you interviewed used highly personal or judgmental language to describe others or the organization, find ways to report these concerns that allow the points to be made clearly yet without provoking defensiveness.

There are several ways to organize the feedback data to help participants understand it. Whatever method you choose, remember that the goal is to focus on a few key issues that the group needs to address, not on a whole laundry list of complaints.

For example, you might organize the feedback by

- Focusing on broad themes (see the accompanying box: "What We Told Lassiter & Tompkins")
- Identifying organizational strengths and weaknesses and external opportunities and threats

- Selecting key strategic issues, with an analysis of the likely consequences of not addressing them
- Turning the feedback into a story or narrative (which itself could be organized along any of the lines just described)

What We Told Lassiter & Tompkins

These are some of the themes that emerged from our interviews with the managers of a midsize advertising agency (which we'll call Lassiter & Tompkins) prior to a strategic planning retreat. (Note that this is a summation. We went into greater detail in the report itself by citing some actual comments that led us to the conclusions we drew.)

Management Group Dynamics

- While you individually have respect for each other, you are not a cohesive team.
- The people in this room have different goals and priorities for the agency.
- Critical decisions are made by the CEO, not by this group.
- You tend to agree with each other in meetings, but then leave and do whatever you want.
- Some women executives feel that there is a strain of male chauvinism among the people who are here today.

Strategic Direction

- Your internal slogan, "Let's do great work, have fun, and make money," doesn't help you determine the strategic direction of the agency. The three ideas conflict in many people's minds.
- Your greatest threat is that one huge account dominates your client list. Everyone is afraid of what would happen if the agency lost that client.
- You're generating lots of new business contacts but not winning a lot of new business.

Organizational Issues

- The creative department is seen as an enclave unto itself, different in spirit and intent from the rest of the agency. The rest of the agency feels shut out of a special club.
- Finance is seen as the "schoolmarm" of the agency, scolding people but not necessarily helping them do their jobs.
- The agency is reluctant to fire marginal performers because "we are too nice."
- The people who will have to guide this agency in the future don't fully understand the succession plan.

And use the words of the people you interviewed when you can (taking care that they can't be identified with specific individuals) rather than your own words. We tend to paraphrase and summarize but also to sprinkle the feedback with quotes from the interviews that capture the themes without identifying any particular person.

Content Segments

A good retreat is an exploration into new territory. As with a challenging trek in mountainous terrain, it takes time to reach your destination. The trip can be arduous or easy, an exhilarating experience or a tedious one. Content segments must provide enough challenge, variety, and flexibility to maintain participants' interest.

Because a retreat takes so much more time than a typical meeting, it would be deadly to seat the participants around a table and have them work their way through a rigid agenda. Instead the content of the retreat—the actual work—should be organized into segments that take people through different processes for thinking, communicating, and planning. Each exercise, or activity, should be appropriate for the specific topic and should flow sequentially into the next. (The following chapter presents an in-depth exploration of these various techniques.)

Keep in mind that people process information in many different ways and have different preferred learning styles. To keep participants engaged, include a variety of experiences in your retreat design, some very active and some more reflective, some aural and some visual.

Decision Making

Because decisions made at a retreat are often complex and involve a change in organizational direction, it is critical that those decisions represent participants' best thinking and have their support.

There are several methods for making decisions, each with its advantages and disadvantages. Typically the group will need to use different methods at different times. But before you help the participants determine what decision-making method they will use, you and they must be clear on the group's mandate: Do participants have the authority to make decisions on their own? About policy? About procedures? Will their decisions have to be reviewed and endorsed by a higher authority? Are the participants charged with making recommendations only? Are they authorized to make action decisions in some areas and recommendations in others? It will be dispiriting to people if they learn after the fact that decisions they thought they were making have been denied, amended beyond recognition, or ignored by top executives.

For more information about decision making, see Chapter 8, "Methods of Decision Making," pp. 162–168.

At each step of the process, participants need to know, Are we deciding, or are we just recommending? If the end product of the retreat is a set of recommendations, the participants will need to spend some time assembling the rationale for their ideas and discussing how the recommendations will be presented to senior management.

Participants also need to know whether the recommendations they are making must fit within the organization's current resources of time, money, and people or if additional resources are available. If it's the former (and it often is), we ask the group to think of ways the current resources can be used more effectively and to assume that these resources won't increase.

Although such a limitation might seem inhibiting to people's creativity, it's far worse to encourage participants to generate a host of terrific ideas only to have senior management respond, "Sorry, we don't have the resources to do that." It's better for people to know in advance the constraints they're working under.

In addition to making final choices about goals and actions, the group will have to make other choices, and you will need a plan for guiding them through each type of decision.

Action Planning

Well before the last few hours of the retreat, you will need to guide the group in making commitments to a specific plan of action. Even if the participants reached agreement on action items as they went along, you will have to put everything together and have them look at this in its totality. (Sometimes, for example, a decision made on Day One will conflict with a decision made on Day Two.) This process will take several hours—possibly an entire morning or afternoon—and it's critical not to rush through it, skip parts of it, or give it short shrift.

Planning how retreat participants will involve others in implementing (and perhaps modifying) recommendations is an important part of action planning—so important in fact that we have devoted Chapter 17 to that topic.

At this point you are approaching the end of the retreat. People's energy may be flagging, but there is still difficult work to be done. If the retreat lasts longer than a day, we suggest you review the notes at the end of the first day and consolidate on a few flip charts the key points that will need to be included in the action plan. The group's work in action planning will be much more streamlined if people aren't trying to pick action points out of a blizzard of flip chart pages covered with abbreviations, arrows, and notes in less than perfect handwriting.

A key part of action planning must focus on how the group will let people back at the office know what happened at the retreat and its likely effect on them. You will need to discuss both the immediate questions that will come up on participants' first day back ("Well, how did it go? What did you all decide?") and the longer-term question of how to introduce, build support for, and implement proposed initiatives and changes. Responding effectively to the concerns of the people who were not at the retreat is critical to the success of any proposed changes.

Closing

At the end of the retreat, allow forty-five minutes to an hour (the time needed depends a lot on how many participants there are) for a closing exercise. (We suggest several possibilities in Chapter 14.) An effective closing exercise allows participants to reflect on the work they've done together, acknowledge and express appreciation for others' contributions, and prepare themselves to integrate what they have learned when they return to the office.

We cover follow-up from the facilitator's perspective in Chapter 14, and we explore it from the client's viewpoint in Chapter 17 (which you can reproduce from the CD), so that your client can be thinking about follow-up even as you are planning the retreat.

Post-Retreat Follow-Up

Part of your thinking as you design the retreat should address how you will follow up. You need explicit agreement with the client about how you (or the client) will report back to those who attended the retreat (as well as those who didn't) about what occurred there. We urge our clients to circulate the retreat report (or at least a summary) to everyone in the organization who will play a role in implementing its recommendations or who will be affected by those recommendations. As part of your planning for post-retreat follow-up, you will also want to discuss with your client whether and how you might be involved after the retreat.

The Importance of Timing

We urge you to remember the importance of pacing throughout the retreat. The check-in that launches the retreat and the exercises that start each day should engage participants fully; if they don't, people are likely to stay indifferent. And the activity that takes place after lunch should be lively. Get people out of their chairs, if possible. Otherwise, participants may fall into the post-lunch doldrums.

You will also need to pay particular attention to the final activities of each day and the closing of the retreat itself.

Each day should, if at all possible, end on an upbeat, hopeful note. If participants end a day discouraged or frustrated or angry, those are the feelings they will take with them to dinner, to their post-dinner interactions with other participants, and to bed. It's better that they end each day looking forward with enthusiasm to resuming the following morning. That being said, it's not necessarily a bad thing if participants are somewhat confused or unsettled at the end of the first day. Working through these feelings overnight may help them make better recommendations the following day.

And the final activities of the retreat should be highly engaging and even inspiring, because the impression made in the final hours is likely to be the one everyone will remember. Just as the first exercise helps set people's expectations, the final activity colors their memory and judgment of the whole offsite.

Retreat Elements

Advance Preparation

Reaching agreement with the client

Conducting interviews and data gathering

Designing the retreat

Opening the Retreat

Welcome

Check-in

Ground rules

Feedback to the group

Doing the Work

Gaining group agreement on issues

Exploring ideas (experiential activities)

Making decisions (experiential activities)

Action planning

Closing the Retreat

Check-out

Post-Retreat Work

Reporting back

Following up

Chapter 5

Structuring the Retreat

The more tricks you have up your facilitator's sleeve and the more practiced you are in using them fluidly as circumstances demand, the more likely you are to keep participants from getting bored or restless.

We mix several techniques in the retreats we design and lead. And the longer the retreat, the more variety we include.

And though we plan to conduct each activity in a certain way—say, by asking groups to "discuss" an issue by creating a picture together in silence—we are willing to change our plan in the moment if the group's energy is too low or tensions seem too high for the activity to be productive when conducted as planned.

We purposely include activities that push participants beyond the confines of their comfort zones because that's how breakthrough work will be accomplished. Occasionally we have felt a twinge of anxiety. Will trauma surgeons put on silly hats to make a point? Will bankers make a collage together? Will nuclear engineers draw on their intuitive sides? You have to know your client, but our experience has been overwhelmingly positive. People have told us repeatedly that some activities they never would have dreamed they would have enjoyed were the most meaningful and memorable of the retreat. So we encourage you not to limit your creativity or the group's by placing too many self-imposed restrictions on what a given group will do.

Group Size and Composition

An important side benefit of a retreat—no matter what its primary purpose—is that participants get to know one another better and appreciate the gifts each brings to the group. By ensuring that participants work in groups of varying size and composition, you help them accomplish this goal and also ensure that they stay engaged and can contribute constructively.

Whole Group Conversation

Virtually every retreat begins and ends with the whole group in the room participating in a single facilitated conversation. If the retreat group is small (twenty or fewer), you can spend more of the total retreat time in whole group conversation. But even with small numbers of people, we recommend introducing other experiential modes to hold the group's interest.

It takes skillful facilitation to make sure everyone is heard and no participants dominate the discussions. You may have to institute a temporary rule, for instance, that no one will speak twice until everyone who wants to has spoken once.

Breakout Group Discussions

See Chapter 2, "Thinking About Logistics," pp. 49–54, for ideas on how to break participants into groups.

If there will be multiple reports on different issues from the same subgroups, be sure to vary the order in which the groups present their information, so that the same group doesn't always go first.

Breaking the whole group into subgroups for simultaneous discussions is a classic retreat technique. Breakout groups, typically consisting of fewer than ten people each, discuss the question at hand and then report their ideas to the entire assembly. Breakout groups may move into smaller rooms or simply pull chairs together in different corners of the main room. We suggest you vary the composition of these subgroups throughout the course of the retreat so the same people are not always working together.

Using subgroups helps ensure that many different voices are heard. Even so, it happens that different groups discussing the same question come to similar conclusions. When they express the same opinion on a topic, breakout group reports can be—let's be honest—boring.

One way to avoid repetition is to give each small group a slightly different assignment. In that way each group's report provides a different perspective on the issue. Another method is to ask each breakout group to report only those elements that are different from the ones other subgroups have already reported. (A third method—which we recommend against—is having one group report one point, then another group report another point, and so on in a round-robin until it's the first group's turn again. This can be a time-consuming process, and it's not really necessary.)

Consider how you will assign people to breakout groups for each activity. Some exercises will yield better results when participants work in particular groupings. Depending on the activity, you might group people in some of the following ways:

- All managers in one group and all subordinates in other groups
- In groups that duplicate their workgroups
- In groups that combine different organizational levels
- In groups that combine different disciplines
- In groups with random cross sections of participants

In determining who will be in which subgroup, you are much more likely to get a truly representational mix if you make the assignments yourself rather than depending on your client or someone else in the organization to do so. This

Forming Subgroups

Limiting subgroups to ten people isn't a hard-and-fast rule. Circumstances may dictate that subgroups be larger. When they have more than ten people, however, subgroups will have the same problem that the whole group has—it may be difficult for everyone to be heard. Subgroups may also be much smaller than ten people, sometimes as small as a pair or a trio.

may include putting participants in the same subgroup who don't especially care for each other or who have had clashes in the past. Often a side benefit of retreats is that they give people a positive experience of working with colleagues with whom they have had previous difficulties or little prior contact.

For certain activities the best way to get people into breakout groups is to allow them to choose, from among several options, the topic they'd most like to talk about. We often write the options on flip chart pages—one per page—and post the pages around the room. Every page also has spaces for a specific number of people to sign up; participants select their own breakout groups by writing their names on the relevant chart. This method is particularly effective when the topics under discussion require specialized knowledge, experience, or interest. Because you limit the number of people in each subgroup, some participants won't get their first choice, and that's okay.

Using breakouts can help a group deal more quickly with large or complex topics, but be careful not to overuse them. A day should not be simply a series of breakouts, followed by small group reports, followed by whole group conversation. Boring!

Switching Groups

The technique of switching groups involves asking participants to start in one group, then having some of the participants move to another group when the facilitator signals that time is up. Each group can be working on a different task, or a different aspect of the same task, and people bring the concerns of their previous group to bear on the current conversation. We might use this technique to have one group suggest actions that the group members should take to accomplish a particular goal, then in a second round another group would look at the obstacles to implementing those actions, and in a third round yet another group would look at how to overcome those obstacles. This technique is very useful when it is important to get many perspectives on an issue or to ensure that participants have contributed to the discussion of key topics. It works best logistically when all the subgroups are meeting in different parts of the same room, though that is not a requirement.

Pairs and Trios

Working in pairs or trios offers everyone the opportunity to speak and be heard. Participants may also feel safer speaking candidly and openly to one or two other people rather than to the whole group. We ask participants to form these small groupings when it's important that everyone have a turn to speak and listen, when it's not necessary for every group to report to the whole, when discussion has bogged down in larger groups, or when too many participants are sitting passively in larger group discussions. Imagine the level of energy in a room when, say, four people, one in each of four breakout groups, are talking at the same time and compare that to the level of energy in a room in which half or a third of the whole group is talking at once.

Varying the Methodologies

Varying the techniques you use to address the agenda items will help participants stay focused and engaged, leading to a better outcome for the group. When structuring a retreat agenda, we're likely to choose several of the methodologies that follow.

Listening

Often, when people need to be brought up to date on an issue, someone is asked to prepare an informational report before the retreat. If possible, ask the client to send this report to participants ahead of time so you won't have to spend precious time at the retreat conveying this basic information to the group.

If it's necessary to have oral reports, however, ask the presenters to keep them short and simple—ideally, no more than ten minutes—and leave those PowerPoint presentations back at the office. It's hard for most people to listen intently and absorb information for very long. If there must be several such reports, intersperse them with other activities.

There will always be someone in the room who didn't do the assigned reading. Bring extra copies of any reports and distribute them early in the retreat to participants who haven't brought their own copies.

Sometimes a deeper kind of listening is called for. When contentious issues haven't been solved satisfactorily in the past, a retreat can be a place where people learn to draw one another out, rather than judging, comparing, or advising one another or dismissing each other's concerns.

Asking and Answering Questions

Participants may have questions they are reluctant to ask, particularly if the retreat includes senior executives with whom they do not have frequent contact. They may not want to appear misinformed or ignorant or to come across as challenging a more senior official. Or they might simply be shy.

You can create a safer environment for asking questions by having people write them down on index cards. After collecting the cards you can read the questions aloud, addressing each one to the appropriate individual or group. Or you might toss them into a paper bag and ask various participants to draw them at random and read them out loud. Both of these methods allow participants to maintain their anonymity while still getting their questions asked. Retreat participants usually appreciate top management's willingness to answer questions in this manner, and they often acquire important new information and perspectives.

But senior managers must be prepared to handle the unexpected. In a retreat we conducted for a federal agency field office, for example, the widely admired leader, Latanya, was asked, "Is it true you're leaving us to go to headquarters in Washington?"

It was indeed true. Latanya hadn't realized that anyone on the staff knew about her upcoming promotion and consequent transfer, and she had to decide on the spot how to handle the issue. Latanya dealt with this potentially awkward situation effectively by confirming that she did expect to be leaving, but that the final paperwork hadn't come through and she had felt it was premature to announce something that wasn't 100 percent final.

If executives invite questions at the retreat, they must be prepared to answer them truthfully or at least explain forthrightly why they cannot provide a full answer. A retreat is not a place to evade or mislead.

If participants hold management's collective feet to the fire by asking follow-up questions when they don't receive satisfactory answers to their queries, your role as facilitator is relatively passive. If, however, executives give unclear or evasive replies and no one in the group challenges them, you may have to play a more active role in encouraging candor.

Observing Others' Actions or Discussions

When participants need to understand other people's viewpoints, you can use a technique in which some participants silently observe other participants discussing an issue or working on a problem. The well-known *fishbowl* is typical of this kind of experience. Chairs are set up in inner and outer circles. People sitting in the inner ring discuss a topic while those in the outer ring simply observe and listen. In the subsequent debriefing of this activity, those who were being observed hear comments about the effectiveness of their behavior, and the observers sharpen their feedback skills.

For a long retreat you can structure more innovative observational opportunities. For a marketing retreat, for instance, you might take the group on an excursion to watch customer behavior in stores and then, back at the retreat, ask the participants to apply what they've learned to their merchandising strategies.

Another possibility is to give one group a task to complete under a time constraint, and then ask other participants to observe patterns in the way members of the group work together. For example, in a retreat we led for an arts organization, we asked half the participants to come up with a creative closing for the offsite while the other half made notes about how the first group worked as a team. This sparked a rich dialogue about how the group's work reflected relationships and teamwork back in the office. And it gave us a very imaginative way to close.

Reflecting on Experiences

The need to be in conversation hour after hour can be exhausting. It's a good idea to provide some time for individual reflection so people can gather their thoughts outside the flurry of activity. You might provide time for participants to take a walk outdoors or make notes in a personal journal.

Writing down their thoughts often helps people clarify their ideas, even to themselves. As you'll see in the exercises in the later chapters of this book, we often ask participants to write their thoughts on Post-it Notes before sharing them with the group. Writing helps extroverts reflect before they speak, allows introverts to be heard. If the activity is structured so that all the Post-its are read prior to discussing any idea, it ensures that participants don't just agree with the first two or three suggestions that are voiced. The group will gain a much greater diversity of options to choose from when people have some focused time to think before they can influence (or be influenced by) others.

Applying Theories to Real Situations

Before participants can fully engage in certain activities, they may need some theoretical background. In a strategic planning retreat, for example, they may need to understand different planning models.

When a theoretical framework is new to people, they frequently need time to try the ideas out before they can fully understand them. Don't assume that just because people have heard something that they fully grasp it—or that they'll even remember it. We believe that theory should be presented in as experiential a manner as possible. It's best to give people small pieces of information, have them use the information in some way, and then move on to the next learning point.

Learning About What Has Happened Elsewhere

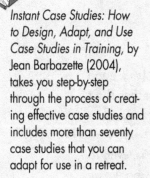

Instant Case Studies: How to Design, Adapt, and Use Case Studies in Training, by Jean Barbazette (2004), takes you step-by-step through the process of creating effective case studies and includes more than seventy case studies that you can adapt for use in a retreat.

Hearing what worked well in another organization confronted by similar issues can give participants a new lens through which to view old problems. As part of a series of planning retreats that we facilitated for a museum, for example, members of the staff conducted a benchmarking study. First, they identified organizations—not just other museums, but amusement parks and department stores as well—that were renowned for areas the museum wanted to improve, such as customer service. Museum staff interviewed people from the selected organizations and brought that information into the retreats. The retreat group then adapted ideas from the benchmarking study to suggest innovative ways for the museum to improve the experience of its visitors.

You might also use case studies to provide a framework for exploring issues in the participants' organization.

Improvisation, Role Playing, and Storytelling

Increasingly, organizations are using improvisation to give people new experiences and tools to express their feelings in a fun and relatively nonthreatening way. As a facilitator, you might find it useful to take an improvisation course to become familiar with the principles and techniques.

Role plays offer another means for people to try out new behaviors and responses to what are often familiar situations. You can custom-design a role play that reflects the organization's particular circumstances (and jargon) or use a role play from a very different field of endeavor that might give participants some useful distance on their situation. Participants can act out (and get coaching for) situations they have found difficult to manage and can put themselves in another's shoes by taking on that person's role. (Caution: Some people have a strong negative reaction against playing roles. We never force anyone to accept a role. Anyone who doesn't want to participate can be an observer.)

Storytelling allows listeners to create mental images that they are much more likely to remember than bullet points on a flip chart. You can suggest the form of the story (science fiction, an urban legend, or a fairy tale, for example) or leave it up to the participants' imaginations. You can also tell a brief story yourself to make a memorable learning point that might encourage participants to take a broader view on an issue. Or you can have the participants tell a story as a group, with each participant providing a sentence of the story when a Koosh ball is tossed to him or her. Stories can be used to give life to a vision for the future, and they can illustrate the behavior that is (or should be) rewarded in the organization. Much like metaphor (discussed later in this chapter), stories can help people raise difficult issues in less threatening ways.

These techniques, which engage participants' emotions and bodies as well as their intellects, tend to be highly memorable. When these forms of adult play are skillfully led, even the shyest participants may raise important issues. These techniques may, however, also leave people feeling awkward if the facilitator doesn't have a mastery of them. You must assess your own ability to create an engaging and meaningful exercise with these techniques.

For inspiration in incorporating improvisation, role playing, and storytelling into your retreats we recommend

- *Stories Trainers Tell,* by Mary B. Wacker and Lori L. Silverman (2003), offers information on types of stories, how to incorporate stories for maximum effect, how to find stories to tell, and how to craft a story. It also includes dozens of stories that can be used or adapted to jump-start conversations about topics such as communication, leadership, motivation, values, collaboration, and creative thinking.

- *Orchestrating Collaboration at Work: Using Music, Improv, Storytelling, and Other Arts to Improve Teamwork,* by Arthur B. VanGundy and Linda Naiman (2003), contains several excellent exercises that use storytelling and improvisation as well as other art forms to help groups explore important issues.

- *Training to Imagine: Practical Improvisational Theatre Techniques to Enhance Creativity, Teamwork, Leadership, and Learning,* by Kat Koppett (2001), also presents improvisational and storytelling activities and an excellent overview of the basic theory of improvisation.

- *Playing Along: 37 Group Learning Activities Borrowed from Improvisational Theater,* by Izzy Gesell (1997), contains several improvisational activities that can be adapted for use in team building, culture change, or creative thinking retreats.

Music and Rhythm

Music can help create a mood, such as contemplation prior to a guided visualization exercise, playfulness at the start of the retreat or the end of the day, liveliness right after lunch, and the like.

Music also has metaphorical possibilities galore. Whether it's Bob Dylan's "The Times They Are A-Changing," The Beatles' "Yesterday," Louis Armstrong singing "What a Wonderful World," or Vivaldi's "Four Seasons," music can evoke strong metaphorical associations.

Making music together can help strengthen bonds among group members. Rather than a boring flip chart presentation, participants can report out their small group discussions using song lyrics or in rhythmic phrases.

We sometimes give rattles and other noisemakers to groups to help them enforce their own ground rules by making noise when the norms are violated. Or we introduce a rain stick that participants request from one another when they want to be heard in the large group; the person holding the stick has the floor.

Skits

You might invite small groups to create short skits that demonstrate some significant points—"Illustrate how we work together," for instance, or, "Create a TV spot, complete with jingle, to promote our new customer relations strategy." Skits are almost always funny and memorable, especially if people are given hats, toys, or objects from their offices to work with.

A group can generally work up a skit in twenty minutes or less. But beware of participants becoming so wrapped up in the humor of their performance that the central point is lost. If your retreat includes an overnight stay, after-dinner skits can be an excellent way to get people working together and having fun at the same time.

Metaphor

Participants may need an indirect way to express their feelings about sensitive issues. We frequently ask people to use metaphors (visual symbols) to describe how they feel. Metaphors can free people up to be more creative and more candid about issues they're reluctant to discuss.

At a retreat we led for a rather formal group of investment fund executives, for instance, we scattered Beanie Babies around the room. When the executives began talking about how they worked together, we asked each person to choose an animal that represented how they saw their role in the group.

These executives told us later that it proved relatively easy for them, high-powered and serious as they were, to grab a couple of stuffed animals to illustrate, for example, that "everybody thinks I'm a shark, but inside I'm really a lamb." It would have been harder for them to say directly, "Hey, you guys think I'm so tough, but my feelings get hurt around here." This activity was memorable, fun, and helped loosen people up.

A Chinese finger trap can be a powerful metaphor for a group that gets stuck. What counterproductive behaviors make it harder

You will find very useful metaphor exercises in the following books:

- *101 Activities for Teaching Creativity and Problem Solving,* by Arthur B. VanGundy (2005), includes dozens of exercises that use metaphor to stimulate creative thinking.
- *Shake, Rattle & Roll: Using the Ordinary to Make Your Training Extraordinary,* by Sharon Bowman (1999, pp. 77–88), presents some excellent metaphor exercises.

Many books contain creative thinking exercises. Some of our favorites are these:

- *101 Activities for Teaching Creativity and Problem Solving*, by Arthur B. VanGundy (2005).
- *The Big Book of Creativity Games: Quick, Fun Activities for Jumpstarting Innovation*, by Robert Epstein (2000).
- *A Whack on the Side of the Head* (1998) and *A Kick in the Seat of the Pants* (1996), by Roger von Oech.
- *Jump Start Your Brain*, by Doug Hall (1996).
- *Thinkertoys: A Handbook of Business Creativity*, by Michael Michalko (1991).

to escape from the traps that people set for themselves? A Rubik's Cube can be used as a metaphor for what is puzzling participants and the kind of fresh thinking they'll have to employ to move forward. The retreat facility's garden can be a metaphor for valuing diversity, planting seeds for the future, needing to weed out unproductive practices, and the like.

If you provide the metaphor, make sure it's one that everyone will understand; be sensitive to cultural and generational differences. Choose your metaphors carefully, as an inappropriate metaphor may unnecessarily limit the group's thinking.

Envisioning Possibilities and Generating New Ideas

We all tend to fall back on what's familiar. It's hard sometimes to imagine what we've never seen. To create positive change in the workplace, however, people must be able to imagine how things could be. You will boost participants' envisioning powers by structuring activities that help them reflect on what's possible. You might bring such materials as photographs and magazines to provide visual symbols that could trigger participants' imaginations.

Drawing, Collage, and Mask Making

Using their aesthetic abilities often helps people think differently about issues. Drawing or making collages can be individual or group activities that help participants express what's on their minds. For instance, you could ask people at the start of a long retreat to make a collage that illustrates how they see the organization and then ask them at the end to create a second collage that expresses the future they're aiming to create. You'd be surprised how many top executives enjoy rolling up their sleeves and really getting into this kind of activity.

> Assure participants they needn't worry about talent when expressing themselves artistically. Most people aren't particularly skilled at these activities, so these exercises actually become a leveling influence among the participants.

Toys and Other Props

We bring a large collection of inexpensive toys and silly hats to most of our retreats. Aside from their usefulness as metaphors and as props for memorable presentations, toys can help us establish a more relaxed environment, engage participants playfully with one another, inject needed humor into a tense session, and involve more of the participants' senses (such as tactile and kinesthetic) in their conversations with one another.

Visual Gallery

Participants can hang pictures they create, meaningful images they find in magazines, or Post-it Notes with written messages along a wall for others to walk past and contemplate. The visual gallery might have messages for the boss, another team, or the organization's customers. This technique allows the messages to be conveyed while the messengers remain anonymous and also often has greater impact for the recipients than hearing the same messages from group report-outs. Also, because it is done in silence, it allows the recipients to think about and absorb the levels of meaning in the messages.

> For our money there is no better book on how to use art forms effectively in a retreat setting than *Orchestrating Collaboration at Work: Using Music, Improv, Storytelling, and Other Arts to Improve Teamwork*, by Arthur B. VanGundy and Linda Naiman (2003).
> We also recommend highly *Visual Explorer: Picturing Approaches to Complex Challenges*, by Charles C. Palus and David M. Horth (2001), with 224 stunning images and a facilitator's guide for helping groups explore complex topics through images.

Physical Activities

Most of us aren't accustomed to sitting in one place all day. Even in desk jobs, we visit other offices, climb up and down stairs, wander the halls, go out for lunch, walk to meetings. Retreat participants need similar opportunities to move around.

On a nice day you can send breakout groups outdoors and ask them to conduct their discussions while walking. (The results will definitely be different from those of a seated discussion.) People can illustrate where processes break down in their office by creating an imaginary machine. Simple aikido principles can help group members see how focusing on obstacles rather than goals is hampering their ability to take action. Or people can place themselves along an imaginary line from one end of the room to the other and designate each end an opposite position: for example, "The front of the room represents throwing out our budgeting process and inventing something completely new. The back of the room represents leaving our budgeting process exactly as it is. Arrange yourselves along a continuum. Where do you stand?" It's a great way to see what people are thinking, and it gets participants' blood circulating. (This sort of exercise is even more energizing when conducted in silence.)

Circus Techniques

Juggling, acrobatics, magic tricks, and clowning can all be used to interesting effect in a retreat setting. The discussion of the competing priorities that we're juggling will be much more memorable if accompanied by group members attempting to juggle balls or beanbags. Encouraging participants to adopt clown personae can help them see the humor in a stressful situation or to speak the truth to authority. A magician can help illustrate a better future when current problems have been resolved, and an acrobat can be a symbol for how the group will have to stretch itself to reach its goals. Participants don't have to be skilled at circus techniques to use them, metaphorically or as a fun adjunct to a story or a skit.

Guided Visualization

Guided visualization can be an excellent technique for helping participants imagine the future they are hoping to create. When we use this technique in a retreat, we create a script for ourselves in advance that encourages participants to relax and visualize a place where they feel creative, adventuresome, playful, or sure of themselves. This place can serve as a springboard for imagining themselves and their colleagues working together more productively toward the achievement of important goals.

If you decide to use guided visualization, be careful about where you place it in the agenda. If you choose after lunch or near the end of the day you can be sure that some of the participants will drift off to sleep. (See *Ask the Genie* in Chapter 11, pp. 294–296 for an example of a guided visualization activity.)

Silence

Almost any retreat activity will be enriched by the judicious use of silence, and we tend to use it liberally. It's a great equalizer between those who talk a great deal and those who are more reticent, and between those who are more powerful and those who are reluctant or uncertain about speaking out. We have found that using silence as a precursor to an important discussion greatly enriches that discussion. As a rule, the more articulate and verbal participants are in our pre-retreat interviews, the more likely we are to include activities that employ silence.

Incorporating Rituals

We like to include rituals that signal that the retreat day is starting or ending or that it's time to transition from one activity to another or to take a break. The ritual might consist of special music, Tibetan chimes, rhythmic hand clapping that the group joins in doing, or a brightly colored ball that you toss in the air. It might be the use of red circles and green squares to signify, "I have a concern about the recommendations that were just made," and, "I agree with those points," respectively. (We recommend using different shapes for anything that contrasts red with green, as a significant minority of people cannot distinguish those colors.)

Be sure to tell people what the rituals mean before you employ them for the first time. If you incorporate rituals that the group understands, you'll have much less difficulty with, for example, bringing the group back to order at the end of an activity without having to shout over the participants' talk. We encourage you to vary the rituals you employ; participants may learn to tune out something highly repetitive.

If appropriate, you might consider giving the group or each individual participant a memento that recalls the rituals that were particularly significant—for example, a CD with the song you played when the group came up with its breakthrough ideas or the picture each participant chose to be a metaphor for what the organization will be known for when the group achieves its goals.

Chapter 6

Leading the Retreat

At the retreat your primary job as facilitator is to manage the process. Your job is not to "fix" what is "wrong" with the organization. It's important that your client has realistic expectations of you and of the retreat itself. No retreat will result in overnight change. When you do your job well, though, you help create an environment in which the hard things can be discussed, and that makes it easier for the retreat participants to achieve their objectives.

In his book *Masterful Facilitation,* A. Glenn Kiser (1998, p. 7) defines facilitation as "a purposeful, systematic intervention into the actions of an individual or group that results in an enhanced, ongoing capability to meet desired objectives." We like that definition, because to be an effective facilitator you have to be purposeful. You must know what you are doing and why you are doing it at all times.

The word *facilitation* comes from the Latin root *facilis,* which means *easy.*

105

Your Effect on the Group

By your very presence—even if you do nothing—you are intervening in the group. Anthropologist Margaret Mead noted that simply by observing another culture you affect and subtly alter it. Similarly, merely by shining a light on participants' typical behavior when they're working together, you foster greater self-awareness, which can lead to changes in their behavior.

A key element of Kiser's definition is "to meet desired objectives." The point of facilitation is not to encourage change for its own sake but to help the group reach its goals. For this reason you must understand these goals and ensure that participants agree on what they are.

You need to monitor what is going on in the room at all times and be able to guide participants through difficult discussions, both by knowing when to prod them forward and when to encourage them to change course.

A facilitator is like a traffic cop—keeping the conversation flowing, noticing when the stoplights are broken, and reacting quickly to prevent nasty accidents. This means you must be very alert to what is happening and anticipate what is about to happen. You must respond skillfully, so participants feel they are being guided to a destination they want to reach.

The key to effective facilitation is your own self-awareness. You should be keenly aware of what you are experiencing at any given moment and be able to elicit responses from the participants about how your experience matches theirs. In addition, you will have to make conscious choices about how you behave when interacting with the group, because they will look to you as a model.

As a facilitator, you'll want to help participants accomplish several things:

- Create a positive, collaborative environment in which they can explore common interests and goals.
- Participate actively.
- Stay on task and complete their work.
- Establish a framework for addressing issues.
- Create a safe space for surfacing, exploring, and addressing difficult issues.

- Distinguish between concerns about content (such as finding a solution to a certain problem) and those about process (such as feeling pressured to come to agreement).
- Manage conflict effectively.
- Ensure that everyone who has something to say is heard.
- Examine and modify behavior that is hampering the group's effectiveness.
- Stimulate the widest range of thinking.
- Identify and solve problems.
- Make intelligent decisions.
- Summarize agreements.
- Determine appropriate action steps.

In their classic book *Theory in Practice: Increasing Professional Effectiveness*, Chris Argyris and Donald A. Schön (1974) talk about three values that we believe are the underpinnings of effective retreat facilitation:

- *Valid information.* Participants share all relevant information in such a way that others can understand it and, if necessary, verify it independently. This means that you as the facilitator must have no hidden agenda and will encourage all retreat participants to be straightforward about what they want and don't want.
- *Free and informed choice.* Participants define their own goals (within larger organizational goals) and determine the methods for achieving them. They are not coerced or manipulated into making choices against their will.
- *Internal commitment to the choice.* Participants take responsibility for their own choices and make those choices because they find them intrinsically rewarding.

We suggest you abide by these values and encourage the group to commit to them as well.

There must be an explicit agreement with the group about what your role is and what it isn't. Although you may deal most directly with your client, it must be clear to your client and the participants that you're working for the good of the whole group. Although this message should be communicated to the participants in advance, we encourage you to reinforce it at the beginning of the retreat itself.

Key Facilitation Practices

See Chapter 5, "Group Size and Composition," pp. 90–93, and "Varying the Methodologies," pp. 93–103.

When we teach the art of retreat facilitation, we spend considerable time helping course participants gain comfort and skill in using a variety of techniques and in working with participant groupings of various sizes. That said, all retreats have periods of whole group discussion, which draw on the following facilitator competencies.

Listen Deeply

This means quieting the little voice in your head that wants to judge, analyze, or come up with a clever response. Show with your body language and eye contact that you are paying attention to what is being said in the room.

Ask Questions

Asking questions effectively is one of the most important techniques for a facilitator to master. Most questions should be open-ended and encourage participants to provide ideas and options. Questions such as, "How should we proceed, Mecha?" "What do others think about Sidney's proposal?" "What options do you suggest, Joan?" and, "How will this move us toward our goal, Daryush?" are the staples of a facilitator's vocabulary.

At times, though, it's advisable to ask questions that elicit a yes or no response to help determine the group's mood. Questions such as, "Should we discuss this after a break?" "Are we ready to move on?" and, "Can we finish this topic before we end for the evening?" are important in assessing the group's energy for a particular topic or course of action.

It's also valuable to know how and when to ask probing questions that draw participants out. "Can you say a bit more about your thinking, Amy?" "How does this relate to the point that George just made?" and, "Can you tell us more about what you're proposing, Elaine?" are all examples of probing questions.

Asking clarifying questions is another key competency for a facilitator. When you don't understand something completely, ask the person to provide more details: "Vilma, will you tell us a bit more about how this new procedure would change your job?" If you aren't sure (or think participants aren't sure) what

Pitfalls of Overusing the Probing Technique

- Group members may feel that you are interrogating them.

- Others may feel left out as you engage in dialogue with one member.

- You may appear to have a hidden agenda or outcome that you are pushing for.

- You may distract the group from the real work they need to do.

Source: Adapted from Rees, 1998.

someone is proposing, check for understanding by asking a question like this: "I'm not certain I understand exactly what you mean, Paula. Are you proposing that we follow Bill's recommendation?"

Ask for Suggestions

As a facilitator, you don't have to have all the answers. Sometimes it's helpful to ask a participant ("Pennie, how would you suggest that we proceed on this?") or the group ("Are there other options we should consider?") for ideas. This technique also encourages the group to look to its own members for answers to its dilemmas, rather than assuming that the facilitator will always provide direction.

Paraphrase

Restate what a participant has said to confirm that you understood him or her. ("Andrea, let me see if I understand your perspective on this issue. Are you saying that . . . ?") If you have paraphrased accurately, other participants will hear a concise summary of the speaker's point to confirm their own understanding. If you have missed the point, chances are that others have too, and your question will give the participant a chance to clarify.

Be careful, however, when you are capturing individuals' comments on a flip chart. You won't be able to write everything in its entirety; you will have to summarize. Even though you'll have to edit for space, try to use as many of the speaker's exact words as possible, ask for help if you need it ("How can I capture that in a few words, Larry?"), and check for accuracy ("Does this reflect your main points?"). Guessing someone else's meaning can make it appear that you don't understand or that you disagree with what the person said or that you are trying to put your own slant on things.

Suggest a Process

Have some procedures handy for those times when the group gets stuck. You might ask the participants if they need to revisit the ground rules, suggest that they take on another person's or office's point of view. Or you might ask for a quick show of hands to see if they are ready to move on.

Help the Group Broaden Its Perspective

Sometimes participants are too focused on why an idea or plan won't work, and they need encouragement to see its potential benefits. ("We've heard a lot of concern about Karen's suggestion. Can anyone think of how we might make it work?"). Or the group may be focused entirely on its internal concerns and not thinking about the implications of proposals for others ("How do you suppose your clients will respond to this new procedure?")

Often groups lose sight of the big picture because they get mired in details. ("Are we stuck in the weeds here?") Alternatively, they may be approaching an issue so broadly that it is difficult to understand specifically what they are recommending. ("Can you help me understand what specific actions we should take, Mary?")

Ask for Options

When the group seems to be concluding a discussion too quickly or members seem unwilling to express divergent viewpoints, you can encourage them to explore other options with questions like these: "Are there other ways to approach this problem, Jon?" "Pat, is there anything else you think we should consider?" "Dottie, do you see another way we can do this?" Don't beat a dead horse, though. When the group is done, it's done.

Pull Ideas Together

Help participants see how their ideas relate to one another and encourage them to build on each other's suggestions. An observation such as, "From what we've heard from Ahmed and Alicia, it seems that you have the resources and commitment to expand sales in the eastern region," can help participants see common ground. When you show how a current point being raised relates to something said earlier, you help participants listen to one another's comments more carefully and also to tease out the differences in their approaches or recommendations. This technique also helps the person who made the original comment feel heard. You can use this technique strategically to encourage the group to build on the contributions of its quieter (and often most thoughtful) members or to call attention to the ideas of participants who are lower in the hierarchy.

Give and Receive Feedback

At times it is important to help the group see its progress or where it has reached an impasse. ("You seem to be having a difficult time narrowing down the goals, yet you were emphatic in the pre-retreat interviews that you don't want to take on too much. How should we handle this apparent contradiction?") It's equally important to ask for and to receive feedback gracefully. ("I sense that my directions for that activity were confusing. What did I leave out?")

Provide Encouragement

Often simply ensuring that key points are written on the flip charts is enough to help participants feel that their ideas are worthwhile. It may also serve to quiet down someone who keeps repeating the same point. ("Did I chart your concern accurately, Rajiv?") Sometimes it's important to recognize individuals (particularly those whose ideas may be ignored by the group) for their contributions. ("That's a really important point, Analía.") At other times, it's useful to praise the work of the whole group. ("You've generated lots of fresh ideas. I think we've got a great deal to move forward with.")

Ask for a Summary or Provide One Yourself

At key points in the conversation it is important to have a summary of what has been proposed or agreed to. You should periodically ask questions such as, "Can someone summarize what you agreed to do?" Do not ask a question like, "Does everyone understand what you agreed to so far?" because people might think they do, even when they don't. Or they might be afraid to admit that they don't.

It's helpful to have participants themselves summarize agreements or action steps. It encourages the group to take responsibility for the commitments being made. If no one else can summarize, however, don't belabor the point. Just provide the summary yourself, check for accuracy, and move on.

Make Transitions

Sometimes a retreat can feel like a series of unrelated exercises. To prevent this the facilitator has to connect one activity to the next. By reviewing what the group has accomplished and relating it to what participants are about to engage in, you help the group see its progress. We also refer back frequently to goals, decisions, or recommendations the group has agreed to, so that participants can see how one thing is building on another. ("We just came to agreement on the strategic direction that will guide your company for the next five years. Now we're going to decide which segments of your activities seem most likely to advance this strategic direction.")

Encouraging Participation

The success of the retreat will depend in large measure on your ability to elicit broad participation. The following examples provide guidelines to help you keep participants involved in the discussion.

Encourage Participants to Engage the Issue

It's natural for people to be reticent when they're dealing with issues that are difficult, even scary. You can help participants overcome this by urging them to say what's on their minds. Ask such questions as, "Rayna, do you have thoughts

Best and Worst Facilitator Practices

Behaviors That Help the Group

- Listening well
- Keeping the attention focused on the participants, not on yourself
- Speaking in simple and direct language
- Displaying energy and enthusiasm
- Treating all participants as equals
- Being willing to change direction as necessary
- Paraphrasing, summarizing, and tying ideas together
- Being open to ideas that you don't personally favor and to participants who "push your buttons"
- Using a wide range of facilitation techniques
- Offering and accepting feedback skillfully
- Staying focused on the group's progress
- Maintaining a calm, pleasant, approachable demeanor
- Being assertive in keeping the group on track

Behaviors That Hinder the Group

- Not monitoring the group's energy
- Losing track of the conversation and key ideas
- Becoming defensive
- Putting people or their ideas down
- Getting into a conflict with the participants
- Allowing the group to wander off track or to be dominated by a few participants
- Pushing ahead with an irrelevant agenda
- Noting participants' key points inaccurately on flip charts
- Being insensitive to diversity concerns
- Using humor inappropriately
- Pursuing a discussion that isn't producing fruitful results

Source: Adapted from Bens, 2000.

about this?" or, "Do you have anything to add, Ari?" When you ask the group, "Does anyone have anything to add?" wait, wait, wait for someone to respond. A moment of silence (even what may seem like an uncomfortably long moment of silence) can stimulate someone to speak up who might otherwise remain silent. Some people tend to be quieter than others and may be fully engaged even if they are not saying much—and often you can't tell unless you ask.

Ask Participants to Pair Up, or Conduct a Round-Robin

When it's very important to give everyone a chance to discuss a key issue, you can ask participants to pair up to discuss something and then report their conclusions back to the group. Or, on rare occasions, you might conduct a round-robin, asking each participant to speak in turn. We recommend reserving this latter technique for times when you absolutely must hear from everyone in the room. Round-robins take a lot of time and grow tedious if participants who have little to add feel compelled to say something anyway. And if someone doesn't want to comment, allow him or her to pass. The point here is to give everyone a chance to speak up, not to force people to say something.

Ask Participants to Write Responses on Post-it Notes or Index Cards

Having people write things down and then post these responses on a flip chart sheet or turn in index cards gives the more reflective participants the opportunity to think things through and break through the talk of the more outspoken participants. It also provides anonymity for more reluctant participants.

Reflect What You Read in Someone's Body Language

Body language can be a more powerful form of communication than words, but don't assume that you know what someone else is thinking just by observing him or her. Ask such questions as, "Jeremy, I sense that you don't agree with Sharon's proposal. Is that right?" or, "Roshana, you seem to be uncomfortable with David's response. Am I right about that?"

Manage the Participation of the Leader(s)

We hope you will give Chapter 16 to the leader (or leaders) in advance of the retreat and that she (or they) will read it. (You can print it out from the CD.) In any case, it's useful to review a few key points with the leader right before the retreat. We always urge leaders to state in their opening remarks that they will use the retreat to listen—really listen—and that they won't be taking the lead in discussions. Then we hold them to this behavior. We remind them on breaks, as necessary, of their commitment not to dominate the conversations, lead the report-outs, or give their opinions first. At times we will have a leader sit out during an activity (or leave the room) if that's necessary to foster candor.

Don't Be Part of the Problem

If you are seen as being critical of a participant's comments, if you interrupt too much, if you give unasked-for advice, or if you fill in the silence when the group grows quiet, you will hinder effective participation.

Barriers to Participation

People may hold back from participating when they

- Are confused about or uninterested in the topic being discussed
- Lack confidence in themselves or in the value of their contributions
- Worry about others' reactions to their ideas
- Have a history of not being listened to
- Lack trust in the group
- Feel "shut down" by more talkative members
- Feel emotional
- Are upset that things aren't going their way

Source: Adapted from Bens, 2000.

Process or Content Facilitator?

Every facilitator has a different approach to leading retreats, and you'll want to make sure yours is compatible with the organization's culture and consistent with your client's expectations.

Your client may expect you to be either a *process facilitator* or a *content facilitator* (content expert) or possibly to play some of both roles.

Acting as a Process Facilitator

When you are acting as a process facilitator, your focus is on helping the participants understand how they are working together to accomplish their tasks. You observe who speaks up and who does not and how participants interact and collaborate with one another. (Do they interrupt each other or listen respectfully? Are ideas considered or are they rejected out of hand? Is communication generally supportive or competitive? Who makes decisions and how are they made?) You help participants set ground rules at the beginning of the retreat and call attention to those rules as needed. You keep the discussions focused and ensure that everyone can be heard.

At appropriate times you may question the participants about the way they are interacting. In doing so, you'll help them see and correct dysfunctional communication patterns.

Even if you are doing pure process facilitation, you should be knowledgeable about the organization and the issues participants are concerned about. If you don't have personal experience in an industry, do some research—read internal reports provided by your client, check out Web sites, review industry trend reports, even conduct some outside interviews—to make sure you understand the business and can speak its language (terms of art, acronyms, expressions, or jargon). Knowledge of the full range of an organization's concerns will pay off in countless ways. No client will be pleased about a retreat—no matter how flawless the process—that has led to decisions that the organization cannot support. If you are not knowledgeable enough about the organization and the issues it faces, you might inadvertently lead a retreat that wastes the group's time.

Acting as a Content Facilitator

If you have content knowledge, you can draw on your experience in the organization (if you're an internal consultant or recent employee) or with other organizations in the same industry as well as your expertise in areas such as strategy or teamwork to help participants make more informed decisions. By paying attention to the content of the work, and not just the processes, you will be able to challenge participants to examine their assumptions, help them make thoughtful decisions, and ask the group tough questions about actions they are proposing to take. In *Organization Consulting: A Gestalt Approach,* author Edwin C. Nevis (1987) describes the kind of distinction we are discussing here as the difference between *evocative* and *provocative* modes of influence.

When working in the evocative mode, the facilitator helps the group gain fresh awareness of its behavior with the aim of fostering action. A facilitator might observe, "You seem to be reluctant to address this issue openly. You're talking around it, and you're stuck. To break through, you'll have to confront the issue head on." The facilitator would then help the group deal with the issue forthrightly and not wander off into a thicket of euphemisms and tangents.

In the provocative mode the facilitator intervenes to sharpen the group's focus and press the participants toward a specific goal or narrow range of possible outcomes. A facilitator might say, "You keep talking about several options for dealing with the problem, yet from what I've heard you say and what I know of your organization, three of the options clearly are beyond the range of what's doable, and two of the others are practically identical. I think you're more likely to come up with a practical action plan if you focus only on X and Y, decide which of these two you prefer, and move on from there."

Although a facilitator typically acts to increase awareness so that participants can find their own way, sometimes provoking people is the only way to help them reach a viable goal. You might, for example, want to press participants to explain their thinking: "How do you know your idea will work? Have you considered . . . ?" The point is not to pass judgment on the participants' proposals or decisions but to urge them to explore every aspect of an issue so they can come up with the most thoughtful and feasible conclusions.

Sometimes content knowledge allows you to play a provocative role by asking just the right naïve or incredulous questions that will stimulate participants to see things more clearly. "Are you saying that if you take this action, you're likely to get this result?" a facilitator might ask. "Hmm," a participant might respond, "I guess that doesn't make a whole lot of sense, does it?"

You and your client should decide in advance whether you will focus strictly on process or become involved with content as well.

When Should the Facilitator Intervene?

You need to help participants recognize behaviors that are fostering or hampering their effectiveness by calling attention to them yourself and by continually making decisions about whether it would be helpful or not to intervene when confronted with specific dysfunctional behaviors.

Our advice is to intervene only when it is truly necessary, after you have allowed time for participants to deal with their own concerns and when you are reasonably sure that your intervention will advance the discussion. Before jumping in to "help" participants, ask yourself these questions. If your answer to any of them is yes, *do not* intervene.

- Does the dysfunctional behavior seem like a one-time occurrence that participants will move beyond easily?
- Is the behavior bothering only you, not the group?
- Will a member of the group likely intervene if you do not?
- Will the intervention distract the group from tackling a tough issue?
- Would intervening later, if necessary, be as useful as intervening now?
- Are you so staked in the outcome that it will upset you if the group rejects your intervention?
- Might the intervention take more time than the group has available to process it?

At the same time, you don't want to adopt a hands-off style that invites participants to waste time on fruitless discussions. If you decide it is appropriate to intervene, you must then determine which of three levels of intervention—personal, interpersonal, or group—is most likely to elicit the best response.

Let's say you have noticed that the participants keep wandering off task, largely because Lisa keeps bringing up extraneous matters and Mike is arguing with her.

A *personal intervention* might be simply to encourage Lisa to remain focused on the agenda. Or it might be to remind Mike of the ground rule "Listen to understand, not to judge."

An *interpersonal intervention* might be to have Mike and Lisa practice giving and receiving feedback effectively.

But in this case the best course of action would probably be a *group intervention*. After all, the whole group is allowing Mike and Lisa to derail the conversation. Reminding the group about the ground rules they agreed to earlier and stressing the need to stick to the agenda (or to decide explicitly that another topic is more important) would probably be the most beneficial intervention.

Or let's say that the group is getting off track because every time Chris raises a question, Ron rolls his eyes and tells Chris that the question is irrelevant to the discussion at hand. Other group members try to defend Chris, who they feel is being attacked, but Ron's behavior does not change. In this case the best intervention would likely be personal—calling Ron's attention to the ground rules, for example, and if Ron's behavior continues, talking with him about it between sessions.

Facilitators, particularly inexperienced ones, are often tempted to intervene anytime there is a strong emotional reaction in the room, especially if someone becomes angry or bursts into tears. This is treacherous terrain. We urge you to curb your natural instincts to "make everything all right." It's perfectly acceptable to remain silent when someone becomes emotional.

Emotional responses might occur when participants are

- Dealing with an issue that has been frustrating them for a long time and just discussing it is releasing pent-up feelings
- Feeling threatened in some way
- Feeling embarrassed or exposed
- Feeling passionate about a particular course of action and concerned that the organization is moving in the "wrong" direction
- Feeling left out, unheard, ignored, or not valued
- Feeling pressured to support the growing consensus in the room, with which they disagree
- Feeling preoccupied with something unrelated to the subject under discussion, such as fatigue, an unresolved work issue, or a family problem

Being Transparent with the Group

Many facilitators get into trouble by trying to appear infallible. But participants will respect you more for show-ing your humanity and acknowledging uncertainty or mistakes than for turning every challenge to your author-ity into a test of wills.

Allowing an airing of these emotions will often reveal the passions in the room and save the group from making costly mistakes. Such mistakes occur when groups rush their discussions because they are riding a wave of emotion or are making a misguided effort to quell that emotion.

It's common for emotions to rise to the surface at retreats, and we think this is generally a positive development because emotions are a sign that par-ticipants care about the issues. Emotions per se shouldn't be of concern; inter-vene only if they lead to dysfunctional behavior such as name-calling, negative stereotyping, or the threat of physical violence.

It's a different story, though, if a participant becomes emotional with you. Then you must respond, not to the emotions but to what triggered them.

Let's say Mary Lou seems to be upset with you. Ask yourself whether her emotional response may have been prompted by something inappropriate that you did or said. If so, don't be defensive. Acknowledge her point of view, explain your intention, and express regret for the impact. This has the added benefit of modeling the kind of behavior that will help the participants them-selves work together most productively. For example, in your desire to move the session along, you might have cut Mary Lou off when she was speaking. And she might be particularly sensitive to not being heard.

However, if you are convinced that Mary Lou's emotional reaction is really an attempt (conscious or not) to distract the group from a difficult issue, it is worth drawing out not only Mary Lou but others as well. Asking the group what you might do to make it easier to discuss a particular issue will often lower the emotional temperature by focusing people on something practical.

Giving Feedback to Retreat Participants

As a facilitator, you have a great deal of power. You can interrupt the proceedings. You can make one participant look good in the eyes of her coworkers or embarrass another.

By the mere act of standing up in the front of the room, you are having an impact on the participants. It may or may not be the impact you intend. Most facilitators have good intentions; they want to help the participants work together better. The key is to match your impact with your intent.

This is especially important when you decide it's absolutely necessary for the work of the group to give feedback to individual participants. If Ed has been interrupting Carolina every time she speaks, for instance, and if subtle reminders of the ground rules haven't made an impact on Ed's behavior, you might want to raise the issue with him privately at the next break (or even call a break if Ed's behavior is disruptive enough that it cannot be allowed to continue). You're not trying to embarrass him, only to make him aware of his behavior and the impact it is having on the group. So don't confront him in public. If you do, everyone else in the room will take note of your action.

Ask permission first ("May I talk with you about something, Ed?") and be sensitive about your timing. Don't give feedback to a participant who is in the throes of an intense emotional reaction. He won't be able to hear it. Then take care to describe specific, observable behavior, not your opinions or judgments. ("I couldn't help noticing that you keep interrupting Carolina, and this is making it very difficult for Carolina to be heard.") Finally, ask Ed for the behavior that would be more helpful. ("You'll have a chance to express yourself, but it would help your colleagues if you'd let Carolina have her say without interrupting her.")

If all else fails, ask your client what she wants you to do. She might then have to tell Ed that if he wants to participate in the retreat, he must abide by the ground rules.

See Chapter 7 for an in-depth look at strategies for dealing effectively with participants who are acting out.

Co-Facilitation Challenges

Participants will observe how you and your co-facilitator work together. If the two of you collaborate smoothly, you are modeling effective teamwork; if not, you'll be a distraction. When you don't work well with one another, you diminish your credibility with the group. And if there is tension between the two of you that mirrors tension that exists in the group (for example, between younger and older, male and female, or African American and white), you will be the screen on which the group projects its own issues. Participants might become so engrossed in taking sides that they lose focus on why they're at the retreat.

See Chapter 2, "Deciding Whether to Work with a Co-Facilitator," pp. 47–49.)

It takes effort and thoughtful planning to work well with a co-facilitator. Rather than focusing entirely on the group and your individual relationship to the group, each of you also has to focus on the other—how you're working together and how the group will *perceive* that you are working together.

You will have to trust one another a great deal. You can't afford to undermine one another or be seen as disrespectful of one another's professionalism. That means that unless one of you has asked for the other's help or guidance, each of you must feel at ease with the other when she is leading the group.

We would make an exception only if something a co-facilitator did might cause harm to the group or keep it from accomplishing its task. In such a case we would still tread lightly. ("May I interrupt, Margarita? I wonder if it wouldn't be more productive if we discussed that issue at a later time. Would it work for you if we finished the conversation about planning goals first?")

It's important for both of you to be in agreement about the division of roles. Who will lead which exercises? What different things will each of you watch for in the room? Who will chart participants' responses for each session? Who will intervene and how if the group is violating its norms or wandering off track? Even where each of you will stand or sit when not presenting should be predetermined, so you can easily catch each other's eye without being disruptive. You might assign respective roles based on each person's level of comfort with particular interventions, substantive knowledge of a topic being discussed, or skill at recording material on flip charts rapidly and legibly.

We recommend that you play to the strengths of co-facilitation by taking turns being in front of the group. Participants will be less likely to become bored when they experience different paces, energy levels, and speaking styles.

Even with the best intentions and extensive preplanning, however, co-facilitators will sometimes disagree about the best course of action to take at a given moment. Here's how we handle this issue:

- We never contradict one another in front of the group, but we do consult with one another frequently. (During breaks, we check in with each other, asking how effectively one of us handled a particular intervention, for example, or if we should change course based on something that happened in the room.)
- We don't "rescue" one another unless explicitly invited to.
- We may add clarification to instructions or ask our co-facilitator to elaborate on instructions if it's clear that the group is lost.
- We ask for help from one another publicly when we need it. One of us might say, for instance, "Did I cover everything I was supposed to?" "How do you think we should proceed?" This creates an opening for the other person to chime in.
- We debrief one another at the end of each session and each day, as well as after the whole retreat, to explore what worked well and what we might do differently next time.

Diversity Issues

Your job requires that you be aware of and sensitive to the role that diversity plays at a retreat. It's a delicate balancing act to remain attuned to possible cultural differences and at the same time not categorize participants' responses as products of their cultural identity. Some of the diversity variables you will have to consider will be related to the organization itself (the part of the organization individuals work in, their position in the hierarchy, the length of their tenure, the breadth of their experience), and some will have to do with individuals' backgrounds (age, gender, race, ethnicity, national origin, religion, and personality).

Cultural disconnects occur when behavior that is the norm in one cultural group (ethnic, racial, religious, and so forth) is inappropriate in another, creating a kind of "we're okay, you're not okay" mentality. Such clashes can be destructive when the individuals involved are unaware that the different behavior stems

Diversity in a global context is a vast, complex, and important topic, which we cannot possibly fully address in this book. For facilitators who want to learn more, we highly recommend the following:

- *The Global Diversity Desk Reference,* by Lee Gardenswartz, Anita Rowe, Patricia Digh, and Martin F. Bennett (2003).

- *International Dimensions of Organizational Behavior,* by Nancy J. Adler (1997).

- *Intercultural Communication in the Global Workplace,* by Iris Varner and Linda Beamer (1995).

- *The Promise of Diversity: Over 40 Voices Discuss Strategies for Eliminating Discrimination in Organizations,* Elsie Cross, J. H. Katz, F. A. Miller, and E. W. Seashore (Eds.) (1994).

from different cultural values and norms and instead judge the behavior in absolute, right or wrong terms.

Cultural differences can come up in many ways at a retreat. Let's say Hélène expresses frustration with Lando because Lando "won't stand up for what he believes." Hélène sees Lando's reticence and reluctance to take issue with others' opinions as evidence of lack of intellect, paucity of ideas, and shameless fawning. But Lando is merely acting in a way that he considers respectful. According to his cultural norms, you simply don't challenge others in public.

As the facilitator you must be mindful of how participants' adherence to different cultural norms might affect their interactions, not only at the retreat itself but back at the office as well. These effects could run the gamut from simple misunderstandings to unexpressed resentment to open and angry confrontation. You will have to help participants manage possible cultural clashes before they hamper the group's effectiveness. At the same time, you must engage everyone in the work of the retreat and foster behavior in keeping with the ground rules the participants agreed to—a balance that is sometimes difficult to maintain.

Culture influences many aspects of participant interactions. For example, culture affects everyone's (including our own)

- Willingness to be direct and candid in a group setting
- Views on appropriate levels of formality and respect
- Perspectives on time and timeliness

- Orientation toward the individual or toward the group
- Degree of ease with showing emotion
- Willingness to express disagreement
- Comfort with physical closeness
- Tolerance for uncertainty
- Use of language
- Use of body language

Willingness to Be Direct and Candid in a Group Setting

Certain cultures rely more on context, implicit and indirect communication, and subtle nonverbal cues to express meaning, whereas others value putting all one's cards on the table. Because the retreat format favors the latter, we recommend that you structure exercises that will encourage the more reticent participants to contribute, particularly when retreat participants represent various levels in the organizational hierarchy.

In addition, some cultures value a thoughtful silence prior to responding, whereas others believe that responding quickly indicates enthusiasm for or knowledge of the subject being discussed. The people who value an initial silence might see the people who speak up promptly as rude, and the people who speak up promptly might see the people who take time to reflect silently as disengaged. To level the playing field, we integrate silent activities into every retreat that we lead.

See Chapter 5, "Varying the Methodologies," pp. 93–103, for ideas on how to vary the exercises to help all participants feel free to contribute.

Views on Appropriate Levels of Formality and Respect

Some cultures are very hierarchical and formal. Titles are important, and people in these cultures typically address strangers, their elders, and social and organizational superiors by titles or last names and may consider the practice of using first names in most situations, even with strangers—which is increasingly common in business settings in the United States—to be disrespectful. People in such cultures also rarely express disagreement with or question their seniors (in both age and rank), particularly in public settings. Contrast that with a culture that is more informal and where leaders value dissenting views. Because the retreat format favors the latter (at least nominally), it's important to take this potential cultural difference into account when structuring and leading the various exercises.

Perspectives on Time and Timeliness

In his book *The Dance of Life: The Other Dimension of Time,* cultural anthropologist Edward Hall (1983) contrasts cultures that value punctuality, adherence to schedules, and accomplishing tasks with those that give interpersonal relations precedence over precise schedules and specific accomplishments.

To more task-oriented cultures, spending time on building relationships can be seen as a waste of time and needlessly touchy-feely. To more relationship-oriented cultures, it's critical to develop a level of personal comfort before delving into the task.

In a retreat setting you will have to manage the push and pull between the two orientations, as participants struggle with task and process issues.

Orientation Toward the Individual or Toward the Group

Some cultures encourage individuals to look after themselves and their immediate families primarily (broadly speaking, majority U.S. culture is an example). Other cultures stress the primary importance of looking after the welfare of the larger groups to which individuals belong. In the former it is perfectly appropriate to recognize the work of an individual. In the latter it might not be. You'll have to keep these differences in mind when structuring activities where the work of individuals might be recognized. These differences might also come up if you ask participants to express their personal views and not represent their teams, departments, or divisions.

Different cultural groups may have different reactions when a person is asserting his leadership of the group. Lee Gardenswartz and colleagues (2003), for example, tell a story about showing a photograph to a group of Chinese and a group of Americans. The photograph showed people in a room with one person standing in the front of the others. When asked who the person in front was, the Americans said that he was the leader and the Chinese identified him as the outcast.

In addition, in more individualistic societies people are encouraged to fight for what they believe to be right. This contrasts with more collectivistic societies, which value harmonious working relationships, compromise, and cooperation. The former might be viewed by the latter as overly aggressive and self-promoting, and the latter might view the former as passive and not supportive of individual achievement. These fundamentally different motivations can make it difficult to find mutually acceptable solutions to issues that might come up in a retreat.

Degree of Ease with Showing Emotion

Some cultures value emotional expression, and others value keeping emotions in check (although there are obviously great individual variations and personal preferences within both traditions). You have to be cognizant of these differences throughout the retreat, as emotional responses often come out during discussions. This will help you guide the group's discussions, balancing sensitivity to differences with the need to avoid (and help the group avoid) stereotyping participants' reactions.

Willingness to Express Disagreement

In certain cultures raising concerns, arguing passionately for a point of view, and challenging others constructively are viewed positively as means to foster fresh thinking and address persistent problems. In other cultures expressing such disagreement or challenging others publicly causes tremendous disharmony and stress.

It's critical to ensure that the feedback participants give to one another and that you provide to participants takes this particular sensitivity into account.

Should conflict break out in a retreat, different cultural groups will tend to take different approaches to managing it. Some will prefer to defer to an authority, some will look to a regulation or a precedent for the "right" way to handle the situation, and some will prefer a back-and-forth exchange of opinions that can lead to a solution accommodating most people's concerns. The latter approach, which is seen as democratic and inclusive in a U.S. context, could also result in some people's deepest concerns not being heard. (See the accompanying box for a model you can use to help participants be more aware of various cultural points of view when conflict surfaces.)

Seven-Step Model for Dealing with Cross-Cultural Conflict

1. *Problem identification.* Agree on the problem, even if various parties view it differently. Describe the situation and the difficulties it presents from all sides.

2. *Problem clarification.* Compare intentions. Is there a gap between the parties' intentions and the impact of their actions on others?

3. *Cultural exploration.* Explore the values of each culture represented in the conflict. What impact do these values have on each party's expectations and assumptions? Examine how these values affect each party's intentions and perceptions of the situation.

4. *Organizational exploration.* Explore the organizational context and the competing pressures that affect the conflict.

5. *Current status.* How is the conflict affecting operations, customers, employees? What goals can we agree on to manage this conflict successfully?

6. *Impact assessment.* Determine the measures or key indicators that will show the conflict has been managed successfully.

7. *Organizational integration.* Record results, celebrate success, institutionalize benefits. Create new stories and incorporate new symbols. Strengthen relationships.

Source: Adapted from Clarke & Lipp, 1998, cited in Gardenswartz et al., 2003.

Comfort with Physical Closeness

The amount of personal space a person requires differs from culture to culture, and also from individual to individual within each culture. What feels intuitively appropriate in one culture might seem like a violation of personal space in another. Because certain retreat exercises may have participants working in closer proximity than some in the group might feel comfortable with, be sensitive to this possibility when designing and leading retreat activities.

Tolerance for Uncertainty

Some cultural groups have a high tolerance for ambiguity, risk, and behavior that doesn't conform to the norm. Other cultural groups seek certainty and want to know what the rules are. The former groups might seem reckless to the latter, and the latter might seem bureaucratic and resistant to change to the former. In a retreat setting you have to be mindful of the kind of change that is being proposed. Will it push some participants further than they can reasonably be expected to go?

Use of Language

Even when all participants are speaking the same language, specific words and phrases may have different meanings to people from different cultures, depending on the context. We were doing some work in Africa with a mixed group of Africans and Americans. During the course of a retreat, Lou, an American participant, expressed some frustration because he had on occasion been told that something would happen "any time from now," and yet nothing transpired while he waited. Lou thought the phrase meant "any minute" or "right away." However, Safietou, one of his African colleagues, explained that it meant "*any* time from now," and probably later rather than sooner (or never. The closest American English equivalent would be "I have no idea when or if this will happen.").

Moreover, people who are communicating in a second or foreign language are likely to miss some of the nuances of meaning associated with certain words—meanings that most native speakers would recognize immediately, usually without thinking about it. As a facilitator, you will find it important to be aware of the potential snares hiding in language, to define terms that might be unclear or might have different meanings to different people, and to notice when people are talking past each other or reacting to meanings they have incorrectly attached to what someone else said.

The potential for misunderstanding is fairly obvious when the participants are an international group; however, you will also inevitably encounter differences of vocabulary and usage among those who ostensibly speak the same language—for instance, operations and marketing staff or program directors and administrative personnel. You'll have to be mindful of these differences as well.

Use of Body Language

In some cultures it's what you say that's important; in others it's how you act. If someone quietly says she's upset about something that happened, members of cultures that tend to focus on body language might ignore her comment or not take it seriously because it was not accompanied by congruent behavior, such as raising her voice. They might not understand that she is accustomed to using words alone, even when expressing a serious concern. And particular behaviors don't necessarily convey the same meaning from culture to culture either. For example, in one culture giggling might mean that someone is terribly embarrassed; in another it might mean that someone finds what's being said amusing.

How can you tell for sure? You can't, so to be sure that people understand what others are saying and are not misinterpreting one another's words or body language, you'll sometimes have to play the role of cultural anthropologist and ask questions that help shed light on possible misunderstandings.

Managing Cultural Differences

Sometimes it's hard to distinguish between cultural norms and personality differences. No behavior is common to all members of a culture, so resist the temptation to stereotype. The authors of the *Global Diversity Desk Reference* (Gardenswartz et al., 2003) present the Three Cultures Model, which illustrates the existence and interrelationship of three cultural dimensions—national culture, personal culture, and corporate culture. They also talk about *terminal* values, or the values that indicate the end result someone is trying to achieve, and *instrumental,* or behavioral, values. Thus two individuals might share the same desired end state of work-life balance, but the way they behave to achieve that balance might be very different. Or two individuals might exhibit similar behavior (for example, deferring to the leader), but the behavior might spring from very different values.

Even though cultural differences are real and are not in any way trivial, they do not have to tie you or the group in knots. Just as you might help participants navigate the communication differences between extroverts and introverts, so might you have to help them bridge cultural differences, which, although more subtle, can still be managed successfully.

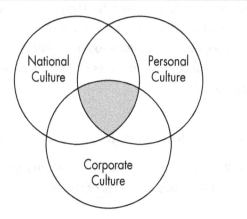

Personal culture is the integration of an individual's traits, skills, and personality formed within the context of his or her ethnic, racial, familial, and educational environments.

National culture is the shared understanding that comes from the integration of beliefs, values, attitudes, and behaviors that have formed the heritage of a nation-state.

Corporate culture represents the integration of an institution's widely shared beliefs and values and its guiding philosophy as frequently espoused in its vision, mission, and values statements.

Source: Gardenswartz et al., 2003, p. 65.

It's important not to ignore these differences or favor one cultural tradition over another. Rather, you'll need to design and lead the retreat in such a way that participants from various cultural backgrounds can contribute in equal measure to its success.

There is no absolute rule for dealing with cultural differences, but this general guideline may be helpful: participants should respect the same behavioral norms they follow in the workplace, in addition to adhering to the ground rules they established for the retreat. Thus, for example, if the organization wouldn't tolerate someone arriving late for an important meeting back at the office, neither should such behavior be allowed at the retreat, even if it is acceptable in the culture of the latecomer.

Similarly, if the ground rules call for everyone to participate actively in discussions and activities, those who are inclined toward reticence (whether as a cultural imperative or as a personality trait) should be encouraged to speak up at the retreat, just as those who tend to be outspoken should be urged to hold back to make space for others to express themselves. Although you'll want to help participants be sensitive to cultural differences, they may all have to get out of their comfort zones at times if they are to accomplish anything meaningful during the retreat.

Being Sensitive to Diversity Concerns in Your Facilitation

You will observe many dimensions of diversity present in any group that you facilitate. Here are some rules of thumb for facilitating a diverse group:

- If you're not familiar with the values of a particular culture represented at a retreat, consult with someone who is, so you don't unintentionally give offense.
- Use straightforward language, without the jargon and cultural references that might be lost on some of the group.
- Help participants recognize and value the gifts their diversity brings to the group.
- Lead a range of activities that will appeal to different styles of working.
- Present retreat activities in a way that is respectful of differing cultural norms; don't force people to participate in activities that violate their core values.
- Check frequently for understanding.
- Don't assume that an individual's membership in one or another cultural group always means that he or she will (or will not) feel comfortable engaging in a given activity.

Recording the Group's Work

What you and the group members write on flip charts will become the record of the group's work. Without adequate charting of the proceedings, people will forget what they decided and will tend to keep repeating their arguments.

Reasons for Charting

- It holds people's attention and keeps everyone focused on the work at hand.

- It creates a *group memory* about key points and action assignments.

- It allows the group to review conclusions from prior activities so that everyone builds on what was already decided.

- It separates an idea or recommendation from its originator, so that it can be considered on its own merits, not on the relative power of the person who brought it up.

- It becomes the basis for the retreat report.

Source: Adapted from Rees, 1998.

Deciding what to record is a key skill for any facilitator. As Fran Rees (1998, p. 71) puts it in *The Facilitator Excellence Handbook,* "Listen carefully to find one or two key words or phrases that will capture the idea—just enough information to jog people's minds later. Remember, you are not selectively listening; you are selectively recording. Your aim is to hear everything and then glean the key message." Sometimes the key points will be clear; at other times you will have to ask participants to help you record the essence of their idea or recommendation. ("Sam, can you help me boil that down to just a few words that I can record?" or, "Miriam, did I capture your main point here?")

At times you will need to record only the key ideas and recommendations; at other times it will be critical to record everyone's contribution. It's important to be clear with yourself—and with the group—why you are recording what you are recording, so that you won't inadvertently slight a participant, even if you're sure that person's point was already made by someone else. ("Michelle, do you see that as relating to the point that Liz made, or is it a separate issue?") And if someone believes her point deserves a separate mention, we never argue. It's far better to record something redundant than inadvertently communicate to a participant that you are not taking her viewpoint seriously.

If your charts aren't legible or attractive, here are some resources to help you:

- *Flip Charts: How to Draw Them and How to Use Them*, by Richard C. Brandt (1986), contains an excellent tutorial on how to print attractively and legibly, use color to best effect, and ensure that the overall effect is balanced and pleasing to the eye.

- *A Picture's Worth 1,000 Words: A Workbook for Visual Communications*, by Jean Westcott and Jennifer Hammond Landau (1997), will teach you lettering and overall flip chart design.

- *The Facilitator Excellence Handbook: Helping People Work Creatively and Productively Together*, by Fran Rees (1998), contains excellent suggestions on the art of charting.

- The Grove Consultants International offers a training workshop in *graphic facilitation*. The course teaches consultants how to use graphics to produce an engaging and well-organized system of work charts that can be copied directly as a record of the session. You can find out more about this technique in the Learning Center section of www.grove.com.

If you are working with a co-facilitator, one of you might record ideas while the other leads the group. If you agree to use this approach, you should be sure to check with each other periodically to ensure that the leader isn't moving the discussion along too rapidly and that the recorder isn't struggling to capture the key points.

In addition to using flip charts to track key points, it is often useful to create one that lists topics that are off the agenda for the retreat but should be dealt with at a later time. Referring such topics to a separate flip chart (sometimes referred to as the "parking lot") can be an excellent quick facilitation device. ("That's an excellent point, Mira. Should I note it on this flip chart so the group doesn't forget to address this issue after the retreat?")

See Chapter 3, "Capturing the Work Product," pp. 67–69, for a discussion of how to organize the charts to help create the retreat report.

Monitoring the Group's Energy

It's very important for facilitators to know how to "read" what's happening in the group. Are participants engaged in the task? Are they yawning and stretching? Are they slumped in their chairs and difficult to draw out?

Sometimes it's evident that people just need a break—when participants start leaving the room to go to the restroom or grab a cup of coffee, for example—in which case we'll just ask, "Do we need a break?" Occasionally groups will surprise us and tell us no, but most often they will readily assent to the invitation.

At times people's energy flags because there isn't any enthusiasm for the topic. When that seems to be the case, we might employ a technique such as listing various topic options on separate flip charts on which we have drawn thermometers, and then asking participants to mark the thermometers to show whether they feel cool or warm toward each topic.

Varying the pace of activities and facilitation techniques, being sure to have some activities that get people moving, and taking special care to use the more active techniques immediately after lunch and toward the end of the day will all help keep the group's energy higher.

Changing the Plan

What's important is not that you follow your retreat plan but that you achieve the outcome. At the end of each segment, ask yourself, "Have we gotten to where we need to be at this point?" If the group has reached agreement on an issue sooner than you expected, you may be able to skip the next planned activity. Or, if things haven't gone as smoothly as you had hoped, you may have to decide on the spot to lead an activity you hadn't planned on.

What comes up spontaneously during a retreat is often a core part of something important enough to propel a change initiative forward or stop it in its tracks. For example, several people we interviewed in preparing a retreat for the international division of a telecommunications company expressed concern that the division was not dealing with diversity issues with enough sensitivity. They told us how people of different nationalities were offending one another without necessarily intending to. We designed activities we thought would help participants get to the root of some of these issues.

In the middle of one of the activities, one participant, Dennis, said testily, "This is stupid! Nobody would respond in real life in the polite ways we're acting in this exercise."

Had we been wedded to our agenda, we might have simply thanked Dennis for his observation and continued the exercise. Instead, we engaged him in a conversation about how he saw the communication issues. Dennis talked about how hurt he felt when he was blamed for offending someone and how much he disliked being thought of as insensitive.

His candor and passion sparked an intense discussion in the group about the causes of conflict in the division and how they might be addressed. As a result, participants got to the source of something that was irritating many of them and agreed on how they wanted to manage the differences that would certainly occur among a multiethnic staff.

The discussion went on much longer than we had planned, but had we ignored what was going on in the room, the participants would not have made such a dramatic breakthrough on this important concern. After all, the point of any activity is to engage participants and get at real issues, not merely to complete the activity and move on.

This is not to suggest that you can get away with developing only a sketchy idea of what you are going to do and then improvise from moment to moment. On the contrary, we typically prepare much more than we'll have time for because we can't be certain what will come up and we want to be able to take advantage of real-time opportunities that arise. And no matter what we plan for, we'll almost always be surprised by what happens in the room and find ourselves designing something on the spot to move the group forward.

Chapter 7

How to Recover
When Things Go Awry

Even in the best-planned retreat, things go wrong. One of the most important skills for you as a facilitator is the ability to think on your feet and change course when necessary. You'll have to recognize and respond in the moment to unanticipated developments such as participants' engaging in emotional conflict, wandering off task, or resisting suggestions for dealing with a highly charged issue.

Let's face it: rather than enforcing their own ground rules themselves, participants almost always prefer the facilitator to confront "difficult" members of the group and deal with any inappropriate behavior. But as we discussed in Chapter 6 ("When Should the Facilitator Intervene?"), facilitators must beware of any tendency to rush in and rescue the group.

In general, when intervening in difficult situations, we tend to follow three rules: describe, discuss, engage. And as with most personal interventions, we prefer to apply these rules privately, not publicly.

First, we use observable data, not our subjective judgment, to *describe* the behavior we are seeing. ("Sara and Sophie, I noticed you came back from the lunch break an hour late today.") Then we *discuss* the impact of that behavior on the group. ("Because you weren't here when we narrowed the goals down to three, the group had to revisit its discussion so that you understood our reasoning. That means we won't have time to get to action planning this afternoon.") Then we *engage* the miscreants in thinking of ways to address the situation moving forward. ("If you need to come in late again, how do you suggest we handle what you missed in the session?") Sometimes it's enough just to bring behavior to a person's attention discretely at a break, without discussing the impact of the behavior or engaging in a long conversation about what might work better in the future.

Before intervening, you have to decide whether the behavior is bothering just you or if it is interfering with the group's ability to do its work. Is something or someone "pushing your buttons"? Does the participant remind you of someone in your own life with whom you have had difficulty? Remain focused and attuned to what is happening in the room. Don't respond impulsively because someone's behavior has gotten on your nerves.

If you decide the person's behavior *is* hindering the group, don't take it personally. Being bent out of shape is a difficult position from which to deliver helpful feedback.

If you feel judgmental when a participant becomes angry or teary or withdraws emotionally, you will be less likely to be empathetic to that person's real distress and therefore less helpful to the person and to the group.

Even when participants are acting out inappropriately and you are thrown off your stride, listen—really listen—to them. Often someone who seems difficult has an important concern. He or she just might have an inelegant way of expressing it. If you get caught up in how the message is delivered and don't pay attention to that person's underlying distress, you risk galvanizing the group into reacting against you.

Bob Dick (1987), in his book *Helping Groups Be Effective: Skills, Processes and Concepts for Group Facilitation,* has a useful formula for confronting, which he calls *inform-invite.* Rather than asserting that a certain behavior is troublesome, a facilitator can state what he has noticed and invite the group to respond. For example, he might say, "The group's energy seems lower today than it was yesterday" (inform), and then say, "Can anyone help me understand what's happening now?" (invite). That's a good core strategy for remaining neutral and calm when faced with a tense situation.

Here are some of the things that might go wrong in a retreat, followed by a discussion of strategies for dealing with each:

- A few participants dominate the discussions.
- The group keeps wandering off task.
- The group's energy is flagging.
- A participant keeps plowing the same ground.
- A participant repeatedly disrupts the conversations.
- Participants refuse to deal with important issues.
- A senior manager violates the ground rules.
- People are misusing humor.
- A participant is overtly hostile or refuses to participate.
- A participant walks out.
- A participant gets furious or defensive or bursts into tears.
- Participants are turning the retreat into a gripe session.
- Participants are resisting new ideas.
- An intense conflict breaks out.
- A participant breaches another's confidence.
- The group is resisting you.

This might seem like a long list, but take our word for it—it's not complete by any means.

A Few Participants Dominate the Discussions

Let's say Peter and Marusa are dominating the conversation, and you sense the group's mounting frustration.

You might first ask if people who haven't spoken yet have anything to say. Next, remind the group of the ground rules (which should include something about listening to others and encouraging everyone to participate). If necessary, politely interrupt Peter or Marusa by saying something such as, "That's an interesting point, Peter. Perhaps we can hear what others think?"

If Peter and Marusa still don't modify their behavior, have a private conversation with them during a break. Explain how their behavior is affecting the group, and ask them to be mindful of the need to allow many voices to be heard.

The Group Keeps Wandering off Task

Off-task conversations happen for a variety of reasons. Some people may feel that another topic is more important than the one being discussed. A topic may elicit strong emotional responses that some in the group would rather avoid. Participants may feel cynical about the possibility of any real change coming out of the retreat.

Keeping the discussions on track is a delicate art, because you must continually assess (and help the group assess) what *on track* means at any given moment. Is a particular comment advancing the conversation or derailing it? Is it helping the group identify and deal with the real issues, or is it permitting participants to avoid them?

One clue that things have gone off track is that you feel ill at ease or lost during the group's discussions. When this happens to us, we tell the group what we are experiencing and ask the participants to consider whether they may have lost focus. But it's important not to get stuck on what *you* think the task should be. Ask the group to assess whether *they* think the current topic is the most appropriate one or if they want to move on to something else.

If the group keeps wandering off task and there is a ground rule about sticking to the topic at hand, call participants' attention to that rule. If there is no such rule, encourage them to develop one.

If you sense that the group is wandering off track to avoid discussing a sensitive but important issue, consider creating a mechanism for participants to communicate anonymously about what may be hampering the discussions and about what, if anything, can be done to allow this issue to be aired safely. For example, you can ask everyone to write a note that outlines what would help the participants feel more comfortable discussing this issue. After collecting the notes, read them aloud to the whole group. (The authors, of course, would remain anonymous.) Or you might ask participants to work in small groups to explore why they're reluctant to discuss the issue, and then report the gist of what they find to the whole group.

Sometimes the group gets sidetracked because someone contributes a valuable idea but at the wrong time. The group is talking about fundraising ideas for next year, for instance, and seemingly out of nowhere, someone suggests a new board member orientation program. That's an interesting topic, so the group takes it up then and there. To keep the participants from being diverted from the main task in such situations, you need to hold that thought for later discussion.

Write the topic, and the name of the person who brought it up, on a flip chart sheet titled "Other Topics." (Some facilitators label it the "Parking Lot.") Keep this sheet on the wall where everyone can see it, adding ideas to it when they come up. And be sure to keep it in mind so you can reintroduce these ideas when there is time to address them.

The Group's Energy Is Flagging

Although you will diminish participant fatigue by having a varied schedule of activities, participants are still bound to get weary in almost any retreat that lasts longer than a day. People are working intensely, and they get tired. Participants are particularly prone to lassitude immediately after lunch (which is why we always try to plan an invigorating exercise for the first session each afternoon).

Our first response when we notice that participants seem to be running low on energy is to express our observation and ask what they want to do. Most often, all they need is a chance to stand up and stretch or take a short break.

See Chapter 5, "Varying the Methodologies," pp. 93–103, for ideas about how to vary the experiential elements in a retreat.

Sometimes, however, they are communicating that they have exhausted (and are exhausted by) the topic. If that's the case, it's time to move on.

Fatigue also can be an indication that the group is avoiding an issue. In that case follow the procedures we outlined earlier for times when the group is wandering off task.

A Participant Keeps Plowing the Same Ground

People tend to repeat themselves when they feel they have not been heard. So if Gabriela keeps inserting the same point into the conversation, the first thing to do is acknowledge that you've heard what she said. Write her words down on a flip chart to demonstrate that you understand and have recorded her point of view. Then, if it's not the right time to deal with the issue, record it on the Other Topics chart and ask the group to identify a more appropriate time to discuss it.

If the topic cannot be addressed at the retreat at all, ask the participants whether they would be willing to discuss it back at the office. Once you get agreement from the group that the issue will be addressed, ask her if she is ready to move on. If you sense that this is an issue of concern to many participants but it can't be resolved at the retreat, ask the participants what they would like to do to move on from this point where they have gotten stuck.

A Participant Repeatedly Disrupts the Conversations

If a participant interrupts once or twice, put it down to enthusiasm. You can handle it just as you would deal with participants who dominate the conversation (as discussed previously). If the interruptions continue, however, none of those techniques will work. If Richard is consistently disrupting discussions by interrupting, interjecting inappropriate comments, or initiating side conversations that distract the group, he might be crying out for attention. As facilitators we may be especially inclined to try to meet participants' needs. But that's not always a good idea.

If you have brought the issue to Richard's attention, privately, between sessions, and he remains disruptive, you will have to stop paying attention to him. Look at other participants and talk to them, not to Richard whose behavior is obstructing the group's progress. If nothing you do works, take your client aside at a break, give him your observations, and ask him how he wants to handle the situation. A private conversation between Richard and his boss might turn the behavior around. Ultimately, if Richard can't or won't stop being disruptive, he may have to be asked to leave. This is a drastic step, but sometimes (although rarely) it's necessary for the good of the whole group.

The Participants Refuse to Deal with Important Issues

We were facilitating a retreat a few years ago for a consortium of nonprofit organizations. In our pre-retreat interviews everyone made it clear that the key issue the consortium faced was its failure to make the hard choices about which programs to pursue and which to eliminate. Yet at the retreat itself the participants were unwilling to think about any cutbacks in programs and services. No matter what technique we employed to encourage them to make some choices (and we have lots of them), they wouldn't address the topic.

We got hooked into pursuing the agenda the participants told us was important; their issue became our issue. They weren't ready to face the difficult decisions they knew they needed to make, and we pushed them too aggressively.

All a facilitator can do is hold a mirror to the group. ("Are you sure you don't want to make some choices at this retreat? You all told me that was a goal you had for our work together.") You can't force the group to do anything. If the participants aren't willing to face a tough issue in a retreat setting, they'll be even less likely to implement their own recommendations. So our advice if this happens to you is to reflect what you see; don't become staked in participants' dealing with an issue until you are sure they are ready to do so.

A Senior Manager Violates the Ground Rules

Rules on paper mean little unless they are observed in practice. For this reason it's important that participants adhere to the ground rules they agreed to. Although all participants should observe the rules, it's especially important that your client and other senior managers be model citizens. If the rules are relaxed or ignored for the boss, the participants are less likely to observe them.

You may have to take special care to keep senior managers in compliance and, if they break a rule, to remind them of their commitment. In fact, in our pre-retreat coaching to senior managers, we emphasize that more than anything else, their behavior will determine the success of the retreat, and we ask how they would like us to remind them of this if they fail to observe the ground rules at the retreat.

Before we conducted a retreat at a military installation, for example, we had a series of conversations with the commanding officer about the need for him to assume a different role at the retreat than he was accustomed to in the command-and-control culture of the base. He understood our point and agreed to acknowledge up front that he was taking on an unusual role. As part of his welcoming words to his staff, he reiterated that he would not be taking the lead in discussions and that he would be listening more than talking. He would allow ideas that he didn't agree with to get a thorough airing without shooting them down. He even asked his staff to refer to him by his first name instead of his rank and to drop the use of "sir" for the duration of the retreat.

But once the retreat got going, he quickly reverted to his typical behavior. He interrupted others frequently, told participants why their ideas wouldn't fly, and was invariably the person who reported out the work of any small group he was a member of.

We called a break and had a private conversation to remind him of his commitment to behave differently. We told him the behavior we had observed and the impact we saw it having on the group.

After hearing our feedback he decided to admit to the group that he had lapsed back into his old habits. He encouraged his staff to remind him of the new behavior he was trying to practice if he forgot his intentions.

Although his acknowledgment did not radically change the underlying culture of the base, it did give participants permission during the retreat to help the commanding officer see how his behavior affected his staff's ability to do their work. And it set a positive tone that paid off in lively discussions and innovative solutions to long-standing problems.

People Are Misusing Humor

During a retreat we led for a trade association, several participants started "teasing" their general counsel, Paul, by trading wisecracks about lawyers. When we called this behavior to the group's attention, they insisted that it was just innocent fun. We asked if they thought it bothered Paul, and they told us, "Of course not. He knows it's just good-natured teasing."

So we asked Paul if that was how he saw it. With his voice cracking, this tough-as-nails attorney responded, "I hate lawyer jokes. I hope I never have to hear another one. I can't tell you how bad they make me feel." The room fell silent, and after the conversation resumed, there were no more "good-natured jokes" about lawyers.

Remarkably, at some offsites (just as in some workplaces), similar "good-natured teasing" of women and minorities still goes on. At one retreat we led, several women expressed anger at the joking behavior of a colleague who had recently immigrated to the United States. He was astonished to hear that people were offended by things he said, which he believed were well accepted in his culture. He told the women publicly that he meant nothing offensive by his remarks, apologized, and asked them to let him know if he ever inadvertently offended them again.

That story had a happy ending, but often people persist in offending others without realizing it.

It's important for you to recognize your own internal reaction to such humor. If something bothers you, chances are it's bothering some of the participants as well. Let the group know how you are reacting to the humor and why. Try to communicate your observations without judgment, and talk about your own discomfort, rather than the inappropriateness of the humor.

If someone seems to withdraw emotionally after being subjected to a "joke," ask the group members (not just the person targeted by the "humor") what they think the impact of such humor is and what would help them work together most productively. You might also encourage the group to point out when people are using humor inappropriately. If you notice that the group uses such humor routinely, suggest adding a ground rule about the appropriate use of humor.

If none of the above works, have a private conversation with participants who insist on skewering others in the name of "good fun."

Don't misunderstand us. We're all for humor. It's the grease that lubricates progress. But it must be respectful and appropriate. Whatever the intentions of the persons teasing others or telling such jokes—and their intentions may in fact be innocent—having fun at someone else's expense isn't fun for the people being teased or for others present who don't like to see their colleagues embarrassed.

A Participant Is Overtly Hostile or Refuses to Participate

A participant may be displaying hostility or refusing to take part in an exercise or the business of the retreat in general because the particular exercise has

See Chapter 2, "Pre-Retreat Interviews with Participants," pp. 33–38, for information on unearthing participants' concerns in advance.

touched a nerve, he is upset about something else, or he is rebelling against your perceived power. Indeed, it's not uncommon for participants who are feeling resentment or anger toward the organization or its leaders to direct that resentment or anger toward the facilitator. Or, judging that it's safe to do so in the context of the retreat, they might express overtly and directly feelings that they would be more circumspect about back at work.

The first rule here is, Don't take it personally. Facilitators get into trouble when they turn such incidents into power struggles. You decrease the likelihood of such a clash when you design a retreat that addresses participants' major concerns, but it still may happen. When it does, it's essential to remain empathetic to the participant's concerns and not become defensive or combative yourself.

In a retreat we led for a government agency that was rife with turf issues, we scheduled a simulation early on the first day to provide a framework for discussing these issues. The nature of the simulation required participants to follow precise instructions for which we could not provide reasons until later in the exercise. Alan, the mailroom supervisor, stood up and declared there was no way we could make him follow those instructions. When a low-key effort to convince him to reconsider failed, we asked him if he could think of an alternative that might help him stay engaged in the exercise. He came up with conditions that he was willing to meet, and we moved on.

Alan turned out to be a very constructive participant, who at several times during the retreat helped people see when they were avoiding tough conversations. Later that day we asked Alan if we might have done anything differently that would have persuaded him to comply with the original instructions. He said that we hadn't earned his trust at that point and that he got pushed around too much at work for him to be pushed around at the retreat.

The next morning, when participants were talking about what they had learned the previous day, several waxed enthusiastic about how useful the simulation had been in helping them identify and address their turf problems. Alan stood up abruptly. (We must confess we were a little nervous.) He told the group that he had learned something by our not having made an issue of his refusal to go along with our instructions and that if we were doing the simulation today he would have followed those instructions.

"I'm Outta Here!": A Participant Walks Out

There are three likely scenarios in which a participant might walk out:

- A discussion becomes too emotionally intense for one of the participants. He gets up and leaves, visibly upset, without saying a word.
- A participant becomes increasingly frustrated with the direction in which the discussion is heading and her inability to affect it. She announces to the whole group, "I don't have time for this. I'm outta here!"
- A participant doesn't show up for the next morning's session or doesn't return from lunch or from a break.

The first two are particularly difficult scenarios to deal with when there is only one facilitator. When there are two facilitators, we recommend that the one who is not leading the group at the moment quietly go after the participant who left to hear what he or she is concerned about.

Obviously, if a participant (we'll call her Tamima) can't stand being in the room any more, she is experiencing intense feelings, so it is crucial that you not fan the emotional flames. Your role should be mostly to listen to the nature of Tamima's concerns. You can reassure her that she will be welcomed back into the group, and you can ask if there is anything that would make it easier to discuss the difficult issue. If she is not ready to come back to the room, ask if there is anyone else she would feel comfortable talking to. If there is, ask that person to speak with Tamima.

If she refuses to return, keep in mind that you are neither a therapist nor a disciplinarian. Talk privately with your client about how he wishes to address the issue. He might decide to speak with Tamima directly and discuss options.

When you are the only facilitator and it's not an appropriate time to call a break, we recommend that you ask if there is anyone who would be willing to listen to the participant's concerns.

Although only one person may leave the room, chances are that others are also feeling intense emotion, both because of the nature of the discussion and because of their colleague's visible distress. That's why it's important to allow participants to talk about how they're feeling, not just plow forward. The worst thing you can do is pretend that nothing happened. Not only has something happened but it has changed the climate in the room, and you must acknowledge that.

If someone doesn't return to a session following a break, the first thing to do is to determine where the missing person is and whether he or she is all right. Perhaps somebody in the group knows what happened and can help head off any rumors that might start. ("Does anyone know where Enrique is? Is he okay? Can someone go and check on him?") If the participants don't know what happened, ask your client how she wants to address the issue of the missing participant.

A Participant Gets Furious or Defensive or Bursts into Tears

Sometimes something comes up in a retreat that is just too much for a participant to handle. Let's say this happened to Juan Carlos, and you have to manage the results of a heated emotional outburst. This is particularly difficult if Juan Carlos happens to be a senior executive. He might feel blamed, overloaded, misunderstood, or disrespected. The discussion might strike a nerve that triggers his angry response. If not managed skillfully, such an event could affect the course of the retreat, usually in a negative way.

As a compassionate human being, your first impulse might be to avoid an awkward situation by calling a break and—after emotions have cooled—resuming as if nothing happened. Or you might be inclined to rush in and "rescue" Juan Carlos, who seems to be having trouble handling tough feedback. Neither of these approaches is the best way to respond.

You can't ignore what happened, and neither can Juan Carlos or the other participants. If you all implicitly conspire to do so, you will be hobbled from that point on by this bit of important unfinished business. But leaping into the fray isn't the best approach either. It is rarely effective to try to engage someone who's in a highly emotional state.

So you need to deal with the situation, but maybe not at precisely that moment.

Know When to Move On

As the facilitator you can't judge what's going on in someone else's head. Only the person having the emotional reaction can decide if he or she can handle more information. If a participant is unwilling to discuss a subject any further, move on to something else, making it clear that you hope the group will return to the topic at another point. Later, during a break, you can try to encourage the person to reintroduce the topic.

We suggest that you call a break. ("I think maybe we should take ten minutes to stretch. Let's all be back in the room ready to resume at 11:30.") Take Juan Carlos aside and ask if he is willing, when the group reconvenes, to continue the conversation that triggered the emotional response. If so, give him the floor to explain what prompted that response and to let the group know that he would like the discussion to resume where it left off.

If Juan Carlos is the boss and he is unwilling to discuss the subject any further, move on to something else, at least for the moment. Later, during another break, you can explain to him how important it is to address the contentious issue and encourage him to reintroduce the topic when he has had a chance to think about it and calm down further.

Participants Are Turning the Retreat into a Gripe Session

Sometimes the group cannot focus on the agenda for the retreat because participants are upset about something else.

It's foolish to attempt to push an agenda through when participants are in the throes of an emotional response to something else. When this happens in a retreat, we encourage participants to look forward, rather than back. ("What can we do going forward to make this better?" "What's in our power to change?" "What steps might we take, no matter how small, to improve this situation?") We might also invoke the appreciative inquiry approach. ("Given that a lot of things have gone wrong in the past, what are some things that have worked well that we can build on?")

Although we don't attempt to suppress the expression of resentments, we do encourage participants to see their own part in creating or sustaining the situation they find intolerable, rather than blaming others entirely for their woes. And we invoke the ground rules to ensure that the session doesn't degenerate into personal attacks.

We also touch base with the whole group before allowing the agenda to be sidetracked. ("How much time should we allow for this discussion?" "Are there others who share Benjamin's concerns?")

Participants Are Resisting New Ideas

Resistance is often used as a pejorative word. Actually, resistance is often a healthy reaction to change initiatives. It can serve as a brake on those who would bring about change for its own sake and as a reality check when new ideas are presented that though perhaps bold and novel aren't very good.

But sometimes resistance is knee-jerk reactive, not a thoughtful response to the prospect of change but simply a digging in of the heels. Such resistance, if you don't manage it well, can stop a change initiative in its tracks.

Holding Onto the Familiar

It's natural for people to want to hold onto things. It is said that the hardest thing for a trapeze artist isn't grabbing hold of the new trapeze as it swings within reach but letting go of the one she's already gripping. So it is with change; it's hard to let go of the familiar and comfortable.

Fear of the unknown is often cited as the reason people resist new ideas, and certainly it plays a role. But a good deal of resistance stems from people's reluctance to give up things they are comfortable with and—more important— things that matter to them. People's concerns about change are valid and should be addressed as soon as they surface. Before focusing on areas for change, we typically ask participants to turn their attention to things that already work, things they're proud of, and things they would particularly like to keep. This helps participants identify the babies they don't want to throw out with the bathwater, and often it's sufficient to resolve the human tendency to resist something new for the sake of resistance.

Often resistance emerges when the group starts making decisions. Just when you think people have reached agreement on a course of action, one or more participants start revisiting the arguments against it.

Because resistance often stems from the anticipation of loss, whether real or imagined, your client or other participants are unlikely to build support simply by restating the wisdom of the proposed change. And dismissing last-minute objections is likely only to increase resistance, if not at the retreat, then back in the office during the implementation effort. So you must help the group address the anticipation of loss.

The first step in dealing with resistance is encouraging it to emerge throughout the retreat. Early on in a discussion, invite dissenting views. ("Does anyone have a different take on this issue?")

In *Beyond the Wall of Resistance,* Rick Maurer (1996) talks about resistance intensity. In what he calls *Level 1 Resistance,* people are *reacting against the idea itself.* When this occurs at a retreat, make sure that participants are communicating clearly with one another and that everyone has a chance to influence the shape of the idea under discussion. You do this by

- Asking your client and other senior leaders to reemphasize that they want to hear and learn from different opinions and that candor will not be punished.
- Encouraging participants to listen carefully to one another's ideas and concerns, without defending their own points of view.
- Urging the group to consider the messages in people's objections: What might they be communicating about the feasibility of these new ideas?

In what Maurer calls *Level 2 Resistance,* which is almost always present when the group is contemplating major changes, people are *reacting to something deeper. Often it's the fear of loss.* When this happens, ask the whole group, not just those resisting the ideas, to identify things they *don't* want to lose. Focusing on what's important to participants, what they want to retain, may help reassure resisters that not everything they care about (indeed, perhaps not anything) will disappear.

Encourage resisters to talk about what they want for the organization, not what they *don't* want. Ask them to be as specific as possible. Ask if anything would help resisters support the new idea. Often a minor adjustment will make an idea acceptable.

Sometimes you'll be confronted with what Maurer calls *Level 3 Resistance.* At this greatest intensity of resistance, people may have *conflicting values or sharply contrasting visions* for the future of the organization, or they may have a history of sabotaging one another's successes.

Ideally, the experience of working together at the retreat and striving to find common ground will diminish resistance at this third level of intensity, but that's not always going to be the case. Sometimes the differences among group members are so sharply delineated that they just cannot be resolved at the retreat. In this case we suggest you encourage the group to table the discussion (see "Drop the Issue . . . for Now," later in this chapter) and to decide on another forum in which it can be addressed.

If resistance asserts itself just as the discussion seems to be winding down and decisions are near, don't dismiss it (or let participants dismiss it) as coming too late. It's important not to let momentum roll over people's concerns or to let impatience carry the day. And don't think of resistance as an attack on you and your well-thought-out retreat plan. Participants who are resisting something may be doing you and the others a favor, even at the eleventh hour.

It's far better to address the resistance openly than to force participants to deal with it later back at the office, where it can derail the effort to implement what they worked so hard throughout the retreat to accomplish.

Remember, though, that you aren't the one who will have to implement the change plan. It's not your job to persuade participants to like some aspect of the plan that they are rejecting.

At the same time, you can't permit last-minute resistance to derail the retreat just as the train is approaching the station. Use your best judgment about how much discussion is necessary at this late stage, and balance that against the need to draw the retreat to a close.

The following activity may help the group deal with its resistance to change.

Gains and Losses

Description

Participants are asked to fill in a four-quadrant diagram that will summarize what they and their work groups stand to lose and to gain as a result of a particular change. Group discussion follows about what the organization should do more of and less of to foster more gains and fewer losses.

Experiential Elements
- Personal reflection
- Whole group discussion

Steps

1. Distribute one Gains and Losses Diagram to each participant (see CD 7):

	Gains	Losses
Me Personally		
My Work Group		

Source: Adapted from Gardenswartz, Rowe, Digh, & Bennett, 2003.

Setup

Make a copy of the "Gains and Losses Diagram" for each participant (see Step 1 and CD 7).

2. Introduce the task: "We will be looking at what you believe you and your work group stand to lose and to gain if this change is implemented."

3. Have participants fill out their four-quadrant diagrams, alone and in silence.

4. Break participants into three subgroups, and ask them to discuss what they wrote on their four-quadrant diagrams.

5. Ask one subgroup to recommend the top actions the organization should take to minimize the losses. Ask the second subgroup to recommend the top actions the organization should take to foster the gains. Ask the third subgroup to look at the current operating principles and ways of working and recommend which ones the organization should be sure to retain. (If each of the three subgroups would be quite large, you can divide participants into more subgroups and have more than one subgroup focus on each topic.)

6. Have each subgroup report to the whole group and make recommendations for specific actions the organization should take to ensure a successful change initiative.

Activities to Help You Recover When Things Go Awry

You will find other activities for managing conflict and helping the group refocus on its work in the Activities for Building Cooperation and Dealing with Sensitive Issues index (p. 495).

An Intense Conflict Breaks Out

Sometimes progress is sidetracked because two or more participants get into an escalating disagreement and cannot listen to one another or back down from their own strongly held positions.

Here are some techniques we use to prevent minor disagreements from getting out of hand:

- *Help participants hear and understand one another.* People involved in a disagreement are often thinking of their rebuttal rather than listening to what others are saying. When you hear someone saying, "Yeah, but . . ." or something similar, stop the action, and make sure each party in the disagreement has really heard and can state the other person's point of view.
- *Look for points of agreement.* Often disputants are in substantial agreement on most points and disagree on only one or two. If you can lead them to discover those areas on which they agree, you greatly enhance the climate for resolving the areas of disagreement.
- *Involve others in the discussion.* Getting others who have not expressed a strong point of view engaged can clarify points of misunderstanding and identify areas of agreement. ("Kevin and Roberta seem to be having a problem understanding each other's point of view. Can anyone help out?" "Bob and Dianne seem to be in agreement on several points. Can anyone help identify these points?")
- *Help participants understand why the issue matters.* Sometimes the people in a conflict are so bogged down in defending their own positions and in attacking others' positions that they are unable to express clearly why the issue matters so much to them. Arguments take on a life of their own, unrelated to the underlying concerns. You can ask participants on both sides of a conflict to restate their concerns in terms of what they're hoping to accomplish and why it is important to them. It's much easier for people to be empathetic about something when they know it matters deeply to someone else. When those engaged in the conflict understand what their "adversaries" want, they may be able to come up with mutually agreeable solutions that neither could think of when both were focused only on defending their positions.

- *Break participants into smaller groups.* Have participants discuss the issue for five to ten minutes in pairs or trios.
- *Have participants write down ideas.* Ask the participants to stop talking and to write down their thoughts. This will often calm emotions and produce a more reflective mind-set. It will also help quieter participants (who might have excellent suggestions for resolving the issue) collect their thoughts and express them.

> For a fuller discussion of how to use breakout groups and silence, see Chapter 5, "Varying the Methodologies," pp. 93–103.

- *Explore options.* Encourage group members who are not at either extreme of the conflict to generate options that might satisfy the needs of all parties in the disagreement.
- *Establish a deadline.* When you say, "OK, let's give this just another five minutes," participants will often focus more intensely, not only on making their arguments but also on reaching an agreement. People who aren't part of the heated discussion are particularly likely to help the others find a solution so the group can move on.
- *Call a break.* A short break can give people a chance to cool off. Often an issue that has seemed impossible to resolve will yield to a solution after people have had a chance to stretch their legs or chat informally with someone else.
- *Change seats.* Ask participants to change their seats. This may seem silly, but it can literally give people a new vantage point. (This action can be combined with taking a break. Ask people to move to different seats upon returning to the room.)
- *Postpone the discussion.* In a multiday retreat it is often useful to delay the discussion of a particularly contentious issue, thus allowing some time for people to reflect or to lower their emotional temperature. People who have advocated strongly for a position usually find it difficult to change their minds on the spot. Postponing the discussion gives participants time to do some research, reflect on the issues, and find common ground without losing face.
- *Drop the issue . . . for now.* If you are convinced that the group is at an impasse, suggest tabling the discussion until it can be resumed at another time and place. Essentially, this means agreeing to disagree on this topic so participants can move on to other matters in the limited time available to

them at the retreat. Emphasize, however, that the disagreement shouldn't be swept under the rug but should be revisited back at the office or at another retreat scheduled specifically to address the issue.

A Participant Breaches Another's Confidence

A breach of confidence is a serious transgression that can threaten the environment of trust you've worked to establish, and you must deal with it immediately. In our experience, it doesn't happen often, but when it does, it's highly corrosive.

Here's how a breach of confidence might play out.

Grace and Lynn are part of the same small breakout group. Lynn suggests to the group members that their supervisor, Susan (who is working in another group), may be responsible for the delays in the production schedule. Others nod their assent, and the group members record what specifically they would like Susan to do differently, which they then report as a group to the other participants. At a break, Grace tells Susan that it was Lynn who raised this issue in the small group. Other participants hear this conversation and report it to you.

If this happened to us, we would tell the group that a breach of confidence had occurred. If the participants had established a ground rule about confidentiality, we would remind them of that rule. If there were no such rule, we'd suggest that the group put one in place.

We would then ask participants how they would prefer to deal with sensitive topics and ask for their suggestions about what might be done to rebuild trust.

The Group Is Resisting You

This is a tough one for most facilitators. To deal with this appropriately you must be very centered and willing to practice what you preach about being open-minded and welcoming to divergent views. Resistance to you is important feedback that you ignore at your peril.

When people perceive themselves to be under attack, they usually have strong fight-or-flight responses. It is critical that you curb those reactions. Participants might be irritated with their boss, but it isn't safe to express that frustration so you—having been hired by the boss—become a convenient target for their anger. Or you might have misunderstood their major concerns and might be moving forward with an agenda that doesn't serve the group's needs. Or the participants might remember that they never implemented the recommendations from past retreats, so retreats in general seem to be a waste of time. Or they might be afraid of the personal consequences of the changes that could result from this retreat.

None of this is your fault, so don't make it about you or your professional competence. Instead draw on the desire you share with the participants that the retreat be a success, and partner with them to get their needs met.

Resistance to you may emerge passively. People might return to the session late from the breaks or might not follow your instructions in their small group work. They might engage in side conversations when you're in the front of the room. Or they might profess not to understand the points you are making.

Sometimes participants will be more overtly challenging. ("Why are we doing this activity now?" or, "Can we cut this retreat short? I'm really behind in my work back at the office," or, "What qualifies you to lead this retreat? You don't know our company.") In such cases don't allow yourself to become defensive about your agenda or your skill as a facilitator.

Whether the resistance is passive or active, we deal with it when it emerges by naming the behavior we're seeing in nonjudgmental terms and then asking the group to tell us what it means. Then we draw the participants out on the things that would make the retreat more relevant to their concerns.

Common Intervention Language

- "I'm noticing that . . ."
- "It strikes me that . . ."
- "I'm wondering if . . ."
- "I'd like to suggest . . ."

- "A pattern I have observed is . . ."
- "I'd like to describe what I'm seeing and get your reaction to it."
- "How do you suggest that we . . .?"

Source: Adapted from Rees, 1998, pp. 27–44.

Chapter 8

Helping Participants Make Decisions and Plan for Action

Retreats are all about making decisions. Participants must decide what their priorities are, what to change, what actions to take after the retreat is over, and how to implement those actions. How participants make these decisions and how careful they are in planning for action are likely to determine the ultimate success or failure of the retreat. A key role for you as facilitator is to help participants make sound decisions and create action plans they will be willing and able to implement.

Just as there are many delicious dishes you can order at a fine restaurant, there are many effective ways to make decisions. Each has advantages and disadvantages, and any of them might be the best, depending on the circumstances and on what the group is trying to accomplish.

Symptoms of Poor Decision Making

- Several group members have tuned out the conversation.

- With time running out, group members make a hasty decision by taking a quick vote with little discussion of the decision's merit.

- Some people say nothing during the conversation but later complain that they weren't asked for their opinion.

- Discussion moves to another topic without a decision having been made.

- The conversation turns into a heated clash of wills rather than a calm debate of ideas.

- People give in, even though they believe the decision is wrongheaded, just to end the conversation.

- After the retreat is over, participants tell others back at the office that they don't support the decision that was made.

_____
Source: Adapted from Bens, 2000.

Methods of Decision Making

See Chapter 4, "Decision Making," pp. 83–84, for further discussion of this issue.

One of the most important things participants must decide is how they are going to make decisions. You'll have to be prepared to help them decide which decision-making methods they will employ and what they will do if they have no success with the method you and they have chosen. And you'll have to reach a clearly understood prior agreement with the person who has the ultimate decision-making power on the limits to the group's authority.

It's important that the discussion on decision making be open and explicit, particularly in organizations that have a history of top-down decisions or of lower-level decisions being routinely overturned by senior executives. To avoid cynicism participants must understand what choices they have and what will happen with the decisions or recommendations they make once the retreat is over.

When participants apply the appropriate decision-making techniques at the right times for decisions they are authorized to make at the retreat, it's more likely that the decisions will stick and gain widespread support.

Here's the decision-making menu:

- *Executive authority.* The leader decides.
- *Consultative executive authority.* The leader decides after seeking the group's perspective.
- *Majority rule.* The decision is made by majority vote.
- *Decision by default.* Someone suggests a course of action and no one raises objections, even though some group members harbor doubts.
- *Moving right along.* An idea is never considered because the group has moved on too quickly to the next idea.
- *Minority activism.* A few people use their influence to make the decision for the group.
- *Compromise.* Everyone gives up something in order to get something they can all live with.
- *Consensus.* Everyone agrees to support the decision.
- *Unanimous consent.* Everyone is enthusiastic about the decision.
- *Roll of the dice or flip of the coin.* Everyone leaves the decision to a random event.

Defining Moments

Many people think *consensus* means the same thing as *majority*. You may hear, "We've achieved an overwhelming consensus." Actually, as with pregnancy, there are no degrees of consensus; you either have it or you don't.

Another common misunderstanding concerns the difference between *consensus* and *unanimous consent*. In both instances everyone is in agreement, but there is a clear difference. In a consensus, everyone agrees to support the decision even if it isn't his or her first choice. In the case of unanimous consent, there is no disagreement; everyone supports the decision without reservation.

Executive Authority

When executive authority is invoked, the most senior person makes the final decision on his or her own, involving few, if any, others in the process. This is a highly efficient way to make decisions, but we don't recommend it for a retreat, as the whole purpose of convening an offsite is to involve the participants in decision making. If an executive *does* intend to make the final decision, however, that fact should be made clear to participants at the outset.

Consultative Executive Authority

When consultative executive authority is employed, the top executive makes the final decision, but only after seeking input. Sometimes the executive might ask for the advice in the form of options to choose from.

This method is better than deciding by executive authority alone, because it takes multiple perspectives into consideration. (In fact, most decisions made by executive authority are really consultative to some extent, because the senior person is likely to have been listening to others all along.) Still, we recommend avoiding this method in a retreat setting, except in cases where the executive has relevant information other participants lack and that for some reason cannot be shared.

Majority Rule

In this method the participants decide by a simple majority (or a predetermined larger majority, such as two-thirds or three-quarters). Although counting hands is a relatively quick and easy way to make a decision, it has a serious disadvantage. Voting creates win-lose situations. Participants who are in the majority win all the marbles, and those who voted with the minority may feel resentful. These "losers" may continue to raise the issue long after others in the group think it has been decided, or they may even work to undermine the implementation.

This winners-take-all situation can be mitigated if participants negotiate compromises (discussed later in this chapter), but even compromise doesn't entirely overcome the disadvantages of using majority rule. So even though voting may be useful to give you a quick survey of how the participants are feeling (and perhaps help the group avoid a long discussion when everyone is in agreement), we recommend using this method only when the stakes for the decision are low.

Decision by Default

In decision by default, someone suggests a course of action, and no one raises questions or objections. It is then assumed that everyone agrees, and the suggestion becomes the decision—even if some participants silently harbor doubts or are actually hostile to the idea. Decisions by default are made most often when an executive who does not like to be challenged offers the suggestion. Such decisions also occur in low-trust or risk-averse groups, when people are exhausted and simply want to end the discussion, or when participants really don't care about the outcome.

Ideally, decisions are never made by default. But if this phenomenon does occur, make it a point to seek positive confirmation that everyone is in agreement or to ask whether anyone has an observation or objection.

Moving Right Along

This is perhaps the most common and least effective method of group decision making. Someone suggests an idea and, before the participants discuss it, someone else makes another proposal, and the first idea is lost. Moving right along gives the illusion of progress, but it creates an environment in which potentially excellent ideas may be left unexplored.

Not only are ideas lost, but participants whose contributions get dismissed are likely to become disgruntled. Bring it to the group's attention when you notice decisions being made this way. Slow down the process, before participants whose ideas are not heard become disengaged.

Minority Activism

Minority activism involves a small group (often made up of senior managers or people with particularly strong personalities) employing tactics that push the rest of the participants into going along with a particular decision. This method can be useful when time is of the essence, but it often results in friction, resentment, and a desire to revisit the issue. ("I went along against my better judgment. Let's look at that again.")

If you sense this is happening, poll the group to see if people are truly in agreement. If you believe that participants might be feeling intimidated by the activists, you can create a mechanism to protect their anonymity, such as asking people to cast their votes or express their concerns in writing and then pass the ballots or comments to you.

Compromise

Compromise is the classic horse trading that occurs in many group situations. ("I'll give in on this if you give in on that.") Sometimes people do have to give up something they want to get something else they want. During a retreat, because people often develop empathy for one another's concerns, the sacrifices may not seem so great. Compromise can also be a good tool for coming up with temporary solutions for complex issues that will be decided later, outside the retreat setting. The problem is that participants might end up with a decision that none of them is really satisfied with, and such decisions are rarely implemented back at work. If you see the participants making compromises on important issues, encourage them to discuss whether they are making decisions everyone is lukewarm about or even opposed to, and if so, suggest an alternative technique.

Consensus

Consensus is reached when all participants in the discussion understand and are prepared to support the decision, even if it isn't their first choice. When people have reached a true consensus, all of them feel that they have had a fair chance to influence the decision and are willing to work to implement it, even if some would prefer another course of action.

Consensus is a valuable tool for making key decisions that require the widest possible support (such as decisions about the core strategies the organization will pursue or about whether to eliminate a signature product or service). It offers the advantage that everyone supports the decision. But it also has the disadvantage of requiring a great deal of time and effort. That's why it is important not to use this method to make decisions about less consequential matters, as doing so may create frustration and disillusionment with consensus building in general.

Participants should come to an agreement, with your help if necessary, about how much time they want to devote to consensus discussions. Then, if the group cannot achieve consensus in the agreed-on time, participants can opt for another decision-making process, such as majority vote, compromise, or executive authority, or even putting off reaching a decision until a later time.

Overuse of consensus is often a sign of a low level of trust. You can help the group see that not every decision requires support from everyone—only those who will be most affected need to decide. You might also explore the issue of trust with the participants if you sense that it is important to do so.

Unanimous Consent

Unanimous consent looks a lot like consensus, but there are key differences. You have unanimous consent only when everyone enthusiastically supports the course of action to be taken. You can achieve consensus with only a willingness on everyone's part to abide by a certain decision. Moreover, unanimous consent is most often achieved quickly and with little dissent. ("Let's break for lunch" is a typical unanimous consent decision.) Consensus, in contrast, typically takes a good deal of time and discussion to build.

Be cautious, however, about accepting unanimous consent at face value. If the participants are simply climbing on the bandwagon, the result can be similar to that of decision by default, and the enthusiasm might fade as reality sets in.

Roll of the Dice or Flip of the Coin

When the participants cannot figure out how to decide, they might flip a coin if choosing between two alternatives or roll a die or a pair of dice if choosing from among several. This isn't as silly a way to make decisions as you might think. Sometimes groups are unwilling to assume risks for bad decisions, and this allows an external force to dictate the decision.

Obviously, we don't stop with the dice roll or coin toss, however. The following activity works very well when groups are having great difficulty making a decision.

Let's Take Our Chances

Description

In this activity participants who seem unwilling to make a decision or choose among options allow a flip of a coin or a roll of the dice to determine the decision; then they discuss whether this is a decision they can support.

Experiential Elements
- Group discussion
- Experimenting with ideas
- Movement and sound

Steps

1. Tell the participants: "Since we seem to be stuck, we're going to decide by rolling the dice [or tossing a coin]."

2. Roll the dice (or toss the coin), and announce to the participants which "decision" they have made.

3. Ask the participants to move to the right side of the room, rotate their hands above their heads, and call out "Yes" if they're happy with the decision they have made; ask them to move to the left side of the room, shake their heads vigorously from side-to-side, and call out "No" if they're not happy with the decision.

4. Ask the group of people who said no what would have to be modified in the decision to make it work for them. Ask the people who said yes if they can live with those modifications.

Setup

Prepare a flip chart with the options under consideration—numbered consecutively if the group is doing the dice roll or labeled "heads" and "tails" if it is doing the coin toss.

Special Supplies

A coin or a pair of dice

Facilitator Notes

- Be sure not to tell participants that there will be a discussion after the dice roll (or coin toss). For this to work well, participants must believe that chance will make the decision for them.

- You will be surprised how effective this method can be when a group is stuck, because it puts them in a different, more playful mind-set. Sometimes knowing that they won't have to agonize over a decision prepares participants to see its positive possibilities.

- This technique helps participants clarify what's important to them in a decision, so that they can make better choices for themselves.

Types of Retreat Decisions

Typically, participants make a variety of decisions, both individual and collective, throughout the course of a retreat. They make decisions to set priorities, for example, or to determine what's core to their organization and what's peripheral. The kinds of decisions retreat participants have to make include

- Ranking importance
- Rating quality
- Categorizing
- Limiting issues
- Prioritizing actions
- Sequencing actions
- Choosing among alternatives

Ranking Importance

The group may have to rank in order of relative importance such things as specific customers, products, services, and training needs. A simple ranking exercise can have a dramatic impact on what the retreat accomplishes.

A paint manufacturer and retailer, for example, had to choose between emphasizing its contractor base, which accounted for 70 percent of sales but yielded very low margins, and emphasizing its homeowner customers, who were fewer in number but whose purchases yielded a much higher profit. If the company ranked homeowners higher in importance than contractors, virtually everything about its marketing and service strategies would have to change (as would relationships with contractors that had been built over the years).

When the relative ranking isn't immediately clear to a group, a quick way to get a snapshot of participants' inclinations is to list the various elements on a flip chart and give each participant three large, colored, self-sticking dots to post next to his three highest priorities. When all participants have posted their dots, they will easily be able to see, from the number of dots next to each item, which items the

Self-sticking dots, available in office supply stores and elsewhere, may be called color-coding labels or garage sale stickers. We refer to them as *voting dots.*

group ranks highest. Although this is a simple method, it can be misused. We don't recommend counting dots and using a difference of one or two to definitively rank one item over another. Use this method only to establish a basis for discussions, *not* as the final determinant of priorities. And in the case of close numbers, invite people to give reasons for how they voted.

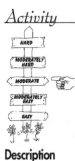

Our Stable of Clients or Resources

Description

This activity focuses on the characteristics of any one of the orga-nization's resource areas—clients, programs, products, services, customers, or other stakeholders. Participants categorize each of the clients (or programs, products, and so forth, depending on the resource area selected) according to its value to the organi-zation. In the course of the activity, different opinions often arise, so group members develop a broad-based concept of how other participants view the contribution of various resources.

Experiential Elements

- Group discussion
- Using metaphor to express ideas
- Individual and group reflection
- Experimenting with ideas

Steps

1. Tell the participants: "We are going to assess one of the resources available to your organization, your clients [or what they will be assessing, if not clients] and what value these clients represent to the organization. We will be assigning each client to one of five categories in the Stable Matrix."

2. Show the Stable Matrix chart. (See the chart on p. 172 for more detail on each category.)

3. Ask participants to call out the organization's current clients, and as they do, write the name of each client on a Post-it Note.

4. Ask the participants to call out the Stable Matrix category to which they would assign each client. Because not everyone will agree initially on the assignments, ask individuals to explain their assessments.

5. When the participants have reached agreement on the category for each client, have them discuss the strategies the organization would have to pursue to turn more of the clients into Stakes Winners.

6. (*Optional.*) Indicate each client's annual revenue value to the company. Total the revenues in each cate-gory, then calculate what percentage of the organization's revenues fall into each category of the stable. Ask the group: "What should these percentages be? What actions would you need to take to increase the number of high-revenue clients in the Stakes Winner category?"

Setup

Prepare a Stable Matrix chart for "Our Stable of Clients" (see p. 172).

Special Supplies

A pad of Post-it Notes and a Sharpie pen for the facilitator

Our Stable of Clients

Category	Description	Comments
Stakes Winners	Vital to our growth and future success	Ideal—profitable, have a solid growth pattern, and are good to work with. Value quality work.
Workhorses	Attractive for the moment, but not for the long run	Often have had a close relationship with the organization for years.
Yearlings	Unproven, but have the potential to become Stakes Winners	Represent the possibility of strong growth in the near future or of doing high-quality, profitable work.
Mules	Inconsequential for the organization's future	Neither particularly profitable nor large. May take more time than they're worth.
Nags	Detrimental to the organization's future success	Unprofitable, difficult to work with, don't value quality work. Actually consume more resources than they provide.

Facilitator Notes

- The facilitator must be able to help participants reach agreement on issues on which they may have very different perspectives. The facilitator with an understanding of the underpinnings of the client's industry will be better prepared to ask appropriate questions to help participants place resources in the categories accurately.

- If something falls into the "Nags" (detrimental) category, the organization should consider ceasing to devote resources to it, because in the group's judgment it is hurting the organization. You may need to press this point with the group.

- Nonprofits can use a variation of this activity to focus on their programs. They can measure each program's capacity to advance the organization's mission vis-à-vis the resources it takes to run the program, as in the chart shown on p. 173.

- In the variation of this activity that focuses on products, for example, the group would put new and existing product lines into the categories.

Our Stable of Programs

Category	Description	Comments
Stakes Winners	Ideal programs	Serve the right groups, operate well, and are well funded, achieve their goals, align with the goals and values of the organization.
Workhorses	Long-running programs	Often large programs with long histories, but whose effectiveness (or the need for the program) may be in gradual decline.
Yearlings	New programs	Seem to have potential to become ideal programs, but it's too soon to tell.
Mules	Programs that serve few people at a high resource cost	May no longer be important to the organization's mission or may not be financially feasible to continue.
Nags	Detrimental to the organization	Programs that don't serve the needs of constituents well and use up more resources than the value they create.

Our Stable of Programs in Practice

In a strategic planning retreat we facilitated for the board of a large metropolitan nonprofit that was hoping to increase the reach and the revenue-generating potential of its programs, we led the group through the "Our Stable of Programs" activity. Participants analyzed the current (and potential) reach of each of the organization's programs and categorized each as "Stakes Winners" (ideal programs); "Workhorses" (long-running programs whose costs are too high or reach too small); "Yearlings" (new programs whose potential is not yet known); "Mules" (programs that serve too few people at too high a resource cost); or "Nags" (programs that are detrimental to the organization). They explored for each program specific actions that might

- Make the programs less labor intensive

- Attract more participants

- Increase revenue (sponsorships, higher fees, and so forth)

- Take advantage of marketing opportunities

Using the results of this analysis, participants determined whether each program should be left as is, scaled back, enhanced, or eliminated.

Rating Quality

Sometimes the group may need to rate certain items for quality. Participants often want an overall picture of how well the organization is performing in various areas. Although empirical data are best for understanding how well the company is doing, sometimes that information isn't available.

At a retreat we led for the sales division of a telecommunications firm, for example, it was important to rate the company on questions such as, "How good are the materials we use to promote ourselves?" and, "How strong are the presentation skills of our new hires?" These are difficult answers to obtain from research, so the executive group had to rate the issues themselves.

The most efficient way to handle rating such issues is simply to ask everyone to write, for each of the issues, a rating number from 1 (lowest) to 10 (highest) on a slip of paper, fold it, and pass it to the facilitator to be tallied and averaged. (Anonymity usually evokes honest responses, so be prepared for the ratings to be lower than the organization's leaders had expected.) Just as with ranking, however, participants shouldn't treat the numbers as empirical data. Encourage them to discuss the initial ratings to see if any adjustments ought to be made.

Rating Resources

Description

In this activity participants create a report card rating the organization's competencies. The ensuing discussion should address issues of how to improve performance and reallocate resources.

Experiential Elements

- Active decision making
- Individual and group reflection
- Shared dialogue and discussion
- Receiving and acting on feedback

Special Supplies

A pad of Post-it Notes and a Sharpie pen for the facilitator

Steps

1. Introduce the activity: "A critical piece of any organization's operational strategy is the scope of work it takes on and how well it performs that work. This activity will help you focus on how you rate [the organization's] competencies. The ratings will allow you to determine where improvements are needed."

2. Ask the group: "What kinds of clients [customers, members, or constituents] do you wish to serve in the future?" As they answer, write the list on a flip chart.

3. Ask the group: "Looking at this list, which competencies would best help you meet the needs of the clients you want to serve?" On a flip chart, list the competencies the group suggests.

4. Then ask: "Are there any competencies you now have that are not on this list?" Add these to the list too.

5. Facilitate a discussion to group the competency suggestions into common themes. Limit the final list of competencies to no more than ten.

6. Hand out small pieces of paper to each participant. Go through the list of competencies one by one. For each competency, ask participants to write on a slip of paper how they rate the organization on a scale of 1 to 10: 1 meaning that the organization has no competency in that area and 10 being perfection.

7. Ask for two volunteers to help calculate the average of the ratings the group will produce.

8. Ask participants to fold their slips of paper and pass them up to the volunteers.

9. Have the volunteers tally the ratings to derive an average score for the competency, while participants are doing their ratings on the next competency.

10. List the competencies and their average ratings on a flip chart, as shown in the flip chart illustration:

COMPETENCY	AVERAGE RATING
A	XX
B	XX
C	XX
D	XX
E	XX

11. Discuss the ratings. Any competency that scores a 7 or less should be considered deficient. Ask the group to consider strategies for improving the organization's rating in that competency.

Facilitator Notes

- This is a straightforward activity that is easy to facilitate unless participants become defensive about the ratings.

- It is often surprising how realistically a group will rate itself. Be prepared for the possibility that the average ratings will be significantly lower than some senior managers might expect them to be.

- For some groups, it might be useful to have the participants rank the competencies in order of importance before you reveal the rating scores.

Rating Resources in Practice

Rating competencies can be especially useful when working with an organization over time. At the first of a series of retreats we led for the senior staff of a government agency, for example, we ask these executives to rate their competencies as a team. At each subsequent retreat they re-rated those competencies, looking for areas where progress had been made and highlighting areas where they had fallen short of their goals. This gave team members a quick and familiar way to track their progress.

Categorizing

If you are facilitating a large retreat with many breakout groups, you will quickly fill up multiple flip chart pages with information, much of it redundant. Before moving on after an important exercise, the participants will often need to collapse this wide range of points and ideas into a smaller number of categories.

Such culling of information usually seems like a relatively easy task, and facilitators are often tempted to do it for the group to save time. But it's good practice for the participants to figure out how to do it themselves. In addition, you'll learn a lot about how decisions are made in the group by observing how the participants approach this effort.

At other times the group may need to sort items into types in order to see them differently. You might want to structure an exercise that helps a company that typically looks at its clients by geographic region, for example, to assess these clients instead according to profitability or the variety of services they buy. Or you might guide the group through a more subjective sorting exercise: "Which of your departments are underperforming, and which deserve more recognition and rewards?" The more subjective the topic, the more dissension you can expect—and the longer it may take to reach agreement.

Limiting Issues

If the organization you're working with does not have an effective process for addressing problems, a retreat can easily unearth many more issues than can be dealt with effectively in the time available. When that happens, help the participants choose which issues must be dealt with at the retreat and which will have to be left to another forum.

Prioritizing Actions

Prioritizing actions is similar to ranking, except that it relates to specific action steps the group is considering. A lively retreat often generates many more ideas than the organization can possibly act on. Choosing the few action steps that will make the most difference isn't merely a matter of selecting the actions that people are most interested in or that can be accomplished most easily.

Among the factors that the participants need to consider in determining their priorities for action are

- The potential impact on their goals.
- The resources needed to implement this action.
- The time required to complete this action.
- The interest in or enthusiasm for the action. (Enthusiasm is important because, even if an action makes sense, someone has to be willing to undertake it.)

When people must consider several factors, it might be helpful to create a matrix on a flip chart, with each action to be considered listed down the left side and the factors the group is weighing listed across the top. For each potential action, ask the group to agree on how important each factor is, on a scale, say, from 1 (least) to 5 (most). The numbers in each cell will give the group a visual summary of how the factors might affect their priorities.

When the actions under consideration are not especially complicated, *energy voting* can be a fast and effective way to make choices. List the options on a flip chart, hand out markers, and tell participants to put a check next to any item they have the energy for—as many as they like. This is not one-person, one-vote democracy. You're trying to identify the ideas people are truly enthusiastic about.

One characteristic of energy voting is that people see how others vote. When the vote isn't particularly sensitive, this can be an advantage: participants may find that their colleagues' energy is a positive reinforcement for their own feelings. But we do not use energy voting for a contentious issue, where individuals might be reluctant to reveal their interest or lack of interest in a particular option.

Criteria Evaluation Grid

Description

This activity helps participants determine evaluation criteria and the relative weight of the criteria before deciding which actions to pursue.

Steps

1. After the group has generated its potential action steps, write each step on a separate Post-it Note.

2. Guide the group as a whole in determining the evaluation criteria they will use for choosing their actions. These criteria might address cost, potential impact, difficulty of implementation, urgency, match with the organization's overall priorities, customer interest, employee enthusiasm, and the like.

3. Lead the group in a discussion to decide on the relative weight of each criterion, based on the overall issues facing the organization and its core priorities, using a scale of 1 to 3, where 1 = *somewhat important,* 2 = *important,* and 3 = *critical.*

4. Divide the group into subgroups, and give each subgroup an equal number of the Post-it Notes with the potential action steps written on them. (For example, if you have three breakout groups, each group will work with one-third of the potential action steps.)

5. Hand out the Criteria Evaluation Grid to each participant (see CD 8). Ask each group member to use the grid to evaluate, alone and in silence, how well each action step the subgroup is considering meets each criterion, using a scale of 1 to 3, where 1 = *meets the criterion poorly,* 2 = *meets the criterion somewhat,* and 3 = *meets criterion very well.*

Experiential Elements
- Active decision making
- Individual and group reflection
- Shared dialogue and discussion

Setup

Prepare a "Criteria Evaluation Grid" on a sheet of butcher paper and individual grids for each participant (see CD 8; also see the sample grid on p. 182).

Special Supplies

A pad of Post-it Notes and a Sharpie pen for the facilitator

6. Ask the participants to share their individual action step rankings with their subgroups. Then ask the subgroups to come up with group rankings for these action steps by averaging the individual action step rankings and adjusting as necessary after discussion among subgroup members and multiplying the group ranking by the relative weight of the criterion (see Step 3).

7. Ask each subgroup to report its rankings and rationales to the group as a whole, and lead a discussion to determine if the whole group agrees with each subgroup's analysis.

Criteria Evaluation Grid in Practice

In a strategic planning retreat for a sporting goods company that aspired to increase its share of the urban youth market by sponsoring inner-city youth programs, the participants came up with a long list of potential actions that they believed would help increase the company's appeal to that community and strengthen the bottom line. To pare down the list they used the Criteria Evaluation Grid to assess which actions would best meet their criteria for success. (An evaluation grid for some of this company's potential action steps is shown in the sample grid on p. 182.) It is important to understand that the participants didn't determine which actions to take based solely on the numbers but rather used the grid as a springboard for discussion. They explored, for example, how to make certain actions easier to implement or more likely to generate revenue or new client streams.

Sample Criteria Evaluation Grid

Criteria (weight)	Potential Actions					
	Raise our prices	Create internship program for inner-city youth	Identify current and target customers and the products they are most interested in	Increase interactivity of Web site so customers can give us timely feedback	Identify target reporters and media outlets to tell our story	Identify community leaders who will be spokespeople for our products and services
Increases revenue (2)	× 3 = 6	× 1 = 2	× 2* = 4 *potentially	× 1 = 2	× 2* = 4 *potentially	× 2* = 4 *potentially
Is easy to implement (1)	× 2 = 2	× 2 = 2	× 1 = 1	× 1 = 1	× 2 = 2	× 1 = 1
Garners favorable publicity (1)	× 1 = 1	× 3 = 3	× 1 = 1	× 2 = 2	× 3 = 3	× 3 = 3
Gives us entrée into a new market (2)	× 1 = 2	× 2 = 4	× 3 = 6	× 1 = 2	× 2* = 4 *potentially	× 3 = 6
Addresses an urgent problem (3)	× 3 = 9	× 1 = 3	× 3 = 9	× 1 = 3	× 2 = 6	× 2 = 6
Totals	20	14	21	10	19	20

Note: "*Potentially" means that a specific action has the potential to achieve a certain outcome, but that it isn't known whether that potential would be realized.

Sequencing Actions

Part of the action planning process may involve putting items in a time sequence. Certain actions may be prerequisites for others, some actions may lead to decision points, or limited resources may dictate hard choices about what to do next. These sequencing decisions, unlike most other retreat decisions, are usually best made not by the entire group but by the people who will have to perform the tasks. We recommend that you structure time-sequencing discussions to give first consideration to the opinions of those who will do the work.

Choosing Among Alternatives

Sometimes a group has many attractive action options it might pursue but insufficient resources to support all of them. The following activity can help groups see the comparative passion they have for one option over another.

Show Me Our Future

Description

In this activity participants work in small groups to imagine positive scenarios associated with the various options they are considering. They use props to tell stories about the positive impact each option may have. The group as a whole decides with its applause which option(s) to pursue.

Experiential Elements

- Group discussion
- Envisioning possibilities
- Role play
- Storytelling
- Using toys and other props

Steps

1. Assign one option to each small group.

2. Tell the participants: "Your job is to make the most compelling case possible for the option your group has been assigned. Even if it's not your personal favorite, each group should present everything that is attractive about this option to the rest of us. You can use any prop in the room to help make a strong and memorable case for pursuing the option your group has been asked to recommend."

Setup

Prepare a flip chart that lists the options under consideration.

Special Supplies

Hats, toys, and other evocative props

3. Give participants ten to fifteen minutes to prepare their stories.

4. Have each subgroup make its case in turn. Then ask the group as a whole to indicate by its applause the most appealing option. Remind the participants not to base their applause on the quality of the presentation but on the attractiveness of the option.

Facilitator Notes

- Encourage the groups to have fun with the presentations, to tell an imaginative story, and to use the props liberally to illustrate their points.

- Each group should participate in the applause section for the strongest case. Subgroup members do not have to vote for their own group's presentation; they should vote for the option most appealing to them personally.

The Nub: Action Planning

Although it is the fashion in planning these days to write long, detailed lists of actions, numbered software style (1.1.1) and intensely cross-referenced, that's not what we recommend for your retreat action plan.

Retreats are much more suited to identifying strategic initiatives—broad blueprints for change aimed at a few specific goals—than to drawing up detailed plans. The more goals and initiatives you have, the less likely they are to be achieved. It's far better to leave the retreat with a few well-thought-out initiatives and an agreement on how the group will achieve them than with a long list of action steps that no one will be able to remember.

Keep the action plan format simple. Even very bright people get stuck on the definitions of terms like *goal, objective, strategy, tactic,* and *action step.* You can capture the essence of the results that participants are aiming to achieve by asking them these questions, in the order shown here:

1. What results do we want to achieve?

2. How will we know we have achieved a result?

3. What do we have to do to achieve each result?

4. Who will do which of these things?

5. Do we have the resources to do these things? If not, how will we get the resources?

6. When will these actions be completed?

7. What obstacles will we have to overcome to complete these actions?

8. How will we overcome these obstacles?

1. What Results Do We Want to Achieve?

The answer to this question outlines the goals the group is committed to. Be careful to frame the answers so that each one reflects a *result,* not an *action.* For instance, "Let's reorganize into cross-discipline teams" is an action, not a result. In this example the result that the group wants to achieve might be, "We want to improve the quality and speed of our response to members' requests." Organizing into cross-discipline teams might be an action step to help the group achieve that goal.

Sometimes it's easier to ask an even more basic question than "What do we want to achieve?" You might ask, for instance, "What do we want to happen as a result of these actions?"

We strongly recommend that the group leave the retreat with no more than three desired results (goals). Most people can remember two or three ideas, but very few can recite a list of six or seven. Unless people can remember day-to-day what they are trying to achieve, it's not likely that the results they commit to achieving will be reflected in their everyday priorities.

If the participants come up with more than three goals, see if you can help them combine several into a single strategic initiative with interim milestones.

2. How Will We Know We Have Achieved a Result?

"What gets measured gets done" is an old adage, but an accurate one, at least in organizations. For each result the group will need to devise a means of indicating progress and noting when that result has been achieved.

The most effective measures are quantifiable or directly observable. If a hands-on science center wanted to increase visitation by 15 percent, the participants setting up a measure for this result would need to know the current visitor counts and that the center will continue to count its visitors.

Often, though, the issues aren't that easy to quantify. If the center's goal was to increase diversity among its visitors, retreat participants would have to

The Five Whys

If the group has trouble differentiating desired results from actions, you might use a variation of the "Five Whys" exercise recommended by Senge, Roberts, Ross, Smith, and Kleiner (1994) in the *Fifth Discipline Fieldbook*. If you're not sure whether something is a result or an action, ask, "Why is that important?" If the answer doesn't help you find what seems core, keep asking, "And why is that important?" for each subsequent answer. By the time you've asked five times or so, you should have the core result people are trying to achieve. (If not, keep asking.)

specify what kind of diversity it was seeking—racial, economic, gender, age, and so forth—and the center might well have no empirical mechanism for collecting that information. So part of the work of the group would be inventing—and finding the funding for—a quantitative measure. Even harder to measure might be visitor satisfaction, and the group would have to be particularly creative in devising a means to measure that.

It's tempting for people to say, "We'll know if we've been successful," or to rely on anecdotal information. Unfortunately, that kind of thinking sets the stage for later debates in which people simply trade opinions rather than focus on fact. It's far better to take the necessary time at the retreat to work out measurement criteria.

3. What Do We Have to Do to Achieve Each Result?

To specify the actions that will move the organization toward achieving each result, the participants will need to create a list of specific actions that they are committing to take.

As facilitator, you'll want to help participants ensure that the proposed actions reflect what people or groups will *do,* rather than what they will think or feel. It's useful to keep asking, "Is this an observable action? Will you be able to see if it happens or not?"

When participants recommend changing how people work together, for example, they often want to list a change of attitude instead of a specific action. "We'll all be more understanding of other people's mistakes" is a nice thought, but it's not likely to survive more than two days back in the real world, nor is it observable or measurable. Instead, the group might plan to hold a monthly meeting to celebrate what they've learned from their mistakes, with an award for the best new ideas that grew out of those mistakes.

You'll also want to make sure the group is not devising actions that are all for *other people* to take. "Let's get the accounting department to start tallying the customer service evaluation forms" is easy to say when no one from accounting is there to protest. Action plans are much more likely to be implemented when they are created by the people who will be taking the actions or by the managers of the ultimate actors. If action plans do require the active assistance of people who aren't in the room, ask the group, for example, "And what do you think the accounting department will say about that? How can you get them involved and committed?"

Although it is important to keep the number of desired results small, each goal may have five to ten action steps. If an action is likely to take months to complete, you might consider breaking it into several shorter pieces. Shorter time frames allow the organization to monitor progress more effectively. (No one wants to get to the six-month mark and find out that essentially nothing has been done.) And having smaller chunks to work on gives people a sense of achievement as they finish each one.

When the participants complete their list of action steps, apply the "necessary and sufficient" test to see whether they have a coherent plan. You do that by asking two questions:

- *If you do all those things, will you achieve the result?* In other words, are all these actions, taken together, *sufficient* for the plan to succeed? A long list of actions may obscure the point that despite a burst of activity the goal is still out of reach. A series of action steps that are insufficient to achieve the desired result may have the long-term effect of discouraging people from taking on new initiatives.
- *Do you have to do all the things you've listed to achieve the result?* Could participants eliminate some of the items and still reach their objective? Sometimes a popular project is built into an action plan when it doesn't actually relate to the results the group is trying to achieve. Or a group can be so enthusiastic about action ideas that the list becomes too long. In both cases the action plan will use up resources that could be saved or applied to other needs.

4. Who Will Do Which of These Things?

Next to each action step should be the name (or names) of a person (or people) *who have accepted responsibility* for ensuring that it is implemented. Notice the emphasis on "who have accepted responsibility." If at all possible, you want people to volunteer or at least agree to take on responsibility for the implementation, whether they are going to do the work themselves, oversee the work of others whom they supervise, or work to build a coalition with others who aren't in the room. Assigning an action step to someone who doesn't want the responsibility or isn't present can be a recipe for disaster.

When there's something the group has agreed to but no one is willing to take on, it's not likely that it will be done well, if at all. If no one volunteers to assume responsibility for a certain action step, an executive may decide to assign it to someone in the room, but it would be prudent first to explore why no one is interested. Is it onerous work? If so, should it be shared by more people? Is it so high risk that people are concerned that failure would put their careers on the line? How could the risk be minimized? Was the item put on the list because someone in power suggested it but no one else actually believes in it?

Reluctance to accept responsibility for action steps can signal many things, including a workforce that is already overtaxed, but it always means that more discussion is necessary before the group can conclude it has an action plan.

Other questions to ask participants who are deciding who will be responsible for what include: How many people do you need for each action step? Can one person do this, or do you need a team? Should the team members all come from one department? Should the team include representatives from several parts of the organization or outside stakeholders?

Finally, the group must consider whether there are people who are not in the room who have a vital role to play in accomplishing these actions. How will the group involve them? For instance, if the company database needs to be reformatted or some market research is needed, those tasks will have to be done by people with the appropriate technical expertise, and they may not be taking part in the retreat. If so, the action plan should include a process for getting input from the people whose collaboration is essential, before the final action steps are decided. These people will often have perspectives that the participants lack.

5. *Do We Have the Resources to Do These Things?*

In the excitement of coming up with new ideas, staying focused on reality can be a tough task. But if participants fail to recognize current reality, the final plan is unlikely to be implemented.

In the course of a board retreat we led for a nonprofit organization, for example, the participants came up with an extensive list of action steps. There was no doubt that these actions would significantly raise the organization's profile—if they got done. But everyone on the board had other full-time obligations, and the staff were already working long days and coming in on weekends. "When do you plan to do all of this?" we asked. That question sent them back to the list, looking for the few actions that would give them the greatest leverage, taking into account their most limited commodity, time.

Another issue is that of information or knowledge. Do the people who will take certain actions have the information they need? They may have to enroll in training courses or do a benchmarking study, for instance, before they set off for unfamiliar territory. If this is the case those prerequisite actions will have to be part of the plan.

If the required time, money, and information are not available, and the action is truly important, participants will have to explore how to come up with these resources. Are there others in the organization who have the necessary skills or information? Could some of the workload of people assigned to this project be transferred to others? Could funds already allocated to one budget item be redistributed?

Of all the reasons a retreat might not meet expectations, one of the most common is that the participants fail to allocate resources to the activities they've agreed to undertake. The resources question is tempting to ignore, but don't let the group shortchange this all-important aspect of action planning.

Organizations, whether strategically or inadvertently, set priorities by budgeting. It's a safe bet that no one wants to see the budget for his or her project cut, much less eliminated. But too often, realistic budget constraints are overlooked in retreats, resulting in unfunded action plans that go nowhere.

Are the budgets for the next year set in stone? If they are, you'll need to remind the group that the money for new initiatives will have to come from some existing program or programs. The participants will have to discuss which current budget items might be valid trade-offs. The group often won't have authority to make budget changes, but the participants should face up to the budget implications of their action plan by making recommendations about how to handle funding constraints.

6. When Will These Actions Be Completed?

For every action step the group should specify a deadline for finishing the task and—for multiple steps—interim target dates as well. Without targets and deadlines, the plans made so enthusiastically at the retreat can slowly decelerate into inaction. Deadlines are best when they are hard dates ("April 25," for instance), rather than inexact estimates ("by early spring").

But just as important as setting realistic deadlines is coordinating them. And such coordination will also help ensure that no one person or office is overloaded by a series of competing demands for immediate action.

The group should decide on a mechanism to monitor agreed-on deadlines. Will a senior executive volunteer to coordinate the whole project? (This is not a responsibility to be handed off to someone without clout or commitment to the initiative.) If there is no one person who can monitor compliance, does the group need to set up a series of regular status meetings of the action plan's champions, or perhaps of department heads, specifically to review progress? The action plan is not a set of unrelated items; people will need to cooperate and keep each other apprised of what's being accomplished and where they are encountering rough patches and roadblocks.

The group will also have to discuss what happens if deadlines aren't met. How will that situation be handled? Will other people share the workload if it looks like a deadline might be missed? Who has the authority to extend a deadline?

7. What Obstacles Will We Have to Overcome to Complete These Actions?

This question is particularly important if the organization has a history of holding retreats that do not result in meaningful change. In that case the group will need to confront the reasons for previous failures. Similarly, if the plans call for significant change, you and the client should expect some resistance and be prepared to bring it to light so it can be managed.

We discuss strategies for dealing with the resistance that might surface at the retreat in Chapter 7, "Participants Are Resisting New Ideas," pp. 150–155.

8. How Will We Overcome These Obstacles?

If obstacles are identified, it is important to take time at the retreat to help participants think about how they will move forward in spite of the predicted impediments. Thinking about how to maneuver around potential roadblocks will be helpful in focusing participants' thinking on desired outcomes no matter what obstacles occur during implementation.

Finally, be wary of action plans that are in effect *plans to plan*. If there are a lot of steps that begin with phrases like, "Think about . . ." or, "Meet to decide . . . ," the group may have avoided making real commitments. The retreat is the time for people to think and consider. But it will only be useful if it leads to real action.

Activities to Help Participants Make Decisions and Plan for Action

You will find other activities for decision making and action planning in the Activities for Making Decisions, Planning, and Evaluating Ideas index (p. 502), as well as throughout Chapter 9, "Leading a Strategic Planning Retreat."

Chapter 9

Leading a Strategic Planning Retreat

Strategic planning is the most common reason organizations hold retreats. Executives convene offsites to help them determine where they want to be in a year, three years or five years, what route they want to take to get there, and what resources they will need for the journey.

This is a tall order, and a single strategic planning retreat won't result in a fully formed blueprint for the future. But it can help participants make great strides in reaching agreement on the key elements of a plan to guide their business decisions. Although the time needed depends on the size and complexity of the organization and the challenges it faces, most groups can agree on overall goals, strategies, and preliminary tactics in one or two retreats. Then working groups tend to be charged with fleshing out the tactics, and someone commits to writing the plan.

Why Strategic Planning?

Organizations are continually presented with unexpected opportunities and unanticipated problems. They must make hard choices quickly, often under conditions in which little is certain. It's easy to become distracted by these challenges, expending time, money, and energy on activities that divert people's attention from the organization's principal goals. To avoid these distractions, organization members—including staff from top to bottom—need to understand clearly what the organization's goals are and what it will take to achieve them.

Before embarking on the strategic planning process, organization leaders must be clear about their own priorities. When you are planning such a retreat, we recommend that you ask the leaders to consider what they personally would like to see happen. It's not that you will try to guide the retreat participants toward what the leaders want, but leaders' views do affect the range and scope of possible outcomes. In the end, if the plan doesn't match what the leaders are willing to support, it won't be implemented.

This is especially true in privately held companies or organizations headed by their founders. For example, to prepare for a retreat for a firm owned by two partners, we asked them to spell out the emotional, intellectual, and financial rewards they wanted from the company. Each declared that he wanted to retire in five years with a multimillion-dollar cash buyout. When we pointed out that the company would have to grow eightfold to finance such large, simultaneous buyouts, the owners realized that they had to redefine their own expectations before they could forge ahead with planning for the company.

Most retreat processes fall into three phases: understanding the current state of things (scanning the environment), setting goals, and devising strategies to fulfill those goals.

In *scanning the environment* the organization examines both the external and internal factors that will have an impact on the success of its plans. In *setting goals* the organization outlines in measurable terms what it hopes to achieve. Finally, in *devising strategies* the organization determines what actions are necessary to meet its goals. The concepts and activities that follow will help you move the participants through the decisions necessary in each of these three planning phases.

For more information about strategy and strategic planning, we recommend these resources:

- *Strategic Planning for Nonprofit Organizations: A Practical Guide and Workbook*, by Michael Allison and Jude Kaye (2005).

- *Good to Great: Why Some Companies Make the Leap . . . And Others Don't*, by Jim Collins (2001).

- *Management Challenges for the 21st Century*, by Peter Drucker (1999).

- *Leading the Revolution*, by Gary Hamel (2000).

- *Strategic Planning for Success: Aligning People, Performance, and Payoffs*, by Roger Kaufman, et al. (2003).

- *Plan or Die! 10 Keys to Organizational Success*, by Timothy Nolan, et al. (1993).

- *What Is Strategy?* Harvard Business Review, pp. 68–69, by Michael Porter (1996, November/December).

- *Scenarios: The Art of Strategic Conversation*, by Kees Van Der Heijden (1996).

Elements of Organization Strategy

There is no universal model of what should go into a strategic plan and no single best format. The planning model you use to guide the retreat discussions must fit the organization's circumstances, expectations, needs, and capacity.

Many successful organizations, realizing the futility of predicting the future, tend to think less about complex analyses of past performance and more about imagining a new future and inspiring people to create it. Here is a model for strategic planning that we often use to help groups begin this process.

A Model for Strategic Planning

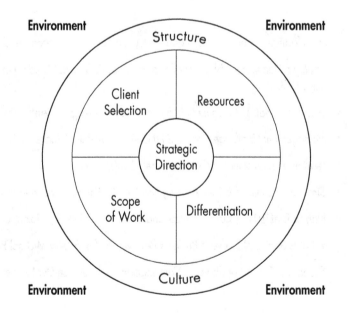

In this model, *strategic direction* is at the core of everything an organization does. It defines the kind of work the organization will do (and what it won't do) and, ultimately, how it will measure success. An appropriate strategic direction will be deeply rooted in the organization's *values*.

Flowing out of strategic direction are four primary aspects of strategy that every organization must address: *client selection, resources, differentiation,* and *scope of work*.

The organization's *structure* and *culture* are shown on the outer edges of the model, because together they both define and restrict what's possible for an organization to achieve. And they are in the same ring because they are so interconnected that changing one almost always requires changing the other. Highly successful organizations may not need to delve deeply into these elements in a planning retreat. But organizations that are struggling will have to explore their structure and culture before they can make real progress in planning.

Finally, every organization operates in an environment it cannot control. Effective strategic planning demands a deep awareness of the rapid changes taking place outside the organization—in its field, in technology, in business, in the economy, in society, in politics, and in the rest of the world at large.

Strategic Direction

Although many organizations like to begin a planning retreat by revisiting their mission statement or coming up with a new vision, starting there is like deciding to route a long hike through a swamp. It's still possible to get where you're going, but it's going to be very messy and take a lot longer than necessary.

The instinct to start with a mission statement isn't a bad one. Obviously, participants have to agree on the organization's core purpose before devising a strategy for achieving it. But the problem with most mission and vision statements is that they typically have been wordsmithed so thoroughly that they no longer reflect anything unique about the organization. They express the organization's commitment to such uncontroversial issues as quality, caring for people, satisfying clients, being environmentally responsible, and oh, by the way, making a profit. They're often so bland that they obscure what the organization is really all about. (That's one reason few employees in most organizations can remember what the mission statement says, let alone what it means.)

Hedgehog or Fox?

"The fox knows many things, but the hedgehog knows one big thing," wrote Archilochus, a Greek poet, circa 650 BCE. In the twentieth century this axiom was popularized by the British philosopher Isaiah Berlin, who used it to classify some of the greatest writers and thinkers of all time as either hedgehogs (single-minded visionaries) or foxes (those who pursued a broader range of interests).

If the organization needs a guiding statement, we recommend focusing on strategic direction. Jim Collins (2001, pp. 95–96), in *Good to Great,* calls it a *Hedgehog Concept:* "a simple, crystalline concept that flows from deep understanding about . . . what you can be the best in the world at, what drives your economic engine [and] what you are deeply passionate about." Because such a statement doesn't pretend to spell out everything—only the single most important thing—it can be written in one sentence.

As Collins explains it, "The Hedgehog Concept is not a goal to be the best, a strategy to be the best, an intention to be the best, a plan to be the best. It's an *understanding* of what you *can* be the best at" (p. 98). What is important for retreat participants to understand is that what the organization "*can* be the best at" is not necessarily synonymous with its core business. As a matter of fact, Collins would say that if an organization can't be best in the world at its core business, its core business cannot form the basis of its Hedgehog Concept.

In formulating their own inspiring Hedgehog Concept (what we call *strategic direction*), retreat participants must be bold. Collins argues that "focusing solely on what [the organization] can potentially do better than any other organization is the only path to greatness" (p. 100).

The last important point that retreat participants should keep in mind is what they're passionate about. Rather than trying to get passionate about what the organization already does, Collins says they should strive for only those things that they are passionate about.

A widely understood strategic direction informs the hundreds of daily decisions that in the end will determine what an organization can achieve.

Read more about the Hedgehog Concept in *Good to Great: Why Some Companies Make the Leap . . . and Others Don't,* by Jim Collins (2001).

No organization will be as effective as it might be until its people understand and support the organization's strategic direction. A muddled direction leads to confusion and allows—indeed, compels—people to decide individually what's important, without any context to guide them. A clear and galvanizing strategic direction, in contrast, focuses everyone's efforts and moves the organization forward in an unambiguous manner.

If your pre-retreat interviews have demonstrated that the organization's mission and vision statements are well understood and influence behavior and decision making, by all means encourage the group to use them as a framework for planning. If not, you'll conserve time and energy by helping the group agree on what the organization's strategic direction ought to be, rather than trying to lead participants through the morass of drafting a mission statement as a group.

Here is an activity we use to help organizations identify their strategic direction.

The Trouble with Mission Statements

Several years ago we were conducting interviews in the conference room of a government agency that had just completed a lengthy process to define its mission. Pleased with the outcome, the planning team had hung large color posters with the mission statement all over the agency's offices.

In the course of an interview we asked a mid-level manager to tell us what the agency's mission was. "Um," she said, "I think we have one. I know we worked on it. I can't quite remember." Meanwhile the mission statement was hanging just over her left shoulder on the conference room wall.

Exploring Strategic Direction

Description

In this activity participants work in silence to create a collective collage that represents what they believe the organization's potential to be. Once the collage has been created, they discuss their individual contributions to it and work together to see how their views converge. Each group presents its collage to the group as a whole, along with a statement of strategic direction that flows from the collage. The whole group looks for common themes and agrees on the elements that belong in the statement of strategic direction. The group then considers whether the elements they propose including in the strategic direction will help the organization make effective decisions. If not, the strategic direction statement is modified.

Experiential Elements

- Collage
- Experimenting with ideas
- Group discussion

Setup

- Prepare the sentence prompt, "Our future potential will be realized when . . ." on a flip chart.
- Put art materials on participants' tables, and words and images that you have clipped from magazines on tables along the sides of the room.

Special Supplies

- Pictures and words clipped from magazines
- Colored paper
- Prismacolor Art Markers for each breakout group
- Glue sticks
- Scissors
- Other inexpensive art materials, such as feathers and beads that can be glued onto a collage

Steps

1. Tell the participants: "This is your chance to be bold and creative in identifying [the organization]'s core purpose. You will work collectively in silence to create a collage that completes the following sentence—with concrete and observable results, not attitudes:

   "'Our potential will be realized when . . .'

   "Examples of concrete results that would complete the sentence are, 'we have offices on every continent,' or, 'we win our industry's Top Company to Work For award.' Attitudes—such as, 'we treat our customers well'—do not easily translate into concrete results, although 'customer complaints drop 90 percent' would.

"In completing the sentence, consider these critical questions:"

- "What could we be the best in the world at?"

- "What is the single best measure of our economic success?"

- "What are we deeply passionate about?"

- "Where can we make the biggest difference?"

2. Divide the participants into subgroups of no more than seven members each.

3. Give the subgroups twenty minutes to select their materials and create their collages. Urge participants not to take too long gathering materials but to pick up the words and images that seem to relate to the organization's potential without dwelling too much on why they are choosing certain images or phrases.

4. Ask participants to discuss in their subgroups what each person contributed to the collage and to look for common themes. Then the subgroup members should work together to come up with a collective conclusion to the statement, "Our potential will be realized when . . ." Once the members of each subgroup agree on a strategic direction, they write it on a separate flip chart as a title for their collage.

5. As each subgroup shows its collage in turn, ask all participants to listen for common themes that can be combined into one or more expressions of strategic direction.

6. Write the themes on a flip chart. Ask participants to suggest which themes belong in a statement of strategic direction.

7. Ask participants to suggest typical strategic issues that arise in the organization, for instance, "Is the timing right for us to expand into other geographic markets?" or, "Should we increase our plant capacity, or outsource new product manufacturing?" List the issues on a separate flip chart.

8. Test the relevance of the strategic direction the group has agreed on by asking, "If this were our strategic direction, would it help us address these issues?"

Facilitator Notes
- This is a difficult activity to lead. The facilitator must reassure participants that this nonlinear activity will lead to the creation of a compelling strategic direction. The facilitator must also be skilled in guiding senior executives in the process of making tough choices about complex issues and narrowing these choices down to a single strategic direction. The facilitator should be comfortable working with visual images and helping people see multiple levels of meaning in the images they choose. Be prepared to overcome objections that this exercise is "childish" or "silly." (It is childish in a way or, more accurately, childlike, which is the whole point. Children know how to create with unfettered imagination, which this activity helps participants reclaim.)

- It takes time to prepare for this activity; clipping enough words and images—and you'll need a lot, more than you think you will—can be tedious. If you have young children, you might be able to enlist them in the effort. That said, when done well, this activity yields brilliant results and can save you from hours of fruitless discussion at the retreat.

- Emphasize the importance of working on the collage in silence. This will make the discussion more meaningful and allow the group to come to agreement on strategic direction much more quickly.

- Don't get trapped into editing the participants' statements or debating the meaning of words. If you do, you may end up spending the entire retreat on this activity.

- The biggest mistake planning groups make is not thinking boldly enough. If the ideas aren't compelling, encourage the group to try again. Or ask the group why their ambitions are so constrained. Try to get at the underlying issues.

Client Selection: Whom Will the Organization Serve?

For companies (and for many nonprofits as well), the question "Whom will the organization serve?" implies difficult marketing considerations: Which customer segments generate the greatest sales volume? Which are the most profitable? Which have the greatest potential for future growth? Without answers to such questions, organizations can fall victim to the tendency to seize any opportunity that comes along, regardless of its strategic value.

Nonprofit organizations face an additional difficulty with client selection because it implies that the organization will not serve all possible constituencies equally and may not serve some at all. Most nonprofits don't have the resources to serve everyone they would like to (or who would like to be served), and they frequently fall into *mission creep,* adding a few more programs every year to address the needs of new constituent groups. Over time these organizations can lose focus and, in attempting to serve everyone to some extent, ultimately end up serving no one well.

It's difficult for many organizations to decide which constituencies will receive priority attention. Organizations that don't establish such priorities, however, can easily overstretch their budgets, muddle their identities, and strain their resources. As painful as the decision may be, organizations must often be explicit about whom they will serve and how, and implicitly, whom they can't or won't serve.

If you sense that an organization is trying to be all things to all people, you might try the following activity to help participants sort out their commitments to various constituency groups.

Prioritizing Constituencies

Description

This identification and ranking activity allows participants to examine and evaluate the organization's various constituencies or clients. After working together to list constituencies, participants get out of their seats and "vote" by sticking colored dots next to their choices.

Experiential Elements

- Group discussion
- Individual and group decision making

Steps

1. Ask participants, working as a whole group, to call out discrete categories of constituents or clients that the organization should serve. List the categories on a flip chart. Allow time for them to name all possible constituents or clients regardless of importance or centrality.

2. Show participants the Core Constituencies flip chart:

Setup

Prepare a "Core Constituencies" flip chart (see Step 2).

Special Supplies

Several large blue, red, and yellow voting dots for each person

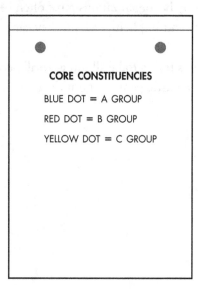

CORE CONSTITUENCIES

BLUE DOT = A GROUP

RED DOT = B GROUP

YELLOW DOT = C GROUP

3. Tell the participants: "The categories you called out must be prioritized to examine the organization's opportunities and ability to serve them.

- "The A Group receives highest priority for resources. This is an enormously important, primary constituency; they are probably regular users of your products and services.

- "The B Group receives targeted resources. This group is important for your future, but is likely to be less familiar with what you do now. They are infrequent or nonusers of your products and services, but have the potential to use them without an extraordinary effort on your part.

- "The C Group receives lower priority for resources. These may be smaller groups of people, perhaps with very specialized or narrow interests compared to your overall purpose, or groups whose needs do not align closely with your current abilities to serve them.

- "The D Group (with no votes) receives no targeted resources. The organization does not have the resources to serve them in light of its focus on members of the A, B, and C Groups."

4. Distribute a generous supply of blue, red, and yellow voting dots to each person. Explain: "The blue dots represent the A Group, red dots the B Group, yellow dots the C Group, and constituencies that receive no dots make up the D Group. Using the dots as 'votes,' you should each place one dot on every constituent category you believe merits at least some of the organization's resources, but you won't have enough dots to rate every constituent group as A. You will have to make some choices."

5. Invite everyone to come up to the chart and place their dots on the constituent categories to indicate each category's group, A, B, C, or D.

6. After the voting, review the votes each constituent category received to see whether the group agrees with the results. For each category, how consistent is the rating? When a constituent category receives a mix of dot colors, that indicates lack of agreement about the importance of that category. Facilitate a discussion to resolve the differences of opinion.

Facilitator Notes
- You must be prepared for some resistance to this activity. Most groups do not like deciding which constituents or clients are more important to the organization's future than others.

- Be sure to explain that the results of this activity will not force the organization to abandon any of its constituents or clients. But it will help the organization focus its resources to best meet the needs of its key constituents.

- Make sure you limit the number of voting dots of each color so that participants must make choices and cannot, for instance, place all constituents in the A Group.

- This activity should spark a discussion about how much effort and resources the organization can and should devote to category C and D constituents and whether it would be a better use of these resources to devote them to the higher priority constituents.

Prioritizing Constituencies in Practice

International relief organizations work in high-stress environments that can threaten field staff and volunteers with burnout. In a retreat for one such group the participants talked of being torn by the competing demands of their many constituents (refugees, suppliers on the ground, government agencies, and local workers) and by not having a system for deciding whose needs to address first. In addition, successful fundraising depended to a large degree on having compelling stories to tell potential donors. As the participants worked through these conflicting needs, they saw that they could reduce their stress if they changed their relationship with the organization's development department. Most of the volunteers saw fundraising work as their lowest priority, well below their work in the field, whereas senior executives rated it near the top. This activity sparked a critical dialogue about how to involve field staff and volunteers in fundraising efforts in less labor-intensive ways.

Differentiation

How will the organization distinguish itself from others in its field? An organization's basis of differentiation might lie in its products, quality, pricing, service, convenience, or philosophy or the overall depth and breadth of its offerings. To understand what makes their organization stand out from others in its field, participants must ask themselves, "What do we do or know that is unique? Do we have any proprietary processes, systems, services, or products? What do we do (or can we do) better than anyone else?"

Too often an organization claims differentiation that is . . . well . . . not really different. To be significant, the difference must be part of the fabric of the organization's everyday work, and it must represent a true difference from the way competing organizations operate.

If identifying significant differences is difficult for businesses, it can be a particular challenge for nonprofits, but it's critical that they too be able to articulate what makes them unique. Unclear differentiation from other groups that do similar work deprives current and potential funders and donors of compelling reasons to support the work of that particular organization, and potential clients of reasons to avail themselves of the group's products and services.

If participants have trouble articulating exactly what sets their organization apart, you might use the following short activity.

Distinctive Competencies

Description

Participants are asked to role-play a situation in which they must quickly and succinctly describe what is unique about their organization. By restricting responses to what can be written on one side of a business card, this activity forces participants to make strategic choices.

Experiential Elements

- Active decision making
- Participation in role play
- Shared dialogue and discussion

Steps

1. Distribute one or more of the blank business cards (see Setup) to each participant. Introduce the scenario: "Imagine that you are attending an important civic event and are introduced to the head of an organization you have been desperate to do business with. You start talking and really seem to connect, when, suddenly, she looks at her watch and says, 'Oops! I'm running late for a meeting. I've got to go. Give me your card.' Then she adds, 'You know, we're very happy with the organization we're already working with. Would you jot down on the back of your card what makes your organization different?'"

2. Give participants thirty seconds to write on the business cards the one thing that makes their organization unique. Tell them to be sure to write clearly—and on one side only—so this potential client will be able to read it when she gets back to her office.

3. Collect all the cards, and read them aloud, without identifying the authors. Note what the cards say on a flip chart.

Setup

Prepare "business cards" for the activity. You can use a paper cutter to cut index cards or paper into 2 inch x 3 1/2 inch cards or you can purchase blank business card templates from an office supply store.

Special Supplies

One 2 inch x 3 1/2 inch "business card" for each participant and one additional business card for each breakout group

4. Review what you wrote on the flip chart. Ask the participants:

   - "Do these cards say anything that others in our field couldn't say?"

   - "Is this our version of 'all things to all people'"?

   - "Do we say things that everyone says, such as, 'We care'?"

   - "Do these cards set us apart from our competitors?"

5. Have the participants form small subgroups and give each subgroup a single blank business card. Ask the members of each subgroup to decide how they could describe what makes their organization unique so succinctly that they could write it on a business card, and then ask them to write their description. Ask each breakout group to present its business card to the rest of the group.

Facilitator Notes
- The only difficulty in this activity is in the debriefing, when the facilitator must feel comfortable challenging the group until participants come up with true distinctive competencies so that round two (Step 5) will be useful.

- The point of this activity is to help participants focus on what sets their organization apart from others: what differentiates their products or services from others in the industry—distinctive product features, exceptional service, new technology, and so on.

- The real-life scenario of this short activity creates insights that can lead to a powerful debriefing.

- The immediacy of this activity helps participants reexamine their assumptions about the organization.

For the qualities that differentiate an organization to be important strategically, they should be perceived as valuable to customers as well as challenging for competitors to copy because these differentiating qualities depend on internal competencies that other organizations cannot easily acquire.

Sometimes organizations have difficulty putting themselves in the shoes of their customers to assess what those customers value and what trade-offs they would be willing to make. When this is the case, the differentiation strategies organizations develop tend to be aligned more with current business operations than with customers' desires or needs.

If an organization has the resources to convene focus groups or conduct in-depth market research with current and potential customers, the planning group might obtain some useful information. We have found, however, that most people cannot imagine products or services that do not yet exist. It can be just as useful for an organization to engage in some creative thinking from various customers' perspectives as it is to engage in lengthy and expensive research processes. Try either of these two activities to encourage retreat participants to put themselves in their customers' shoes.

Our "Proverbial" Differentiation

Description

Participants are asked to free associate on ideas from proverbs to generate principles of differentiation that would add value for the organization's customers.

Steps

1. Distribute "Our 'Proverbial' Differentiation" handout— a list of several dozen proverbs from various cultures (see CD 9A).

2. Give participants ten minutes to write as many associations as they can for the various proverbs. Encourage them to skip around in the list of proverbs. If one proverb does not inspire them, they should select another.

3. Call time, and then give participants another ten minutes to turn their associations into ideas about what could differentiate the organization in a way that its customers would value. Participants should write each idea on a separate Post-it Note.

4. Have the participants form small subgroups, read their proverbs and associations to each other, and then post their ideas on a wall.

5. After a discussion of these ideas in their subgroups, the members should decide on two or three things that might differentiate the organization in ways its customers would value.

6. Each subgroup reports out in turn, and the whole group selects the top differentiation that customers would see as value-added.

Experiential Elements
- Creative thinking and wordplay
- Shared dialogue and discussion

Setup

Copy one "Our 'Proverbial' Differentiation" handout for each participant (see CD 9A).

Special Supplies

A pad of Post-it Notes and a Sharpie pen for each participant

Facilitator Note

Some participants will not have an easy time making the associations, and others will make dozens and dozens. You should be prepared to help individuals who are frustrated with this activity to see the associations that are possible.

This activity is adapted from *101 Activities for Teaching Creativity and Problem Solving*, by Arthur B. VanGundy, and is used with permission.

Our "Proverbial" Differentiation in Practice

In a retreat we facilitated for a developer of major downtown office buildings and cultural facilities the group used Our "Proverbial" Differentiation to identify which characteristics distinguished this developer from its competition. The group free-associated with the proverb "a stitch in time saves nine," and came up with "planning ahead saves effort, time, and money." This led the group to state: "What differentiates our company is our meticulous planning with our clients' every need in mind. This results in our buildings being finished on time, under budget, and to exact client specifications."

Sell Me Glamour

Description

Participants are asked to think about customers' hopes and needs in the broadest sense and what role the organization can play in meeting them.

Experiential Elements
- Creative thinking
- Shared dialogue and discussion
- Self-selecting breakout groups

Special Supplies
A pad of Post-it Notes and a Sharpie pen for each participant

Steps

1. Once the participants have established the organization's strategic direction, work with the group to create a succinct expression of the organization's purpose. You might give participants some examples from other organizations, such as

   - Google: "to organize the world's information and make it universally accessible and useful"

   - Disney: "to produce unparalleled entertainment experiences"

   - Amnesty International: "to protect human rights worldwide"

   - Elderhostel: "to provide extraordinary learning adventures for people 55 and over"

2. Write the agreed-on statement of purpose on a flip chart where all participants can see it.

3. Tell participants: "What we are looking for is why customers would choose one product, service, or experience over another. Let me give you some examples of this concept. Don't sell me a car, sell me safety. Don't sell me a new haircut, sell me glamour. Don't sell me a room in a hotel, sell me pampering. Don't sell me a gym membership, sell me admiring looks."

4. Tell participants: "Complete the phrase, 'Don't sell me [statement of purpose], sell me . . .' Write at least a dozen separate Post-it Notes stating what [the organization's] customers want to be sold. Write as quickly as possible, and don't worry whether your ideas make sense. Let yourself tap into your intuition and gut instincts about what people want. You'll have seven minutes to come up with your ideas."

This activity is adapted from *Jump Start Your Brain*, by Doug Hall, and is used with permission.

5. Ask the participants to post their ideas on a wall and then to take a break.

6. During the break, sort the Post-it Notes into categories of customer wants and needs, and write each of these categories on a separate flip chart sheet. (They might be such categories as easy to use, money-saving, time-saving, safe, informative, entertaining, and the like. Obviously the categories will vary according to the product or service the group is exploring.)

7. Ask each participant to sign up on the flip chart sheet that corresponds to the category he or she is most interested in discussing. (You will have to ensure that this sign-up process yields manageably sized subgroups. If not, ask some participants to move to a second-choice topic.)

8. Taking inspiration from the Post-it Notes on their flip chart sheets, participants in each subgroup should discuss how the organization should differentiate itself to address customers' needs and wants.

9. Ask each subgroup to report its recommended differentiation, and have the whole group decide which aspects of potential differentiation would best meet customers' needs and desires.

Sell Me Glamour in Practice

We used Sell Me Glamour in a retreat for an association of leading research scientists whose board wanted to differentiate the association from its competitors. Through this exercise, the board members realized that the association's members did not want to be sold easy access to publishing in the association's journal. Rather, they wanted to be sold the prestige of belonging to the professional association that published the top-rated journal in their field. Therefore the board decided to maintain the high review standards for publication as a core differentiation and not to offer relaxed standards for members as a benefit of belonging to the association.

Scope of Work

What are the reach and focus of the organization's day-to-day operations? Does the organization concentrate on just one thing it can do particularly well, or are its activities highly diversified? Does it have sufficient financial resources to support all its programs adequately, or should some be scaled back or eliminated so that others can receive sufficient support?

We tell our clients that no organization can distinguish itself in everything. Even organizations that are known for the highest quality don't do everything equally well. But by doing a few things exceptionally well, the "brand" comes to stand for high quality.

The following activity can help participants determine what the centers of excellence for their organization should be.

Centers of Excellence

Description

Participants are asked to draw a metaphor for the organization at its best and to explain why it is an appropriate metaphor for excellence. The metaphor serves as a springboard for a discussion of centers of excellence for the organization—those areas that will define its brand.

Experiential Elements
- Drawing
- Using metaphor
- Self-selecting breakout groups

Special Supplies
A selection of Prismacolor Art Markers for each breakout group

Steps

1. Divide the group into subgroups of five to seven people.

2. Ask each subgroup: "Please come up with a metaphor for the organization at its best. Draw the metaphor, and then come up with at least six reasons why this is an appropriate metaphor."

3. Tell the group: "Once you have agreed on the metaphor, discuss the products, services, programs, and so forth, that are (or have the potential to be) the exemplars of the organization at its best. Then narrow your list down to the top two or three things that exemplify the organization at its best. What two to three things should [the organization] be known for? By saying this, you are saying that these areas should have priority for [the organization]'s limited resources."

4. Ask each subgroup to show its metaphor, to state its reasons for choosing that metaphor, and to identify its two or three proposed centers of excellence.

5. The whole group listens for common themes in the metaphors and centers of excellence and then narrows all the proposed centers of excellence down to no more than three.

Facilitator Note

Most groups enjoy talking metaphorically and have fun drawing the metaphor.

Centers of Excellence in Practice

In a retreat we facilitated for a large dance company, one of the metaphors for excellence the group came up with was a planet with many lines orbiting around it. This metaphor represented for the participants "a guiding light," "wonder," "possibility," "universe," "eternal," "energy," and "grounded." The participants decided that rather than having a multipronged focus for its efforts, the company should put its resources toward developing world-class choreography of universal appeal that would evoke in audiences a sense of wonder and possibility, that would showcase the energy and athleticism of the dancers, and that would be grounded in the rigorous technique that had made the company famous around the world.

Resources

How will the organization ensure its future success? This issue is not simply a measure of profitability or growth. Strategically, looking at resources means understanding the economic drivers of the business—the determinants of financial success. If an organization is faced with insufficient financial or human resources to achieve its goals, it must examine how it generates revenue, budget allocations, or donations; the prices it charges for its products or services; how it deploys its current staff; and how expenses are allocated.

In addition, all strategic plans have resource implications for the organization. Where will it get the resources to implement the plan? (See "Checking Against Resources" later in this chapter, pp. 239–242.)

Discerning the Organization's Values

Many organizations recognize the influence their culture and values have on how people work together and what they can achieve. We often include an exploration of values in our planning retreats, as the plan that emerges from the process is much more likely to be implemented successfully when it supports people's core values and what people perceive to be the organization's highest values.

No matter what is written in a values statement, the people who work in an organization know instinctively what the organization stands for in practice. If a company allows a particular customer to abuse the staff because that customer gives the company a lot of business, employees will consider the organization's statement that "employees are our most important asset" to be a sham. Conversely, if the organization grants liberal paternity leave and permits some employees to leave on the dot of 4:00 P.M. every day to pick up their kids from preschool, there is no need for a formal statement that the organization is "family oriented." Everyone knows.

Many of the planning issues for a healthy organization center on making course corrections and taking advantage of opportunities. But if the organization is foundering and people seem to be working at cross-purposes, it's important to spend time at the retreat helping the group identify a guiding philosophy and governing values.

One way to determine an organization's values is for the participants to reflect individually and then collectively on what they believe in. Once they've agreed on a list of their core values, you can help them whittle the list down by asking, "If this value became a competitive disadvantage, would you cling to it anyway?" Only those values that receive a strong yes should be considered core values.

Just as with a mission statement, you want a statement of values that people can recall. If an organization lists more than three or four values, chances are people won't be able to keep them in mind. Encourage participants to limit their values list—by combining similar values and eliminating those that are less central—to those they genuinely care about and would make personal sacrifices to achieve. And if senior leaders don't visibly exemplify the organization's values, the statement will be meaningless, or worse.

Either of the following values exercises will help generate a thought-provoking conversation about values.

Values Vignettes

Description

In this activity participants act out vignettes to express in a memorable manner their view of the values the organization practices and those the participants aspire to.

Steps

1. Introduce the task: "We are going to explore the values that your organization practices and the values that you would like it to practice. We'll do this by creating vignettes that express how these values play out in the organization."

2. Divide the participants into an even number of subgroups of five to ten members each.

3. Show the two flip chart pages: Our Current Values and The Values We Should Aspire To. Say: "The first group [or groups if there are more than two subgroups] will consider Our Current Values in creating their vignettes. You should think about what values seem to be in place now—even if unspoken—judging by the way people behave and get things done in [the organization].

   "The second group [or groups] will consider The Values We Should Aspire To. You will keep in mind the values that you think [the organization] should have.

   "You will have thirty minutes to create your vignettes using any props you find in the room. The vignettes can be funny or serious. The only rule is that every member of the group must participate in presenting your vignettes."

4. After the first group of participants presents its vignettes, ask the other participants, "What values does this group see in the organization right now?" Make a list on the flip chart.

Experiential Elements

- Reflecting back on experiences
- Producing skits
- Using props and toys
- Individual reflection
- Group decision making

Setup

- Prepare a flip chart labeled "Our Current Values" (see Step 3).
- Prepare a flip chart labeled "The Values We Should Aspire To" (see Step 3).

Special Supplies

A selection of evocative toys, silly hats, noisemakers, and other props

The Fifth Discipline Fieldbook, by Senge, Roberts, Ross, Smith, and Kleiner (1994), is an excellent resource for examination of values in the workplace.

5. Then ask the second group to present its vignettes. Ask members of the first group: "What values does this group wish the organization would have?" Make a list on the flip chart.

6. Compare the two lists. How closely does the Our Current Values list match the Values We Should Aspire To list? If they match closely, what are the three or four most important of these values? If the values don't match, facilitate a discussion of what would have to change for the organization to live up to the new values suggested.

Facilitator Note   It's important not to let participants get so carried away by the production values of their vignettes that they lose track of the assignment, which is to convey in a memorable way the values that are practiced and those that should be practiced.

Values Vignettes in Practice

In a culture change retreat we facilitated for the office of the head of an international organization, the group used Values Vignettes to explore the values their behavior was communicating to their internal clients in the rest of the organization and to spark a discussion of the values they would like to live by. This group of intensely serious and committed professionals (we discovered in our interviews that many of them worked twelve- to fourteen-hour days and some hadn't taken a vacation in years) produced laugh-out-loud funny vignettes using a variety of silly props that made a serious and memorable point about the chasm between how they believed they were seen and how they would like to be seen. The vignettes about their current values made a compelling statement about how they seemed to value being powerful, intimidating, and authoritative; blocking access; hoarding information; and engaging in one-way communication. In the Values We Should Aspire To segment the participants made clear they wanted to be perceived as accessible, knowledgeable, smart, gentle, diplomatic, good listeners, and fun colleagues.

Values Auction

Description

In this activity participants bid competitively on the most important values for the organization.

Steps

1. Introduce the task: "We are going to explore the values that you would most like to see this organization practice. These are the values that are very important to you personally—so important, in fact, that you'd be willing to pay for them."

2. Read the values from the values handout you created (see CD 9B). Ask participants if any important organizational values are missing. (Create a certificate for every value that the group adds; see CD 9C.)

3. Give each participant $300 in play money. Tell the group: "I am going to auction off the values on the list. Use your money to purchase the values that are most important to you.

   "These are the rules: you must bid in multiples of $20. Once you have spent your $300, you are out of the auction. There is no pooling of money among participants or reselling of values. If you don't obtain the value that is most important to you, there is no guarantee that the value will be adopted by your organization, so it's important to try to acquire all the values that are very important to you personally. If there is a tie between two bidders, the value will be removed from the auction and no one will be able to claim it for the organization.

Experiential Elements

- Role playing
- Individual reflection
- Group discussion

Setup

- Create a handout of organizational values for each participant (see CD 9B for some values to get you started, but be sure to use values appropriate for the organization).
- Create a certificate for each value (see CD 9C for a sample certificate) and some blank certificates for any values the participants might add.
- Make one copy of the "Values Reflection" handout for each participant (see CD 9D).

Special Supplies

- $300 (in $20 bills) in play money for each participant
- A gavel

"You will have two minutes to create your bidding strategy. You may bid on several values, or you may save all your money for the single value that is most important to you."

4. Begin the auction by randomly selecting a certificate representing a value. Open the bidding for that value, and "sell" it to the person with the highest bid. Give that person the certificate and collect the bidder's money.

5. Continue until all the values are "sold" or the participants have expended their funds.

6. Ask participants to fill out the Values Reflection handout (see CD 9D).

7. Divide the participants into small groups and ask them to discuss their answers to these questions.

8. Ask each subgroup to come up with three to five values to present to the whole group, values that they all believe are critical for the organization's success.

9. Help the group find commonalities among the presentations. Work with the whole group to narrow the list down to three to five values the participants all believe are critical for the organization.

Facilitator Note The facilitator has to take on the role of an auctioneer to create a fun and frenetic atmosphere during the auction so participants will bid quickly.

Understanding the Environment

Even when an organization has a clear purpose and explicit values, participants cannot begin to plan for the future without first understanding the environment in which the organization functions. In addition to internal factors, an organization's work may be affected by external economic, social, political, and technological changes. A retreat provides an ideal forum for reflecting on what is changing externally and what impact these changes might have on the organization's future.

A key underpinning of a successful strategic planning process is increased awareness among the planning team members of trends occurring inside and outside the organization that might have an impact on it. The more the planning group is aware of trends in the internal and external environment, the more likely the plan is to reflect an urgency for needed change.

In *Plan or Die!* Nolan, Goodstein, and Pfeiffer (1993) refer to five overlapping environments that should be monitored throughout the planning process. They are *internal* (trends in areas such as staff skills, production capability, quality, labor-management relations, cross-department cooperation, and the like); *customer* (trends in areas such as the demographics, expectations, interests, concerns, and competing pressures of current and potential customers); *competitive* (trends in areas such as what direct and indirect competitors are doing, who is entering and leaving the market, and how the company measures up in terms of price, quality, innovation, customer service, and on-time delivery); *industry* (trends in the organization's field, such as industry-specific regulations, prices, quality, cycle time, and percentage of new products launched annually); and *macro* (trends in society, politics, the economy, international relations, consumer preferences, and the like), as illustrated in the figure titled "Environments to Be Monitored" on page 225.

When a change in the environment occurs unexpectedly, people often resist acknowledging it and therefore are unable to come up with strategies to address it. But when retreat participants start thinking about what might happen, these scenarios form what Swedish neuroscientist David Ingvar (1985) calls "memories of the future." According to Kees van der Heijden (1996), author of *Scenarios: The Art of Strategic Conversation*, when people practice developing such scenarios, they learn to recognize new trends more quickly and can take more

Environments to Be Monitored

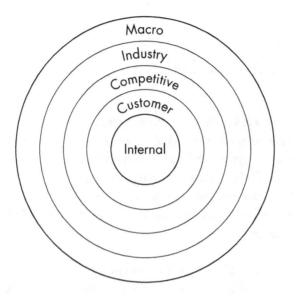

Source: Nolan, Goodstein, & Pfeiffer, 1993, p. 129.

appropriate action in response to changes that occur. "Even if the specific rehearsed scenario never plays out in reality," he writes, "the mind has nevertheless built up a readily available set of concepts" that will increase the scenario maker's ability to see what's really happening and to respond accordingly.

There's no way to predict the future, of course, but you can help the group explore the ramifications of several possible scenarios. We have found that either of the following activities can elicit dramatic pictures of possible futures that can help organizations make more informed strategic choices.

Glimpses into the Future

Description

This activity promotes discussion of present and future trends in the organization's external environment (including sociocultural, economic, technological, legal, political, and international trends and any additional trends affecting customers, competitors, suppliers, and the labor market). Participants list trends on Post-it Notes; then, working in small groups, they choose several trends that might influence possible futures.

Experiential Elements

- Individual and group reflection
- Group discussion
- Experimenting with ideas
- Storytelling and group presentations

Steps

1. Introduce the activity: "Clues to the future environment [the organization] will be operating in can be found by looking at current trends and considering where they might lead. These are the trends that occur in your professional field, trends inside [the organization], and external trends (in economics, technology, politics, and society at large, for instance).

   "Refer to the three major areas of trends identified on the three Trend flip chart sheets [*see Setup*]: trends in [our field], in [our organization], and in society as a whole.

   "List as many trends as you can think of in each of the trend areas, writing one trend per Post-it Note."

2. After the participants have written their ideas, ask them to post their notes on the appropriate flip chart sheets on the wall. Encourage them to take a moment to read what others have written.

Setup

- Prepare three "trend" flip charts, labeled as follows, and post them on the wall:

  "Trends in [Our Field]"

  "Trends in [Our Organization]"

  "Trends in Society"

- Prepare and copy "Glimpses into the Future" sheets for each group (see CD 9E).

Special Supplies

A pad of 3 inch x 5 inch Post-it Notes and a Sharpie pen for each participant

3. Divide the participants into subgroups of four to six people, preferably mixed by department, discipline, or organizational level. Ask each subgroup to select four trends—including at least one from each of the three trend areas. Each subgroup should take back to its table the four Post-it Notes that represent the trends that group has chosen.

4. Hand out the Glimpses into the Future sheets (see CD 9E).

5. Ask the breakout groups to address the questions on the Glimpses into the Future sheets, using the trends they selected, and to prepare a presentation for the entire group on flip chart paper. Ask each breakout group to make a presentation of its assignment to the rest of the group.

6. Facilitate a discussion on the strategies the organization would need to pursue to thrive in the different possible futures.

Facilitator Notes

• A strong understanding of the client's industry and of the business environment in general will allow the facilitator to ask probing questions that will help make the glimpses into the future compelling for the participants.

• Most strategic planning groups are composed of the managers who were responsible for creating the status quo. It can be hard for them to look critically at their own work, but solid planning must be based on a realistic appraisal of the organization's current state. This activity helps participants learn to challenge their own assumptions and innate complacency and to engage in a new way of thinking. Ask the participants: "If you keep operating the way you do now—even if you keep getting better at what you already do—could you survive and thrive should these possible scenarios come to pass?"

• Don't let the group get caught up in choosing among the scenarios. The point of this activity is to encourage the group to think about all the possibilities, not to try to predict the future.

Glimpses into the Future in Practice

At a retreat for a midsize advertising agency the entire staff participated in examining trends in the industry. Although most people thought at the outset that the agency had been responsive to industry changes, at the end of the exercise they were astounded at the "previously unthinkable" ideas that had emerged. They realized that the agency, although adding new services such as interactive and Web design and sales promotion, had not actually changed its business model to reflect the substantive changes in the industry. As a result the new services were not profitable.

Once the staff recognized how deeply the changes in technology, client relationships, media, and compensation would affect their future, they were able to review with open minds their processes for getting work done, how work was organized, whom they hired, what kinds of clients they needed to pursue, and how they priced their services.

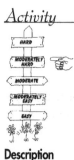

Alternative Futures

Description

This activity involves the discussion of three alternative change scenarios: one in which there is little change in key trends; one in which one or two key trends change; and one in which factors different from the ones anticipated change. Participants create a metaphor for the organization in each scenario and suggest guiding principles for thriving in each environment.

Steps

1. Introduce the activity: "We're going to explore some scenarios to see what might change for our department [or organization] if certain trends changed.

   "One-third of you will imagine a scenario in which very little changes in our environment over the next ten years; one-third of you will imagine a scenario in which there are one or two significant changes in our environment in the next ten years; and one-third of you will imagine a scenario in which there are dramatic changes in our environment in the next ten years.

   "The first group will imagine that our operations have not grown or been scaled back; that we have no measurable change in the rate of staff turnover; that no new program, technology, or service has been created by our competitors that would diminish the need for what we provide; that customers have approximately the same disposable income as they do now; that other units in our organization are just as supportive of our work as they are

Experiential Elements

- Individual reflection
- Group discussion
- Experimenting with ideas
- Using metaphor
- Drawing
- Group presentations

Setup

- Prepare and post on the wall these three change scenario flip charts:

  "There is little change"

  "One or two factors change"

  "Dramatic changes"

- Prepare and copy "Alternative Futures" sheets for each group (see CD 9F).

Special Supplies

- A pad of Post-it Notes and a Sharpie pen for each participant
- Prismacolor Art Markers for each breakout group

This activity is adapted from *Performance-Based Evaluation* by Judith Hale. Copyright © 2002 by John Wiley & Sons, Inc. Published by Pfeiffer, San Francisco, CA.

now. In essence you're going to imagine that not much will change in our external environment in the next ten years.

"The second group will imagine that one or two areas will change significantly in the next ten years. Our operations will be much larger or will have been seriously scaled back. Or that we have great staff turnover, with most employees leaving within a year. Or that we will have had no turnover at all, our staff will be aging, and there will be no opportunities to bring in fresh blood. Or that a new program, service, or technology will have been created by our competitors and will diminish the need for what we provide. Or that the economy will be very weak so that customers have very little disposable income or it will be quite strong and we will have the potential for a much greater market share. Or that other units in our organization will no longer support our work and will believe our department should be abolished. Decide collectively which changes you want to consider and imagine what the impact would be of a few significant changes in our external environment in the next ten years.

"The third group will imagine dramatic changes in our external environment over the next ten years. The changes could be in any of the dimensions we've talked about or in any other dimension that might radically alter what we do or how we do it. Decide collectively which changes you want to consider, and imagine what the impact would be of some dramatic changes in our external environment in the next ten years."

2. Divide the participants into three breakout groups.

3. Tell participants: "List as many effects on our operations and on how we might work as you can think of in the scenario you are exploring, writing one idea per Post-it Note."

4. After the participants have written down their ideas, ask them to stick their notes on flip chart sheets on the wall. Encourage them to take a moment to read what others in their breakout group have posted.

5. Hand out the Alternative Futures sheets (see CD 9F).

6. Ask the breakout groups to address the questions in their assignment, then draw a metaphor for the department [or organization] in that scenario and also guiding principles for thriving in that environment.

7. Ask each breakout group to make a presentation of its assignment to the rest of the group.

8. Look for commonalities in the different scenarios and facilitate a discussion of the guiding principles the organization would need to live by to thrive in the different possible futures.

Facilitator Note A strong understanding of the client's industry and of the business environment in general will allow the facilitator to ask probing questions to help spur participants' thinking about different environments and the need for flexible approaches. In addition, some groups may have difficulty generating an appropriate metaphor and may require guidance from the facilitator.

Evaluating Work Processes

When an organization is considering major changes, such as reorganizing, adding new products or services, changing compensation structures, or moving to teams, it's helpful to have participants examine their current operating processes first.

In his book *The Process Edge,* consultant Peter Keen (1997) posits that all work processes fall into one of five categories: *identity, priority, background, mandated,* and *folklore.* He suggests that determining which category an organization's work processes fall into will help leaders decide whether each is a net asset or a net cost (that is, does it generate revenue or other benefits to the organization, or is it an expense?).

Having retreat participants classify their work processes in this way will help them determine where process improvement would help the organization achieve its goals.

Identity Processes

Identity processes define what the organization stands for (to its customers, its employees, its members, its funders—to everyone who has a stake in its success). These processes are almost always net assets; they are what attracts new clients to the organization.

For a history museum, for instance, an identity process might be the way it plans, produces, and promotes special exhibits. For a retail hardware chain, an identity process might be how its personnel help customers find just the right tool for the job.

Investing in these identity processes, says Keen, will usually result in a direct payoff in terms of improved operations and long-term viability.

Priority Processes

Priority processes support an organization's identity processes. They're not necessarily visible to an outsider, but they're critical to an organization's success because without them the organization wouldn't be able to maintain its identity processes.

An example of a priority process for a museum might be conservation of its materials. For a computer design firm, it might be its in-house programming ability. For an association, it might be its research capability.

Background Processes

Background processes, such as billing, compensation, benefits, and accounts payable, help the day-to-day business run.

Most background processes are net costs. They're all necessary, but, says Keen, it can be a mistake to spend massive amounts of money to improve them, because no matter how much better they are, they won't bring revenues into the organization. Yet it is in precisely these areas that many organizations often spend the most in process improvement. That's not to say an organization shouldn't work to improve these processes and make them more cost effective, but only after paying attention to its identity and priority processes.

Mandated Processes

Mandated processes are the things an organization is required to do by law, such as filing employee withholding taxes. They are almost always net costs. Spending money to improve them usually doesn't bring any significant return on investment. Just as with background processes, an organization may find ways to accomplish mandated processes more efficiently, but it should focus most of its effort on its identity and priority processes.

Folklore Processes

Folklore processes are the things an organization has always done, although the reason for doing them is lost in the mists of history. They no longer serve a real purpose and create no value for the organization. People have done these things for so long, however, that it's almost impossible for them to see how they could get rid of them without changing the nature of the organization. Typical folklore processes are producing reports that no one has any use for or holding weekly meetings that take up more time than they're worth. One organization we worked with devoted many staff hours every spring to preparing a report that a previous CEO had demanded but that the current CEO couldn't have cared less about.

If folklore processes no longer serve a purpose they should be eliminated. They burn up the organization's time and money for little or no return.

Planning for Action

Once the group has worked through thinking about the organization's environment and possible futures and has rated current performance, participants will have a good sense of the areas in which change is called for. But it's almost certain that they won't be able to implement all the changes they have thought of.

Good strategy involves making trade-offs. It's practically a law of nature that unless resources are increased, paying more attention to one thing means devoting less attention to another. If an organization tries to take on too many things, it will be expert at none, and may fail at all. Venerable companies have gone out of business or have been acquired by more successful firms because they bit off more than they could swallow.

Such trade-offs—do less, but do it better—are not only inevitable, but according to strategy expert Michael Porter (1996), they serve a useful purpose for these three reasons:

* Making choices forces an organization to resolve inconsistencies in image or reputation.

- Different strategic choices require different activities, people with different competencies, and different ways to deploy resources. If an organization isn't willing to make hard choices, its energies will be dispersed.
- Strategic trade-offs make organizational priorities clear to the staff.

Determining Desired Results

Often participants become entangled in discussions about vocabulary. Is there a difference between *goals* and *objectives?* What is a *strategy?* Is this idea a *strategy* or a *tactic?* In reality the terminology isn't important; what's critical is the quality of the thinking. For that reason we often substitute *results* for *goals* or *objectives,* and *key actions* for *tactics.* It may be helpful to remind the group of these simple definitions:

- *Results* answer the question, What specifically do we want to achieve?
- *Strategies* answer the question, What major initiatives will we have to undertake to achieve these results?
- *Key actions* specify who will do what by when.

You might think of it this way. *Result:* we will arrive in Chicago tomorrow evening. *Strategy:* we'll drive. *Key actions:* we will rent a car from A-1 Auto Rentals down on Third Street; we will leave tomorrow at 7:00 A.M.; we will trade off the driving every two hours; we will head north to Pennsylvania and then west to Chicago.

Brief Activity

Remind the group that the list of results should be short, so people can remember them and focus their work on achieving them. You can help the participants refine their list by asking these questions:

- If you achieved this result, would it move you toward your strategic direction? (See the activity "Exploring Strategic Direction," pp. 200–202.) If not, why do you have it as a result?

- Which of these results will make the greatest contribution to fulfilling the organization's most deeply held aspirations? Which will move the organization ahead faster?

- What would happen if the organization took no action on one or more of these results? Would it make a serious difference in your ability to achieve your strategic direction?

See Chapter 11, "Wouldn't It Be Great If . . . ?" pp. 287–289, for another goal-setting activity.

It may take an organization several years to achieve its strategic direction. In the meantime, senior managers need to establish measurable shorter-term goals so they can monitor progress. Five-year goals, common in plans of several years ago, are practically useless for guiding people as they make day-to-day decisions about how to use their resources, so we recommend establishing some shorter time frames and nearer milestones.

Desired results outline what an organization (or work group) intends to accomplish, where the participants want to go, like the destination of a journey. If there is no agreement on desired results, people will pull in different directions and expend great energy while making little forward progress.

Although a corporation may think about results in financial terms and a nonprofit may focus more on the reach, quality, and effectiveness of its services, results should always be expressed in terms that are measurable.

To help retreat participants determine the results they want, you will want to guide them in an exploration of these key areas:

Financial results. For a company you might ask: "From the total gross revenue (or percentage increases in revenue, profit margins, or changes in sources of business), will you achieve the results you want? If not, what could be done to change that?" For a nonprofit organization the question might be: "What are the trends in total income, changes in sources of income, ratio of earned to contributed income, or membership totals, and what are the implications of those trends for your organization?"

Products and services. "Are changes necessary in the products or services the organization now offers?" "Should new products or services be developed?" "To whom are or should the organization's services be directed?" "How satisfied with its offerings are the people the organization currently serves?" (See CD 9G, 9H, and 9I for some program analysis tools.)

Internal management. "To achieve the results the group has agreed on, does the organization need to take steps to improve organizational effectiveness?" "Are some operating ratios out of whack?" "Do certain operational processes need to be overhauled?" "Are any changes called for so that the organization can function more in accordance with its values?"

Learning. "What new skills and knowledge must the organization obtain to thrive in the future?" "What competencies must employees possess or acquire?"

Prioritizing Results

One of the hard decisions organizations have to make is prioritizing among goals. You might use the following activity to help the retreat participants do just that.

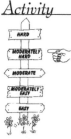

Targeting Results

Description

Participants use the power of visually prioritizing the results they would like to achieve on a bull's-eye target, making forced choices to sharpen their thinking.

Steps

1. Divide the participants into subgroups of five to seven people. Direct each subgroup to a flip chart on which you have drawn concentric quarter circles, like a quarter of a bull's-eye target, as shown in the sample that follows.

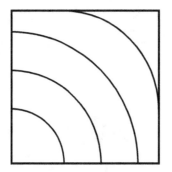

2. Ask each subgroup to work in silence to rearrange by importance the Desired Results you placed in random order on the target, placing only one note per ring, putting the result they judge to be the least core in the outermost ring, and the result that is most core in the bull's-eye.

   Tell the group: "You are free to write new Desired Results to replace any that are on the Post-it Notes. (Again, working in silence.) If someone does this, he or she must remove one of the original Post-its from the target and place it to the side of the flip chart. Don't add a new Desired Result without removing another Desired Result."

Experiential Elements

- Group discussion
- Visualizing relationships
- Group decision making

Setup

- Draw one quadrant of a large bull's-eye target on flip chart paper for each subgroup (see Step 1). (A quadrant is all you can fit on a sheet of flip chart paper because each concentric ring must be wide enough to accommodate a 3 inch x 5 inch Post-it Note.) Make sure you have one ring for each of the group's identified desired results (no more than six or seven).
- Write the desired results (these could relate to program areas, financial targets, types of activities) on 3 inch x 5 inch Post-it Notes, one result per note.

3. Show the group the How to Decide on Results flip chart. Tell participants to silently consider the four questions when making their determinations of the most important results.

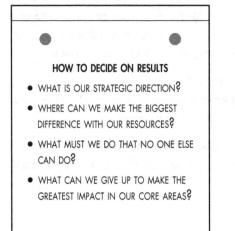

HOW TO DECIDE ON RESULTS

- WHAT IS OUR STRATEGIC DIRECTION?
- WHERE CAN WE MAKE THE BIGGEST DIFFERENCE WITH OUR RESOURCES?
- WHAT MUST WE DO THAT NO ONE ELSE CAN DO?
- WHAT CAN WE GIVE UP TO MAKE THE GREATEST IMPACT IN OUR CORE AREAS?

4. Encourage the participants to stay engaged in the activity until they are satisfied that the results are arranged in priority order. The fact that someone has moved a Post-it from where another participant thinks it belongs doesn't mean the activity is over. All participants should keep moving the Post-it Notes into the priority order they believe is best.

5. When everyone can agree with the order of the note placement, or if the subgroups reach an impasse, have the subgroups sit down. Ask each subgroup to tell the whole group why subgroup members put the priorities in the order they did, where they got stuck, and why that happened. (No one person will know that, of course, because the participants were working in silence. The debrief will encourage many participants to discuss their perspectives on the experience.) Facilitate a discussion with the whole group to see whether participants can come to an agreement on priorities.

Setup (continued)

- Create a set of Post-it Notes for each subgroup ensuring that the same desired result is written on the same color Post-it Note for all subgroups (for example, Desired Result X on pink notes, Desired Result Y on blue notes, and so forth).
- Place the notes in random order on each group's bull's-eye (so that Desired Result Y, for example, is on the outer ring for one subgroup and closer to the bull's-eye for another), with only one Desired Result in each ring (see Step 1).
- Prepare "How to Decide on Results" flip chart (see Step 3).

Special Supplies

A pad of Post-it Notes and a Sharpie pen for each participant

Activity (continued)

_____

Facilitator Notes

- The facilitator should be expert in formulating and working with concrete results. Familiarity with business principles in general and with the organization's operations and financial resources is a plus.

- If this activity follows the "Determining Desired Results" discussion (see pp. 233–234), write the Desired Results the group came up with on the Post-it Notes. Otherwise, use the organization's previously stated general goals or priorities for the activity. You should be able to find these goals in your pre-retreat research. They are often listed on an organization's Web site or in an annual report.

- It's important to keep this activity lively and fun and to encourage participants to continue to push for what they'd like to see happen, even if it means moving notes back and forth several times. Remind participants to maintain silence when they are working in their subgroups.

- If this activity is debriefed well, it can be one of the most powerful focusing activities of the retreat. For this to happen, participants must keep pushing for their priorities in their subgroups and in the larger group.

Checking Against Resources

Many strategic planning retreats are tied only loosely to an organization's formal budgeting process. But the answers to such basic questions as, "How much can we spend?" and, "Will we be able to hire new staff to work on this project, or must we redeploy existing staff?" define (and limit) how ambitious a plan can be.

You will need to include ample time in the retreat for the group to review, at least in broad strokes, the current year's operating budget and revenue projections for the coming year. You can help ensure that this review happens by alerting your client well in advance that budget and revenue information will be required. Guide the participants in a discussion of such questions as these:

- "How did you spend your financial resources this year (both in absolute dollars and in percentage of budget)?"
- "In which budget categories do you need to spend more to achieve the results you have agreed on?"
- "Which budget percentages must be reduced next year?"
- *For corporations,* "Are you budgeting to hit your profit or margin goals? If not, where will you cut expenses or increase revenues to become more profitable?"

In the end, every organization needs an operating budget that is consistent with its desired results, as well as results that are consistent with its budget. This is an activity we use to help participants look at the impact of the results they want to achieve and the resources needed to achieve them.

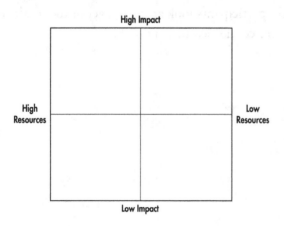

Resource/Impact Matrix

Description

This activity helps participants examine the results they want to hold themselves accountable for achieving, considering both the resources needed and the potential impact on the organization of achieving those results. The relative value of those two considerations becomes dramatically visible when participants create a large matrix and plot each result on it.

Experiential Elements
- Using visual means to clarify ideas
- Discussion of ideas

Steps

1. Ask the group to list the organization's available resources (such as staff time, money, office space, brand recognition), and write them on the flip chart labeled "Resources."

2. Then ask the group to list the impact achieving a goal might have on the organization (such as increasing sales, raising brand awareness, attracting new clients), and write them on the flip chart labeled "Impact."

3. Present the Resource/Impact Matrix to the group, defining the labels on the matrix:

Setup
- Create a flip chart labeled "Resources" (see Step 1).
- Create a flip chart labeled "Impact" (see Step 2).
- Create a large "Resource/ Impact Matrix," using four sheets of flip chart paper (see Step 3).

Special Supplies

A pad of 3 inch x 5 inch Post-it Notes and a Sharpie pen for each participant

```
                        High Impact
        ┌──────────────────┬──────────────────┐
        │                  │                  │
        │                  │                  │
High    │                  │                  │   Low
Resources                  │                  │   Resources
        │                  │                  │
        │                  │                  │
        └──────────────────┴──────────────────┘
                        Low Impact
```

- High Impact/Low Resource Use = Winner (represents high return on investment)

- High Impact/High Resource Use = Future Potential (needs assessment to see if the high resource cost is justified)

- Low Impact/Low Resource Use = Small Potatoes (Can the impact be increased? Otherwise, it should also be abandoned, because it's probably a distraction.)

- Low Impact/High Resource Use = Abandon (low return on investment)

4. Write the group's previously determined results on Post-it Notes, one result per note. Results should include quantitative and qualitative measures.

5. Ask for a group of four or five volunteers to place the Post-it Notes with the results into the appropriate squares of the matrix. The volunteers should keep working until they come to consensus on the placement of each result. The rest of the group observes their actions and listens to their deliberations.

6. After all results are placed, conduct a whole group discussion about the choices the volunteers made. Based on the discussion, rank the goals as

- Top priority

- Secondary priority

- Low priority

Facilitator Notes   In addition to helping the group assess results, this activity can be used when an organization wants to examine current programs, products, or services in terms of their impact and the resources they consume.

Resource-Impact in Practice

In a retreat we facilitated for the management team of a marketing consortium of hotels that catered to a discriminating clientele, the group used the Resource-Impact Matrix to decide which of its programs were highest priority, which required additional investment, and which could be scaled back or eliminated. The Resource-Impact Matrix activity sparked a lively discussion that led this consortium to focus its marketing efforts on developing more Web-based and direct group sales and spending fewer of its marketing dollars on trade shows. The participants also decided to scale back some of their member services, such as an internal newsletter, that were labor intensive to produce and not particularly valued by the members.

Sample Resource-Impact Matrix for Hotel Consortium

High Impact

High Resources		Low Resources
High I/High R Distribution system Web site maintenance Advertising Member services Reservations center Strategic partnerships		**High I/Low R** Gift certificates Direct sales Web-based meetings Group sales
Low I/High R Print directory Trade shows Quarterly newsletter		**Low I/Low R** Database management Vendor members

Low Impact

Devising Strategies

Once the results are determined, the participants can start working on strategies that outline how they plan to achieve those results. Strategies address what people need to do to achieve those results.

When the participants reflect on the organization's strategic direction and on the shorter-term desired results, the process may feel overwhelming. The best advice you can give them is: don't try to do everything at once.

For each result, ask the group, "What do you have to *change* to make this happen?" And perhaps even more important, "Are you willing to make those changes?" The answers to these questions will help the group focus on initial strategies. There's no sense including something in the plan if the organization isn't ready to make it happen.

Encourage the group to list everything the organization needs to do to achieve the results. At this stage you're still looking at broad-strokes ideas. For instance, the group might say, "Improve customer satisfaction ratings by 10 percent each year," without having to specify that the organization will send front-line employees to customer service training.

Testing Strategies

To make sure the recommended strategies are cohesive, ask the planning group these key questions:

- "Have you planned strategies for achieving each result?" (If the group doesn't have a strategy, nothing will happen with respect to that result.)
- "Does every strategy contribute to at least one result?" (Make sure the group hasn't included strategies that are "nice to do" but don't really move the organization ahead.)
- "Is each one of these strategies *necessary* for you to achieve those results?" (The organization doesn't want to spend resources on unnecessary activities.)
- "If you carry out all of these strategies, will they, taken together, be *sufficient* for you to achieve those results?" (There's no sense starting something that's doomed to failure because the planned actions won't lead to the desired result.)

See Chapter 10, "Obstacle Busters II," pp. 273–274, and Chapter 14, "Obstacle Busters III," pp. 423–424, for other versions of this exercise.

Once the participants are convinced that they have ascertained the appropriate broad strategies, they need to stipulate the specific actions individuals and work units will take to implement the strategies. The participants should assign responsibilities and deadlines—and sufficient resources—to the task. You will probably have to help them be realistic. If most of the responsibilities are assigned to people who have little control over their workloads, the tasks are not likely to be completed. Finally, help participants determine how they will monitor progress toward achieving the results. What will happen if a person or department fails to accomplish the assigned tasks?

The following activity will help participants anticipate and eliminate obstacles to implementing their goals.

Obstacle Busters I

Description

Each participant identifies the biggest obstacle to achieving the organization's desired results and writes this barrier on a strip of paper. The participants insert the obstacles into their balloons, inflate the balloons, and then tie them off. Everyone tosses the balloons around the room until the facilitator calls a stop. At this point, participants pop the balloons nearest to them and take the slips of paper to their subgroups, where members discuss ways to overcome the obstacles named on the papers or reduce their impact.

Experiential Elements
- Individual reflection
- Play
- Envisioning possibilities and generating new ideas

Setup

Stretch and pre-inflate all the balloons with a hand pump and then deflate them.

Special Supplies
- Multicolored balloons (one per participant)
- 1 inch x 4 inch strips of paper (one per participant)
- Multicolored, 1 1/4 inch, glass-head straight pins (available at sewing stores and drug stores)
- A few small hand-pump balloon inflators (available at party stores and toy stores)

Steps

1. Introduce the task: "We're going to look at the impediments you might face in implementing this plan and discuss how you might overcome them."

2. Ask each participant to write a major obstacle that might interfere with achieving the plan's goals on a 1 inch x 4 inch slip of paper and to put that slip of paper inside a balloon.

3. Ask the participants to inflate their balloons and toss them around the room for a few minutes.

4. Give the participants glass-head straight pins and ask them to pop the balloons nearest to them, reading the slips of paper inside the balloons they are holding.

5. Create subgroups of five to seven people, and ask them to discuss the obstacles found in group members' balloons.

6. Tell each subgroup: "Determine specifically what the people in this room can do to eliminate or reduce the obstacles you discussed. Consider only the actions that are within the power of the people here, not actions that you wish others would take. You have thirty minutes to work."

7. After thirty minutes have each group report on its findings. Facilitate a whole group discussion of what actions the group should take to address the obstacles. Help the group come up with an action plan of three to ten items. (Keep it simple.)

Go to Chapter 8, "The Nub: Action Planning," pp. 186–192, to review the action planning necessary to conclude the strategic planning retreat.

Writing the Plan

It's deadly to write a strategic plan by committee, so we discourage our clients from drafting the plan at the retreat. Ideally, before the planning retreat is over, someone will volunteer to be lead author of the plan. It really doesn't matter who writes the plan. What matters is that what is written down faithfully reflects the decisions of the strategic planning group and that those who will implement the recommendations want to see the plan succeed.

Often small task forces work on fleshing out discrete action plans for different areas of the plan. One task force might look at new program, product, or service development. Another might look at financial and human resource implications. And another might look at sales and marketing. However the work is subdivided, it needs to be coordinated with the person who will synthesize others' contributions and commit the plan to paper.

Sample Strategic Plan Format

    I. Executive summary with key recommendations

    II. Critical issues facing the organization

        a. Customer needs and competitive position

        b. External stakeholder analysis

    III. Overall strategic direction

    IV. Desired organization and department results

    V. Core strategies to achieve the results (with resource implications)

    VI. Action planning

    VII. Resources required

    VIII. Evaluation

One of the difficulties many people face in writing strategic plans is making them succinct and memorable. One of our clients showed us a previous strategic plan; it was practically the size of the New York City phone book. When we asked if it guided the staff's day-to-day decisions, we were told that no one had referred to it in years. The more complex and lengthy you make your plan, the likelier it is to gather dust on the shelf. It's fine to have each department create a detailed operational plan, but the overall plan should be as concise as possible.

We tend to favor a simple format for strategic plans. We don't encourage clients to include long statements of the organization's history, a detailed analysis of the issues, or a justification for every statement and conclusion. If for some reason a record of those things is needed, we encourage the client to create appendixes so the plan itself can be kept brief.

Once a first draft of the strategic plan has been written, we recommend that our clients create a process that allows anyone who will be involved in implementing the plan a chance to review the draft prior to its being set in stone. Clear ground rules need to be established for this reviewing phase, however, so people don't get bogged down in minutia but focus instead on the big picture and on what each individual person and department can do to ensure the plan's success.

Other Suggested Activities for a Strategic Planning Retreat

You will find other activities to incorporate into a strategic planning retreat in the Activities for Making Decisions, Planning, and Evaluating Ideas index (p. 502) and the Activities to Use in Any Retreat index (p. 490).

Chapter 10

Leading a Culture Change Retreat

Let's be realistic: you can't take a bunch of people to an offsite retreat and expect an immediate and dramatic turnaround in the organization's culture. It isn't going to happen. Organization cultures are like aircraft carriers making thirty knots. They have a lot of momentum and they can't be turned on a dime. A retreat can, however, be a significant event in the life of an organization. It can begin the process of redirection and in this way can have a powerful effect on the culture.

An organization's culture builds slowly. The process starts when a company is founded. Even in older companies the principles that the founders believed in probably still have some influence today on how employees view events and react to them. As people observed the founders and the decisions they made, especially in hard times, the organization's culture started to solidify. When those choices worked out well, employees learned, "This is the way we do things here." And when things went wrong, they learned what *not* to do. As the organization grows the culture is handed down from each generation of staff to the next, just as parents teach their children, by word and—arguably more significant—by example.

Employees start learning the culture from their first contact with the company. How were the help-wanted ads worded? How was the interview handled? What were the conditions of employment? And as soon as they join the organization they are exposed to a barrage of stories, each one carrying the same cultural message: "This is the way we do things here."

New employees are taught the formal rules (regulations, policies, and procedures). At the same time, they begin observing for themselves how things

See Chapter 9, "Discerning the Organization's Values," pp. 218–223, for activities that can be used to explore values in a culture change retreat.

really work. They quickly become aware of any disparity between what Harvard Business School professor Chris Argyris calls the company's *espoused* values—those it professes to believe in—and its values *in use*—those it actually practices (Argyris, 1993). And it's the values that are practiced, rather than those that are merely preached, that have the most powerful effect on employees' perceptions of the organization's culture.

Although influenced powerfully by its founders, an organization's culture is not static. Culture continues to evolve over time, largely as a result of major events in the organization's history and the leaders' responses to them. Take, for example, the way a major layoff was managed at one company.

On a Friday morning the organization announced a large layoff. Those who were affected were asked to clean out their desks and were escorted out of the building before lunchtime. They had little time to say good-bye to colleagues who were staying on.

Worse, when the remaining employees came to work the next week, they were confronted with the sight of tables in the hall piled high with the telephones that had belonged only a couple of days before to their long-standing friends and associates. Employees looked at those phones and saw the extension numbers of colleagues they used to call.

Message: "We treat people like expendable office equipment."

Another organization, in contrast, established a job placement center in anticipation of staff cuts and allowed laid-off employees to use its facilities for several weeks to receive counseling and seek other jobs.

Message: "People matter to us here."

Great Expectations: What Can Realistically Be Accomplished at a Retreat

Most retreats are convened to address particular business-related issues. Rarely are they intended specifically to influence the organization's culture. But it's hard to make significant changes in response to business needs without first addressing cultural issues. For example, Ursula, the CEO of a company whose top managers seemed unable to work together cooperatively, asked us to focus a retreat on helping those managers improve their communication skills. In our pre-retreat assessment, however, we found that the managers were quite skilled at communicating. They communicated well with the employees they supervised and with Ursula. But they did not communicate well with one another because the culture encouraged internal competition. The managers had learned that they had to protect their turf, and one way they did this was by withholding information from one another. The company didn't have a communication problem; it had a culture problem. And we had to design a very different sort of retreat than Ursula had originally requested.

To help an organization explore its culture while still focusing on specific business needs, include activities that will help participants

- Discuss how they view the organization's culture and what they would like to be different
- Understand their own contributions to the prevailing culture
- Explore why various teams or departments work the way they do
- Examine why disagreements arise
- Identify and discuss strategies for changing their own counterproductive practices
- Assess obstacles to a more positive environment, and generate ideas on how to overcome them

We all know that human beings tend to resist change, especially change to conditions they themselves have helped create and sustain. So it's important to help participants identify how the culture is contributing to the problems they are experiencing.

Both the half-day and the daylong version of the Organization Workshop (see Chapter 1, "Using a Specialized Retreat Format," pp. 24–32) can provide an outstanding foundation for participants who need to understand the systemic forces that have helped to create their organization's culture.

For an excellent assessment of organizational culture, we recommend KEYS: Assessing the Climate for Creativity. For a description of this instrument, see Chapter 2, "Using Behavioral Assessments," p. 57.

If the retreat is dedicated to cultural issues, you'll probably want to begin with a diagnostic activity that helps people see their culture more clearly. It's often difficult for groups to assess their own culture because they can't easily get enough distance from it to make objective observations. We find that the following activity, which asks people to examine their culture not from their own perspective but from that of "anthropologists," yields remarkable results.

Visit Our Village

Description

Participants are asked to observe the culture they work in by looking at its rituals and practices through an objective lens. They respond to questions anthropologists might use to study a culture, and post their observations on a wall. All participants then review the postings and draw conclusions about their culture.

Steps

1. Introduce the task: "As you know, anthropologists study cultures by observing the behavior and rituals of people of those cultures. To learn about the culture you are a part of, please imagine that you are anthropologists about to make a report on your village, Village [organization or department name].

   "You have been living in and studying this village for some time. What observations have you made about how things work here?"

2. Give each participant the list of Anthropologists' Questions (see CD 10A). Tell the group: "You won't have time to answer all the questions on your lists, so pick the ones that interest you the most. Write your answers, one per Post-it, and when you have written several, walk up to the wall and stick them under the appropriate questions. Then write and post answers to more questions. You have twenty minutes to write and post your answers."

3. After twenty minutes, ask the participants to walk along the wall and read everyone's notes.

Experiential Elements

- Personal reflection
- Observing and reflecting on other people's actions
- Applying theories to real-life situations

Setup

- Create a list of eight to ten "Anthropologists' Questions" (see CD 10A for questions to choose from), and make a copy for each participant.
- Select a long wall with ample space for participants to walk along it to post and review written material.
- Print each question you select, separately on 8 1/2 inch x 11 inch paper in 48 point type. Tape these question sheets on the wall, above a few flip chart sheets on which participants will affix Post-it Notes.

Special Supplies

A pad of Post-it Notes and a Sharpie pen for each participant

4. When everyone has read the notes and is seated again, ask: "What themes emerge from your observations?"

   Facilitate a discussion to help the group agree on five or six themes.

   For each theme ask: "Is this a positive or negative aspect of your culture? If it's positive, how can you support it? If it's negative, what changes must you make to reduce or eliminate it?"

Facilitator Notes
- The facilitator must be skilled enough to manage potential defensive reactions from leaders who don't like and may dispute the image of the culture that emerges from this activity, or who—as guardians of the existing culture—might want to maintain the status quo.

- The key to the success of this activity is to have the participants discuss how cultural issues and perceptions affect their behavior back at work. Sometimes it's helpful for participants to understand how the culture they've described in the Visit Our Village activity evolved in the first place; this can assist them in determining what can and ought to be changed.

The next three activities are all wonderful means of assessing key aspects of the culture that retreat participants would like to see changed.

Visit Our Village in Practice

We used this exercise when working with senior staff of a marketing organization. After all the answers were posted and the participants read what was on the wall, they were stunned. "It's our Wall of Horror," the CEO gasped.

"Yes, and we created it," a senior vice president responded.

Frankly, it took the participants a while to cope with how dismayed they were at their own culture. It wasn't until the next day that they were able to move on, identifying specific behaviors and policies they practiced, and looking at the unintended consequences of each. They accepted collective responsibility for having neglected the organization's culture. They agreed to eliminate several policies that dampened morale in the company, and prepared behavioral agreements that they would hold themselves and everyone else in the company accountable for. And they promised to revisit their village annually to assess their progress.

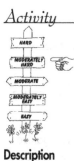

How We Behave

Description

In this activity a small group role-plays holding a meeting to which various participants arrive late. Each latecomer responds to questions posed by the facilitator. The latecomer may use gestures, sounds, body language, and movements to highlight elements of the culture that do not work well. Everyone in the meeting mimics the sounds and gestures of each latecomer in turn. The observers indicate by their applause which latecomers have painted the most accurate portrayal of negative aspects of the culture.

Experiential Elements

- Improvisation
- Role play
- Observing other people's actions or discussions
- Whole group discussion
- Small group discussion

Setup

Create a list of relevant questions to ask each volunteer in turn (see CD 10B for sample questions).

Steps

1. Ask for five volunteers to role-play having a meeting on how to improve [the organization, team, or department]'s culture.

2. Ask for five to eight volunteers (depending on the size of the group) to be latecomers who will embody aspects of the organization's culture.

3. Introduce the task by telling the volunteers who will be holding the meeting: "You should know that there will be some latecomers. When each arrives, he or she will embody a characteristic of [the organization, team, or department]'s culture. You should interrupt the meeting and all mimic whatever you see and hear the latecomer do. After a latecomer arrives and you have mimicked his or her gestures, one of you will allow that latecomer to take your seat at the meeting and then will leave the meeting. Once someone leaves the meeting, he or she will join the observers."

Tell the volunteer latecomers: "You should decide the order in which you will enter the room. When you arrive at the meeting, you will embody the behavior that corresponds to the situation I will be asking you about (such as, 'How do people in this organization behave when they want to resist a change?') using facial expressions, body language, sounds, and movements. You'll be thinking of what most or many people in this organization do in the given situation, not just how one or two people might behave. Have some fun with this. There are no wrong responses."

Tell the observers: "You who are observing will indicate by your applause when you feel that the latecomer has accurately reflected elements of the culture."

4. Allow two minutes for the meeting participants to gather their thoughts and for the latecomers to decide the order in which they will enter the meeting.

5. As each latecomer is about to enter the meeting, ask that person to embody an aspect of the organization's culture in response to a question you ask: such as, "In general, how do people in this organization behave when they want to be promoted?" (See CD 10B for more sample questions. When you construct your own questions, make sure that each starts with, "In general, how do people in this organization behave when . . .?")

6. After the last latecomer has arrived at the meeting, facilitate a whole group discussion. Ask questions such as: "What elements of your culture emerged from how you tend to behave in various circumstances?" "What might you do to change your culture for the better?"

Facilitator Note   This activity requires that the facilitator be skilled in creating an atmosphere where the people who volunteer to be latecomers will feel comfortable improvising a genuine response to the questions that are posed and where the observers will be willing to encourage accurate depictions of the culture.

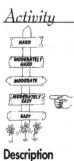

Timeline of Our History

Description   This activity encourages participants to identify the defining events that have shaped their organization's culture and to explore how those events have influenced their (and others') subsequent beliefs and behaviors. They affix Post-it Notes recording their own thoughts on a large timeline sheet posted on the wall. Then they walk along this timeline to see how others perceive the same periods and events in the organization's history.

Experiential Elements
- Personal reflection
- Discussion
- Listening to the ideas of others
- Observing while walking around the room

Steps
1. Introduce the task: "We're going to look at how your reactions to important events have shaped your working culture. Think about what has happened here in the past ten years, and write down on Post-it Notes the events that are most significant to you and, briefly, the reasons why each event was important to you. Write one event per Post-it Note."

2. After five or six minutes, invite the participants to transfer their Post-it Notes onto the big timeline.

Setup
- On a fifteen-foot-long (or longer) sheet of butcher paper, write "Events in Our Organization." Tape this long sheet of paper horizontally on a wall.
- Across the top of the sheet, write the years that the timeline will cover, leaving spaces between the years. A typical timeline might cover ten years; allow more space between the most recent years. For example:

Events in Our Organization

97	98	99	00	01	02	03	04	05	06	07

Special Supplies
- A roll of butcher paper and tape
- A pad of Post-it Notes and a Sharpie pen for each participant

3. Invite the participants to tour the timeline and read what others have written. Facilitate a discussion around these questions:

- "Are there any significant themes suggested by this timeline?"

- "How would you complete this sentence: 'Judging from our timeline, we are an organization that . . .'"

- "What similarities did you see in the events other people chose, compared to the ones you selected?"

Facilitator Notes
- The facilitator must be able to ensure that all viewpoints expressed get a fair hearing, including those not shared by most members of the group.

- Rarely do two individuals assess the impact of a specific event in the same way, so walking along the timeline can be a profound learning experience.

Timeline of Our History in Practice

We began a retreat for a large and diverse nonprofit organization with this exercise. At the end, participants were surprised to see how different their memories were of specific events and of their impact on the organization. Where some saw progress and exciting new programs, others saw segments of their membership disenfranchised.

The ensuing conversation uncovered buried feelings of disagreement and distrust among various groups in the organization. The discussion caused the group to reexamine its goals as the participants realized that they wanted not only to achieve their program and revenue targets but also to ensure that they lived up to their stated values.

Significant Stories

Description Small breakout groups are asked to identify and tell a story of an event inside the organization that they believe illustrates an important principle about the culture. After the small groups report out, the participants discuss their reactions to the stories and what they learned.

Experiential Elements
- Storytelling
- Personal reflection
- Listening to others

Steps

1. Create subgroups of four to six participants. Define the task: "Each group will tell us a brief story about an event that happened in this organization [or department] in the past two years. Choose an event that you believe exemplifies how things work here. Each subgroup needs to agree on a story and be prepared to tell the story to the rest of the group. Avoid mentioning names if possible. Please tell us what rewards and punishments—both formal and informal—occurred as a result of this incident and what this story says about what this organization values and how it operates."

2. After they have heard each subgroup's presentation, ask participants how these events might be interpreted differently by different people or departments in the organization. Guide the participants in a discussion of the underlying meanings of the stories they chose. Ask such questions as

   - "Why is this story significant to you?"

   - "What does it represent?"

   - "Is it significant to other people as well?"

   - "What impact have these events had on the culture and on your perception of the way things work in this organization?"

3. Invite the participants to suggest the stories they would prefer to be telling about the organization. Then ask them: "What do these stories say about this group's aspirations?"

Facilitator Notes
- The facilitator must be able to work with individuals sensitively to help them keep their stories brief, relevant to the task, and not embarrassing to any individual, whether present in the room or not.

- This activity encourages participants to identify and study significant events in their organization's history. The discussion is likely to surface divergent perspectives on the same events.

Significant Stories in Practice

In a retreat for the senior management group of a midsize printing company, the participants told their stories. At the end we asked, "Did you notice that every one of your positive stories was about something that happened internally, and that all your negative stories were about your customers?"

The group then attempted to think of positive customer stories, but they weren't nearly as powerful as the internal stories. That activity led to a discussion of the company's relationships with its customers. "How much do we truly value each customer?" they asked. And, "Do we get close enough to our customers to understand them and their business needs?" The managers agreed that even though they had a right to be proud of how well they took care of their own people, the long-term success of the company depended on creating the same kind of positive stories about their relationship with their customers.

Working with Sensitive or Controversial Issues

Many leaders are reluctant to have controversial issues raised at a retreat for fear that the discussions might trigger open conflict. And even when top managers are willing to discuss sensitive topics, very often participants are hesitant to speak openly. They may not want to hurt anyone's feelings. They may worry that candid comments about how the culture is perceived will be taken as a criticism of management. Also, some people just don't have the skill to speak articulately about delicate issues. These are legitimate concerns.

When it's important for participants to address issues they believe are "undiscussable," you may have to structure an activity that allows them to raise their concerns less directly. The following activity helps people bring difficult issues to the surface by working through these issues in small groups and in silence. It almost always elicits responses that go straight to the heart of people's concerns.

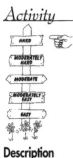

Silent Dialogue

Description

Participants express their reactions to a sensitive issue in the organization by drawing a picture together. Small groups work together in silence, using line and color to express feelings. The post-drawing discussion of the pictures opens the door for the group to speak honestly about the issue.

Experiential Elements

- Personal reflection
- Giving feedback
- Using drawing to express thoughts and feelings
- Listening
- Group discussion

Steps

1. Create subgroups of four to six participants at each table. Each table is prepared with a double-sized sheet of flip chart paper with an oval drawn on it.

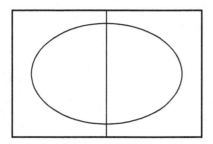

Setup

- Create a double-sized sheet of flip chart paper for each table by placing two blank sheets side by side and taping them together (on the back, so people can draw wherever they want on the front). Then draw an oval a couple of inches inside the edges of the paper—freehand is fine (see Step 1).
- Place one double sheet in the center of each table. Place markers in glasses or mugs on the table.
- Write the concern the group will address on a flip chart (see Step 2).
- Write "The Rules" flip chart (see Step 3).

Special Supplies

Sixteen Prismacolor Art Markers in various colors for each table (see Facilitator Notes); four glasses or mugs per table

2. Introduce the task: "This activity will focus on [the organization's issue]. Please think about all the ways you might answer the question that's on the flip chart."

   Show the flip chart with the question to be covered: such as, "What is it like to work in this company since the merger?" Take a moment to ensure that everyone understands the question.

   Tell the group, "You will draw your thoughts and feelings in silence to make a group picture that answers this question."

3. Show The Rules flip chart.

   Explain the task: "We are going to conduct this activity in silence. Please don't speak or communicate with anyone else in any way. In fact, don't even make eye contact with anyone while you are working on the picture.

   "You are going to use color and line to express your thoughts and feelings, independently and simultaneously.

   "Don't write any words or draw a picture of anything. For instance, if I wanted to express feeling hopeful, I might use a yellow color and draw lines like this [demonstrate], but the rules say I couldn't draw a happy face. Or if I were angry, I might take a black marker and make short powerful lines like this. But I wouldn't draw pictures of lightning strikes.

   "After we start, I will come by and move the paper, but just continue working after I do that. Don't change where you are sitting."

4. Make sure everyone understands the task; then ask the participants to begin drawing in silence. After three or four minutes, turn each subgroup's paper so that each participant is now sitting as far as possible from what he or she was drawing. (It doesn't matter that a corner of the paper might be in front of someone or hanging off the edge of the table.) Participants begin adding to whatever art they find in front of them.

5. After three or four more minutes, rotate the paper at each table again so each participant is working on an entirely new section of the drawing.

6. After four more minutes, make the final move, turning the paper once more so that each participant is working on yet another section of the drawing.

7. Finally, after another few minutes, ask the participants to bring the silent drawing to a close.

8. Instruct each subgroup to spend some time talking about its picture. Suggest that each participant start with, "Here's where I first began drawing," and then explain what the drawing stands for.

9. Ask each subgroup to develop three or four major themes that its picture illustrates and write them on a sheet of flip chart paper. Each subgroup should then title its picture and post it, along with the summary of themes, on the wall.

10. In the whole group debriefing, each subgroup should describe its picture and tell the others in the room the title and the themes the picture surfaced.

11. Facilitate a discussion about what the group has learned about the issue as a result of the Silent Dialogue. Here are some sample questions:

    • "What do the themes and how you worked together in this activity say about [the organization]?"

    • "How did you feel when other people started drawing on your work?"

    • "Did your group decide to draw outside the oval line? [*See Setup.*] If so, did someone take the lead? Did others follow? Does the way that decision was made mirror the way decisions are commonly made in [the organization]?"

    • "How does this experience reflect your behavior back at work?"

    Because every picture will have its own harmony of appearance, you might also ask participants how they achieved that harmony without talking.

Facilitator Notes

- This activity requires very skillful facilitation. Some participants may react negatively to your request that they engage in what they see as "therapy." Some may have difficulty translating their visual expressions to verbal ones. In addition, the facilitator must have the skill to deal with the possibility of uncomfortable revelations that may emerge during the debriefing of the drawings.

- Working in silence allows participants to access more intuitive thinking.

- This activity does not work well with ordinary felt-tip markers. We recommend you use art markers or another medium that offers a large variety of colors. (Prismacolor Double-Ended Markers are an excellent choice. They come in 144 colors and are available at art supply stores.) Other materials you might consider are art pastels (although they smear easily) and crayons (a low-cost alternative). Art markers will create the most striking pictures, however.

- There will be a few moments at the beginning of the activity when no one knows what to do, but eventually someone at each table will pick up a marker and start drawing. Soon, everyone will join in.

- Remember, don't speak to the group as you are moving the paper or at any time once the activity has started; this reinforces the no-talking rule.

- Some people will confine their drawing to a space they have defined for themselves. Others, however, will reach over into other spaces and draw outside the oval line (the oval line's only purpose is to compel people to decide whether or not they want to cross it). Sometimes a group will even add more paper and extend the drawing. Let every group work in its own way. Don't give any further instructions.

- Often, groups want to bring their pictures back to the workplace and hang them up. Some groups we have facilitated have even decided to have the pictures laminated (Kinko's or similar shops can do large-scale laminating) or framed. Displaying these dramatic and emotional works in hallways or gathering places helps remind people of the power they have to create beauty out of confusion.

Silent Dialogue in Practice

A participant in a retreat we facilitated for a company that had just be acquired by a larger, long-time competitor analyzed his contribution to the drawing in this way: "I was drawing these little purple dots to represent that I feel that everybody is very separated here since the merger. And this black line indicates how senior management watches over us. Then the paper turned and I got this big blue wavy thing. I thought that it looked like indecision, so I started putting yellow lines around it to illuminate our thoughts. Then I saw that Loretta was drawing overlapping circles all around my purple dots. I made big yellow circles around her circles because it occurred to me that we should all try to become a more cohesive team, not just hang out with the people we worked with before the merger."

Reward Structures Help Shape Culture

Another important element of an organization's culture is the effectiveness of its reward structure. (Keep in mind that rewards aren't limited to salary and benefits. They are whatever makes work more enjoyable, from an office with a door to an extra day off to celebrate a particular achievement to public recognition for a job well done.)

Do the organization's rewards produce heightened commitment and a strong sense of loyalty? Or are they inappropriate or inadequate, leading to cynicism, apathy, and high turnover?

In one large nonprofit organization, for example, performance awards were centralized in the human resource office, which processed nominations from supervisors. This office decided which candidates would receive recognition and what form that recognition would take. Employees didn't consider the process to be fair. They believed that some people received performance awards who should not have, and some people who deserved awards were passed over. Many also thought that awards were often given for the wrong reasons. They didn't take the awards seriously, so the awards didn't serve as incentives for improved performance.

In the course of a retreat we facilitated, the CEO, Simon, heard that employees thought the current award system was counterproductive. He asked retreat participants how they would design a more equitable incentive program. Employees suggested that any employee, not just supervisors, be able to nominate another employee for an award and that a wide range of employees, not just a central office, be involved in deciding who would actually receive awards. And they suggested that additional categories of recognition be established.

Simon accepted the proposition. Employees formed committees and designed and administered the employee recognition system, with Simon's blessing. Awards soon came to be seen as legitimate recognition for excellence. Recipients appreciated them, and others aspired to them.

Here's an activity to help the group assess whether the organization is rewarding what it intends to reward.

What Gets Rewarded Here?

Description

This activity provides an opportunity to explore the current reward systems, both formal and informal. In addition, participants examine other ways in which people might be rewarded.

Experiential Elements
- Group listing and ranking
- Group presentations
- Listening

Steps

1. Divide the participants into groups of five to eight people. Half will be designated A Groups and half B Groups.

2. Introduce the task: "We're going to explore all the ways in which this organization might reward or reinforce certain actions. The A Groups will list on their flip charts all the elements of the formal reward system—promotions, raises, awards, and so forth—and the B Groups will list the components of the informal reward system—personal attention, recognition of achievements, peer group opinions, top management interest, and so forth. Recognition and reinforcement might come from inside the organization, from one's own team, or from outside the organization.

   "You have five minutes to make a comprehensive list of all the rewards an employee might receive."

3. After five minutes ask the groups to discuss this question: "What would a person have to do to earn each reward you listed?" Give the groups ten minutes to write their answers on flip charts.

4. In round-robin style, have each group report to the other groups one of the behaviors or actions they chose and why they chose it, until all groups have reported what they came up with. (To avoid repetition, groups should only report on behaviors and actions not previously addressed by another group. Yes, this is an exception to our general disinclination to use round-robins in this way. See Chapter 5, Breakout Group Discussions, pp. 90–92.)

5. Discuss the implications for the organization (or office) that emerge from the group reports. Ask: "What might need to change so that the organization rewards what it intends to?" and, "What type of reward or reward system would you find most motivating?"

Reward Sonatas

Description

This activity allows participants to perform as an orchestra, calling out, when signaled by the "conductor," something that gets rewarded in the culture currently or something they would like to see rewarded.

Experiential Elements
- Improvisation
- Whole group discussion
- Small group discussion

Steps

1. Ask a participant to volunteer to be the conductor.

2. Divide the remaining participants into two groups. The first group will be Today's Orchestra and the second will be The Orchestra of a Better Future.

3. Introduce the task: "You are the individual instruments in your respective orchestras. When the conductor points to someone in Today's Orchestra, that person will call out something significant that is currently rewarded in [the organization]'s culture (whether you believe the organization intends to reward that behavior or not). So, for example, if you believe that the organization rewards internal competition when the culture says it values teamwork, you would call out, 'competition', not 'teamwork,' if you are a musician in Today's Orchestra. If you are in the Orchestra of a Better Future, you would call out something you would like to see rewarded that isn't currently rewarded enough. Keep repeating what you are calling out until the conductor signals for you to be quiet. If the conductor calls on you a second time, feel free to say something different."

4. Allow the orchestras to continue to play for about three minutes.

5. Facilitate a discussion in which the participants report on the key "musical strands" that they heard in their own orchestra and in the other. What does the organization reward now? What specifically would they like the organization to be rewarding? Chart their responses on flip charts.

6. Ask the participants to form self-selecting breakout groups, with each group working on a different topic chosen from the flip chart list of what participants would like the organization to be rewarding. (For example, one breakout group might discuss rewarding risk taking and another might discuss rewarding thinking about the good of the whole organization rather than just of one's own department.)

7. Ask the members of each breakout group to come up with one or two concrete actions the organization might take to reward people in the area that group is discussing, and then to report their recommendations to the whole group.

8. Ask the whole group to add relevant reward ideas as each group reports its recommendations.

Facilitator Note   This activity requires that the facilitator be skilled in creating an atmosphere where people will have fun with the orchestra and also be unafraid to speak out about what is rewarded and what they would prefer to see rewarded.

How Individuals Foster Culture Change

Experts differ on how long it takes to change an organization's culture, but everyone agrees it can't be done overnight. The biggest mistake a group can make at a retreat is to try to change everything at once.

Often when people talk about their organization's culture, they speak in terms of attitudes: "Nobody really cares about quality around here," "We're all obsessed with what the CEO thinks," or, "If we could just move beyond office politics, we'd all work together better." Colleagues typically make assumptions about one another's motivations and attitudes. And although they behave as if these assumptions were the truth, no one can know for sure what is going on in another person's mind.

At the retreat, then, you'll need to help participants translate their *assumptions* or *perceptions of attitude* into *observations of behavior*. Ask, "What does it look like when people are obsessed with what your department head thinks? How does that play out in your work?"

The culture won't change because someone says, "Let's stop being obsessed with what the department head thinks." But people can change some of their behaviors. You might ask the group about the impact of that perception in meetings, for instance. If it means that people aren't willing to state an opinion until they see which way the wind is blowing, ask participants to suggest ways to change that behavior. They might decide, for example, to have everyone write down his or her opinions and read them aloud (or to exchange papers and read each other's opinions aloud) before the department head declares himself on an important issue.

Remember, too, that all organization cultures contain positive and supportive elements. It will be reassuring to the participants if you take time to help them focus on what they appreciate and want to maintain in their culture, not only on what they want to change. The following activity can help participants focus on what they want to keep in the midst of change.

We'll Keep . . .

Description

This activity encourages participants to use props in the room (or elements from the retreat center's outdoor wooded area, if there is one) to symbolize aspects of the organization's culture they want to keep (or strengthen). Each participant adds an offering to the "culture mound" in the center of the circle.

Experiential Elements

- Reflection
- Using metaphor
- Using toys and other props
- Listening

Special Supplies

Hats, toys, and other evocative props

Steps

1. Introduce the task: "You are each going to find an object anywhere in this room or elsewhere in the building or on the grounds of the retreat center that symbolizes an aspect of this culture that is very important for [the organization] to keep. You will have ten minutes to find that object and come up with the reasons it is a good symbol for an important element of [the organization]'s culture."

2. When the participants return to the room, ask them to sit in a circle around a table in the center of the room, which represents the culture mound.

3. Tell the participants: "I would like each of you in turn to come to the center of the circle and offer your symbol representing an element of the culture that [the organization] should be sure to preserve. If someone else has already used the same item or used another item to represent the same thing, use your item or name the same thing anyway."

4. As the participants offer their symbols in turn, write down on a flip chart the elements of the culture the group wants to keep.

5. Facilitate a conversation with the group. Ask: "How can we ensure that we don't lose the elements of our culture that matter most to us?"

Recognizing and Removing Obstacles to Change

Even after participating in the decisions on how to foster changes in the organization's culture, many people still won't make a wholehearted commitment to modify their own behaviors. It's easy for people to see insurmountable obstacles, both for themselves and the organization. "Oh, we've tried to change things before, but it never works," some people say. "Here we go again." Such sentiments obstruct forward movement because they can become self-fulfilling prophecies.

At a retreat we facilitated for the online department of a national magazine, the participants readily identified specific changes that were within their power to make. They agreed that they would work better together if they made these few changes. But when we asked what obstacles stood in the way of implementing these changes, they quickly generated a list of more than forty reasons that these changes couldn't happen.

See Chapter 7, "Participants Are Resisting New Ideas," pp. 150–155, for techniques to manage resistance when it emerges.

This group wasn't any more negative than the participants in an average retreat. It's easier for most people to see why things won't work than to figure out how to make them work. So you will probably want to include time for people to confront the impediments they anticipate. The following activity offers a structured way to address these concerns.

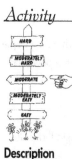

Obstacle Busters II

Description

Working first in small groups, participants discuss what might hamper their ability to achieve their goals. After identifying the obstacles, they discuss ways to overcome them or reduce their impact.

Steps

1. Create subgroups of six to eight people. Introduce the task: "Too often we get into the habit of thinking we can't achieve things because there are too many obstacles in the way. Some of these obstacles are real, but very often we find that what we perceive to be insurmountable obstacles can be removed. And some are simply embedded in the way we usually do things."

2. Ask the subgroups to take ten minutes to list on a flip chart every obstacle they can think of that might interfere with achieving the desired results.

3. Reassemble the whole group, but don't review the subgroups' work yet. First, show the participants the Thinking About Obstacles flip chart.

4. Define the next task: "Sort the obstacles you identified into these three categories: Obstacles within our power to remove or minimize, insurmountable obstacles, and obstacles that exist primarily in our minds."

Experiential Elements

- Reflecting back on experiences
- Listening to the ideas of others
- Envisioning possibilities and generating new ideas

Setup

Write "Thinking About Obstacles" flip chart (see Step 3).

Special Supplies

A pad of Post-it Notes and a Sharpie pen for each participant

---

THINKING ABOUT OBSTACLES

- WHICH OBSTACLES COULD BE REMOVED OR MINIMIZED BY GROUP EFFORT AND AGREEMENT?
- WHICH OBSTACLES ARE INSURMOUNTABLE?
- WHICH OBSTACLES EXIST PRIMARILY IN OUR MINDS?

5. Instruct each subgroup: "Choose at least six major obstacles, and determine specifically what the people in this room can do to eliminate or reduce them. Consider only the actions that are within the power of the people here, not actions that you wish others would take. You have thirty minutes to work."

6. After thirty minutes have each subgroup report on its findings to the whole.

7. Tell the participants: "Since we can't eliminate obstacles that are out of our control, we'll skip that category and go on to obstacles that are in our heads. Using a separate Post-it Note for each idea, answer the question: 'What assumptions can we get rid of?'" After participants have written down their ideas, they should read their thoughts aloud in turn and post them on the wall.

8. Facilitate a discussion of these questions:

   • "How will we implement the obstacle-busting ideas back at work?"

   • "In the future, how can we avoid making erroneous assumptions about what's possible?"

Facilitator Note   The facilitator must be skilled enough to prevent cynics from carrying the day and to prod reluctant participants to take personal responsibility for addressing the obstacles and negative attitudes that are identified in this activity.

See Chapter 9, "Obstacle Busters I," pp. 245–246, and Chapter 14, "Obstacle Busters III," pp. 423–424, for other versions of this exercise.

Feedback for Senior Executives

A retreat is a great opportunity for senior executives to learn about the impact of their behavior on the organization's culture. How open are they to new ideas and to adapting their leadership styles to best serve the organization? How willing are they to try new approaches, help others grow, and encourage risk taking? Do they foster internal cooperation or competition?

It's very hard for leaders to get honest feedback from employees, who may fear the consequences of speaking out. Thus executives often lack valuable perspectives that could help them lead their organizations more effectively.

When we conduct retreats, we often ask senior executives if they want feedback from the people they supervise. If they do (and most *say* they do), we give them the feedback about them and their leadership styles that emerged from the interviews and surveys we conducted (while being very careful to protect the sources), and we discuss the implications of this feedback with them. We encourage leaders to talk with the participants about what they've learned, what they're willing to change, and also where their boundaries are firm.

Talking about this feedback at the retreat gives executives the opportunity to learn about and acknowledge behaviors that may be hindering the staff from doing their best, to pledge to modify leadership and management styles or make other changes, and to ask the staff for their help in doing so successfully. It also affords executives the opportunity to clear up any misconceptions that may have arisen because people have ascribed erroneous motives to their leadership practices. When participants see it is safe to request changes from their leaders, trust improves exponentially. Executives often find that by making small changes they can make significant improvements in the working environment.

Other Suggested Activities for a Culture Change Retreat

You will find other activities to incorporate into a culture change retreat in the Activities for Culture Change, Team-Building, and Board Retreats index (p. 493) and the Activities to Use in Any Retreat index (p. 490).

Chapter 11

Leading a
Team-Building Retreat

Employees seem to work at cross-purposes. Too many things keep falling through the cracks. One department head won't cooperate with another. Managers find themselves spending an inordinate amount of time mediating subordinates' disputes. Such symptoms often lead executives to conclude that it's time for a team-building retreat.

There are other reasons as well why managers might want to convene a team-building retreat. If staff members are just beginning to work in formal teams or if different working units are being merged, a retreat can help the group get off to a good start.

If You're Asked to Lead a Team-Building Retreat

It's often tempting—for executives and employees alike—to believe that most of an organization's problems would disappear if people would only stop behaving badly and learn to cooperate with one another.

Management wants people to work more effectively together and believes that changing the behavior of individual employees would accomplish this end.

Although the behavior of individual employees often contributes to an organization's problems, it is rarely the root cause. A perceived lack of teamwork may really stem from a fundamental disagreement about where the organization is heading or from trust issues rather than from "difficult" employees. Team-building retreats are unlikely to produce lasting results if they focus mainly on interpersonal issues when the real problem is something else entirely. That being said, we've seen many instances of relationships that changed dramatically for the better as a by-product of work done at a retreat.

Many dysfunctional relationships, often ascribed to "personality differences," result from the assumptions people make about each other and the conclusions they draw from those assumptions. When participants use the retreat setting to address real issues together with colleagues with whom they may have had difficulty in the past, they might learn to see one another in a new light. Their new insights often lay the groundwork for more constructive professional relationships. Although a retreat is unlikely to be the most effective setting for resolving a long-standing personal issue between two individuals, it can establish a framework for dealing with that issue more effectively back at work. It can also be a forum for people to begin to address larger issues that rankle work groups and departments.

Characteristics of a Productive Team

It is not uncommon for managers, when confronted with a major problem, to rename it, in the apparent hope that this will also solve it. The Personnel Department isn't performing? Call it Human Resources. If a division isn't performing well, call it a team. But calling the office staff a team doesn't make them a team. And if you don't have a real team, a team-building retreat is likely to fall short of solving the problems it is intended to address.

The first targets for a successful team-building retreat are for team members to understand the functions or characteristics of a productive team, to analyze where their team may fall short, and to develop plans to improve their weaker areas. In retreats we lead for teams we often help them focus on the following areas (also see the accompanying figure):

Purpose and goals. Do all team members understand and support the team's core purpose, its reason for being? A clear and galvanizing purpose will help move the team forward in an unambiguous direction and will focus the efforts of its members. A muddled sense of purpose will lead to confusion and conflict. Does the team have clear goals? Do the goals support the team's purpose?

Rewards. What is the team's reward structure? (And team members should keep in mind that rewards aren't limited to salary and tangible benefits.) Do rewards produce heightened commitment, positive motivation, high morale, and a strong sense of loyalty? Or are the rewards inappropriate or inadequate, leading to cynicism, apathy, an ethic of self-interest, and high turnover?

See Chapter 10, "Reward Structures Help Shape Culture," pp. 266–269, for activities that focus on identifying appropriate rewards.

Structure. How is the team structured to accomplish its work? Is the distribution of work seen as fair and equitable? Does work proceed in a coordinated fashion or is it fraught with redundancies and shortfalls? Do people clearly understand their roles and responsibilities?

Collaboration. Do team members collaborate, take a broad view of the whole team, and support each other's efforts? Or do they mistrust each other and engage in turf battles that result in lack of coordination and a sense of disjointedness?

Risk taking. What happens when a team member makes a mistake? If mistakes are seen as opportunities to learn, the team is likely to take appropriate risks for the sake of innovation. If mistakes are to be avoided at all costs, team members are likely to be timid and resistant to trying out new ideas.

Decision making. What is the quality of the decisions the team has made, particularly in stressful times? Sound decision-making practices will help the team respond appropriately to members' needs and devise creative solutions to internal and external concerns.

Leadership. How open are the leaders to new ideas and to adapting their management styles to best serve their team?

Managing conflict. How is conflict dealt with in the team? If it is managed openly and cooperatively, it leads to resolution and trust. If it is stifled, buried, or denied, it tends to foster defensiveness, blame, and long-standing grudges and creates distractions from work.

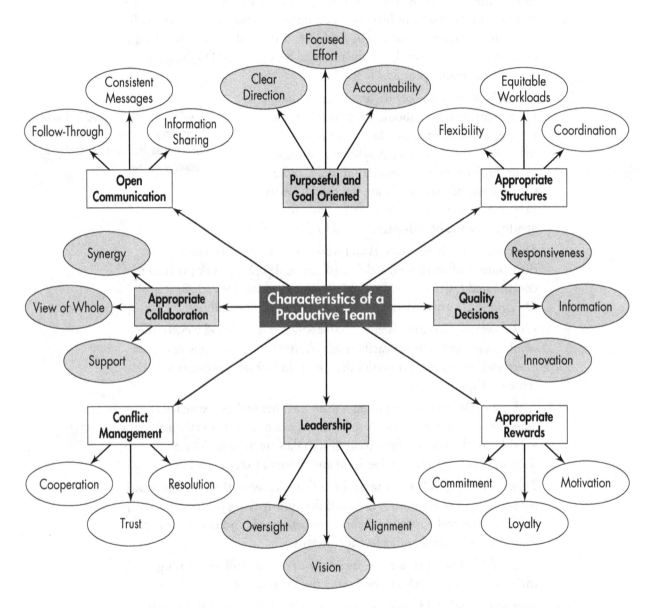

Productive teams manage their relationships and work processes, as well as their production. This model helps teams look in a structured way for evidence of how well they are working together and what areas need improvement.

Communication. Do team members share information, follow through, and give and receive helpful and timely feedback? Or is there an atmosphere of secrecy, gossip, and mistrust, with team members and their internal and external customers receiving mixed messages?

 We have included our favorite team-building activities in this chapter. If you want access to a wealth of other team-building exercises, we recommend these resources:

- *The Pfeiffer Book of Successful Team-Building Tools,* by Elaine Biech (Ed.) (2001).

- *The Fieldbook of Team Interventions: Step-by-Step Guide to High Performance Teams,* by C. Harry Eggleton and Judy Rice (1996).

- *Pfeiffer's Classic Activities for Building Better Teams,* by Jack Gordon (Ed.) (2003a).

- *Pfeiffer's Classic Activities for Developing Leaders,* by Jack Gordon (Ed.) (2003b).

- *Pfeiffer's Classic Activities for Managing Conflict at Work,* by Jack Gordon (Ed.) (2003c).

- *Pfeiffer's Classic Activities for Interpersonal Communication,* by Jack Gordon (Ed.) (2004a).

- *The Pfeiffer Handbook of Structured Experiences: Learning Activities for Intact Teams and Workgroups,* by Jack Gordon (Ed.) (2004b).

- *Team Depot: A Warehouse of Over 585 Tools to Reassess, Rejuvenate, and Rehabilitate Your Team,* by Glenn Parker (2002).

- *25 Activities for Developing Team Leaders,* by Fran Rees (2005).

- *The Fifth Discipline Fieldbook,* by Peter Senge, et al. (1994).

- *Teamwork and Teamplay: Games and Activities for Building and Training Teams,* by Sivasailam "Thiagi" Thiagarajan and Glenn Parker (1999).

- *Working Together: 55 Team Games,* by Lorraine Ukens (1997b).

- *101 Great Games and Activities,* by Arthur VanGundy (1998).

The activities that follow will help team members focus on what they can do to create a more productive and harmonious team.

Are We Dropping the Ball?

Description

In this activity participants review a model for a productive team, use juggling beanbags as a metaphor for where the team is "dropping the ball," and tell stories to illustrate their conclusions.

Steps

1. Review the Characteristics of a Productive Team model, and answer any questions about the model (see CD 11A).

2. Divide the participants into subgroups of five to eight people.

3. Assign each subgroup one or two sections of the model (depending on the number of participants).

4. Show the Your Group's Task flip chart:

> **YOUR GROUP'S TASK**
>
> 1. DECIDE IF THE TEAM IS LIVING UP TO ITS POTENTIAL IN THE ASPECT OF THE MODEL YOUR GROUP IS REVIEWING.
>
> 2. COME UP WITH ONE OR TWO STORIES TO ILLUSTRATE YOUR CONCLUSION.
>
> 3. PRESENT YOUR CONCLUSIONS BY SHOWING THAT THE TEAM IS EITHER "JUGGLING" THIS ASPECT EFFECTIVELY OR "DROPPING THE BALL."
>
> 4. TELL US YOUR BEST STORY.

Experiential Elements

- Group discussion
- Juggling
- Using metaphor
- Storytelling

Setup

- Provide a copy of the "Characteristics of a Productive Team" model to each participant (see CD 11A).
- Prepare one "Your Group's Task" flip chart (see Step 4).

Special Supplies

One set of three juggling beanbags for each small group

5. Introduce the task: "You will assess whether the team is 'juggling' effectively the aspect(s) of its productivity that your subgroup is reviewing or is 'dropping the ball.' Be prepared to tell a story to the whole group that illustrates your conclusion. So that we remember your conclusion, illustrate it for us when you present your findings, using the beanbags that are at your table. Even if you don't know how to juggle, you can catch the beanbags that you toss to one another to signify 'juggling effectively,' and you can let them drop to signify 'dropping the ball.'"

6. Ask the participants to applaud if they agree with each subgroup's assessment and to refrain from applauding if they disagree.

7. Facilitate a discussion about the aspects of its functioning in which the team seems to be dropping the ball most consistently and note any concrete action steps to improve the situation.

Facilitator Notes
- You may choose to lead this activity without the juggling beanbags, but it will be more memorable and fun for the participants if you include them.

- The subgroups may juggle the beanbags in any way they choose when they present to the whole group. The juggling can be done by one or more people and may involve one, two, or all three beanbags.

Purpose and Goals

Effective teams, whether long-term work units or short-term task forces, need to know why they exist and what they contribute to the organization and its customers. In addition, team members need to know what is expected of them so they can formulate goals to meet those expectations.

We have worked with many organizations where everyone says, "Sure, I understand our core purpose." But when we have probed more deeply, we have often found that each person's "clear understanding" was different from everyone else's.

The following activity will help the team assess how much common understanding there is of the team's purpose.

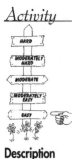

Purpose Check

Description

In this activity each participant writes the team's purpose on a Post-it Note. The participants read the resulting collection of Post-it Notes and discuss whether they all agree on the purpose for the team.

Experiential Elements

- Personal reflection
- Writing
- Visual gallery
- Group discussion

Steps

1. Describe the activity: "Please write this team's purpose on a Post-it Note, and post what you have written on the flip chart paper along the wall. Your purpose statement should be no more than one sentence."

2. When everyone has posted a purpose statement, instruct participants: "View what is posted on the wall. Take a notepad with you, and write down the common themes you see among the various expressions of purpose."

3. Facilitate a discussion of how much similarity and how much difference participants noted in their statements of team purpose. Ask questions such as these:

   - "Were there any themes common to most of the purpose statements? What do those themes say about this team?"

   - "What differences did you notice among the purpose statements? How might these differences be playing out in the team? Can anyone think of examples of how you work at cross-purposes?"

   - "Did anything surprise you in the purpose statements? What impact might those surprises be having on how the team functions?"

Setup

Tape several sheets of flip chart paper to the wall.

Special Supplies

- A pad of Post-it Notes and a Sharpie pen for each participant
- A notepad for each participant

For a newly constituted team or one that seems rudderless, you can use the following activity to help the team create a statement of purpose.

Or use the "Exploring Strategic Direction" activity in Chapter 9, pp. 200–202.

"Purposeful" Poetry

Description

In this activity participants write limericks that reflect their view of the team's purpose.

Steps

1. Divide the participants into subgroups of no more than five people.

2. Review the Limerick Instructions (see CD 11B), and make sure participants understand them and know how to use the rhyming dictionaries.

3. Give the subgroups ten minutes to create their limericks.

4. Have each subgroup read its limerick to the whole group, and ask the participants to listen for similarities in the limericks.

5. Facilitate a discussion of the themes that were common in the various limericks, and note them on a flip chart.

Facilitator Note

The facilitator must be able to help groups that get stuck and encourage them to have fun while still focusing on the team's purpose.

Experiential Elements

- Personal reflection
- Writing poetry
- Group discussion

Setup

Prepare one copy of the "Limerick Instructions" for each participant (see CD 11B).

Special Supplies

- A rhyming dictionary, such as *The Complete Rhyming Dictionary* (Wood, 1991) or *The New Comprehensive American Rhyming Dictionary* (Young, 1991), for each subgroup
- A notepad for each participant

Also see Chapter 9, "Exploring Strategic Direction," pp. 200–202, for a discussion of how to establish concrete results.

The following activity will help the team establish tangible goals.

Wouldn't It Be Great If . . . ?

Description

In this activity participants create goals for which the team will hold itself accountable.

Steps

1. Describe the activity: "Now we're going to give you a chance to explore your ambitions for [the organization]. We're sitting here at our reunion five years down the road. What would you want [the organization] to have accomplished? What is the headline in [the major local or industry paper]? What are your customers saying? Ask yourself, 'Wouldn't it be great if . . . ?'"

2. Show the Wouldn't It Be Great If . . . ? flip chart.

Experiential Elements
- Personal reflection
- Group discussion

Setup
- Prepare the "Wouldn't It Be Great If . . . ?" flip chart (see Step 2).
- Prepare the "Make Your Goals SMART" flip chart (see Step 8).

Special Supplies

A pad of Post-it Notes and a Sharpie pen for each participant

WOULDN'T IT BE GREAT IF . . . ?
CONSIDER:
- ACHIEVEMENTS
- REPUTATION
- SCOPE OF WORK
- CUSTOMERS SERVED
- RECOGNITION
- IMPACT ON ORGANIZATION
- YOUR ROLE
- ANYTHING ELSE

3. Tell participants: "Think about all aspects of your ambitions for the team. You might have multiple desires for one aspect and none for another.

   "Working alone and in silence, please write your ambitions on Post-it Notes (one ambition per Post-it Note), and post what you have written on the wall. Allow yourself to be bold in your ambitions, and write as many ambitions as you can think of."

4. Give participants five minutes to write their ambitions.

5. Ask for volunteers to work together to sort the Post-it Notes into categories and to label each category.

6. Give each participant five voting dots, and then ask the participants to use the dots to vote for their preferred categories of ambitions.

7. Ask participants to form breakout groups. Each group will discuss a different category of ambitions that received many votes.

8. Show the Make Your Goals SMART flip chart.

MAKE YOUR GOALS *SMART*
- SPECIFIC
- MEASURABLE
- AMBITIOUS
- REALISTIC
- TIME-BASED

9. Explain the concept of SMART goals. Help the group as a whole to come up with examples of goals that aren't SMART (such as, "We will be more productive") and examples that are SMART (such as, "By May of next year, we will have every customer query processed within 48 hours").

10. Ask each breakout group to come up with no more than three SMART goals for the category of ambitions it is exploring.

11. Ask each breakout group to report its SMART goals to the whole group, and ask the whole group to judge whether the goals are SMART and whether they are desirable and reasonable goals for the team.

Facilitator Notes
- The facilitator must be able to help groups create SMART goals and limit the number of goals so that the team doesn't take on too much.

- Groups sometimes have difficulty coming up with SMART goals, so spend some time in the discussion helping people see the difference between SMART goals and goals that are vague or unfocused.

- If the groups come up with too many goals for the team, you might want to follow this activity with one of the prioritization activities in Chapter 9.

Wouldn't It Be Great If . . . ? in Practice

We used Wouldn't It Be Great If . . . ? at the beginning of a retreat for a company that had recently gone through some tough times. Employees had been laid off and budgets were tight for the following year. Nevertheless people were ready to imagine future outcomes and to make them specific.

It was a two-day retreat. On the morning of the second day the president of the company asked if the group could revisit its ideas from the day before: "Are these goals big enough, or did we pull our punches yesterday?" Indeed, the group had. Most of the managers present, having had some time to think it over, agreed that they had been reluctant to push themselves too hard. But after a day of working together, they were willing to go back and do the exercise again. This time, their outlooks were more optimistic, and they set more ambitious and challenging goals for themselves.

Exploring How Things Are and How Participants Would Like Them to Be

People often express what they want to be different in the workplace by complaining about what's wrong. But it's not possible to deal constructively with "what's wrong" unless people have a full view of the larger picture, which also includes what's right. A gripe session, however satisfying it might feel in the moment, won't change anything (and could make things worse).

That's why it's important to have participants take a balanced look at how things *really* are. People typically come away from such an activity with a greater appreciation for all the things that are "right" with their working relationships and a clearer sense of where to focus their energies to make things better.

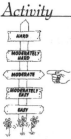

Vehicle for Change I

Description

This activity uses vehicles as a metaphor to stimulate thinking about what working relationships are like now and what they could be like in the future.

Experiential Elements

- Using metaphor to express thoughts and feelings
- Personal reflection
- Drawing
- Group presentations
- Giving and receiving feedback

Steps

1. Divide participants into subgroups of four to five people. Introduce the task: "Imagine your organization [or department] as if it were a vehicle of some kind. Take a moment to picture the organization as it is now—its characteristics and its environment—in terms you might use to describe an automobile, a truck, a cement mixer, an eighteen-wheeler, whatever.

   "I will be asking you to draw a vehicle that represents the organization, but first, here are some questions you should consider."

2. Show participants the Questions flip chart.

Setup

- Prepare "Questions" flip chart (see Step 2).
- Prepare "The Rules" flip chart (see Step 3).
- Prepare "Organization Characteristics" flip chart (see Step 4).

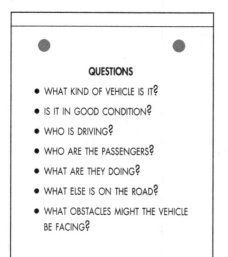

QUESTIONS
- WHAT KIND OF VEHICLE IS IT?
- IS IT IN GOOD CONDITION?
- WHO IS DRIVING?
- WHO ARE THE PASSENGERS?
- WHAT ARE THEY DOING?
- WHAT ELSE IS ON THE ROAD?
- WHAT OBSTACLES MIGHT THE VEHICLE BE FACING?

3. Ask participants to take a moment—without talking—to get a clear picture in their minds of a vehicle. Show participants The Rules flip chart, and explain the rules.

THE RULES

- WORK IN SILENCE.
- EVERYONE MUST DRAW.
- EVERYONE MUST PARTICIPATE IN THE REPORT.

4. Advise participants to look for symbolic ways to convey their organization's (or department's) characteristics. Show participants the Organization Characteristics flip chart.

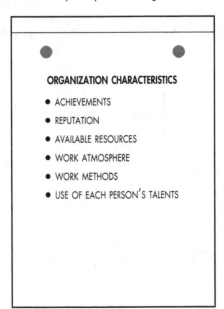

ORGANIZATION CHARACTERISTICS

- ACHIEVEMENTS
- REPUTATION
- AVAILABLE RESOURCES
- WORK ATMOSPHERE
- WORK METHODS
- USE OF EACH PERSON'S TALENTS

5. Ask each subgroup to work in silence to draw a vehicle on a sheet of flip chart paper.

6. After calling time, have the members of each subgroup describe in turn their picture to the larger group and explain what each element of the drawing means. Because participants will have been working in silence, they themselves won't know what it all means until they hear other members of their group report out loud.

7. Explain the task: "Now, draw another vehicle, or the same vehicle under different conditions, that represents [the organization or department] as you would like it to be. This time, you can talk with each other as you design your vehicle."

8. After calling time, have the subgroups, as before, describe their pictures to the larger group and explain what they mean. Ask such questions as these:

   - "Were there any themes common to most of the drawings? What do those themes say about this organization [or department]?"

   - "What would this group like to be different in this organization?"

   - "What steps can you take to change from the vehicle you are in now to the vehicle you'd like to be in?"

Facilitator Notes
- This activity requires skillful facilitation to draw groups out on the real significance of their pictures.

- This activity can help a group discover and sort out issues that may be causing confusion and anxiety. Using the symbol of the vehicle, the group can quickly see what is on everyone's mind and come up with strategies for change.

- The use of metaphors and silent work in groups can help the participants surface difficult issues in relative anonymity.

Vehicle for Change in Practice

We used this exercise in a retreat for a large international organization with participants from throughout Latin America. Although it was important that these virtual team members coordinate their efforts, by necessity they interacted primarily by phone and e-mail.

People interpreted their vehicles very differently, and looking at the drawings sparked much good-natured laughter. At the same time, the pictures brought excellent ideas to light for improving the performance of this geographically dispersed team. The participants chose five major areas in which they wanted to improve their teamwork and developed action plans for each one.

Ask the Genie

Description

In this activity participants practice a guided visualization that helps them reflect on what they wish for the team. Each participant writes his or her top wish, and then another team member comes up with concrete steps to implement that wish.

Steps

1. Introduce the activity: "We're going to explore your aspirations for this team, and then you will receive help from a benevolent genie to make your wishes come true."

2. Instruct the participants: "First, I'd like to take you on a brief guided visualization.

   "Please make yourself as comfortable as possible. Uncross your legs and arms.

   "Please close your eyes.

   "Notice your breathing and try to slow it down just a bit. [*Pause.*]

   "Now slow it down just a bit more. [*Pause.*]

   "Now imagine that you are at work. [*Pause.*]

   "Go to your desk. Try to see everything with fresh eyes, taking in as many details as you can. What do you notice? [*Pause.*]

   "See yourself working. What do you need to be more effective in your job? [*Pause.*]

Experiential Elements
- Personal reflection
- Guided visualization
- Group presentations
- Using toys and other props
- Group voting
- Whole group discussion

Setup

Prepare "Guidelines for Genies" flip chart (see Step 6).

Special Supplies
- Colored photocopy paper and a Sharpie pen for each participant
- A box that you can fit the papers into
- Toys and other props
- Three voting dots for each participant
- Flip chart paper and colored markers for each participant

This activity is adapted from "The Genie's Wish: Identifying and Addressing Team Needs," by Thomas F. Penderghast, in *Pfeiffer's Classic Activities for Building Better Teams*, and is used with permission.

"Now travel through your team's entire workspace. See each member of the team working. What does the team need to work as effectively as possible? [*Pause.*]

"When you are ready, please open your eyes and return to the room."

3. Tell participants: "Now is your chance to ask for help from that benevolent genie. What is the wish you would most like the genie to grant?

"Write your wish neatly so the genie can read it. Use your Sharpie pen, and confine your wish to the top half of the paper. Make your wish as specific as possible so the genie will know what to grant you. Frame your wish in positive terms: tell the genie what you want, not what you don't want."

4. When participants have finished writing their wishes, ask them to fold their papers in half, so that their wishes are hidden from view, and deposit them in the box.

5. Mix the papers up in the box, and ask each participant to draw one and take a quick look at it. If a participant draws his own wish, he should refold the paper and select another.

6. Tell participants that they will be one another's genies, coming up with implementation plans for the wishes they have drawn. Go over the Guidelines for Genies flip chart.

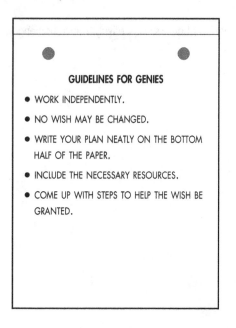

GUIDELINES FOR GENIES

- WORK INDEPENDENTLY.
- NO WISH MAY BE CHANGED.
- WRITE YOUR PLAN NEATLY ON THE BOTTOM HALF OF THE PAPER.
- INCLUDE THE NECESSARY RESOURCES.
- COME UP WITH STEPS TO HELP THE WISH BE GRANTED.

7. When participants finish their implementation plans, ask them to write them on the bottom half of the papers and then to refold the papers and deposit them in the box. Mix the papers up in the box again, and ask each participant to draw one. If a participant draws her own wish or implementation plan, she should refold the paper and select another.

8. Tell participants: "You will have ten minutes to come up with a short presentation that will 'sell' the wish and the implementation plan you have drawn. You should work independently. If you can guess who wrote the wish or the implementation plan, please don't identify either person. Don't change the wish or implementation plan in any way, even if you aren't personally enthusiastic about them. Write the key points of your presentation on a flip chart. Use any of the props you find in this room to make your presentation memorable and compelling."

9. Ask each participant to present in turn his or her best sales pitch.

10. When the presentations are over, give participants three voting dots, and ask them to vote for the ideas they would most like to see implemented by placing their dots on the appropriate flip charts.

11. Facilitate a whole group discussion of what it would take to begin to implement the wishes that received the most votes.

Facilitator Note   It's important to focus the group on thinking about issues positively, rather than engaging in griping or cynicism.

Clarifying Individuals' Roles and Responsibilities

No one person in an organization can be responsible for doing everything, but everything that has to be done must be someone's responsibility. Most organizations struggle to achieve the proper distribution of responsibility. Typically, some people are given or take on too much, and others are assigned or are willing to undertake too little. The result can be resentment, frustration, duplication of effort, and important tasks not accomplished.

Individuals' expectations for themselves and for others should advance the organization's or work group's overall purpose, and individual roles should be clearly defined and understood by all when actions are planned and tasks are assigned. The more people know about what their colleagues are doing, the more able they will be to collaborate with one another, complement each other's efforts, and provide one another with appropriate support and assistance.

> You'll find two excellent activities on responsibility charting and workflow mapping in *The Fieldbook of Team Interventions: Step-by-Step Guide to High Performance Teams*, by C. Harry Eggleton and Judy C. Rice (1996), pp. 161–178.

Picturing Our Roles

Description

In this activity participants produce crests that highlight different aspects of their primary job role on the team, and they receive feedback on what their teammates perceive and would prefer.

Steps

1. Ask the participants to form subgroups of four to five people with whom they work closely on the team.

2. Introduce the task: "As I have noted on this flip chart, according to theory developed by psychologist Gordon Allport, there are four aspects of role." Show the Four Aspects of Role flip chart.

FOUR ASPECTS OF ROLE

- ROLE EXPECTATIONS — WHAT OTHERS THINK OUR JOB IS

- ROLE CONCEPTION — WHAT WE BELIEVE OUR JOB IS

- ROLE ACCEPTANCE — WHAT WE ARE WILLING TO DO

- ROLE BEHAVIOR — WHAT WE ACTUALLY DO

Experiential Elements

- Using metaphor to express thoughts and feelings
- Personal reflection
- Drawing
- Group presentations
- Receiving feedback

Setup

- Prepare the "Four Aspects of Role" flip chart (see Step 2).
- Copy one "Team Roles Crest" for each participant (see CD 11C).

Special Supplies

Prismacolor Art Markers in various colors for each table

This activity is adapted from "Role Clarification: Developing a Team Norm," by John E. Jones, in *The Pfeiffer Handbook of Structured Experiences: Learning Activities for Intact Teams and Workgroups,* and is used with permission.

3. Tell the members of each subgroup to make notes about their own jobs in terms of these four aspects of their own roles. Once they have completed this, they should create an image of each aspect of their role, that is, one image for each of the quadrants in their personal team crest. (See CD 11C for an image of a crest.)

4. Each participant in turn should share the meaning of his or her crest with the other subgroup members and receive feedback from them on their actual expectations and how closely these expectations match what the participant thought others' expectations were.

5. The subgroups report to the whole group what they learned about others' expectations of them and what they are willing to do differently. The whole group provides any additional feedback on expectations and helpful behavior.

This Could Be Me

Description

In this activity participants reflect on their ideal role in the team and ask for help in achieving their ideal.

Experiential Elements
- Personal reflection
- Group presentations
- Receiving feedback

Steps

1. Introduce the activity: "We're going to explore what more each of us would like to contribute to this team. We all have skills and abilities that help us do our job and also skills and abilities that are not fully exploited in our current work that we might contribute to the team. We'll use the This Could Be Me Reflection sheet [*see CD 11D*] to help us think about what we contribute to this team now and what more we could contribute.

   "So, for example, I might say that I am very detail oriented and that helps me catch errors in our budget submissions. And I might add that I am also very creative and that my current work doesn't take advantage of my creativity. I could come up with innovative ways to organize our budgets that would be more user-friendly for our internal customers."

2. Give participants fifteen minutes to fill out their handouts.

3. Have each participant read his or her handout to the whole group, and ask the group members to give the participant feedback on what they hear. Individual group members might also offer specific support.

4. After listening to the feedback, have the participant make a public commitment to take one specific step toward creating a more ideal role in the team.

Setup

Prepare one "This Could Be Me Reflection" handout for each participant (see CD 11D).

This activity is adapted from "Kaleidoscope: Team Building Through Role Expansion," by Carlo E. Cetti and Mary Kirkpatrick Craig, in *Pfeiffer's Classic Activities for Building Better Teams*, and is used with permission.

Improving Work Processes

Often circumstances change over time, but an organization's work processes do not keep pace.

For example, one of our clients, a federal government agency, found it could not respond adequately to the great number of requests for information it received. Agency officials were deeply concerned about the increasing number of complaints from irate customers (and members of Congress) about backlogs and slow processing times.

The agency had recently lost approximately 15 percent of its workforce (including many of its most experienced employees) in government-mandated downsizings; at the same time, the demand for information was increasing steadily. To make matters worse, the agency had not modernized its technology in years, so its database was woefully out of date.

We facilitated an offsite for senior managers and staff to explore how they might fundamentally redesign the work processes. By giving employees information about the urgency of the change and by involving them in modifying the work processes, the managers generated broader commitment for a new course of action.

When the participants grasped the full picture of how the work was being done, they were surprised to discover that they were undertaking many unnecessary tasks, with much duplication of effort. By taking their attention away from what they couldn't control (the federal budget) and redirecting it to what they could control (eliminating or reducing these redundancies), they were able to come up with new processes that significantly increased their productivity and reduced their response time—and the number of complaints.

> We know of no better activity to create a framework for discussing work process improvements than a half-day version of the Organization Workshop. See Chapter 1, "Using a Specialized Retreat Format," pp. 24–32.

Strengthening Communication

Here's an activity to help participants examine the effectiveness of their organization's communication processes so they can take steps to improve how they share information with one another and with outsiders.

How We Communicate

Description

In this activity participants focus on how they and their colleagues typically communicate. They take on the viewpoint of outsiders—sociologists sent to study their organization—and their observations then inform discussions about the positive or negative value of various communication patterns.

Experiential Elements

- Personal reflection
- Discussion
- Giving and receiving feedback
- Observing other people's actions

Setup

Prepare a "How We Communicate Reflection" handout for each participant (see CD 11E).

Steps

1. Give this introduction: "Imagine you're a group of sociologists sent to study communication in [the organization or office]. As you consider what you have observed, what patterns do you see in the ways people convey, withhold, distort, use, misuse, understand, and misunderstand information?

   "Concentrate on the way most people communicate, not on individual communication styles. Look for anomalies—disparities between what people are trying to communicate and how they're going about it.

   "For example, do managers praise subordinates in private but not in public? Might a subordinate wonder whether the manager really means it?

   "Pay attention to patterns, not to the behaviors of one or two individuals. So you might observe, for example, that 'most people avoid confrontations,' rather than that 'Arlyne and Jim avoid confrontations, but Shari and Dan love to mix it up.' If there's no clear pattern, you might note, for instance, that 'many people seem to dislike confrontations while an equal number seem to relish them.'

   "In a moment I'm going to divide you into small groups. In your group you'll make a list of the five to ten most important questions you want to study from a sociologist's perspective. Look over the examples I'll show you in a moment to get some ideas, but feel free to add to them or to make up your own list."

2. Distribute the How We Communicate Reflection sheet (see CD 11E).

3. Have participants work in groups of three to five to identify and then answer their five to ten most important How We Communicate questions.

4. Ask each group to identify its top three answers—those that seem to give the best idea of what communication is like in the organization—and then write those answers on a flip chart.

5. Invite participants in each subgroup to explain to the whole group why they chose the examples they did and why they think people communicate in the ways they identified.

6. Explore in a whole group discussion the implications for the organization. What might need to change to foster better communication throughout the organization?

Facilitator Note   This activity needs particularly skilled facilitation to guide the group in addressing previously unarticulated—and sensitive—communication issues.

Exploring the Importance of Feedback

"You're cold. You're getting warmer. Now you're hot!" You probably played that game as a child. Without feedback, people may reach their destinations accidentally—and sometimes without even realizing it. More likely, however, is that they'll wander aimlessly, never finding what they're looking for.

People need to know, in a timely manner, specifically how they're doing, what's working well, and what's not. And feedback must be well timed and respectfully delivered. If not, it's not likely to be very effective.

You can use either of the following activities to help participants practice giving and receiving feedback.

Speed Feedback Rounds

Description

This activity provides a means for the participants to receive feedback from their teammates.

Steps

1. Introduce the task: "Giving feedback to colleagues—whether subordinates, higher-ups, or peers—is often very difficult. One reason for this is that we don't want to risk the consequences of how we imagine our colleagues might respond. Yet giving feedback is among the most important things we can do to improve teamwork. We're going to conduct mini-feedback sessions with one another.

    "Feedback can be positive, of course, as well as what many of us think of as negative, but even then we may be reluctant to provide it. 'Will the boss think I'm trying to butter her up?' 'Will my assistant think I want something from him?' 'Will my coworker think I'm not being sincere?'"

2. Go over the Speed Feedback Guide flip chart, and explain that participants should use this guide when giving one another feedback.

Experiential Elements

- Giving and receiving feedback
- Reflection
- Pairs discussion
- Whole group discussion

Setup

- Prepare a "Speed Feedback Guide" flip chart (see Step 2).
- Prepare a "Guidelines for Receiving Feedback" sheet for each participant (see CD 11F).
- Prepare a "My Feedback" sheet for each participant (see CD 11G).
- Prepare a "Responses to My Feedback" sheet for each participant (see CD 11H).

Special Supplies

A pen and notepad for each participant

This activity is adapted from "I Hear That You . . . : Giving and Receiving Feedback," based on material by Drew P. Danko and Rich Cherry, in *Pfeiffer's Classic Activities for Building Better Teams*, and is used with permission.

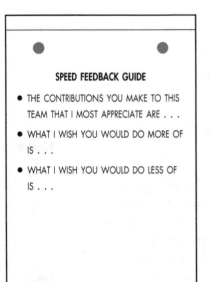

SPEED FEEDBACK GUIDE

- THE CONTRIBUTIONS YOU MAKE TO THIS TEAM THAT I MOST APPRECIATE ARE . . .
- WHAT I WISH YOU WOULD DO MORE OF IS . . .
- WHAT I WISH YOU WOULD DO LESS OF IS . . .

Ask participants to describe specific behaviors—such as, "I wish you would interrupt me less in staff meetings"—rather than attitudes or judgments—such as, "I wish you would be less rude."

3. Tell participants: "You will pair off in rounds with every other person on the team. During each round you will give feedback to and then receive feedback from each other. You will have three minutes each before I will ask you to reverse roles. When you are giving feedback to the person you just received it from, remember that it's feedback, not payback. When you are receiving feedback, you should follow the suggestions on the Guidelines for Receiving Feedback sheet [*see CD 11F*]. I will take a few minutes to go over those guidelines now."

4. Ask participants to write down the feedback they believe they will receive in each of the three categories described in the Speed Feedback Guide flip chart.

5. Have participants form their first pairs. Signal when the three minutes are up for each participant.

6. Hand out the My Feedback sheets (see CD 11G). Give participants one minute to write down the feedback they received.

7. Ask participants to form new pairs.

8. Repeat the process until everyone has spoken with every other member of the team.

9. Hand out the Responses to My Feedback sheets (see CD 11H). Give participants ten minutes to fill them out. Ask participants to reflect on the feedback they received and how it compared to what they expected to hear.

10. Ask participants to summarize the most important things they learned in these speed feedback sessions and to tell the whole group in turn what, specifically, they are willing to do differently (even if that means doing more of a good thing) in response to the feedback.

Facilitator Note   The facilitator must ensure that the groups follow the feedback guidelines and don't engage in attacking one another or in defensive responses to feedback they receive.

How Do I Contribute?

Description

In this activity participants use Post-it Notes to give one another feedback on the roles they each play and wish they would play more of in helping the team to accomplish its goals and team members to work together effectively.

Experiential Elements
- Personal reflection
- Giving and receiving feedback

Steps

1. Introduce the activity: "It is important that we all have an accurate perception of how we help this team accomplish its tasks and work together smoothly. We're going to practice giving one another feedback on the roles each member plays on this team."

2. Hand out the Team Member Behavior Grid (see CD 11J) and the Task and Process Behaviors list (see CD 11K).

Setup

- Make self-adhering labels that represent group member behavior and stick them on separate 3 inch by 5 inch Post-it Notes; make enough so that each participant has one label of each behavior for every member of the group (see CD 11I for the label template—Avery 5162).
- For each participant, prepare one flip chart sheet divided into two columns labeled "My helpful roles" and "Roles my teammates would like me to play," and also write the participant's name on a Post-it Note. Post these charts, with a participant's name on a note above each one, around the room.
- Prepare a "Team Member Behavior Grid" with everyone's name on it for each participant (see CD 11J).
- Make a copy of "Task and Process Behaviors" for each participant (see CD 11K).
- Make a copy of the "Responses to My Feedback" sheet for each participant (see CD 11H).

Special Supplies

- A pad of Post-it Notes, with labels for each participant (see Setup)
- A Sharpie pen for each participant

3. Tell participants: "Please work at your seat and fill out the behavior grid for every member of the team, including yourself. The list of helpful task and process behaviors will get you started, but feel free to add behaviors that are not on the list.

"So that everyone on this team will know the part he or she plays, please write down for each member of the team at least one positive contribution he or she makes to the team and at least one contribution you wish that team member would make or increase. Make sure you include yourself in this. What do you contribute that is positive, and what contributions do you wish you made or made more of to the team?"

4. Tell participants: "When you have completed your grid, copy the feedback onto separate Post-it Notes for each team member. Post your feedback notes in the appropriate column on each person's flip chart, including your own."

5. Hand out the Responses to My Feedback sheet (see CD 11H).

6. When participants have posted their feedback, ask each person to take his flip chart sheet to a quiet corner to reflect and to answer the questions on the Responses to My Feedback sheet.

7. Ask each participant to tell the whole group one behavior she will adopt to increase her contribution to the team. After participants have spoken, they should write that behavior on their own flip chart sheet.

Facilitator Note   This activity needs skilled facilitation to help participants respond thoughtfully to the feedback they receive.

Probing for Sources of Conflict

In many organizations conflict is a taboo subject, as if denying its existence would make it go away or acknowledging it would destroy the illusion of a happy family of coworkers. But conflict is inevitable in any relationship, and it's healthier and actually helpful when it's expressed openly and respectfully, rather than buried. Conflict, like resistance, can act as a reality check on decisions and directions.

Where there is no apparent conflict, there may be apathy. Or conflict may have gone underground, where it can fester and, like a hidden abscess, reemerge in damaging ways at the worst possible times. When dissent and disagreement are not allowed to surface, the organization becomes inflexible and unable to respond to opportunities that might arise. At the same time, you don't want unbridled conflict that turns into personal animosities, name-calling, active or passive resistance, or even open warfare.

Conflict is a natural and healthy response when people deal with issues that are important to them. Trying to suppress it is as futile as it is counterproductive. Conflict leads to tension when it is ignored or denied or when an organization's culture demonizes it as a "bad thing" that is to be avoided. Managing conflict well, however, will often help an organization progress.

Organizations that create a climate of trust at a retreat allow difficult issues to surface. Greater trust helps participants discover better and more satisfying ways of doing their work, which often translates into enhanced collegiality, communication, and cooperation back in the workplace. Managed effectively, the energy that drives conflict can be channeled to foster greater understanding and more respect among colleagues.

The following activity is designed to generate discussion about the impact of conflict on retreat participants.

How Conflict Affects Us

Description

This activity is a facilitated discussion, both in small groups and in the group as a whole, about how people respond to conflict. The design is simple, but the questions provide participants with a framework for discussing difficult issues.

Experiential Elements
- Personal reflection
- Discussion
- Giving and receiving feedback

Steps

1. Distribute one Questions on Conflict sheet to each participant (see CD 11L).

2. Introduce the task: "Please write your answers to the questions on the sheet I just passed out. You will have ten minutes."

3. After the participants complete the sheet, divide them into subgroups of three to five people, and have them discuss what they wrote. Have each group record its members' responses on a flip chart and report to the whole group.

4. Ask the participants to explore the similarities and differences in the various subgroups' responses. Ask: "What do these similarities and differences tell you about the perceptions of conflict in this team?"

Setup

Make one copy of the "Questions on Conflict" sheet for each participant (see CD 11L).

Facilitator Note

It's particularly important for the facilitator to discourage participants from blaming others for conflicts that occur.

The following activity can help retreat participants get to the root of a deep-seated conflict and make a commitment to change for the better.

Taking Responsibility

Description

This activity causes people to reflect individually and in groups about the impact of their own behavior. The group reports are often surprising—and occasionally moving.

Steps

1. Divide participants into subgroups of people who usually work together.

2. Introduce the task: "Everyone here is aware that we have a particular issue we need to grapple with: [name or description of the issue]. Before we can begin to resolve it, we have to understand everyone's role in making this an issue.

   "Working individually and silently, write down your Sources of Satisfaction, that is, the contribution your department [or team] has made toward resolving the issue. Use one Post-it Note for every new idea, and write down as many Sources of Satisfaction items as you can come up with. Then have one person in your subgroup collect all the Post-it Notes."

3. Continue the activity: "Just as you might be pleased about many things your department [or team] has done, there may also be actions your department [or team] has taken in relation to this issue that you regret or wish had been done differently. Please list the things that your department [or team] or you personally have done, or have failed to do, that you regret, again using one Post-it Note for each Sources of Regret item. Give all your ideas to a person in your subgroup (not the same one who collected the Sources of Satisfaction)."

Experiential Elements

- Personal reflection
- Active listening
- Giving and receiving feedback

Setup

Prepare three flip chart pages with the following titles: "Sources of Satisfaction," "Sources of Regret," and "Good Intentions," and post them on the wall.

Special Supplies

A pad of Post-it Notes and a Sharpie pen for each participant

4. Ask the person who collected the Sources of Satisfaction Post-its in each subgroup to read aloud all the items and post them on the appropriate flip chart. Then ask the person who collected the Sources of Regret Post-it Notes to read them aloud and post them on the appropriate flip chart.

5. Now ask the members of each subgroup to list their Good Intentions for the future—the specific actions or changes they are prepared to undertake. Again, each item should be written on a separate Post-it Note.

6. Have a third representative from each subgroup collect and read aloud all the Good Intention items and post them on the appropriate flip chart. Then ask the whole group: "What have you learned from hearing how other groups or individuals view their contributions to this issue? Did you hear anything that surprised you?"

After facilitating the discussion on contributions and surprises, ask: "Are there some Good Intentions that you can all agree on?" Record participants' ideas on a flip chart, and seek consensus from the group.

Facilitator Notes
- You'll need to be prepared to deal with any defensiveness that might crop up during the discussions about Sources of Regret. In addition, during the Good Intentions discussions you may need to prod participants to come up with specific actions (not just changes in attitude) they will commit to take.

- The results of this activity are easy to integrate into the workplace after the retreat. The participants can take the three flip charts listing the Sources of Satisfaction, Sources of Regret, and Good Intentions back to the office and leave them posted on a wall for a week or two. You might suggest that the organization use the technique of asking for Sources of Satisfaction, Sources of Regret, and Good Intentions to begin meetings that include issues about which people or groups have different views and have taken opposing positions.

The following activity can help participants understand their personal conflict triggers and plan their responses in a measured way.

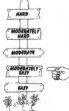

My Conflict Triggers

Description

This activity allows participants to reflect on the conflict cycles that trap them into unproductive behaviors. After reflection, participants work in pairs to get feedback on how they might more effectively handle conflict that triggers their "hot buttons."

Experiential Elements

- Personal reflection
- Pairs discussion
- Whole group discussion

Steps

1. Distribute and review the Conflict Cycle model (see CD 11M), and illustrate it with examples from your own experience.

    You might say something like this: "One of my emotional triggers is when someone ignores me. A conflict I had with a colleague, Chuck, occurred because I told him that I needed some information from him by the following Friday to complete a report that our boss, Debby, had requested. Although I raised this with Chuck several times, he never gave me the information or explained why he wouldn't or couldn't provide it.

    "The perceived threat was that I was going to look incompetent to Debby, and I didn't want to be in the position of having to complain to her about Chuck. I assumed that Chuck didn't care about my needs or about maintaining a productive relationship with me. I assumed he had other priorities but hadn't bothered to explain what they were. I felt angry and hurt that Chuck didn't care enough about me to deal with my concerns.

    "I responded by withdrawing from Chuck and sending copies of the e-mails I had sent to him to Debby. I told Debby that the report was complete except for what was missing from Chuck and asked her to intercede on my behalf.

Setup

- Make one copy of the "Conflict Cycle" model for each participant (see CD 11M).
- Make one copy of the "My Conflict Triggers Reflection" sheet for each participant (see CD 11N).

This activity is adapted from "Retaliatory Cycle: Introducing the Elements of Conflict," by Daniel Dana, in *Pfeiffer's Classic Activities for Managing Conflict at Work*, and is used with permission.

"Chuck was furious with me for taking this matter to our boss. He said that I had purposely tried to make him look bad and that I had no consideration for the other work he had to do that was more urgent.

"I decided that I needed to repair this relationship, so I let a little time pass and then invited Chuck for coffee. I asked him how I might have handled the situation in a more productive way and how we might negotiate schedules when we have conflicting pressures. We decided that in the future we would ask Debby to help us prioritize work with tight deadlines, so each of us would be working on highest priority tasks. We developed a much more congenial working relationship after that."

2. Distribute one My Conflict Triggers worksheet to each participant (see CD 11N).

3. Introduce the task: "Please write your answers to the questions on the worksheet I just passed out. You will have ten minutes."

4. After the participants complete their worksheets, ask them to form pairs. If there are an odd number of participants, you might pair up with one of them or have three participants form a trio.

5. Instruct the pairs to go over their worksheets in turn. The person who is listening should help draw out his partner on the emotional triggers. Has the person speaking identified all his hot buttons? The person listening should also ask the person speaking questions about what more he might have done to resolve the conflict and maintain a positive relationship.

6. Ask the group to analyze the conflict you talked about in terms of the model. Then ask a participant to volunteer to tell the whole group about her conflict situation. Have the group help complete the cycle from the other person's perspective. What might have been that person's emotional triggers? What might have been the perceived threat? What emotions might that person have been feeling? How did that person respond? How might that person perceive that the participant had escalated the conflict? What can we learn from this about not letting emotional conflict get out of hand?

7. Ask each participant to reflect on what the other person's conflict triggers might have been for their own conflict situation and what steps he or she might take to create a more productive working relationship.

Facilitator Note It's particularly important for the facilitator to encourage participants to be reflective both about what triggers them to respond to conflict in nonproductive ways and about strategies that might be more effective.

Exploring How Individuals Can
Change Their Own Behaviors

The following activity will help individuals and work groups bring to the surface issues that may have blocked effective working relationships.

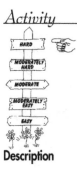

Star Performers

Description

Participants are asked to list the individual talents that help them be effective at work and the individual traits that hinder their effectiveness. They then participate in a role play, presenting themselves to others in the group as one of the hindering characteristics. Individual reflection and group discussion follow to examine what might be different for the participants and the organization if people didn't feel a need to hide hindering characteristics.

Experiential Elements
- Personal reflection
- Participating in role play and improvisation
- Experimentation

Setup
- Prepare a "My Talents" flip chart (see Step 2).
- Prepare a "Things That Hinder Me" flip chart (see Step 4).

Special Supplies

For each participant, a brightly colored sheet of paper on which you have printed the outline of a large five-pointed star on the front and back (see CD 110 for a template), large enough for participants to write a word or two on each point of the star. (If you are feeling particularly ambitious, you can cut out the stars.)

Steps

1. Distribute one sheet of paper with a star printed on both sides (or one cut-out star) to each participant.

2. Introduce the task: "We will be looking at some of the talents we possess that help us do our work successfully, as well as some of the traits we have that may hinder our effectiveness." Display the My Talents flip chart:

MY TALENTS
WRITE ONE TALENT IN EACH POINT OF THE STAR.

GIFT
GIFT   GIFT
GIFT GIFT

3. Explain: "Write down your five most significant personal talents, one on each point of the star on your paper. Choose the five that most help you achieve success in the workplace. For instance, you might write things like 'helpful to others,' 'good presenter,' 'creative thinker,' or 'positive outlook.'"

4. After the participants have written their five talents, display the Things That Hinder Me flip chart:

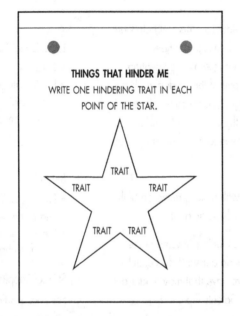

5. Say: "Now flip your papers [or your stars (*if they're cutouts*)] over. On each point of the star on the other side of your paper [or cut-out], write a trait that defines a bit about who you are but that may *hamper* your effectiveness at work. For instance, you might write things like 'perfectionist,' 'dislike details,' 'impatient with others,' or 'avoid conflict.'"

6. Introduce the next task: "Even if we recognize that these traits we identified do not help us at work or in life, most of us are also aware that at least one of them defines a bit of who we are. We may be proud of this trait even though we know it gets in our way. For example, I might say, 'I'm a perfectionist [*substitute your own example here*], and although I know I stay up too many nights fussing over the details of some project, I'm kind of proud of my high standards.' Or I might say, 'I need to be right, and I know that sometimes my coworkers see me as a know-it-all, but the truth is, I do like to be right.' Or, 'I'd rather be spontaneous than plan ahead.' So think about what your principal hindering characteristic is, and circle it on your star."

7. Tell participants: "Now pretend that this gathering is a party and that you want to meet as many people as possible. Each of you will stand, mill about, and introduce yourself to everyone else in the room, not by your job title but as the hindering trait that most gets in your way. So a person might say, 'Hi, my name is Carol, and I need to be right'; 'Hi, I'm Frank, and I'm a perfectionist'; or, 'Hello, my name is Ken, and I don't plan ahead.' After introducing yourself, move on as quickly as possible to the next person at the party." Verify that everyone understands the instructions.

8. After two or three minutes, have the participants return to their seats. Ask them to write down their personal reflections: "Take a moment to write down how you felt when you introduced yourself to others as a characteristic that you perceive hinders you. Also write down the feelings you had when others introduced themselves to you as a characteristic that hinders them. Finally, write down the feelings you had if someone introduced himself or herself to you as a characteristic you share."

9. Ask participants to take a moment to reflect on why a particular characteristic seems to exert an influence over them and whether this is a characteristic they would normally disclose about themselves. If not, why not?

10. Ask the participants to think about how the energy changed in the room when people started introducing themselves by characteristics that hinder their effectiveness. Ask participants: "Imagine what would happen if you all could be more forthcoming about acknowledging areas in which you could stand to improve:

   • "How might things change for you personally?

   • "How might your relationships with colleagues change?

   • "How might this enhance your effectiveness at work?"

11. Finally, invite participants to share their experiences: "Would a few people be willing to tell us what they learned when reflecting on this activity? Might you deal with some of the traits that hinder your effectiveness in a different way now, based on what you learned?"

Facilitator Notes
   • This activity requires particularly sensitive facilitation to encourage people to disclose their talents and hindering traits. When it is led in a lighthearted, judgment-free manner, participants can gain considerable insight.

   • This activity requires that participants open up to one another. Don't use it in a group where there is low trust.

   • Suggest that people report occasionally to others back at work (at meetings, for example, or informally) on progress they have made in letting go of habits that hinder their effectiveness and that they also ask for feedback on how successful they've been.

Collaborative Decision Making

See Chapter 8, "Methods of Decision Making," pp. 162–168, for a discussion of decision-making processes.

Teams need to know how they will make decisions, and should have methods for making them effectively. The following activity will help the team explore the dynamics of collaborative decision making and learn just how collaborative they are when making decisions.

Incident at Coyote Canyon

Description

A subgroup of retreat participants make up an ad hoc team to carry out a specific task under the watchful eyes of the rest of the group, who will be looking for specific behaviors related to collaboration and decision making. The observers record the noteworthy behaviors that help or hinder the group in its task. After the activity all retreat participants discuss the observations and draw conclusions about how they collaborate and make decisions at work.

Experiential Elements

- Unstructured interactivity
- Observation of others' actions
- Small and whole group discussions

Steps

1. Ask half the group (up to ten people) to volunteer to be the "task participants" who will take part in a decision-making activity. Encourage quieter participants to volunteer. Or randomly select the task participants. (Random selection increases the likelihood of a representative sample of the whole group.)

2. Instruct the task participants that they will not be playing roles but acting as themselves in dealing with the task they will be given. Tell them they should behave in ways that are typical for them, not in any atypical ways.

3. Have the task participants sit anywhere they want in the inner circle, and ask the rest of the retreat participants to arrange themselves anywhere they want in the outer circle.

Setup

- Prepare a copy of "Incident at Coyote Canyon Scenario" for each participant (see CD 11P).
- Prepare a copy of "Anthropologist's Notes" for each observer (see CD 11Q).
- Have participants arrange chairs in two concentric circles, an inner circle with enough chairs for the task participants and an outer circle with enough chairs for the observers. (Use no more than ten task participants. If there are more than twenty people in the whole group, ten should be task participants and the rest observers.)

Special Supplies

Pens and notepads for all participants

4. Tell the task participants: "This is the task. I will give you a story to read, and you will have ten minutes to read it and twenty minutes to determine as a group who among the characters is most *ethically* responsible for how the events played out and who is least *ethically* responsible. You must take everyone's opinion into account and achieve consensus without voting."

    Do not embellish these instructions. If the activity participants ask clarifying questions, repeat the instructions and add, "That is all I can tell you."

5. Distribute the Incident at Coyote Canyon Scenario (see CD 11O). Give task participants and observers ten minutes to read the story.

6. Give each observer a copy of the Anthropologist's Notes (see CD 11P). Tell the observers: "You will be acting as anthropologists. This handout will prompt you to look for and record examples of certain behaviors. Please do so silently."

7. After twenty minutes, declare that the activity is over, whether or not the task participants have achieved consensus. (In the unlikely event that the task participants come to agreement in less than twenty minutes, declare the activity over at that point.)

8. Facilitate a debriefing by the observers, who will use the questions on the Anthropologist's Notes sheet.

9. Ask the task participants to contribute their own thoughts about their behavior and about the points made by the observers.

Facilitator Notes
- The facilitator must be able to lead a discussion among observers, who may be making comments that task participants might consider critical of them or of their performance, and task participants, who might be frustrated at not being clear on what they were supposed to do, at not having enough time to complete their task, or at not being able to convince others of their points of view. The discussion is likely to focus on the "answers," and why task participants felt that this character or that one was more or less responsible for the outcome of the scenario. The facilitator will have to refocus the group on the process and the insights the group might have gained about collaboration and decision making.

- There are no "right" solutions in this activity; in fact the task participants are unlikely to reach consensus, which is fine.

- The instructions to the participants are minimal, and there may be as much discussion among the task participants about what they are supposed to do as about the task itself. (This never happens in real life, does it?)

Incident at Coyote Canyon in Practice

We used this activity to great effect at a retreat for a large group that we divided into smaller breakouts. All the breakout groups believed that their conclusions were correct and thus were quite surprised at how strongly other groups felt about their differing decisions.

We asked the groups that came to strong agreement to talk about what worked for them, and the groups that couldn't achieve consensus to talk about the process they used. Not surprisingly, these processes mirrored those that typically played out in real decision making in the organization.

Other Suggested Activities for a Team-Building Retreat

You will find other activities to incorporate into a team-building retreat in the Activities for Culture Change, Team-Building, and Board Retreats index (p. 493) and the Activities to Use in Any Retreat index (p. 490).

Chapter 12

Leading a Creativity and Innovation Retreat

One hallmark of a successful organization is that it continually seeks innovative ways to improve its products, services, and processes to lower costs, retain current customers, and attract new ones. But where will the creative thinkers come from? Chances are they're already working in your client's organization. And not just in jobs that are generally thought of as requiring creativity.

Human brains are wired for creativity. Each of us is a natural problem solver. Watch young children at play: an everyday object becomes a spacecraft. A spoon is a snowball catapult. A cardboard box is a sports car. But by the time most of us enter the workplace, we have learned to follow rules and procedures. We are often too self-conscious to risk suggesting an unconventional idea. Moreover, most of us tend to see ourselves as either creative or not. If we don't think we're creative, we are likely to leave the innovation to others.

Yet creative thinking is a skill that can be recaptured and—like most skills—improved with practice. Just as people learn to drive a car, play soccer, or win at bridge—and to become better at these things by doing them over and over—they can learn to sharpen their creative thinking skills.

If you want to learn more about creative thinking techniques, we recommend these resources:

- *The Big Book of Creativity Games,* by Robert Epstein (2000).

- *Jump Start Your Brain,* by Doug Hall (1996).

- *De Bono's Thinking Course* (revised edition), by Edward de Bono (1994).

- *Thinkertoys,* by Michael Michalko (1991).

- *101 Activities for Teaching Creativity and Problem Solving,* by Arthur B. VanGundy (2005).

- *Orchestrating Collaboration at Work,* by Arthur B. VanGundy and Linda Naiman (2003).

- *A Kick in the Seat of the Pants,* by Roger von Oech (1986).

- *A Whack on the Side of the Head,* by Roger von Oech (1998).

Preparing Participants to Think Creatively

There are three types of thinking involved in creating fresh approaches to old problems. A good creativity retreat will engage all three.

The first is *synthetic thinking.* This thinking allows us to see novel connections and redefine problems. A wonderful example of synthetic thinking comes from the hotel industry. Years ago executives at a major hotel chain spent a fortune on studies trying to figure out how to get the hotel elevators to move faster in response to frequent customer complaints that "they were just too slow." They looked at the costs of retrofitting the elevators with different motors and pulleys or of adding banks of elevators to all their hotels and found them prohibitive. Somehow someone realized that the problem wasn't that the elevators weren't fast enough but that customers became bored waiting for them. This led to synthetic thinking about what would help engage customers while waiting for the elevators. And *voilà,* mirrors started appearing outside elevator doors. After the mirrors were installed, the hotel chain had many fewer complaints about the elevators.

The second dimension is *analytic thinking.* This thinking allows us to evaluate the value or potential in an idea. Many of us are very skilled at this kind of thinking, also called *judging*. So skilled, in fact, that we often kill potentially brilliant ideas before they ever see the light of day. One of your major jobs in structuring a creativity retreat is to help participants separate synthetic thinking from analytic thinking. If every time a participant generates an idea someone else engages in premature analytic thinking about why that idea won't work, there will be less effective synthetic and analytic thinking throughout the retreat. (And often we squelch our own synthetic ideas with our own analytic thinking.)

The third type of thinking needed for a creativity retreat is *practical thinking*. This is the thinking that leads us to see how we might implement the ideas we generate.

These three types of thinking are relatively independent of one another. We may be very good at one of these thinking dimensions and have much more

How Creative People Think

They generate many ideas. A study at University of California at Davis found that most well-known scientists have many more bad ideas than good ones; it's just that they're not famous for the bad ones. Similarly, baseball legend Babe Ruth struck out a record number of times in his career, but it's his home run record he's famous for.

They aren't discouraged by failure. When Einstein was asked the difference between the way he thought and how others thought, he used the image of trying to find the proverbial needle in a haystack: he would just keep looking.

They use metaphor and other visual stimuli. Einstein imagined himself on a beam of light to visualize the theory of relativity. By thinking metaphorically he could see patterns and relationships.

They make novel combinations. Picasso did not start from a blank page when coming up with analytical cubism; he learned from the work of Paul Cézanne.

They synthesize ideas from unrelated fields. Samuel Morse developed the telegraph but couldn't figure out how to make the signal strong enough to go long distances. He saw horses being exchanged at a relay station and was inspired to put power boosting stations along the way.

They play with paradox and ambiguity. Truly creative thinkers can hold opposing ideas in their minds. The physicist Niels Bohr was able to conceive of light as a particle and a wave at the same time, even though that didn't "make sense."

They give themselves quotas and goals. Edison had a goal of one minor invention every ten days and one major invention every six months.

difficulty with the others. A well-structured creativity retreat will help participants practice and strengthen all three aspects of the thinking necessary to develop innovative approaches to thorny issues.

In a creativity retreat some participants may worry about appearing foolish. But you can help them see that just as stretching is important to an athlete before exercising, playing with unusual ideas is critical to loosening up our thinking muscles and releasing people's innate ability to exercise their creativity.

A revered ballet master was once asked—while looking at a class of three- and four-year-olds taking their first dance lessons—whether he could predict which would become great dancers. "Oh, yes," he said, "it's quite simple. You look for the ones who fling themselves around the room and make utter fools of themselves. They are the ones who will do *anything* to be great."

These next activities will help participants mentally "fling themselves around the room" so they can limber up their creative thinking muscles.

Creative Limbering

Description

Participants use Limbering Free Associations sheets to make creative associations that will move them as far away from the original idea as possible.

Steps

1. Give each participant a Limbering Free Associations sheet with one word or phrase from the Limbering Stream on the top (see CD 12A and 12B).

2. Introduce the activity: "Starting with the word on the top of your Limbering Free Associations sheet, you will work in silence to create twenty free associations, trying with each association to move further away from the original idea, but building on associations that the idea brings up for you.

   "Here's how this might work. Let's say my sheet has *a flat tire* on the top. I might say, 'That makes me think of *automobile,* and that makes me think of *accident,* and that makes me think of *roadside assistance,* and that makes me think of *waiting in the car,* and that makes me think of *a dark road,* and that makes me think of *being afraid.*'

   "Or I might say, 'That makes me think of *automobile,* and that makes me think of *sports car,* and that makes me think of *Silvio's Lamborghini,* and that makes me think of *Italy,* and that makes me think of *pizza,* and that makes me think of *what I had for lunch yesterday.*'"

3. Ask participants to note the differences between these two examples. In which did you move further from the original idea? Go over your second example again and help participants identify the "left turns" you took. Left turns are the points where your associations, while building on one another, took you away from the original concept of the flat tire. For example, they might notice how *sports car* led you to *Silvio's Lamborghini,* which led you to *Italy.*

Experiential Elements

- Reflection
- Envisioning possibilities and generating new ideas
- Small group discussion
- Whole group discussion

Setup

Create one "Limbering Free Associations" sheet for each participant by sticking one "Limbering Stream" word or phrase label on the top of each sheet (see CD 12A and 12B).

4. Tell participants: "For this exercise, you should try to take as many left turns as possible. And don't censor your ideas. Keep your pen moving and write the first association that comes to your mind, no matter how wacky."

5. Give participants five minutes to write their associations.

6. Divide the participants into subgroups of about five people. Have them read their associations to one another, take note of the left turns, and then select the limbering sheet in their group that moved furthest away from the original idea to read to the whole group.

7. As each subgroup presents to the whole group the limbering sheet that moved furthest from the original idea, encourage participants to notice the left turns.

8. Facilitate a discussion in which participants talk about the value of the left turns in generating fresh ideas.

Creative Limbering in Practice

We often use this exercise to warm people up when it's important for them to think differently. But it has other uses as well. In the process of making free associations, participants tap into their own experiences and memories and unleash their own unique ways of making mental connections. As a result, Creative Limbering helps team members come to know each other better. That's not its purpose, but it's a very useful side benefit.

How Would I Use It?

Description Participants think of as many uses for a coffee mug as possible.

Steps

1. Give each participant a pad of Post-it Notes and a Sharpie pen.

2. Introduce the activity: "We're going to try to come up with as many uses as possible for this coffee mug. Can you tell me some uses that you can think of?"

3. Note participants' responses on a flip chart.

4. Ask participants: "To help yourself come up with more uses, imagine you are someone else. How might Martha Stewart use this coffee cup? How might a dentist use this coffee cup? How might a choreographer use this coffee cup?"

5. Note the participants' responses on a flip chart.

6. Tell participants: "You'll have five minutes to come up with at least thirty ideas for how to use a coffee cup. Write the ideas on Post-it Notes, one idea per note. Let yourself have some fun coming up with some unconventional uses for this cup."

7. Divide the participants into subgroups of about five people. Have them read the uses they come up with, and post their responses on a flip chart.

Experiential Elements

- Writing down ideas individually
- Envisioning possibilities and generating new ideas
- Breakout group discussion
- Listening to others

Setup

- A pad of Post-it Notes and a Sharpie pen for each participant
- A coffee mug

This activity is adapted from "Getting Ready: Different Uses Warm-Up Exercise," in *101 Activities for Teaching Creativity and Problem Solving*, by Arthur B. VanGundy, and is used with permission.

8. Ask the subgroups to categorize the uses. The uses might fall into categories such as these:

   - To hold liquid foods

   - To hold solid foods

   - To hold nonfood items

   - To construct something

   - To weigh something down

   - To prop something up

   - To protect oneself

9. Ask the subgroups to use the categories to come up with more ideas for using the cup.

10. Tell participants: "If you expanded your thinking, you may have come up with some unusual categories that involved, for example, altering the cup in some way. You might have painted it with the company's logo and given it away as a prize. Or you might have crushed the cup and spread it on your sidewalk to give you better traction in the snow."

11. Facilitate a discussion of any unusual categories the participants came up with and how the more unusual categories generated more interesting ideas.

Generating Wacky Ideas

Most people's primary experience with creative thinking is through *brainstorming* (a method for generating ideas developed in the 1950s by advertising executive Alex Osborn), so chances are your client will assume that a creative thinking retreat is basically a long brainstorming session. If this point comes up in your discussions, encourage her to think back to the last brainstorming session she participated in. Your client may have enjoyed the fun and high energy and thought that the session generated lots of ideas. But chances are, the group didn't come up with nearly the quantity and breadth of ideas it was capable of.

Why not?

Because people are often so concerned with what others will think that they don't articulate their most audacious ideas. Because groups fall in love with an idea too soon and group members stop pushing themselves for more. Because quieter, more reflective people can easily be ignored or can "hide out" in a group setting. Because people who are in positions of authority or who are the most aggressive often intimidate others and carry the day, even if they don't have the most original or useful ideas.

> For a discussion of the Big Kahuna Effect, see Chapter 3, "Sins of Omission: The Top Retreat Design Mistakes," pp. 62–65.)

Or perhaps most important, because people are *talking*. When do you get your best ideas? Many people say, "in the shower," or, "driving in my car," or, "just before I fall asleep." In other words, when they're *not talking*. Recent research provides a neurological explanation for this phenomenon. Human speech centers are primarily located on the left side of the brain, and intuitive and creative thinking are primarily right-side functions. The more we talk, the less likely we are to come up with big new ideas. Basically, the left side of the brain drowns out the right side. To be creative, we need some silence.

Here is an alternative to traditional brainstorming, a way of fostering creative thinking that uses the power of silence and gets everyone's ideas on the table.

> "Genius is 1 percent inspiration and 99 percent perspiration. As a result, a genius is often a talented person who has simply done all of his homework." —Thomas Edison

Wide-Open Thinking

Description

This activity introduces a new way of coming up with solutions to a problem. Individuals write their ideas on Post-it Notes in silence, generating as many ideas as possible. In small groups, participants then share their ideas and post them on flip charts. This is an extremely lively activity that generates good humor while still addressing real issues.

Experiential Elements

- Writing down ideas individually
- Envisioning possibilities and generating new ideas
- Breakout group discussion
- Listening to others

Setup

- Prepare the two "Organizations" flip charts (see Step 4).
- Provide each subgroup with its own flip chart or tape blank flip chart pages near each table.

Special Supplies

A pad of Post-it Notes and a Sharpie pen for each participant

Steps

1. Divide the participants into subgroups of five to eight people. Introduce the task: "Coming up with lots of new ideas should be easy, but usually it is not. Typically, we think of a few ideas and then dissect, evaluate, and either accept or reject them. What we end up with is rarely the best we could do if we knew more about idea-generation technique, which is what we're going to focus on in this activity."

2. Introduce the issue by presenting a current problem or simple question for the group to think about. Tell participants: "Let's take a look at [the issue]." This issue should be a real one for the participants—such as, "How can you improve employee morale?"—and it must be open-ended enough to have many possible solutions.

3. Say: "I'd like each of you to write the names of five organizations that you feel have a lot of character and personality and that anyone in the room would recognize. For instance, Nike or the *New York Times* would probably conjure up a vivid image for anyone here, but a small regional company or a niche magazine would not. You can choose any organization, in any area of human endeavor. Here are some examples."

4. Show the two Organizations flip charts.

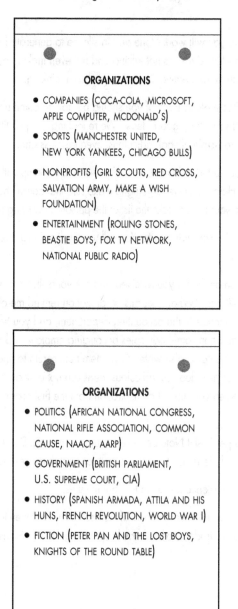

ORGANIZATIONS

- COMPANIES (COCA-COLA, MICROSOFT, APPLE COMPUTER, MCDONALD'S)
- SPORTS (MANCHESTER UNITED, NEW YORK YANKEES, CHICAGO BULLS)
- NONPROFITS (GIRL SCOUTS, RED CROSS, SALVATION ARMY, MAKE A WISH FOUNDATION)
- ENTERTAINMENT (ROLLING STONES, BEASTIE BOYS, FOX TV NETWORK, NATIONAL PUBLIC RADIO)

ORGANIZATIONS

- POLITICS (AFRICAN NATIONAL CONGRESS, NATIONAL RIFLE ASSOCIATION, COMMON CAUSE, NAACP, AARP)
- GOVERNMENT (BRITISH PARLIAMENT, U.S. SUPREME COURT, CIA)
- HISTORY (SPANISH ARMADA, ATTILA AND HIS HUNS, FRENCH REVOLUTION, WORLD WAR I)
- FICTION (PETER PAN AND THE LOST BOYS, KNIGHTS OF THE ROUND TABLE)

5. Tell participants to write their list of five organizations on one Post-it Note. When they have finished, they should set their lists aside.

6. Define the procedure: "Each of you will work alone and in silence to generate ideas to address [the issue the group identified]. 'In silence' means not talking and not even making eye contact with each other. Your silence will facilitate more creative, intuitive, right-brain thinking.

   "You will write one idea per Post-it Note. Each of you should be able to come up with at least thirty ideas. Please note that I didn't say, 'thirty *good* ideas.' We're looking for quantity at this stage, so any idea will do, including silly, impossible, illegal, ridiculous, even tasteless ones.

   "If I gave you the issue and you started right now, most of you would come up with only six or seven ideas, and then you would be stuck. Here's how we're going to make sure that doesn't happen. Give your list of organizations to the person on your left and take the list of the person on your right.

   "Now you should each have a list you didn't write. You will use this list of organizations to help spark new ideas.

   "Start with the first organization on the list you received and ask yourself, 'How would this organization go about solving this problem?' and, 'What does this organization remind me of?' For instance, if the problem were how to improve morale in the accounting department, and you have the CIA on your list, you might write, 'Give rewards when somebody spies accounting employees doing something helpful,' which could be a good idea. You could also write, 'Give them truth serum to find out what the real problems are.' Now that is an outlandish idea, but ridiculous ideas are not only acceptable but very valuable at this stage of the process. When you run out of inspiration from the first organization on your list, move on to the next one.

   "Remember to write one idea per Post-it Note and keep your pen moving. Don't censor your ideas. Focus on quantity, not quality, of ideas. Try to come up with at least thirty fresh ideas."

7. Allow the participants to work in silence for seven to eight minutes.

8. Ask participants to read their ideas to other members of their subgroup and then to stick the Post-it Notes on a flip chart. When people read their ideas, others may keep writing, as new ideas are sparked by what they're hearing.

9. After all the ideas have been read and posted, ask each group to discuss those that are the most appealing to its members, considering these questions:

- "Are there common themes?"

- "Could some ideas be combined?"

- "Can you improve on some of the ideas?"

- "Can you take a really bad idea and turn it into a good one?"

10. Ask each subgroup to share its members' best ideas. Facilitate a discussion around these questions:

- "Which ideas might be implemented?"

- "What conditions helped you be more creative in this activity?"

- "Is there anything about how you worked that you want to take back to the office?"

Facilitator Notes
- Create a lighthearted atmosphere that helps participants enjoy the playfulness of this activity.

- Using the names of organizations helps spur new ideas that people might not normally feel free to express—or even think of. Suggest that participants tell other members of their breakout groups which organizations they had in mind as they generated their ideas.

- The target of thirty ideas is given only so that people won't stop working after they have a few ideas they like. Urging the participants to write down thirty ideas encourages them to stretch to come up with some illogical ideas. Most people, however, will not actually reach the target of thirty ideas in the time allotted.

- It's important to celebrate the potential usefulness even of the bad ideas. Encourage participants to take their most bizarre ideas and turn them into good ones.

- A variation of this activity is to have the facilitator generate the lists of organizations in advance and cut them into strips (one name per strip) that are scattered around each table. In this variation, when the participants have exhausted the possibilities that one name triggers, they grab another name strip from the table.

Wide-Open Thinking in Practice

We used this exercise with a group of engineers who needed to improve their operational efficiency in response to budget cutbacks. They were skeptical at first; they thought of themselves as analytical, not creative. But they took pride in their abilities as problem solvers. By the end of one round they had resolved a major storage problem by rethinking their entire concept of how materials can be warehoused and by imagining new uses for existing structures surrounding their plant.

They were so surprised at their results (they had been thinking about these issues for a long time) that they subsequently began using this and similar techniques at their monthly status meetings.

Wacky ideas generated when people are mentally flinging themselves around the room often contain the germ of something brilliant. These next activities reinforce participants' willingness to take the risks necessary to come up with extraordinary ideas.

Really Bad Ideas

Description

Participants identify an issue or problem and come up with possible solutions by, first, reversing the problem and thinking about how to make the situation worse, and only then thinking about how they can make it better.

Experiential Elements

- Small group discussion
- Listening
- Reflecting on prior experiences
- Envisioning possibilities and generating new ideas

Steps

1. Have the whole group agree on a clear and concise statement of a vital problem or issue. For example: "Our procedures for dealing with customer complaints are too labor intensive."

2. Reverse the problem statement and present it to the whole group. For example: "Our customer relations procedures are not labor intensive enough."

3. Divide the participants into subgroups of three to five people. Have the participants—working alone and in silence—write down as many ideas as they can that would solve the reverse of the real problem, that is, ideas that would make the real problem worse. (For example, they might work on this question, "How can you make your customer relations procedures as labor intensive and unproductive as possible?") Allow five minutes for participants to write, one idea per Post-it Note.

Encourage people to be really silly in generating these ideas. (For the example being used here, ideas might include ordering minute-by-minute reports on customer complaints, requiring that every customer complaint be routed to a supervisor for assignment back to someone to work on the problem, or urging customers to set up picket lines at your company's headquarters until their issues are resolved.)

Setup

A pad of Post-it Notes and a Sharpie pen for each participant

4. Have participants read their ideas to one another, and post the notes on a flip chart. Then each group should take two or three of the ideas and discuss how their opposites might generate practical ideas to address the real issue. For example, if making the problem worse would require minute-by-minute reporting, maybe there's a way to eliminate some existing routine reports that take a lot of time to produce. If requiring a supervisor's approval in advance would make things worse, maybe freeing employees to solve more problems themselves would improve the process.

5. Lead a whole group discussion about the ideas raised in the subgroups.

Facilitator Note It's important for the facilitator to create an environment in which participants feel free to come up with "really bad" ideas.

Really Bad Ideas in Practice

We introduced this activity at a retreat for a nonprofit cultural facility whose staff had tried without success to engage members of the diverse community surrounding the center. The participants conceived of some outrageous ways to ensure that community residents would never feel welcome in their building and then turned those ideas around to generate concrete plans to create a more inviting gathering place for the community.

Villains in Charge

Description

Participants identify "evil" characters in history or fiction and put them in charge of solving a problem.

Steps

1. Have the whole group agree on a clear and concise statement of a vital problem or issue. For example: "We have too many customer complaints about the cost of our service."

2. Introduce the activity: "We've decided we need some tough-minded outsiders to help us resolve this problem. We are authorized to create a task force of villains from history or fiction who will compel us to face some harsh realities so we can solve this problem once and for all."

3. Ask the group: "Whom do we want on this task force? I hear that Boris Badanov might be willing to participate. Or how about Iago? Or Attila the Hun? Or Snow White's wicked stepmother? We must recruit five or six 'villains' who will be willing to tell us what we really need to hear. Whom should we approach for this task?"

4. Record the group's suggestions. Once the group has identified several villains, you can move on.

5. Divide the participants into subgroups of about five people.

6. Ask each member of each subgroup to select a different villain to engage with; these villains do not have to be on the whole group's list.

7. Once each subgroup member has identified his or her villain, the participants—working alone and in silence—write down as many "villainous" suggestions as possible to solve the problem, one suggestion per Post-it Note. Allow five minutes.

Encourage people to allow themselves to be really outrageous in generating their villainous suggestions. Such suggestions might include poisoning customers who complain or retrofitting the products that customers complain about with self-destructing devices or moving all the company's assets into numbered Swiss bank accounts.

Experiential Elements

- Writing down ideas individually
- Envisioning possibilities and generating new ideas
- Breakout group discussion
- Listening to others

Special Supplies

A pad of Post-it Notes and a Sharpie pen for each participant

8. Participants should listen to all the ideas generated in their subgroup; each person should read his or her ideas aloud in turn and then stick the Post-it Notes on a flip chart.

9. Ask each group to take two or three of the villains' outrageous ideas and discuss how they might generate practical positive ideas to address the real issue. For example, if a villain suggested poisoning the customers, what else might the company give customers—rather than poison—that might reduce the number of customer complaints?

10. Have each subgroup present its ideas.

11. Lead a whole group discussion about the suggestions raised in the subgroups.

Facilitator Note It's important for the facilitator to create an environment in which participants feel free to embody the characters of their villains.

Villains in Charge in Practice

We used this activity in a retreat for a company whose CEO was known to be mercurial. His volatile temper had contributed to a culture in which most employees were afraid to speak their minds publicly. We had heard many positive suggestions for improving work processes in our confidential interviews, yet no one was willing to speak them aloud. With the help of Villains in Charge, many of these excellent ideas (and others that no one had thought of before) emerged.

It's Music to My Ears

Description

Participants look for clues in musical passages to address an issue they are facing.

Steps

1. Have the whole group agree on a clear and concise statement of a vital problem or issue.

2. Introduce the activity: "We're going to take inspiration from the music we are about to hear to see what insights we gain that might help us address this issue."

3. Play the musical selection. Ask the participants to jot down any general associations from the music. What do they notice about the mood or tempo or complexity of the music?

4. Play the musical selection again. Ask the participants to focus on what the music might mean for the problem at hand. For example, does a sudden change in tempo mean that it's necessary to prepare for the future so that there are no unpleasant surprises? Does a slow passage indicate the need to proceed with caution? Do complex chord patterns indicate the need to leverage the company's diversity more fully?

5. Divide the participants into subgroups of about five people.

6. Ask the subgroups to use the associations from the music to come up with answers to the problem they are working on.

7. Have each subgroup present its ideas.

Experiential Elements

- Listening to music
- Individual reflection
- Envisioning possibilities and generating new ideas
- Breakout group discussion

Special Supplies

- A CD player and a CD of music that has some complexity to it
- A pad of paper and pen for each participant

This activity is adapted from "Music Mania," in *101 Activities for Teaching Creativity and Problem Solving*, by Arthur B. VanGundy, and is used with permission.

Headline Buzz

Description

Participants come up with problem solutions that are worthy of a tabloid headline.

Steps

1. Divide the group into subgroups of about five participants each.

2. Give each subgroup a few tabloids, such as the *National Enquirer, Star, Globe,* and *National Examiner,* and ask the participants to take note of the headlines that are particularly intriguing or amusing to them.

3. Have the whole group agree on a clear and concise statement of a vital problem or issue. A nonprofit theater company might say, for example: "We need to find innovative, money-making uses for our theater space when we're not using it for our productions."

4. Introduce the activity: "Take inspiration from these tabloids to generate some headlines of your own. These headlines should be just as outlandish as the headlines you just read in these tabloids. We're looking for headlines such as, 'Herd of Three-Head Rhinos in Face-Off with Invaders from Mars.'"

5. The participants—working alone and in silence—write down as many sensational tabloid-style headlines as they can think of, one headline per Post-it Note. Allow five minutes.

6. Participants should listen to all the headlines generated in their subgroup; each person should read his or her headlines aloud in turn, and then stick the Post-it Notes on a flip chart.

7. Ask each group to take two or three of the headlines and discuss how they might generate practical ideas to address the real issue. For example, if the group selected the headline, "Herd of Three-Head Rhinos in Face-Off with Invaders from Mars," it might lead the participants to recommend hosting costume balls at the theater using costumes from the theater's design shop, or inviting other theater companies to rent their space and their costumes.

Experiential Elements

- Writing down ideas individually
- Envisioning possibilities and generating new ideas
- Breakout group discussion
- Listening to others

Special Supplies

- A pad of Post-it Notes and a Sharpie pen for each participant
- A selection of tabloids such as the *National Enquirer, Star, Globe,* and *National Examiner*

8. Have each subgroup present its ideas.

9. Lead a whole group discussion about the ideas the subgroups generated.

Facilitator Note Facilitators must be able to assist participants who cannot think of headlines or cannot convert the headlines into ideas.

Headline Buzz in Practice

At a retreat for the board of a university that had received some unfavorable press and whose leaders had become very concerned about negative publicity, we used Headline Buzz to encourage them to think more playfully about what the university might do to merit an article in the tabloids. This generated a lively discussion about the university's desired profile in the community and inventive approaches for garnering positive media attention.

Minimizing Groupthink

Groupthink occurs when people are more interested in getting on with things or gaining others' approval than in challenging themselves to come up with breakthrough ideas. It's important to encourage participants to remain independent and not agree with the first idea that comes along.

To minimize groupthink, select from the following activities, which compel people to come up with their own ideas and interpretations.

Activity

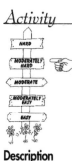

Impressions

Description

This activity helps participants think in fresh ways by having them imagine relationships between a random picture and an existing issue.

Experiential Elements

• Using visual materials
• Individual reflection
• Experimenting with ideas

Steps

1. Distribute one Issue Sheet to each participant.

2. Define the task: "We're going to use visual stimuli to give us new perspectives on this question. Think for a few moments about the question. Then, in silence, walk over to the table and pick up a picture. Make your choice quickly. Don't analyze the pictures; just select the first one that attracts you."

3. Tell participants: "When you sit down again, continue to maintain silence. Look at the picture, and consider how it suggests answers to the question at the top of your issue sheet. Write down your thoughts, using these questions to guide your thinking."

Setup

• Cut as many large pictures as you can find from magazines such as *National Geographic* or from remaindered books of photographs. They should represent a wide variety of subjects or designs. None should be larger than 8 1/2 inches x 11 inches. You will need at least three photographs for each participant.
• Put each picture, backed by blank paper, in a transparent page protector.
• Place all the pictures face up on a large table so that participants can walk around the table and view the images.
• Prepare an "Issue Statement" flip chart. This flip chart should have the question that everyone will answer, such as, "How can I help create a climate of innovation in my department?" or, "What kinds of insights or ideas would help me achieve my goal?"
• Prepare "How to Look at Your Picture" flip chart (see Step 4).

This activity is derived from the authors' experience in the Center for Creative Leadership's Leading Creatively program. As an alternative to clipping their own illustrations, facilitators can purchase a collection of photographs and illustrations CCL has assembled for groups to use, called Visual Explorer®. The Visual Explorer package includes instructions on a number of different ways to use visual stimuli. It can be acquired through www.ccl.org

4. Show the How to Look at Your Picture flip chart.

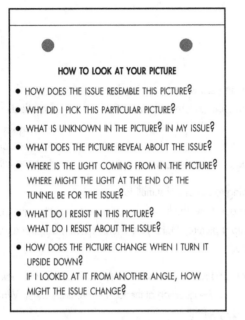

It is helpful to demonstrate to the group how you might get ideas from a picture. Choose one from the table yourself, and tell the group the messages you read in it. For instance: "My picture shows an animal's legs, which are bound together. This makes me think how I limit my thinking about what's possible. Because I cannot see the animal's head, I don't know what kind of animal it is. That makes me think that when I censor my unconventional ideas because I'm afraid of appearing foolish, I don't let the rest of you see who I am and how I think and maybe that's a loss for our department. When I turn the picture upside down, it seems like it would be easier for someone to come along and unknot the rope without getting kicked in the head. This makes me think that I should bounce my weirder ideas off other people and not let myself feel kicked in the head if they don't love those ideas right away."

5. While participants are writing, mix up the remaining pictures and turn them all face down on the table.

6. After seven or eight minutes, ask participants to return to the table, still in silence, and pick up another picture, this time without looking at it. Ask participants to respond to these questions: "What do I typically overlook concerning this issue?" and, "What does this picture remind me of that I must not forget?"

7. After a few minutes, ask for volunteers to show their pictures and share what they wrote with the rest of the group.

Facilitator Notes
- This activity requires a strong ability to model the imaginative use of visual stimuli. It requires comfort in debriefing nonlinear data.

- It's important to use neutral pictures. Don't choose pictures that are related to the group's industry or issues.

Impressions in Practice

At a retreat for a major chemical manufacturing corporation, we introduced Impressions as a method for thinking in fresh ways about an issue the group could not resolve. At the end, several people reported that they had been able to come up with radical new approaches, including an innovative packaging concept and a bold marketing strategy.

We also use this technique to help participants explore relationship issues at work. Participants regularly report that they gain insights into their own behaviors and how they become trapped in counterproductive patterns of thinking.

We had planned to collect the pictures at the end of one such retreat, but a number of people asked to keep their pictures. One woman told us, "I can't go back to work without this. I need to keep it on my desk to remind me to focus on what's really important." Ever since, we have given people the option of keeping their pictures as visual reminders of their commitments to themselves.

Reporters from Planet Arimira

Description

Participants work in small groups to create a skit that shows how a certain product, process, service, or problem would look to visitors from another planet.

Steps

1. Show the flip chart that names the product, process, service, or problem the group will be exploring.

2. Introduce the activity: "You are advance scouts from the Planet Arimira. You and your fellow Arimirans have been sent to Earth to research and report to your Council of Leaders on Earthling behavior. Your task is to make a detailed analysis of [the product, process, service, or problem named on the flip chart]. In your report be sure to create a vivid picture of [the product, process, service, or problem] so that the Council of Leaders, who know nothing about it, will understand it clearly.

   "Let's say you are reporting on a professional American football game. Your description might sound something like this:

   "'Tens of thousands of Earthlings gather once a week during the cooler months in large open-air structures for an enthusiastic worship service. Some of the religious leaders, dressed alike in black-and-white striped garb, officiate while acolytes in other costumes perform the ritual of carrying or throwing a sacred object in the form of an air-filled ovoid made of the skin of an animal up and down a grassy area divided into ten sections by lines that appear at intervals of 10 yards.

   "'In their religious ecstasy the acolytes often jump on one another and form human mountains on the grass.

Experiential Elements

- Reflection
- Envisioning possibilities and generating new ideas
- Skits
- Using toys and other props
- Whole group presentations

Setup

Create a flip chart with the product, process, service, or problem the group will be exploring written on it.

Special Supplies

An assortment of toys and other props

"'The religious leadership seems to be limited to men, though there are worshipers of both sexes in the pews, who participate by drinking liquids, which apparently have a sacred significance, and joining in chanting, standing, and waving in a coordinated fashion.

"'The service seems to be over when a man is drenched by some of the religious acolytes with a mysterious green substance, whereupon the leaders repair to changing rooms away from public view and the congregants leave their pews for their homes, wearing or carrying such religious regalia as collarless short sleeve shirts with spiritual messages printed on them, flags, banners, and large representations of human hands with one finger pointed upward to heaven, no doubt as a sign of their spiritual ecstasy.'"

3. Tell participants: "You should write your key points on a flip chart and then use any of the props in this room to make your presentations to the Council."

4. Divide the participants into subgroups of about five to seven people. Give the subgroups twenty-five minutes to prepare their presentations.

5. After the subgroups have presented their reports, ask the whole group—who will be playing the role of the Council of Leaders—to summarize what they learned about [the product, process, service, or problem].

6. Facilitate a discussion in which participants use their superior Arimiran intelligence to improve the product, process, service or solve the problem.

Facilitator Note   This activity requires a strong ability to encourage participants to engage fully in an activity that doesn't feel "logical."

Reporters from Planet Arimira in Practice

At a retreat for a corporation that had received numerous complaints about its impenetrable customer service operations, we sent scouts from Planet Arimira to describe the levels of complexity a customer had to navigate. While sharing a good laugh, the participants realized that they had created unnecessary obstacles to resolving issues quickly and generating greater customer loyalty. They came up with several concrete proposals for eliminating unnecessary steps.

Cultivating the Creativity Habit

We all have our habits and our ruts—our established ways of doing things. A certain amount of routine is fine; otherwise we'd start each day by reinventing the proverbial wheel. But we can become so accustomed to operating in particular ways that we can't imagine any other possibilities. It may be difficult for us even to acknowledge that there could be better ways.

The great philosopher Isaiah Berlin (1909–1997) ascribed his inquisitiveness as an adult to the habit his father had of asking the young Isaiah each evening at dinner not "What did you learn in school today?" but rather "What did you ask in school today?" "Philosophers," Berlin once famously said, "are adults who persist in asking childish questions."

Not only that, but when we look at something new, we tend to make assumptions based on what we already know. These assumptions can be very useful (we wouldn't want to have to wonder what to do with a chair every time we saw one, for instance), but they also limit our thinking (What other uses could we make of this chair? What other forms can a chair take? What else can I use as a chair?).

How can we break out of this limited way of thinking? "The important thing," Albert Einstein once said, "is to never stop questioning." The more questions we ask, the closer we come to understanding the problem. A creative thinking retreat provides an opportunity for participants to ask the all-important question Why? And also Who, What, Where, When, How, and Why not?

Here is an activity that helps participants move beyond their assumptions and generate new ideas.

Isolated Words

Description

In this activity participants use a simple verbal manipulation to help them challenge the way they habitually see things and to find new solutions to familiar problems.

Experiential Elements
- Individual reflection
- Whole group discussion
- Applying theories to real-life situations

Steps

1. Divide participants into subgroups of three to five people. Introduce the task: "We are going to work on coming up with new ideas in relation to [a specific issue]." Write the issue on a flip chart.

   Tell the participants: "Sometimes we become so caught up in what we know about a problem that we have difficulty getting a fresh perspective on it. So we must reframe the issue, that is, reposition it to try to see it differently.

   "In your group, write down your assumptions about what characterizes this issue. For instance, if our issue were, 'How can we increase repeat sales to our customers?' we might have these assumptions: 'Customers don't read our direct mail. Our product line lacks variety. Our prices are too high. Our competition sells harder.'"

2. "Now, challenge your assumptions by placing emphasis in turn on each noun, verb, adjective, or term in your statement. Using the example I've been using, we might say: '*Customers* don't read our direct mail.' 'Customers don't **read** our direct mail.' Each time you do this, write down how the issue or problem might be different if another word were substituted for the stressed word. What new ideas do you get for solving the problem?

   "Consider the example, '**Customers** don't read our direct mail.' If customers won't read it, might someone else in the customer's organization read the mail? The customer's assistant? His boss? A purchasing agent? An IT specialist? The CEO?

   "If customers don't **read** our direct mail, what else could we get them to do with it? Pass it along to someone else? Post it on a bulletin board? File it? Scan it into their computers? Eat it like candy? Listen to it on their CD players?

"If customers don't read ***our*** direct mail, whose direct mail might they read? A celebrity's? A friend's?

"If customers don't read our ***direct mail***, what would they read? Personal letters? Technical white papers? Journal articles? News releases? Faxes? E-mail?"

3. Allow fifteen minutes for the groups to work through their lists of assumptions.

4. Ask the subgroups to present their ideas. What other ways can participants think of to view the problem differently? Can they invent a fresh solution?

Facilitator Notes
- Facilitators must be able to assist participants in challenging their own assumptions.

- Many of us create self-limiting assumptions that constrain how we look at a problem, issue, or process. This activity gives participants a way to challenge their assumptions by revisiting and reframing their observations.

- This is a quick activity that can spur participants to eliminate the self-limiting assumptions that may be hampering their success.

Besides being too entrenched in our own assumptions, we often fail to realize that others see things through different lenses. Being able to view a situation from other people's perspectives can help retreat participants devise solutions that work for all concerned. The following activity will help participants gain various perspectives on an issue.

Multiple Perspectives

Description

This activity requires participants to view an issue from their own perspectives and then to adopt the points of view of other stakeholders. To encourage empathetic listening, participants must write in someone else's "voice."

Experiential Elements

- Individual reflection
- Imagining other people's interests
- Listening

Steps

1. Write an issue or problem that affects the group on a flip chart. Define the task: "Take a look at the issue on the chart, and then consider where you stand on the issue, in your own words. On a Post-it Note complete this sentence: 'What I wish would happen is . . .' You don't have to be comprehensive. You need only cover one facet of the issue, but choose one that really concerns you.

"For instance, if our issue were, 'How can we make our sales presentations more effective?' I might write: 'I wish we would start a presentations training class for our sales reps.'"

Allow time for participants to write their sentences.

2. "Now, on other Post-it Notes, complete that same sentence about the issue as you think it would be answered by at least four other people involved—a customer, a vendor, your spouse, your supervisor, someone from another department, and so on. Note whose perspective you are adopting, and state it in quotes, as if the sentence were in the person's own words.

"So, in the example, I might write: 'Sales Manager: . . . our reps would learn to listen better to customer needs.' 'Spouse of Sales Rep: . . . my wife would get home at a reasonable hour every night.' 'Customer: . . . my sales rep would understand our industry and wouldn't ask me such elementary questions.' 'Sales Rep's Assistant: . . . I never had to prepare another boring PowerPoint presentation.'

"Please work independently and in silence."

Allow five minutes for people to write their responses.

Setup

Tape several sheets of flip chart paper, each titled "What I wish would happen is . . ." (see Step 1) to a wall.

Special Supplies

A pad of Post-it Notes and a Sharpie pen for each participant

3. Have participants stick their Post-it Notes on flip chart paper mounted on the wall.

4. Ask participants to choose three perspectives from the wall that do not reflect their own opinions. Have them work individually to come up with new ways to address the issue, inspired by the various perspectives they chose.

5. Invite participants to share their ideas. Ask: "What new ideas or insights come from looking at the problem through the eyes of other people?"

Facilitator Notes
- The facilitator may need to prod participants a bit before they are able to see things from others' perspectives.

- This activity can be conducted in one large group or in breakout groups.

Participants won't come up with good ideas if they are paralyzed by fear of failure or of appearing foolish. If the corporate culture looks askance at anything that diverges from "the way we've always done things," chances are participants will be reluctant to come up with truly creative ideas to address pressing issues.

Sometimes you can encourage new thinking by giving people "cover" for their new ideas—by asking them, for instance, to project what they believe someone else would think. This activity makes it easy for reluctant participants to imagine new solutions.

Expert Opinion

Description

This activity helps participants think creatively by having them imagine what an expert would say about an important issue or problem.

Experiential Elements
- Individual reflection
- Imaginative writing and storytelling
- Generating ideas

Steps

1. Present a problem or issue in the form of a question to the entire group. For example, "How can we gain an advantage over our low-price competitor who's cutting into our market share?"

2. Ask each participant to think of someone they've never met whom they believe would be a good person to consult about this question. This expert could be someone they know by name (such as Steve Jobs of Apple Computer) or just by title (such as the marketing director of the Ritz Carlton Hotels). The person could be an inspirational figure outside of business (the Dalai Lama, for example) or someone deceased (such as Leonardo da Vinci). He or she could be a fictional character (like James Bond, Hercules, or Wonder Woman). Each participant selects his or her expert without disclosing the identity of that person to anyone else in the group.

3. Define the task: "Working alone, imagine that you run into your expert. Think up a story of how you meet (on a plane, at a coffee shop, attending an imaginary conference for geniuses or superheroes, whatever). You strike up a conversation about the issue. And your expert says, 'I've been thinking about that very issue. Let me tell you what I've learned and what I think your company should do.' Write down the advice the person gives you, focusing specifically on what he or she tells you to do to resolve the issue."

   Allow fifteen to twenty minutes for people to imagine their conversations and make notes.

4. Have participants read aloud their invented conversations. A note taker should collect all the ideas on a flip chart. Ask participants to consider the ideas they've come up with:

   - "What were the themes that came out of your stories?"

   - "What did your choice of expert tell you about the way you view this problem?"

Facilitator Note

The facilitator needs to be able to create an environment that encourages participants to let their expert say things they might be reluctant to say on their own.

Letting Go of Judgment

We've all learned to analyze, evaluate, critique, and pass judgment on anything new. But while the ability to think critically is a valuable attribute, critical thinking is not creative thinking. Throughout the retreat, you will need to encourage participants to suspend their inclination to look for what's wrong with a new idea and instead focus on how they might make it work.

> Creative thinking is critical, but critical thinking is not creative.

The next activity will help participants look for the positive in new ideas and communicate what's good about those ideas to others.

Gibberish Press Conference

Description

Four volunteers participate in a "gibberish" press conference on the benefits of an idea. Two volunteers sell the idea enthusiastically in gibberish and the other two volunteers interpret for them.

Experiential Elements

- Envisioning possibilities and generating new ideas
- Improvisation
- Using toys and other props
- Whole group presentations

Special Supplies

An assortment of toys and other props

Steps

1. Select an idea that the group generated in one of the earlier creative exercises in this chapter.

2. Introduce the activity: "I will need four volunteers who would be willing to be enthusiastic 'sellers' of this idea to the rest of us. Two of you will be high-level officials who have called a press conference to talk about how excited you are about the idea you are rolling out. You only speak gibberish—a nonsense language. The other two volunteers will interpret your meaning for us.

"Gibberish can be random words that do not make logical sense, such as 'competitiveness a bureaucrat of our customers' beauty' or it can be nonsense syllables, such as 'VEK-ZIB-EBA-WAP.' Gibberish can sound like a foreign language, such as French: 'maison, non, booque, bébé.'

"So no one feels nervous about the need to generate gibberish, we will all practice together."

3. Ask the participants to form a circle.

4. Tell participants: "I'll start us off by giving a gibberish greeting to the person on my right, and you will each imitate me in turn by repeating that greeting to the person on your right."

5. Once the greeting has gone around the circle, tell the participants: "Now I'd like a volunteer who would be willing to talk to the person on your left in the character of a used-car salesperson who hasn't made your quota of sales this month. Using gibberish, convince the person on your left to buy a car from you. Who would like to give this a try?"

6. After a few participants have practiced the used-car salesperson warm-up activity, ask for four volunteers to conduct the press conference. Two will be gibberish speakers and each of the other two participants will "interpret" the gibberish for the rest of the group. Tell the volunteer gibberish speakers: "Please convey your enthusiasm for this extraordinary idea in the gibberish you speak, your tone of voice, and with your body language and gestures."

7. Tell the volunteer interpreters: "Remember *we* don't speak gibberish. Only *you* understand what the words, the tone of voice, and the body language and gestures of the person you're interpreting for mean."

8. Tell the audience members: "When you hear the interpretation of what the gibberish speakers are saying, please convey your excitement by clapping, stomping your feet, whistling, or yelling 'yay!'"

9. Allow the gibberish press conference to go on for a few minutes.

10. If there is enough time convene another press conference for another idea. If not, ask the whole group what they learned about looking for the positive in ideas from this exercise.

Facilitator Note   The facilitator must be able to think quickly, create an environment in which participants won't mind taking a risk, and help volunteers if they are struggling to speak or interpret gibberish.

What are the risks in coming up with new ideas? Actually, if you have created an environment of trust at the retreat, there are few risks associated with idea generation. The difficulty rarely lies in *creative thinking*. The challenge is to move those ideas to *creative doing*.

One way to help the participants find the courage to try new things is to have them assess the risk realistically.

Considering Risk

Description

Participants first consider the nature of personal and organizational risk. Then each one works on a proposed action to evaluate how risky it actually is and to formulate strategies to reduce the risk.

Experiential Elements

- Reflecting back on experiences
- Applying theories to real situations
- Group discussion
- Experimenting with ideas

Steps

1. Divide participants into subgroups of three or four people. Introduce the task: "In your groups, describe to one another in turn the biggest risk you have ever taken, either personally or at work. Tell whether taking the risk turned out well or not. Either way, what did you learn from having taken the risk?"

2. Bring the whole group together. Ask the participants: "Did taking your risks mostly turn out well?" "What contributed to successful risk taking?" "What lessons did you learn from the risks that did not turn out well?"

3. Present the Considering Risk flip chart.

Setup

Prepare the "Considering Risk" flip chart (see Step 3).

CONSIDERING RISK

- THE RISK I'D LIKE US TO TAKE IS . . .
- THE POSSIBLE DOWNSIDES ARE . . .
- I STILL CONSIDER IT WORTH TAKING BECAUSE . . .
- WE COULD MINIMIZE THE DOWNSIDES BY . . .

---

4. Ask participants to write down their responses to these four statements as completely as they can.

5. Divide participants into subgroups of three to five people (not the same groups as in Step 1). Have participants read their ideas to one another. After each participant has presented his or her ideas, ask the group to explore whether there are other possible downsides and, if there are, to come up with strategies to minimize them.

6. If the participants aren't members of the senior leadership team, make sure they know that they cannot decide for themselves what an acceptable level of risk is for the organization to assume. Ask the subgroups to choose one of the risks they discussed and to prepare a case for management that lays out the key points.

7. Have the subgroups present their cases. Facilitate a discussion about the information senior managers need to make intelligent assessments of risk.

Evaluating Ideas

Typically people are trained from their first day at school to make judgments about themselves and others. The work is good or bad. The answers are right or wrong. The ideas are smart or dumb. And thus *they* are good or bad, right or wrong, smart or dumb. Most managers climb the corporate ladder on the basis of their ability to assess a situation accurately and rapidly and to exercise good judgment. Indeed, people's capacity for sound judgment *is* important. But it can also stifle their ability to think creatively.

How? When someone offers a fresh idea, people tend to evaluate it, make a snap judgment about it, and begin marshalling their arguments for or against it. Usually, people judge their own ideas before they express them—"How will this sound to others?" "Will this really work?" "What will people think?" And often our self-judgment keeps us from presenting our own ideas.

But the process of *generating* ideas is the polar opposite of evaluating them, and the two poles produce effects as different as north and south. Idea generation works best when people come up with as many ideas as possible. Great minds do *not* think alike.

Idea generation ≠ idea evaluation.

In contrast, *evaluation* is the process of culling the best ideas and eliminating the rest. Idea generation is inclusive; evaluation is exclusive. If retreat participants engage in both processes at once, they won't do either well.

The best way to help the group come away from the retreat with great ideas is to encourage people to put lots of ideas on the table, build on one another's proposals, and defer judgment for as long as possible. Evaluation and selection can wait.

This next activity, which is inspired by the theories of Edward de Bono, encourages participants to evaluate from various perspectives.

Put on Your Thinking Cap

Description

This activity helps participants evaluate ideas by assuming the roles indicated by the colors of their hats or headbands.

Steps

1. Present the Thinking Caps flip chart to the group.

THINKING CAPS

- WHITE = NEUTRAL, "OBJECTIVE," FACTS AND FIGURES

- RED = EMOTIONS, FEELINGS, INTUITION, "GUT FEELING"

- BLACK = CAREFUL, CAUTIOUS, REASONS WHY IT WON'T WORK

- YELLOW = SUNNY, POSITIVE, OPTIMISTIC, SEES OPPORTUNITIES

- GREEN = CREATIVE, MAKES CONNECTIONS, SEES POSSIBILITIES AND NEW IDEAS

- BLUE = FOCUS, SYNTHESIS, MODERATION, CONTROL, CONCLUSIONS, ORGANIZATION

Experiential Elements

- Categorizing
- Using visual means to clarify ideas
- Role playing
- Small group discussion
- Large group discussion

Setup

Prepare a "Thinking Caps" flip chart for each subgroup (see Step 1).

Special Supplies

Six headbands or hats made of construction paper for each subgroup, each one of a different color: white, red, black, yellow, green, and blue.

2. Divide the group into subgroups of six members each, giving each member of the subgroup a different color construction paper Thinking Cap headband or hat. Each of the six thinking styles must be represented in each group. (If any subgroup has fewer than six members, ask for a volunteer or volunteers to wear more than one hat. If you have one extra person in a subgroup, let two members of that subgroup wear the same color hat. Be creative.)

3. Give each subgroup an equal share of the ideas that the group has generated to evaluate.

4. Explain the activity: "You will evaluate the ideas from the perspectives of the thinking cap each of you is wearing. Don't evaluate the ideas the way you personally would, but assume the persona of the thinking cap you are wearing. For each idea your subgroup explores, please ensure that it is evaluated from each thinking cap perspective.

   "Once you have analyzed the idea from the six perspectives, make a recommendation whether this idea should be pursued further or not and note your finding on your flip chart."

5. Ask each subgroup in turn to present a brief resume of its thinking cap perspectives on each idea and its recommendation whether this idea should be pursued further or not.

In a well-structured creativity retreat, it's important to leave a substantial amount of time at the end for the participants to cull from the many ideas they have generated the few that they want to implement. We use the following activity to help participants decide which ideas are worth further exploration. If at the end of this next activity the group still has more good ideas than capacity to implement them, we use the "Targeting Results" activity (see Chapter 9, pp. 236–238) to help participants focus on their top priorities.

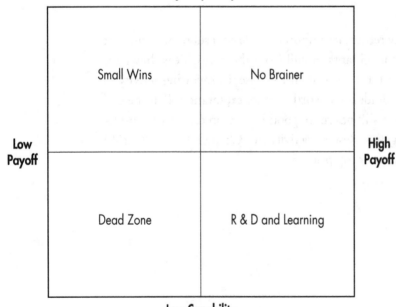

Payoffs and Capabilities

Description

This activity helps participants evaluate ideas, considering both the organization's current capabilities to implement those ideas and the potential payoffs to the organization of putting those ideas into action. The relative value of these two considerations becomes visible when participants plot each idea on a matrix.

Steps

1. Present the Payoff and Capability Matrix to the group, defining the labels:

High Capability

Small Wins	No Brainer
Dead Zone	R & D and Learning

Low Payoff (left)   **High Payoff** (right)

Low Capability

Experiential Elements

- Categorizing
- Using visual means to clarify ideas
- Small group discussion
- Large group discussion

Setup

- Prepare a "Payoff and Capability Matrix" flip chart for each subgroup (see Step 1).
- For each subgroup, create a set of Post-it Notes with the ideas under consideration written on them, one idea per note. Use Post-it Notes of various colors, and assign one color to each idea. (For example, Idea 1 would always be written on a blue Post-it Note, Idea 2 on a green note, Idea 3 on a orange note, and so forth.) By color-coding the ideas, the facilitator and the participants can see at a glance how the subgroups classified each idea on their respective matrixes.

- High Capability/High Payoff = No Brainer

- Low Capability/High Payoff = R&D and Learning

- High Capability/Low Payoff = Small Wins

- Low Capability/Low Payoff = Dead Zone

Special Supplies
Several pads of different colored Post-it Notes and a Sharpie pen for the facilitator

2. Divide the group into subgroups of five to seven members each. Ask each subgroup to work to place the Post-it Notes with the ideas in the appropriate squares of its copy of the matrix. Each subgroup should keep working until its members come to consensus on the placement of each idea. If a subgroup's members cannot come to agreement on the placement of a particular idea, that idea should be placed to the side of the matrix.

3. After the subgroups have placed the ideas on their own matrix, have them look at one another's matrixes to see which ideas fell in the No Brainer or R&D and Learning squares on more than one matrix.

4. For the ideas that fell into the No Brainer or R&D and Learning categories, ask participants to rank them as

- Top priority

- Secondary priority

- Low priority

Other Suggested Activities for a Creativity Retreat

You will find other activities to incorporate into a creativity retreat in the Activities for Idea Generation index (p. 500) and the Activities to Use in Any Retreat index (p. 490).

Chapter 13

Specialized Retreats

All retreats are specialized in the sense that they are designed with a particular client, set of circumstances, and hoped-for outcome in mind. And most retreats are staff retreats, typically bringing together employees from different levels in the same organization or unit to focus on issues of general or widespread concern to them.

In addition, there are what we refer to as *specialized retreats,* which bring together different groups or have different purposes than a typical department staff retreat does. Examples of such specialized retreats include

- Nonprofit board retreats
- Corporate board retreats
- Peers-only retreats
- Abandonment retreats

The Board Retreat

Boards of directors, whether for corporations or nonprofits, have much in common with one another, and we've seen some recurring patterns in the boards we have worked with.

Although board members share goals with an organization's leaders and staff, they are not employees. They bring a variety of different experiences and perspectives to their work for the organization and have different goals and responsibilities (many of them legally mandated).

Nonprofit Boards

Boards of nonprofit organizations typically are composed of unpaid volunteers who donate their time, expertise, and money because they care about the organization's work. Some (such as nurses on the board of a public health clinic) may know a great deal about the substance of the organization's mission and less about management and business issues. Others (such as corporate executives on the board of a museum) may be knowledgeable about business but have little expertise in the substance of the organization's mission or in the different demands and limitations placed on nonprofit boards and different expectations of their members. For this reason, board members may use different "languages" and speak past each other.

Bringing this diversity of interests and experience to bear on the challenges many nonprofits face can be a daunting task. Although retreats don't guarantee more effective boards, they can foster significant changes in the ways boards function and contribute to their organizations' success.

This is what we often observe in nonprofit boards:

- A small fraction of the members (usually the executive committee and maybe a few others) do the lion's share of the work. As a consequence, these individuals may be headed for burnout and often grow resentful of others who don't pull their weight.
- From the staff's perspective, the board often either meddles and micromanages or does too little to help the organization. Sometimes both.

- The board doesn't seem to "get" that fundraising is one of its central responsibilities. Precious time is taken up figuring out how to move the organization beyond short-term crises precipitated by insufficient operating funds.
- Board members perceive that there are *in* groups (who can influence the direction of the organization) and *out* groups (who resent being asked for money when they have little input into what the organization does with that money).
- There are signs of dissension—griping after meetings, whispering or raised eyebrows when certain issues are discussed, or a general lack of interest in the board's discussions—that may not manifest themselves openly and directly.
- It's a struggle to get people to attend meetings or to participate constructively when they do.

When we plan a retreat for the board of a nonprofit organization, we focus on what the board and the staff jointly agree are the key strategic issues and on ways the board can help the organization achieve its mission. These retreats can involve

- Clarifying the organization's purpose and goals, identifying strategic issues, jump-starting a strategic planning process, and measuring progress against goals.
- Orienting new board members to the issues facing the organization and what they can do to address them, as well as to the ways in which nonprofit boards differ from the corporate boards with which members from the business world might be more familiar. (This often has the added benefit of engaging the more senior board members in the process of mentoring new members, thus reinforcing their own commitment.)

For more about strategic planning and making trade-offs and choices about programs and services, see Chapter 9, "Leading a Strategic Planning Retreat," pp. 193–248.

- Increasing the board's involvement in the choices and trade-offs necessary when the organization is deciding which programs and services it should offer.
- Engaging the board in creative thinking about programs, services, processes, or constituents.

To read more about creative thinking, see Chapter 12, "Leading a Creativity and Innovation Retreat," pp. 325–367.

Chapter 10, "Leading a Culture Change Retreat," and Chapter 11, "Leading a Team-Building Retreat," describe activities that can be used at board retreats as well as at staff retreats to clarify roles and to improve internal communications.

- Defining board and staff roles and responsibilities.
- Improving how board members work together and with the staff by addressing such issues as communication, conflict management, and decision making.
- Dealing with a significant issue, such as a public affairs crisis or the need to change the organization's leadership.
- Evaluating the board's effectiveness and agreeing on future performance standards.
- Exploring and modifying, if necessary, the board's policies and structure.
- Enhancing the board's operations by delving into such issues as how members use their time at meetings and how the board's committee system functions.

But here's the rub: be aware when you plan a board retreat that executive directors don't necessarily want a strong board that will challenge their thinking or demand extensive documentation of the organization's expenditures and activities.

Many executive directors believe they know how to run their programs and would prefer that their boards concentrate exclusively on raising (or giving) money to support these programs. But it's not realistic to expect board members to care enough to accept the responsibility for fiscal, legal, and policy oversight as well as fundraising and at the same time not to want to be involved to some extent in program and service decisions. After all, their interest in what the organization does is probably what inspired them to become board members in the first place.

In essence, then, you may have two clients, the board on one hand and the director and staff on the other, each with different outcomes in mind. When we plan a nonprofit board retreat, we include activities that help the staff and board members bring these issues to the surface and deal with their differences while still focusing on what they have in common: their passion for the mission.

A well-conceived retreat for a nonprofit board offers an outstanding opportunity for board members both to learn the staff's thinking about program and service offerings and to communicate to the staff their own priorities and concerns. Most important, perhaps, it can help board members see how their efforts affect the organization's operations and what they can do individually and collectively to contribute more meaningfully to its success.

Corporate Boards

Corporate boards differ from nonprofit boards in significant ways. Members tend to come to such boards with executive experience in industry or government, and they may be paid handsomely for their time and expertise. Even members of boards of small companies are likely to have experience in business, law, or finance. Corporate boards don't often hold retreats but usually conduct their business at regular meetings, which some members may travel great distances to attend.

Yet increasing public and government scrutiny of how these boards direct the fortunes of their companies and look after the interests of their stockholders has led many companies to search for better ways to harness board members' collective expertise. This is all the more true in the United States since the passage of the Sarbanes-Oxley Act of 2002, which mandates much greater accountability from both nonprofit and corporate board members. This additional fiduciary responsibility has prompted a deepening interest in corporate board retreats.

Such retreats can be effective in improving communication among board members, increasing their understanding of significant business issues and problems, and—perhaps most important—fostering disclosure of and honest discussion about concerns that lie beneath the surface, waiting to snare the unwary executive or uninformed investor.

Many of the issues we outlined for nonprofit boards also apply to the board and staff dynamic found in corporations. Senior executives may see their boards as potentially interfering with and challenging the way they run their companies. Some boards are composed of members who serve with the support of major stockholders and whose points of view might therefore be skewed in one direction or another.

Corporate board meetings are typically highly formal, and the comparatively informal atmosphere of a retreat can encourage greater information sharing, more candid discussion, and deeper inquiry into important issues.

Like nonprofit board retreats, corporate board retreats are not a cure-all, but a well-designed offsite can play a significant role in helping corporate boards become more effective in carrying out the increasingly important and public role they play.

Suggested Activities for a Board Retreat

You will find a wealth of possible activities to incorporate into your board retreat in the Activities for Culture Change, Team-Building, and Board Retreats index (p. 493) if you are focusing on relationship-building; the Activities for Making Decisions, Planning, and Evaluating Ideas index (p. 502) if you are focusing on planning; and the Activities to Use in Any Retreat index (p. 490) if you want to consider a variety of methodologies.

Activity

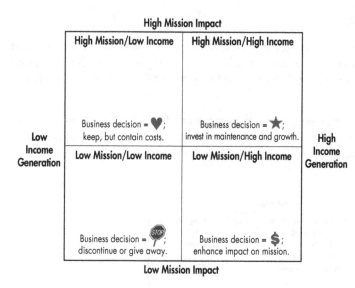

Bottom-Line Matrix

Description

This activity helps members of boards and staffs of nonprofit organizations decide which activities to pursue, based on each activity's contribution to the organization's mission and to the bottom line.

Steps

1. Present the Bottom-Line Matrix to the group, defining the labels on the matrix.

Experiential Elements
• Using visual means to clarify ideas
• Discussion of ideas

Setup

Create a "Bottom-Line Matrix" on a flip chart sheet for each subgroup (see Step 1).

Special Supplies

A pad of 3 inch x 5 inch Post-it Notes and a Sharpie pen for each subgroup

- High Mission Impact/Low Income Generation = Heart; keep, but contain costs.
- High Mission Impact/High Income Generation = Star; invest in maintenance and growth.
- Low Mission Impact/Low Income Generation = Stop Sign; discontinue or give away.
- Low Mission Impact/High Income Generation = Dollar Sign; look for ways to increase centrality to the mission.

This activity is adapted from *Strategic Planning for Nonprofit Organizations,* by Michael Allison and Jude Kaye, and is used with permission.

2. Ask each subgroup of five or six participants to place Post-it Notes labeled with the organization's programs and services in the appropriate squares of the matrix. The members of each subgroup should keep working until they come to consensus on the placement of each program and service.

3. After all programs and services are placed, conduct a whole group discussion about the choices each subgroup made. Look for consensus among the groups about which programs and services contribute the most to the bottom line and also to the organization's mission. Based on the discussion, rank each program and service as

- Keep

- Enhance

- Discontinue

Bottom-Line Matrix in Practice

At a retreat we facilitated for the board of a large membership association (the "XYZ Association") whose major source of income was threatened due to circumstances beyond its control, we used the Bottom-Line Matrix to help board members make some difficult decisions about how to focus XYZ's programs on those that would have the greatest impact.

Through a vigorous debate, board members came to consensus on which activities were most mission-critical and which had the greatest potential to contribute to XYZ's financial stability. This exercise helped the board gain clarity on the activities the association should pursue with its limited financial and human resources.

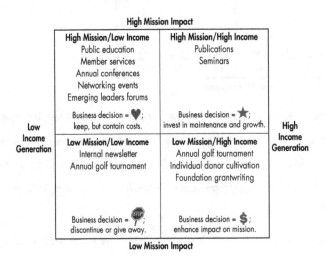

The Peers-Only Retreat

A peers-only retreat would involve people at the same (or approximately the same) level. A peers-only retreat could be convened for a group of team leaders or department heads or vice presidents. There are many excellent reasons to convene such a retreat. It might help improve lateral coordination when several departments need to interact in a given process. Or it might serve as a forum for open information sharing removed from the pressure of impressing the boss. Or it might create the basis for peer managers to identify and solve problems at their own levels, rather than dumping problems on more senior leaders.

Often managers and employees see their colleagues in other parts of the organization less as partners than as competitors. They may resist cooperation and resolutely defend their turf against all who would encroach on it. Some executives even consciously encourage this behavior by fostering internal competition as a way of keeping subordinates on their toes.

If you discover in the preliminary interviews that the organization is having problems getting different departments to cooperate, you might discuss with your client the possibility of holding a retreat for managerial peers only, across the organization chart, with none of the higher-ups or direct reports present. The goal of such a retreat would be for colleagues to figure out better ways of working together, thinking together, resolving problems together, sharing information, and taking collective responsibility for the organization's success.

Early on in such a peers-only retreat, participants need to talk about what's working and what's not working in each part of the organization, which collectively they represent. From this discussion they will gain a comprehensive view of what is happening throughout the organization.

As participants get to know each other and come to realize that they have common interests, aspirations, and concerns, they can begin to break down artificial barriers that have been inhibiting cooperation and interfering with communication. They will then be able to make decisions or recommendations that benefit the entire organization, not just their respective pieces of it. The more they work to support one another's goals, the more likely they are to overcome the mistrust and competition that can hobble an organization.

But better relationships don't happen automatically. Participants must make a commitment to address explicitly not only the ways they would like to work together but also the behaviors and practices that currently hamper effective collaboration.

For example, we facilitated a retreat for a hotel management company in which only mid-level managers took part for the first two days, before the senior managers joined them for a third day of discussion. The middle managers discovered common problems they had not realized were affecting them all. In the course of the retreat these participants shared information and cleared up misunderstandings. They made several joint recommendations when the senior managers came on the third day of the retreat. Most important, they decided to keep meeting as a group when they returned to their office.

The middle managers were pleased to find that they could communicate quickly and directly with each other, solve problems together, and share best practices. This new cooperation allowed them to develop consistent policies and resolve many issues at their level rather than having to buck everything up the chain of command. Senior executives, freed from having to deal with these issues themselves, were pleased because they were now able to devote more time to the larger issues they were supposed to be dealing with. Even the middle managers' subordinates were pleased, because the organization was more responsive to their concerns and more consistent across department lines in its policies.

There are many activities in other chapters of this book that work very well in a retreat for peers (as described later). In addition, we offer several activities in this chapter that focus specifically on issues that peers face.

The following activity allows retreat participants to explore individual and team methods for managing conflict when they must come to consensus on how to allocate scarce resources.

You'll find a more detailed explanation of how working relationships among middle managers and other peers can be improved in *Seeing Systems: Unlocking the Mysteries of Organizational Life,* by organization consultant Barry Oshry (1996), who refers to this improvement as "middle integration."

I Want Those Resources!

Description

Participants in this activity take part in a simulation in which they must decide how to allocate budget resources.

Experiential Elements

- Role playing
- Small group discussion
- Presentations
- Whole group discussion

Steps

1. Divide participants into groups of up to seven people. (Six people will be participants in the simulation and one will be an observer. If the groups don't divide evenly into seven, you can have an extra observer or two, but make sure you have at least five participants and one observer in each subgroup.)

2. Tell the participants: "Six [or five] people in each subgroup will be managers of different plants of the Ace Manufacturing Company. One [or more] of you will be observing a meeting the managers will have to discuss how to cut the company's budget by $500,000."

Setup

- Prepare six "Budget-Cutting Priorities" sheets (for Plants A, B, C, D, E, and F) for each subgroup (see CD 13A), one set to distribute among the "managers" and one set for each subgroup's observer(s).
- Prepare one [or two] "Observer's Comments" sheet(s) for each subgroup (see CD 13B).
- Prepare a copy of the "Budget-Cutting Instructions" sheet for each participant (see CD 13C).
- Prepare a copy of the "Budget-Cutting Key Facts" sheet for each participant (see CD 13D).

Special Supplies

- A set of name tags—labeled A, B, C, D, E, F, and Observer—for each subgroup.
- A pen and pad of paper for each participant

This activity is adapted from "Budget Cutting: Conflict and Consensus Seeking," by Terry L. Maris, in *Pfeiffer's Classic Activities for Managing Conflict at Work*, and is used with permission.

3. Give each person in the subgroups a name tag—A, B, C, D, E, F, or Observer—and then give each person with a letter name tag (each manager) the Budget-Cutting Priorities sheet that corresponds to his or her letter (see CD 13A), and give an Observer's Comments sheet to each observer (see CD 13B). Give all participants a copy of the Budget-Cutting Instructions sheet (see CD 13C) and the Budget-Cutting Key Facts sheet (see CD 13D).

4. Give participants fifteen minutes to read their Budget-Cutting Priorities sheet, Budget-Cutting Instructions sheet, and Budget-Cutting Key Facts sheet and to prepare for the meeting. Give the observers the entire subgroup packet (including copies of all the managers' Budget-Cutting Priorities sheets) to look over.

5. Give participants thirty minutes to hold their budget meetings in their subgroups.

6. Give observers ten minutes to provide feedback to the group on how they managed the process.

7. Ask subgroups to report to the whole group on the behaviors that helped resolve conflict. Then facilitate a discussion of what the team might do when faced with similar circumstances in which different members have apparently conflicting objectives.

What "Blocks" Cooperation

Description

In this activity participants take part in a simulation in which they are asked to use blocks to complete a task in a cross-functional team representing three departments that have different skills and work norms.

Experiential Elements

- Role playing
- Small group discussion
- Whole group discussion

Steps

1. Ask the participants to write out the impediments to working effectively with their peers in other departments; have them write on Post-it Notes using their Sharpie pens (one impediment per Post-it Note). Ask them to post the notes with their responses on flip chart sheets on the wall and then to read and make note of all the posted responses. Do not discuss the responses. Indicate that the group will return to the Post-it Notes later in the session.

Setup

- Prepare a copy of the "Department A" handout for each member of Department A (see CD 13E).
- Prepare a copy of the "Department B" handout for each member of Department B (see CD 13F).
- Prepare a copy of the "Department C" handout for each member of Department C (see CD 13G).
- Prepare a copy of the "Memo from the Office of the CEO" for each participant (see CD 13H).
- Prepare a copy of the "Observer Guidelines" for each observer (see CD 13I).
- Prepare a copy of the "Memo from the Office of the CEO—Update" for each participant (see CD 13J).
- Prepare a copy of the "Memo from the Department A Manager" for each member of Department A (see CD 13K).
- Prepare a copy of the "Team Process Review" for each participant (see CD 13L).

Special Supplies

- About twenty-five colored wooden or plastic blocks in a variety of shapes and colors
- A pad of Post-it Notes and a Sharpie pen for each participant
- A pen and pad of paper for each participant

This activity is adapted from "Three-Way Teamwork," in *Team Depot: A Warehouse of Over 585 Tools to Reassess, Rejuvenate, and Rehabilitate Your Team*, by Glenn Parker, and is used with permission.

2. Form three subgroups with equal numbers of participants (or as equal as possible), and assign them to tables. Designate the groups as Departments A, B, and C. Give each group the appropriate department handout (see CD 13E, 13F, and 13G), and ask the members to follow the handout instructions. Allow fifteen minutes for the groups to develop their norms.

3. Distribute the Memo from the Office of the CEO to all participants (see CD 13H).

4. Ask for one volunteer from each department to serve as an observer. Give the volunteers the Observer Guidelines (see CD 13I), and ask them to take a few minutes to study them.

5. Ask everyone else to come together at the conference table to form the cross-functional team. Place all the colored blocks on the table. Allow twenty minutes for the team to design the structure.

6. At the end of the design period, ask the observers to give their reports.

7. Ask the departments to meet separately to discuss how the team is doing and how their norms are helping or hurting the cross-functional team.

8. Distribute the Memo from the Office of the CEO—Update to everyone (see CD 13J).

9. Just as the team is about to begin its work, pull out the members of Department A and bring them over to their original table. Give them the Memo from the Department A Manager (see CD 13K). If the remaining members of the cross-functional team ask where the Department A people have gone, explain that their boss has a priority project for them to complete but that they expect to return. Remove some of the blocks from the table, explaining that a "corporate cost-containment initiative" has reduced the team's available resources.

10. Allow fifteen minutes for the team to build the structure, taking into account the new requirements from the CEO.

11. Ask the team members to complete the Team Process Review (see CD 13L). At the same time, ask the observers to meet to discuss their data.

12. Facilitate a discussion about

- How the team members felt as they worked on the project

- The feedback from the observers

13. Return to the Post-it Notes on the wall, and ask if the participants

- Noticed any of the impediments that they wrote about previously occurred during the simulation

- Can now think of other impediments that they hadn't noted that also hamper their cooperation with one another

14. Facilitate a discussion about specific actions that participants might take back at the office to increase their ability to collaborate effectively as peers.

Trust Me

Description

In this activity participants form a continuum to show how much trust they believe exists among their peers. They reflect on behaviors that enhance trust in peer relationships. They rate themselves on aspects of emotional intelligence that tend to increase trust among peers.

Experiential Elements
- Line-up continuum
- Reflection
- Pairs discussion
- Whole group discussion

Setup

Prepare a customized version of the "Emotional Intelligence Self-Assessment" (one copy for each participant), focusing on the competencies most important to this peer group (see CD 13M for descriptions of the competencies you will choose from and CD 13N for a self-assessment you can customize).

Special Supplies

A pen and pad of paper for each participant

Steps

1. Introduce the task: "Please line up in a continuum along this wall, in silence, according to how much trust you believe there is among this group of peers. If you believe there is a great deal of trust among all of you, please position yourself near this corner [*walk to one end of the wall*]. If you believe there is very little trust among all of you, please position yourself near that corner [*walk to the other end of the wall*]. If you believe something in the middle, please position yourself somewhere between the two extremes, more toward the side that represents higher or lower trust, depending on which you think is the case. Remember, no talking or communicating with each other in any way as you line up."

2. Interview participants in their groupings along the wall, ranging from high to low trust assessments. Ask participants in each grouping what behaviors they see that indicate there is (or isn't) a great deal of trust among them.

3. Tell the whole group: "The Emotional Intelligence Self-Assessments are based on the work of Daniel Goleman and the Consortium for Research on Emotional Intelligence. Research has shown that people with a high degree of emotional intelligence tend to be more trusted by their colleagues."

4. Distribute the Emotional Intelligence Self-Assessments to participants and ask them to rate themselves (see CD 13M and 13N).

5. For each competence rated by the Emotional Intelligence Self-Assessment in turn, ask participants to place themselves in silence on a continuum along the wall to reflect the ratings they gave themselves: Do they exhibit the competency frequently, sometimes, infrequently, or rarely?

6. Ask each participant in turn to make a commitment to his or her peers to change one behavior to help increase trust in the peer group as a whole.

HARD
MODERATELY HARD
MODERATE
MODERATELY EASY
EASY

Conflicting Interests

Description

In this activity participants take part in a role play in which they must decide who can take vacation the following week.

Steps

1. Introduce the task: "You will take part in a role play. Four of you in each subgroup will play a role and will receive information about your character as well as some information about the immediate situation in your office. Beyond the information supplied, you should be yourself in the situation that is described."

2. Divide the participants into subgroups of five members each. Four will play roles and the other one will observe. If some groups must have more than five participants, the ones who are not assigned roles will also be observers.

3. Give each of the role players in each subgroup the scenario for one of the four roles (see CD 13O), and give the observers an Observer's Notes (see CD 13P). Allow five minutes for the members to read their sheets and prepare for the activity.

4. Give the subgroups fifteen minutes to hold their discussions.

5. Facilitate a whole group discussion about

   • How the VPs felt they collaborated to make a decision

   • The feedback from the observers

6. Ask participants what conditions would encourage them to think about the good of the whole organization rather than their personal interests or those of the departments they lead.

Experiential Elements

• Role playing
• Small group discussion
• Whole group discussion

Setup

• Prepare one copy per breakout group of each of the four "Vacation Decision" scenarios (see CD 13O) and one copy of the "Observer's Notes" (see CD 13P) for each observer.

This activity is adapted from "Vacation Schedule: Group Problem Solving," by L. B. Day and Meeky Blizzard, in *The Pfeiffer Handbook of Structured Experiences: Learning Activities for Intact Teams and Workgroups,* and is used with permission.

Metaphorical Management

Description

Using visual symbols, managers first discuss how they would like to be perceived by their peers. Then in small groups, again using metaphors, participants receive feedback about the impact of their management styles and explore ways to modify these styles to be more effective.

Experiential Elements

- Personal reflection
- Using metaphor to express thoughts and feelings
- Giving and receiving feedback
- Active decision making

Special Requirement

Ask the participants to form small groups composed only of people with whom they work regularly.

Steps

1. Introduce the task: "This activity will help you look at the impact of your management style on others and think about the style you aspire to. We're going to use metaphors—visual symbols—for this exploration.

   Using metaphors helps people come up with more creative ideas. And having a visual symbol will help you organize your thinking and remember these ideas back at the office.

Setup

- Prepare "My Ideal Management Style" flip chart (see Step 3).
- Prepare "Differences Between My Two Metaphors" flip chart (see Step 8).

"Let's begin by exploring your ideal management style.

Think about the kind of work you do and what's critical for success in that work. You might want to make some notes. Then think of a metaphor—a symbol—that represents your ideal management style."

2. To help participants understand the task, offer a personal example: "For instance, I might say that my ideal management style would be symbolized by an eagle [*the facilitator should substitute his or her own metaphor here*]. Why? An eagle is farsighted and sees the big picture. She flies high above all the activity on the ground and doesn't worry about the little stuff. The eagle is also very target directed. She sees her prey, zooms in on it, and swoops it up quickly. I like the symbol of the eagle because I think I get too wrapped up in the minutia of my job and don't look up often enough to remember the big picture. I want to focus on more important projects, instead of always chasing after little details that don't seem to make much difference in the long run."

3. Display the My Ideal Management Style flip chart.

4. Have participants select a symbol that represents their ideal style. The symbol can be anything—an animal, a place, an object, a tool, even an admired person. Tell participants not to worry if their symbol isn't a perfect fit; the idea is to choose something that helps them remember the essence of their ideal style.

5. Ask participants to list five or six reasons why they chose this metaphor.

6. Ask the participants to form subgroups of three or four people with whom they work closely. Tell them that each subgroup is to focus on one of its members at a time and to choose a metaphor to describe that person's style. Once the group agrees on a metaphor, one of the members should write it down, along with the reasons the group chose it. After the metaphor is discussed, the selected person reveals the metaphor she chose for herself and her reasons for choosing that symbol.

7. Have each group talk about the differences between the symbol the group chose and the symbol the group member chose for herself. The groups repeat this process with each member in turn.

8. Display the Differences Between My Two Metaphors flip chart.

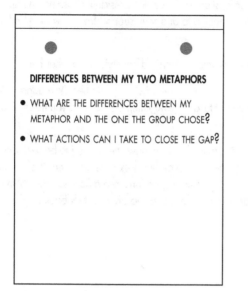

DIFFERENCES BETWEEN MY TWO METAPHORS

- WHAT ARE THE DIFFERENCES BETWEEN MY METAPHOR AND THE ONE THE GROUP CHOSE?
- WHAT ACTIONS CAN I TAKE TO CLOSE THE GAP?

9. Ask participants, working alone and in silence, to reflect on what they learned from their group. For their own use, the participants should write their answers to the two questions on a sheet of paper they can take back to the office.

Facilitator Notes

- This activity may elicit feelings of personal vulnerability for some participants, so it is imperative that the facilitator be skilled in creating a safe and supportive environment for everyone.

- This activity is less threatening than a direct discussion of management styles. People feel safer talking about a personal issue, such as management style, through metaphors, and the activity can be fun, which nearly always reduces tension. The visual symbols become memory hooks that enable participants to recall what they learned even long after the session.

- We encourage participants to find a picture or object, when they get back to the office, that illustrates the metaphor they chose. At the next meeting of their retreat peer group or within their own departments, retreat participants show their symbols and explain how they reminded them of the changes they were hoping to make. We recommend that people keep the picture or object visible in their offices. We have seen executives with stuffed toy eagles and bears on their bookshelves as a result of this activity.

If you are interested in using a leadership assessment, we recommend the *Leadership Practices Inventory* or the *Campbell Leadership Descriptor*. For a discussion of these instruments, see Chapter 2, "Using Behavioral Assessments," p. 56.

Metaphorical Management in Practice

At a retreat we facilitated for a large corporation, a senior vice president chose her metaphor quickly. "I want to be like a lion," she said, "someone others look up to and seek support from. I want to be known as a leader, a visionary."

Imagine her surprise when the group of coworkers described her style as "mother hen."

"You're always clucking around and taking care of everybody," they told her. "We appreciate all the support you give us, but you also micromanage. You want to know everything we do, and you never let us take the chance to exercise leadership ourselves."

There was a significant and memorable difference between how she wanted to be seen and the perceptions of her behavior. She bought a small lion figurine to keep on her desk to remind herself of her desired management style. When she suspected she wasn't living up to her aspirations, she asked her staff, "Am I being a mother hen or a lion today?" It became a nonthreatening way for people to give her feedback.

It's Important

Description

Participants determine collectively which results are important to their immediate team and which to the organization as a whole, and decide on this basis where to focus their efforts.

Steps

1. Introduce the task: "We're going to explore performance results that are important to your particular team or to the organization as a whole. Such results might involve increasing customer satisfaction, improving quality, reducing accidents, or anything else you can think of that is particularly important to your team or to the organization as a whole."

2. Tell participants: "Please use your Sharpie pens to write on Post-it Notes the performance results that you believe are important either to your own team or to the organization as a whole. Write one result per Post-it, and make each result as concrete and specific as possible, so that we would recognize it if your team achieved it."

3. Give participants five minutes to write results.

4. Ask participants to post their results on flip chart paper on the wall.

5. During a break for the participants, categorize the Post-it Notes by logical groupings, such as productivity, growth, customer satisfaction, and the like.

Experiential Elements

- Reflection
- Small group discussion
- Whole group discussion

Setup

Prepare one copy of the "Matrix of Importance" flip chart for each subgroup (see Step 6).

Special Supplies

A pad of Post-it Notes and a Sharpie pen for each participant

---

This activity is adapted from "TeamScores: Measuring and Communicating Performance," by Peter R. Garber, in *The Pfeiffer Book of Successful Team-Building Tools*, and is used with permission.

6. Divide the participants into subgroups to discuss a category (or categories) of results. Each subgroup should have a Matrix of Importance flip chart.

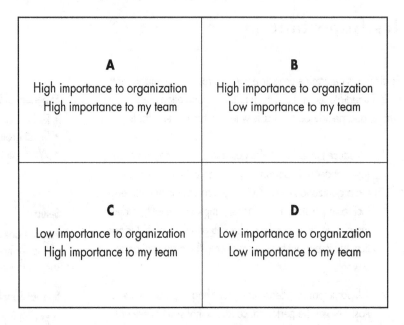

A	**B**
High importance to organization High importance to my team	High importance to organization Low importance to my team
C	**D**
Low importance to organization High importance to my team	Low importance to organization Low importance to my team

7. Instruct participants to take the Post-it Notes that relate to their categories to their subgroup locations. Tell the groups that they may eliminate any duplicate Post-it Notes.

8. Ask the subgroup members to work together to place the Post-it Notes in the relevant quadrants of the matrix and then to discuss the reasons they categorized these results as they did. They should note particularly where they had difficulty reaching agreement (for example, because results that were important to one team were less important to another team).

9. Have each group present its matrix in turn, with the group members' rationales for placing the Post-it Notes where they did and a discussion of the results that they could not agree on.

10. As the whole group listens to each presentation, participants may ask for clarification or suggest that a Post-it be moved from one quadrant to another.

11. Discuss the implications of the completed matrixes with the group: "The results that are in Quadrant A in the various matrixes are those you determined were the most important to your individual teams and to the organization as a whole, and they should receive the most attention from you. The results in Quadrant D are the opposite: least important to your teams and to the organization as a whole and should receive the least of your attention. You will need to do more analysis of Quadrants B and C to determine how much attention they warrant."

12. Facilitate a discussion of each quadrant. Ask:

    • "What specific measures can each team take to ensure that its members focus their efforts on Quadrant A results?"

    • "Are there any results that were placed in Quadrants B or C that are really Quadrant A results?"

    • "Are there any Quadrant D results that you would recommend discarding?"

Other Suggested Activities for a Peers-Only Retreat

You will find a wealth of possible activities to incorporate into a peers-only retreat in the Activities for Culture Change, Team-Building, and Board Retreats index (p. 493) if you are focusing on relationship building; the Activities for Making Decisions, Planning, and Evaluating Ideas index (p. 502) if you are focusing on planning; and the Activities to Use in Any Retreat index (p. 490) for a variety of methodologies to consider.

Abandonment Retreats

You might consider recommending to your client a retreat to address what management guru Peter Drucker called "organized abandonment," in which you "put every product, every service, every process, every market, every distribution channel, and every customer and end-user on trial for its life" (Drucker, 1999, pp. 74–80).

It might sound scary to your client, but an abandonment retreat simply means bringing representatives from all areas of her organization (or department) together offsite and putting everything on the table. The ultimate goal is to eliminate those aspects of the operations that are holding the group back—even if they worked in the past. Done properly, it is a powerful event that can set new and urgently needed directions for the organization.

We often recommend abandonment retreats as precursors to strategic planning or creative thinking retreats. They provide a needed house cleaning before an organization can move in new directions.

A reevaluation of such magnitude is bound to trigger highly charged emotions, so if you recommend one of these retreats, plan it especially carefully and take it slow and easy. Don't push the organization further and faster than it's ready to move.

These are some guidelines we urge our clients to follow to create a successful abandonment retreat:

1. Don't Think in Terms of a Single Meeting

A complex change often requires several offsite retreats and onsite meetings over a period of months. If you think of this as a multisession process rather than discrete events, you can help the participants build on what they have developed and bring new group members up to speed more quickly. A series of retreats or mini-retreats gives participants time between sessions to reflect on what has taken place, test new ideas, solicit input from colleagues who weren't present, and think about how best to contribute to the next session.

2. Make Sure There Is Consensus on the Organization's Strategic Direction

A broad consensus helps drive the hundreds of daily decisions that determine whether an organization will succeed, whereas a muddled strategy allows people to decide individually what is important, without having a context to guide them. Participants in an abandonment retreat must decide in which direction to steer their organization and what it is renouncing. A comprehensive dialogue will identify the activities that will move the organization forward, as well as those that are marginal and may be abandoned.

For instance, the participants may decide to give up certain specialty services that have had a lackluster performance and instead choose new areas of service, place greater emphasis on core services, or restructure their work groups.

See Chapter 9, "Exploring Strategic Direction," pp. 200–202.

3. Evaluate Work Processes

During abandonment retreats, participants examine work processes to determine which are a net asset and which are a net cost. They determine which processes define what the organization stands for to its clients and staff and also which processes are critical to the organization's success, even though not necessarily visible to an outsider. Once they have concluded this analysis, they can eliminate processes that no longer serve a purpose or create value for their organization.

See Chapter 9, "Evaluating Work Processes," pp. 230–232.

See Chapter 7, "Participants are Resisting New Ideas," pp. 150–155, for a discussion of how to deal effectively with resistance.

4. Be Prepared for Resistance

By their very nature, abandonment retreats require people to move out of their comfort zones. Participants want to hold onto what's familiar. It's very hard to let go.

5. Encourage Fresh Thinking

See Chapter 12, "Leading a Creativity and Innovation Retreat," for creative thinking activities.

Some participants will let go of outmoded ways only when they can see other possibilities. In an abandonment retreat we use creative thinking activities to help participants gain new perspectives.

6. Encourage the Group to Make Strategic Choices

See Chapter 8, "Methods of Decision Making," pp. 162–168, and Chapter 9 throughout for decision-making and priority-setting activities.

The word *choice* itself defines the difficulty of the activity. To choose one thing means not to choose an alternative or to give up something else, and for many people, particularly ambitious, competent, high achievers, this is very hard to do. That's why such people are typically overburdened with work; they take on everything and give up nothing. They're not being strategic—and they are paying a price.

7. Recognize and Remove Obstacles to Change

See Chapter 10, "Obstacle Busters II," pp. 273–274, for an activity that will help participants forecast and deal appropriately with impediments.

It's unfortunate when people see obstacles to change as insurmountable, both for themselves and for their organizations. Deal with this before it becomes a self-fulfilling prophecy. Include time for members of the organization to explain the hurdles they foresee rising as change gets underway.

In an abandonment retreat participants look closely at how the organization (or their department) operates. Then they choose to eliminate what doesn't work anymore. Yes, they are spending some time focusing on what doesn't work, but when they do away with that, they are left with what does work. This provides a solid foundation on which to build a great future. In the end the participants in abandonment retreats feel good about what they have done. It's like throwing away all the junk in the attic—they have lightened their load. Best of all, the group is taking control, and the participants are making the tough choices together.

Suggested Activities for an Abandonment Retreat

You will find many activities to consider when you design an abandonment retreat in the Activities for Making Decisions, Planning, and Evaluating Ideas index (p. 502) as well as the Activities to Use in Any Retreat index (p. 490).

Chapter 14

Closing the Retreat and Working on Implementation

N o matter how well-planned and executed a retreat is, it won't be judged a success unless it leads to the changes participants want to make. And it can't lead to significant change unless participants make concrete commitments for action before leaving the retreat (and unless they honor those commitments once they are back at work).

Before the retreat adjourns, as we noted in Chapter 8, participants must determine action steps, assign responsibility for carrying them out, decide on interim and final target dates, and devise ways to measure progress toward meeting the goals they set.

See Chapter 8, "The Nub: Action Planning," pp. 185–192, for a full discussion of action planning.

Summing Up and Preparing to Follow Through

The purpose of a formal retreat closure is to help participants reflect on what they've learned, make commitments to specific actions, and think about how they will integrate back at the office what they accomplished at the retreat. You might use one or two of the following activities to close your retreat.

The Messy Room

Description   The facilitator presents the Four-Room Apartment model (see Step 1). Participants discuss how the model might help them anticipate and deal with adverse reactions that might occur as they attempt to implement the changes they have recommended or decided on at the retreat.

Steps   1. Present the Four-Room Apartment flip chart.

Illustration by Sachia Long.

Experiential Elements

- Shared dialogue and discussion
- Personal and group reflection
- Experimenting with ideas

Setup

- Prepare "The Four-Room Apartment" flip chart (see Step 1).
- Prepare the "Exploring the Rooms" flip chart (see Step 3).

Introduce the activity with this mini-presentation: "Imagine yourselves living in a metaphorical four-room apartment. You as individuals, and your group, team, department, and organization as entities, move from room to room in response to things that happen inside and outside your organization. As shown by the arrows in the diagram, the movement is cyclical and continual—meaning that it is a process that you continually revisit, not something you experience just once and are done with.

"The first room is the Room of Satisfaction, where you are pretty happy with how things are and content to leave them be.

"But let's say you begin to notice that not everything is perfect. Or you're compelled—by changing circumstances, by upper management, whatever—to rethink how you've been working. You then leave the Room of Satisfaction and enter the Room of Denial.

"In this second room you feel anxious about a possible change or deny the need for change, although you may not be conscious of why you are feeling that way. You have to stay in this room, though, where you may be perceived as resisting change, until you come to terms with your denial. Once that takes place you move to the Messy Room.

"If any of you have teenagers whose rooms you don't like to walk into, you know what a messy room is like. In this room you start to question everything. You feel unsure of yourself and your environment. Thoughts that once were neat are now disorderly. Things that you once held to be true now do not seem so true, and you do not yet know what is true.

"Although it is extremely uncomfortable for most people to hang out in the Messy Room, it is probably the most important room in the apartment. For it is in the Messy Room that you are open to new ideas and perspectives. Only by passing through it can you get to the fourth room, the Room of Renewal.

"In this last room you are able to embrace change, to see how it benefits you and others and the organization as a whole.

"Organizations often try to institute changes after retreats by trying to push everyone straight from satisfaction to renewal. But change doesn't happen that way. If you don't work through the resistance in the Room of Denial and the doubts and discomfort of the Messy Room, you will not reach the Room of Renewal. So the key to reaching this last room is recognizing that change is a process. Then you can develop strategies that are appropriate for the room you are in that will help you manage the change successfully.

"Remember also that change is a cycle. Even if you were able to implement every change you have imagined at this retreat, eventually you would become satisfied with the status quo and the cycle would start over again."

2. Ask the group what room they think they are in now with regard to the changes they want to make and why they believe they are in that room. Discuss similarities and differences among participants' responses, and ask for preliminary thoughts about what those differences might mean for the success of these changes.

3. Divide the participants into four subgroups and assign each group the task of exploring one of the four rooms. Present the Exploring the Rooms flip chart.

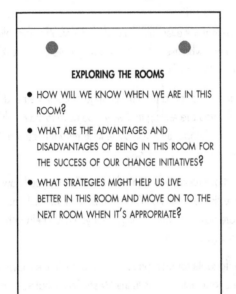

EXPLORING THE ROOMS

- HOW WILL WE KNOW WHEN WE ARE IN THIS ROOM?

- WHAT ARE THE ADVANTAGES AND DISADVANTAGES OF BEING IN THIS ROOM FOR THE SUCCESS OF OUR CHANGE INITIATIVES?

- WHAT STRATEGIES MIGHT HELP US LIVE BETTER IN THIS ROOM AND MOVE ON TO THE NEXT ROOM WHEN IT'S APPROPRIATE?

4. Ask the members of each group to write their answers to the questions about their room on a flip chart.

5. Have each subgroup present its work. Facilitate a discussion that answers these questions:

- "How might being aware of the dynamics of the change process help you back at work?"

- "How can members of this group help one another when some are struggling in the Room of Denial or the Messy Room or some are staying in the Room of Satisfaction even though things aren't as rosy as they might seem?"

Read more about the theory and application of the Four-Room Apartment in *Productive Workplaces*, by Marvin Weisbord (1987).

If the participants came up with a number of action steps, as they likely will, they will have to plan how to accomplish them and decide on their relative priority. The next activity helps the group focus on what needs to be done to achieve the greatest impact.

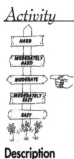

Top Priorities

Description

This activity requires participants to focus on their top three priorities and reach agreement on the actions they will take to accomplish these priorities.

Steps

1. Using a priority-setting activity from Chapter 8 or 9, facilitate a discussion that concludes with agreement on the top three priorities.

2. Show the What Can the People in This Room Do to Accomplish These Priorities? flip chart.

> **WHAT CAN THE PEOPLE IN THIS ROOM DO TO ACCOMPLISH THESE PRIORITIES?**
>
> - WHO WILL DO WHAT BY WHEN?
> - HOW WILL YOU COMMUNICATE THIS PRIORITY TO OTHERS?
> - HOW WILL YOU ENCOURAGE YOUR STAKEHOLDERS TO EMBRACE THIS PRIORITY?
> - HOW WILL YOU HANDLE PRESSURE TO SPEND TIME ON NONPRIORITIES?

Experiential Elements

- Shared dialogue and discussion
- Personal and group reflection

Setup

Create "What Can the People in This Room Do to Accomplish These Priorities?" flip chart (see Step 2).

3. Divide the group into three subgroups. Have each subgroup address one of the top priorities by answering the questions listed on the flip chart.

4. Have each subgroup report back to the rest of the group.

5. Discuss with the whole group of participants how realistic their priorities are, given what it will take to accomplish them. Ask: "Can you accomplish all of these priorities? Do you need to scale back by dropping one or two?"

   Ask the group: "Would some actions support more than one of the priorities? Should those actions be undertaken first?"

Facilitator Note   The facilitator may have to press participants to make hard choices.

The next several activities all wrap up the work of the retreat in different ways. They may be used singly or in combination.

Closing Thoughts

Description

In this activity participants write on individual Post-it Notes and then share their thoughts in three areas: something they learned, something they will commit to do, and a hope they have for the whole group.

Steps

1. Introduce the activity: "You have taken time away from the office to consider issues that you identified as important. This time should pay off as an investment in making things better in [the organization]. But change will take place only when you, the people in this room, make commitments to change how you have been doing things.

   "So, thinking back on everything we have discussed in this retreat, write on three separate Post-it Notes:

   - "One thing you learned

   - "One thing you personally commit to doing differently

   - "One thing you hope the whole group will do differently"

2. Have participants read their resolutions aloud and post their notes on the appropriate flip chart.

Facilitator Note

This is a closing activity, not an opening for further discussion. No one should comment on what any individual says. Encourage participants to listen and absorb the ideas suggested.

Experiential Elements

- Reflecting back on experiences
- Writing down ideas individually
- Listening

Setup

Create three flip charts with these titles:

- "I learned . . ."
- "I will . . ."
- "I hope we all will . . ."

Special Supplies

A pad of Post-it Notes and a Sharpie pen for each participant

---

Letter to Myself

Description

In this activity participants write letters to themselves about the commitments they made during the retreat. The letters are sealed in envelopes, collected, and later sent back to the individuals who wrote them.

Experiential Elements
- Reflecting back on experiences
- Writing down ideas

Steps

1. Distribute the stationery and envelopes to the participants. Ask them to write their names and office addresses on their envelopes.

2. Introduce the activity: "Please write a letter to yourself that summarizes what you commit to do differently as a result of this retreat. Be as specific as possible in making your commitments.

   - "What will you do?

   - "By what date will you do it?

   - "How will you know when you have done it?"

3. Inform participants that you will send the letters to them to remind them of their commitments within the next week or two. Assure them that no one will see the contents of their sealed envelopes but themselves.

4. Give participants ten minutes to write their letters and seal them in envelopes.

5. Collect the letters.

6. A week or so later send the letters to the participants.

Special Supplies
- Two sheets of organization stationery for each participant, plus several extra
- One envelope for each participant
- Postage stamps (if the envelopes will be mailed rather than hand-delivered)

Facilitator Note

Having participants write letters to themselves reinforces their commitment to the decisions they've reached at the retreat. When they receive their letters, they will be reminded of their intentions even as they are faced with competing priorities back at work.

Appreciation

Description

In this activity, participants take turns openly expressing appreciation to each other for the contributions they have made during the retreat.

Experiential Elements
- Personal reflection
- Listening
- Conversations with others

Special Requirement

This activity works best for groups of twelve or fewer participants. Variations for larger groups are given in the Facilitator Notes.

Steps

1. Have the participants sit in a circle. (If the group is large, have people sit in two concentric circles.)

2. Introduce the activity: "Please look around the room. Everybody here has made a contribution to the success of this retreat. When we are busy at work, we don't often take the time to appreciate one another's efforts. So we are going to take some time to do that now.

   "Throughout this retreat, you worked with each other in new ways. You now have the opportunity to express your appreciation for something that people in this room did—taking a risk by bringing up a difficult subject, clarifying a misunderstanding, suggesting an idea for the group to consider, and so forth."

   Demonstrate an appreciation: "For instance, 'I want to express appreciation to Nancy [*substitute an example from your retreat*]. Nancy, I really appreciated how you didn't just go along with a decision you thought would be bad for customer relations. Your persistence—in the face of some frustration from colleagues who wanted to come to closure—helped the group make a better decision.'

   "Notice that while I was expressing my appreciation to Nancy, I made eye contact with her."

3. Invite other participants to contribute: "Now I would like to ask the rest of the group to think about Nancy's contributions over the course of the retreat, whether in small group discussions, in the whole group, or even on a break. We will all take a turn appreciating something that Nancy did.

   "Roxanna, why don't you start? And then we will go around the circle."

4. When everyone has appreciated the person you began with, the group repeats the process with others until everyone has been appreciated by everyone else.

Facilitator Notes
- This is a wonderful activity to end a retreat in which the participants have grappled with really tough issues. It helps participants reflect on the hard work everyone has done and leaves people feeling good that others recognize their contributions. Only use this activity, though, if you feel confident that participants will recognize one another's contributions willingly, without feeling manipulated or forced. You don't want to inadvertently create a situation in which someone does not receive an appreciation.

- After starting the process you should stay out of the circle. Although it might be nice to bask in participants' comments about your work, it is more important to have the participants focus on their appreciation for one another and what they did to make the retreat a success.

- People often find being openly acknowledged for their contributions a moving experience. Be prepared for the possibility that some participants (both men and women) will become teary-eyed when being appreciated.

- This version of the activity will take too long if the group is larger than twelve people. Here are some quicker variations for larger groups:

  The circle. Have participants go around the circle, with each person giving an appreciation to the person on his or her right.

  The Koosh ball. Use a Koosh ball, a small, soft, easily caught, rubbery object found in toy or novelty stores. One person tosses the ball to someone else in the group while expressing appreciation for what that person contributed. Then that person tosses the ball to someone else and expresses appreciation for that person, and so on, until everyone has had the ball and received an appreciation. (Remind participants not to toss the ball to someone who already has received it. In the interest of time and equity, limit appreciations to one per participant.)

  The yarn ball. Introduce a ball of yarn, with each participant holding onto the unwinding string of yarn somewhere along its length as he or she tosses the yarn ball to another participant. This creates a memorable visual (a *web of appreciation*) that demonstrates how the whole group is interconnected. You'll be surprised by how much yarn you'll need. You don't want to run out in the middle of the appreciations.

> **Facilitator Note**
>
> Despite its simple structure this activity calls for skillful facilitation. The facilitator must be able to redirect anyone who gives a backhanded compliment (a comment that sounds positive but implies a negative, such as, "I want to thank Marlene for not being as long-winded as usual"). You should use this activity only if you are sure enough good feeling has built up over the course of the retreat that everyone in the group will respond positively.

What I See for Me . . .

Description

This activity helps participants think in fresh ways about their roles in helping their organization reach its potential. They use visual stimuli to help themselves make associations about what they might do differently after the retreat.

Experiential Elements

- Using visual materials
- Individual reflection
- Paired discussion
- Using metaphor
- Experimenting with ideas

Steps

1. Show the What Do I Need to Do to Help [the Organization] Fulfill its Potential? flip chart, and define the task: "We're going to use visual stimuli to give us new perspectives on the question of what you need to do to help [the organization] fulfill its potential. Think for a few moments about the question. Then, in silence, walk over to the table and pick up a picture. Make your choice quickly. Don't analyze the pictures; just select the first one that attracts you.

"When you sit down again, continue to maintain silence. Look at the picture, and consider how it suggests answers to the question of what you need to do to help [the organization] fulfill its potential. Write down your thoughts, using these questions to guide your thinking."

Setup

- Cut large pictures with as wide a variety of subjects as you can find from magazines such as *National Geographic* or from remaindered books of photographs. You will need at least three pictures for each participant.
- Put each picture, backed by blank paper, in a transparent sheet protector.
- Place all the pictures face up on a large table, so participants can walk around it and view them.
- Prepare a flip chart sheet titled, "What Do I Need to Do to Help [the Organization] Fulfill its Potential?" (see Step 1).
- Prepare the "How to Look at Your Picture" flip chart (see Step 2).

This activity is derived from the authors' experience in the Center for Creative Leadership's Leading Creatively program. As an alternative to clipping their own illustrations, facilitators can purchase a collection of photographs and illustrations CCL has assembled for groups to use, called Visual Explorer®. The Visual Explorer package includes instructions on a number of different ways to use visual stimuli. It can be acquired through www.ccl.org.

2. Show the How to Look at Your Picture flip chart.

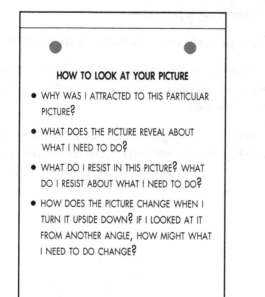

3. Demonstrate to the participants how they might get ideas from a picture. Choose one from the table yourself, and tell the group the messages you read from it. For instance: "This picture is of very straight rows of trees, very orderly. And that tells me that I must plan in a more ordered and organized way how I can encourage more interdepartmental cooperation among my staff. I can't just expect it to happen spontaneously. These trees look old; someone planted the seeds a long time ago. So I have to plant the seeds and be patient, not expecting everything to change all at once. There are some people in the background having a picnic, and that reminds me that I must make the changes fun for people. When I turn the picture upside down, I notice how the trunks of the trees connect to the ground, and I think about keeping us all rooted in the good things we have already achieved."

4. Give participants ten minutes to contemplate their pictures and ten more minutes to share the results with a partner at their tables.

5. After a few minutes, ask for volunteers to show their pictures and share what they wrote with the rest of the group.

Facilitator Notes
- This activity requires a strong ability to model the imaginative use of visual stimuli. It requires comfort in debriefing nonlinear and occasionally highly personal data.

- Use neutral pictures; don't choose pictures that are related to the group's industry or issues.

- Participants should not be pushed to talk publicly about their reactions. Often people who are initially reticent will—after hearing others speak—become eager to explain their pictures. Others will prefer to keep their reactions to themselves, and that's perfectly all right.

- Sometimes one or two participants have such a significant response to their pictures that they wish to take them home. We generally let participants in our retreats do so, and you may wish to do the same if you can spare the photos.

Vehicle for Change II

Description

This activity uses a vehicle as a metaphor to stimulate thinking about the changes the participants will make collectively after the retreat.

Steps

1. Divide participants into subgroups of four to five people. Introduce the task: "You are going to represent this group as a drawing of a vehicle of some sort. It could be an automobile, a truck, a cement mixer, an eighteen-wheeler, a spacecraft, whatever."

2. Show the Vehicle for Change flip chart, and tell participants: "The vehicle you draw should include all these things."

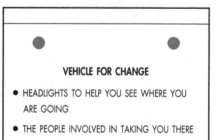

VEHICLE FOR CHANGE

- HEADLIGHTS TO HELP YOU SEE WHERE YOU ARE GOING
- THE PEOPLE INVOLVED IN TAKING YOU THERE
- CARGO (WHAT YOU ARE TAKING AWAY WITH YOU FROM THIS RETREAT)
- THE FUEL THAT WILL MOTIVATE YOU MOVING FORWARD
- THE EXHAUST SYSTEM THAT FILTERS OUT WHAT YOU ARE LEAVING BEHIND

Experiential Elements
- Using metaphor to express thoughts and feelings
- Personal reflection
- Drawing
- Group presentations

Setup

Create the "Vehicle for Change" flip chart (see Step 1).

Special Supplies

Prismacolor Art Markers

This activity is adapted from "Transfer Vehicle," by Tim Richardson, in *50 Creative Training Closers: Innovative Ways to End Your Training with IMPACT!* and is used with permission.

3. Give each subgroup twenty minutes to draw a vehicle on a sheet of flip chart paper.

4. After calling time, have each subgroup describe its picture to the larger group and explain what each element of the drawing means.

Expectations and Outcomes

Description

This activity is started at the beginning of the retreat. Participants write down their expectations for the retreat, as an opening activity, then put these notes into envelopes and seal them. At the end of the retreat the envelopes are returned, and participants reflect on the difference between what they thought would happen and what actually took place.

Experiential Elements
- Personal reflection
- Writing down ideas
- Personal and group discussion

Steps

1. Part I: *At the beginning of the retreat,* distribute the My Expectations form (see CD 14) and an envelope to each person.

2. Introduce the activity: "We are going to reflect on your expectations of this retreat we are about to begin. Please fill out the form with the first thing that comes to mind. Don't censor yourself in any way. No one else will see what you write." Allow five minutes for participants to fill in their forms.

Setup

Make one copy of the "My Expectations" form for each participant (see CD 14).

Special Supplies

One envelope for each participant

3. Have the participants place their forms in the envelopes, write their names on the envelopes, and seal them. Collect the envelopes, and tell participants that you will return their unopened envelopes to them later.

4. Part II: *At the end of the retreat,* give the envelopes back to the participants. Ask them to open the envelopes and look at what they wrote at the beginning of the retreat.

5. In small groups of three to five people, ask participants to reflect on what they wrote. Do they still see things the same way as they did at the beginning of the retreat? If not, what accounts for the change?

6. Ask for volunteers to tell the whole group how they saw things at the beginning of the retreat and how they see them now.

Facilitator Note

This is an excellent way to demonstrate how individual and group perceptions can change when a group puts in a good effort. Be aware, however, that there is always the risk that some people will express disappointment rather than approval.

The Road We've Traveled

Description

In this activity, small groups of participants draw road maps of the progress made in the retreat.

Experiential Elements
- Personal reflection
- Personal and group discussion
- Visual expression

Steps

1. Divide the participants into groups of three to five people. Introduce the activity: "We have traveled a long way over the course of this retreat. The road may have been bumpy, with a few blind curves, but we are now in a different place than we were when we started.

   "While it's important to remain focused on the future, on the road ahead, it's also important to glance over our shoulders to see how far we've already traveled. In your groups, draw a road map of this retreat on a flip chart, showing graphically what the journey was like, what landmarks we passed along the way, and where the road seems to be leading." Allow ten minutes for the groups to work.

2. Ask each group to post its road map on a wall around the room. Facilitate a discussion around these questions:

   - "What are some of the most striking features of the road maps?"

   - "What picture do they collectively paint of what was accomplished at the retreat and where the group seems to be heading?"

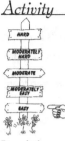

I'm Committing . . .

Description

In this activity participants create mini-posters of their commitments and then tape them to a speech bubble made of foam core. Participants are photographed with their speech bubbles, as if they were voicing their commitments. The photographs are e-mailed to participants a week or so after the retreat as a visible reminder of their commitments.

Steps

1. Ask participants to make mini-posters, on 8 1/2 inch x 11 inch white copy paper, that illustrate with words or pictures, or both, a commitment they are willing to make based on the work that took place in the retreat.

2. Each participant in turn attaches a poster to the speech bubble, shown below:

(This works best when participants attach their posters to the speech bubble with a couple of pieces of masking tape. The tape should be doubled over and stuck to the back of the paper, so that it doesn't show from the front.)

Experiential Elements
- Personal reflection
- Visual expression

Setup

Prepare an oval-shaped speech bubble with a tail (like the ones used for characters in the comics), as shown below. It should be made of foam core at least 1/4 inch thick. The oval area should be at least 18 inches in diameter, large enough so that 8 1/2 inch x 11 inch paper placed vertically (portrait) or horizontally (landscape) will fit inside it. Outline the edges of the speech bubble in dark blue or black marker to give it a border, and attach a handle, made of folded foam core and masking tape, to the back.

Special Supplies
- A foam core speech bubble (see Setup)
- 8 1/2 inch x 11 inch white copy paper
- A variety of dark and brightly colored markers
- A digital camera

3. Ask participants to tell the group what their commitment is and to hold the speech bubble by its handle to the side of their face, so that the pointed end is near their mouth. Take a photograph of each participant.

4. Approximately one week after the retreat, e-mail to each participant his or her photo to serve as a tangible reminder of the commitments made at the retreat.

Facilitator Notes

- Make sure you have everyone's current e-mail address.

- Check out your camera in advance. Make sure the flash is working. Check each photo after you take it to make sure it's a good picture—and take a second one if necessary.

- And if you are working with a co-facilitator, you should both be involved in moving the process along smoothly and quickly.

Activity

Collective Quilt

Description

In this activity participants create their own "quilt pieces," on 8 1/2 inch x 11 inch sheets of paper, that show what they will do differently. The quilt pieces are posted on a long sheet of butcher paper. Participants view the collectively created quilt to see how they will work together to make the changes that they agreed on.

Steps

1. Ask each participant to use the collage materials to make a quilt section on a 8 1/2 inch x 11 inch sheet of paper; the collage will illustrate with words or pictures, or both, a commitment the participant is willing to make based on the work that took place in the retreat.

2. Give participants ten minutes to select their materials and create their collages. Urge participants not to take too long gathering materials but to pick up the words and images that seem to relate to what they would like to do differently without dwelling too much on why they're choosing certain images or phrases.

3. Ask the participants to tape their quilt sections onto the long piece of butcher paper, which you will have hung on a wall.

4. Invite the participants to tour the collective quilt. Then ask each participant to say in turn what his or her quilt piece means.

Facilitator Note

Clip a lot of words and pictures from magazines in preparation for this activity—many more than you expect you'll need. You want to have lots for participants to choose from. And allow yourself sufficient setup time. It can take a while to spread out hundreds of small clippings on a table, face side (the side with the picture or words on it) up.

Experiential Elements

- Personal reflection
- Collage making
- Drawing
- Listening to the ideas of others
- Observing while walking around the room

Setup

- Post a fifteen-foot-long (or longer) sheet of butcher paper on a wall.
- Put collage supplies on each table.

Special Supplies

- A roll of butcher paper
- Pictures and words clipped from magazines
- Colored paper
- Colored markers
- Glue sticks
- Scissors
- 8 1/2 inch x 11 inch sheets of paper

You Can Count on Me

Description

In this activity participants write their names, contact information, and commitments they intend to keep after the retreat on sheets of 8 1/2 inch x 11 inch paper. They crumple the papers into balls and toss them around the room. The participants then pick up commitments that are not their own and take responsibility for checking in with one another to encourage each person to keep his or her commitments.

Steps

1. Distribute the sheets of paper and Sharpie markers, and ask each participant to write his or her name, phone number, and e-mail address on the top of a piece of paper.

2. Introduce the activity: "Please write what you commit to do differently as a result of this retreat. Be as specific as possible in making your commitments."

3. Show the What I Will Do flip chart.

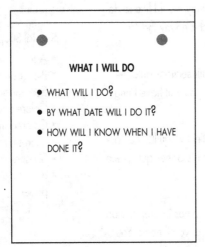

WHAT I WILL DO

- WHAT WILL I DO?
- BY WHAT DATE WILL I DO IT?
- HOW WILL I KNOW WHEN I HAVE DONE IT?

Experiential Elements
- Reflecting back on experiences
- Writing down ideas
- Play

Setup
- Create the "What I Will Do" flip chart (see Step 3).
- Create the "What I Need" flip chart (see Step 4).

Special Supplies
- Several sheets of 8 1/2 inch x 11 inch paper for each participant
- Sharpie fine-point markers

This activity is adapted from "Secret Support," in *50 Creative Training Closers: Innovative Ways to End Your Training with IMPACT!* by Lynn Solem and Bob Pike, and is used with permission.

4. Then show participants the What I Need flip chart.

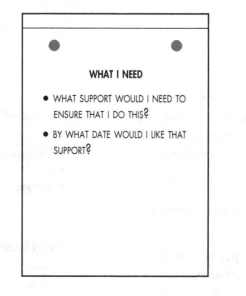

5. Give participants five minutes to write their commitments and what they need.

6. Ask participants to crumple their papers into balls and toss them around the room. After they've tossed their own, participants can pick up any papers that land near them to throw. Allow the tossing to go on for a few minutes.

7. Tell the participants that in a minute they will each pick up a piece of paper that is not their own. Seek agreement from participants that they will support the person who made the commitment they find on the paper they pick up.

8. Ask participants to pick up a crumpled piece of paper. Tell them: "If you happen to pick up your own paper, toss it back and pick up another." Repeat that each participant, without telling anyone whose commitment they have picked up, agrees to provide support in the way requested on the paper.

Facilitator Note   When participants make contact with one another to follow up, they will be reminded of their intentions even as they are faced with competing priorities back at work.

Change Conga

Description

In this activity participants create mini-posters of their commitments. Table by table, participants form a conga line. They dance around the other tables saying their commitments in turn in rhythm while showing their posters to the rest of the participants.

Steps

1. Divide participants into subgroups of five to seven members each.

2. Ask participants to make mini-posters, on 8 1/2 inch x 11 inch paper, that illustrate with words or pictures, or both, a commitment they are willing to make based on the work that took place in the retreat.

3. Ask the first subgroup to form a conga line. Each participant in that subgroup should show his or her poster to the other participants and state in a rhythmic fashion his or her commitment.

4. The last person to show his or her poster in the first subgroup picks the next subgroup to form a new conga line, and then the first subgroup sits down. This continues until all the members of all the subgroups have shared their commitments.

Facilitator Note

The facilitator must be able to deal effectively with a bit of noise and confusion and should feel comfortable working with movement in a playful way.

Experiential Elements

- Dance
- Rhythm and music
- Play
- Drawing

Special Supplies

- Several sheets of 8 1/2 inch x 11 inch paper for each participant
- Prismacolor Art Markers in various colors for each table

Obstacle Busters III

Description

Working individually, participants identify what might hamper their ability to make the changes they want to make. They walk across the room twice, aiming to maneuver around obstacles that have been placed in their path. The first time they focus on the obstacles, and the second time they focus on their destination.

Experiential Elements
• Individual reflection
• Movement

Steps

1. Introduce the task: "We're going to use some aikido principles to help you look at the impediments you might face in implementing the changes you said you want to make and at how your mind-set might help or hinder you in overcoming those obstacles."

2. Tell the participants: "Really focus on all the obstacles you face in implementing the changes you want to make. Let yourself feel the heaviness of the load of these obstacles in your body. Get a sense of how dragged down you'll feel by obstacles such as not enough time, other priorities, demanding customers, and the like."

Setup

Put obstacles, such as chairs, tables, or boxes, around the room in a way that makes it difficult, but not impossible, for participants to walk from one side of the room to the other.

3. Tell the participants: "Now I'd like you to walk from one side of the room to the other, focusing not just on the obstacles you'll face when you get back to the office but on the physical obstacles as well. It's not going to be easy to get from one side of the room to another."

4. While participants are walking from one side of the room to another, move into people's paths, trying to block briefly (without touching anyone) as many participants as you can.

5. Ask participants what the experience of trying to get across the room was like with all those obstacles.

6. Tell the participants: "Now focus on what it would be like if you were successful in making changes you want to make. How would the office change for the better? Let yourself feel in your body the pride at accomplishing what you have set out to do. And when you cross the room this time, focus on where you are heading. Know that you *will* get to the other side of the room, no matter how many obstacles are thrown in your way."

7. While participants are walking from one side of the room to another, once again try to block (without touching anyone) as many participants as you can.

8. Ask participants what the experience of trying to get across the room was like this time.

9. Facilitate a whole group discussion of what actions the group might take to keep their efforts and energy focused on the positive results they plan to achieve rather than on the impediments to achieving those results.

Facilitator Note   The facilitator must be comfortable talking about how participants' states of mind affect their abilities.

See Chapter 9, "Obstacle Busters I," pp. 245–246, and Chapter 10, "Obstacle Busters II," pp. 273–274, for other versions of this exercise.

Writing the Follow-Up Report

Before you leave the retreat site, as all the others head for their cars, take the time necessary to separate all the flip charts that chronicle decisions and action steps from those that just reflect group brainstorming. Organizing the charts in this way while everything's fresh in your mind will be a big help to whoever will be writing the retreat report. Ideally, the report should be completed within a day or two of the retreat, so be sure to give the sorted charts to that person before he or she leaves the site. (If you're that person, of course, you'll take these charts with you.)

Read more about tracking what the group has done in Chapter 6, "Recording the Group's Work," pp. 132–134.

Because it's so important to write and distribute the report quickly, a simple record of what happened at the retreat is far better than elaborate documentation that takes weeks to produce. If a strategic plan is to come out of the retreat, that plan can be written with the aid of the retreat report, but the report is not the plan.

The report should not be a chronological record of everything that took place at the offsite. A more useful structure for the report might include these few points, in the following order:

- Key decisions
- Action steps
- Pending items
- Transcriptions of flip chart notes and handouts

Key decisions. These should include the goals, and the strategies for achieving them, that the group has agreed on. This section of the report is, in essence, the executive summary, so it should be short, clear, and easy to read.

Action steps. These provide the details of what people will actually do: who will take what action, by what date, and with what resources. Make sure you separate out all action steps so that individuals and departments can find and track their assignments easily.

Pending items. These include the topics that were never fully discussed. They should go on the agenda for a later meeting or a future retreat. Other pending items might be information still needed before a decision can be made or a decision that requires the involvement of people who were not at the retreat.

Transcriptions. These contain the actual words on the flip charts created at the retreat and copies of the handouts. It is important to have these records, so that participants can go back to the in-the-moment notes for the details of the various discussions. These transcriptions are also a resource for people when questions come up later. The best place for them is in an appendix at the end of the report. Our practice is to put them in chronological order or by topic so readers can find the ones they want easily.

In capturing flip chart records of open discussions, we usually do not arrange the ideas in bulleted lists because such lists often connote order of importance. Especially when participants have used Post-it Notes to place their thoughts on a flip chart, organizing these thoughts into lists means losing the original sense of free-flowing communication. You might consider using graphics software to present the Post-its as rectangles floating on a page. Or add a note that clarifies that the lists are arranged in random order. We also typically do not edit the points on flip charts (except to correct an obvious spelling error or to spell out an abbreviation that might not be understood by all readers).

An inexpensive software program that allows you to present ideas graphically is Inspiration, available at www.inspiration.com.

What's Your Role After the Retreat?

Ideally, as part of your initial contracting with your client (see Chapter 1, "Aligning Yourself with the Client," pp. 17–21), you and the client discussed what your role would be after the retreat. We may contract, for example, to check in with the group at predetermined intervals (such as one month and three months after the offsite) or to make ourselves available as needed, such as when the group becomes stuck.

In addition to the retreat report, we almost always write a detailed letter to our clients telling them what specifically we recommend that they do (and don't do) to keep the retreat spirit alive. Many of the points we typically include are outlined in Chapter 17 (which is available on the CD, should you wish to print it out and then edit it for your clients). Then we stay engaged with the client organization as much as we have contracted to do.

That sometimes means letting go before *we* feel ready. It is the participants' organization, not ours, and we cannot take implementation responsibility away from them. They—not we—must decide if, how, and when they will implement the plans they made at the retreat.

This isn't as easy to do as it may sound. We have had an intense engagement with the participants. We may like them very much and may find ourselves feeling left out when they no longer seem to need us. People in our line of work are often motivated by a desire to help others, and we may want to remain engaged in the implementation process to keep helping. These are normal human reactions, but one cannot allow them to override the more important concern, which is to ensure that the participants themselves "own" their implementation plans.

If the participants want our help, immediately after the offsite or later, they will ask us. If not, we have to let go.

No matter what we have contracted with our clients to do for them following a retreat, we always contract with ourselves to evaluate our own performance as facilitators. We ask our clients for feedback. We ask ourselves what worked well, what we might have done differently, how we collaborated with our co-facilitators, and which techniques worked best and which less well and why. When two or all three of us work together, we give each other feedback that helps us learn and grow. When we work with an internal facilitator, we ask for his or her feedback and also ask if he or she wants feedback from us. This is valuable for everyone's professional development.

We take this time to reflect and to learn about ourselves because we never want to be facilitating by rote. To be effective for our clients we need to remain open to learning. We can never afford to believe that we're "too expert" to learn. And as we all know, we all often learn a great deal more from our failures—when things don't work out as we expected—than from our successes. That being said, we don't beat ourselves over the head either. We gently probe into what we might do differently when faced with similar circumstances in the future.

Summary of Retreat Roles and Responsibilities

	Convener	Facilitator	Administrator	Participants
Preparation	• Establish clear goals • Demonstrate openness to new ideas • Express willingness to change • Come to clear agreement with facilitator on goals and roles	• Clarify roles • Align with convener's goals • Gather data • Design retreat	• Work with facilitator on logistics issues • Make arrangements for facility • Manage and communicate logistics, including meals and refreshments	• Participate in any retreat planning task forces • Answer the facilitator's questions openly and thoroughly • Make hopes and concerns for the retreat known to the convener and the facilitator
During retreat	• Set stage for retreat • Acknowledge and manage "Big Kahuna" Effect • Set boundaries • Model candor • Be present	• Set stage for retreat • Manage flow of retreat • Maintain focus • Keep moving toward goal • Deal with change • Urge group toward decision making and action planning • Assist in the creation of a clear action plan	• Handle all interaction with retreat facility • Ensure that appropriate supplies and equipment are in the room • Ensure that space is arranged correctly • Ensure that meals and refreshments are made available at the right times	• Engage fully and constructively • Listen to other participants • Raise concerns • Move out of comfort zones (consider new ideas and approaches) • Explore means to overcome obstacles • Get to know people you don't know personally
Follow-up	• Overcommunicate • Make outcomes important • Show top-management commitment • Remove obstacles	• Give work product from the retreat to the client • Assist, as needed, in the implementation of the action plan • Check in on process	• Distribute work product from the retreat • Assist in the logistics of follow-up meetings and communications	• Participate actively in task forces • Be willing to try new approaches to make things better • Ask for guidance in incorporating retreat goals into your daily work

What's Next for You?

We hope we have provided you with tools and tips that will help you avoid many of the mistakes that we made when we started this work. We have incorporated the feedback we received on our first book, *Retreats That Work,* into this book, and we now hope to get feedback from you on this book. Please e-mail us with your questions, comments, and critiques at partners@retreatsthatwork. com. We'd love to hear of successful variations of the activities and techniques that you tried, and any stories about your experiences you might want to share (changing the names, of course).

We hope this book will inspire you to venture out of your comfort zones. To try a technique that you wouldn't have considered before. To seek feedback about your impact on groups that will help you be a more positive force when you're facilitating retreats.

Maybe you will find a mentor—someone who is more experienced in this field than you are, or who has different expertise or become a mentor to someone else. Perhaps he or she will be someone with whom you can co-facilitate and whose work you can observe. It's tremendously important to see how others handle situations that might have confounded you.

It's quite a gift to work with and learn from one another. And it's reassuring to see that even very seasoned facilitators have days when the group doesn't respond well to their interventions.

When we teach internal facilitators the art of retreat design and facilitation, one of the things they tell us they find most useful is the opportunity after the course to co-facilitate with one of us. And frankly, we find it just as useful to partner with our students. Their questions have refined our thinking, and their fresh approaches have expanded our repertoire of possible interventions. So your more experienced colleagues would likely benefit just as much as you would from a collaboration, as less experienced colleagues would benefit from partnering with you, now or in the future.

Mostly we hope that you will take care of yourself. It takes a great deal of energy to facilitate quality retreats, so we urge you not to take on more than you can handle. Let perfectionism go, believe that success is possible, and do your best for each and every client organization.

The rest of this book is focused on the client's role. It is available on the CD, for you to reproduce for your clients.

SECTION TWO

Materials for the Client

Chapter 15

Working with the Facilitator to Plan the Retreat

Retreats, by definition, are distinct from people's everyday work lives. That's good, because it means participants will not be distracted by ringing phones and chiming e-mail notices. Out of their everyday environment, they will be able to devote hours—perhaps even days—of focused, uninterrupted attention to exploring problems and opportunities and determining solutions and strategies.

Unlike meetings, retreats often proceed in nonlinear fashion. At a typical meeting, participants make and hear reports, cover a long list of topics, and work on immediate problems. Participants in retreats are usually focused on coming up with innovative responses to substantive and long-term issues that lie beneath the surface.

The informality of retreats helps loosen people up so they can talk openly and do some real work. But the separation from everyday work life can also be a problem: it's easy to come up with strategies and action plans while cocooned away from the outside world; it's much harder to go back to the office and actually carry them out.

To increase the likelihood that ideas developed at your offsite will be translated into action at your workplace, every retreat should be conceived backward—starting with a vision of what you want to be different in the workplace.

Last Things First: What Do You Want to Be Different?

As an executive, director, manager, board chair, or leader, you have decided that an offsite retreat would be a good means of addressing important issues you and your organization or unit are facing. How to begin?

Your first step—long before selecting a date—is to ask, "What do we want to be different after this retreat?" The point is not to specify the ideas you want the retreat to generate—the *how*—but to identify clearly the organization's goals for holding the retreat—the *why*.

Your answer should be pretty simple. Retreats typically last only a few days at most, so overly ambitious expectations are likely to result in frustration or even failure.

At the same time, retreats are expensive, and most organizations can't afford them unless they have serious reasons for holding one.

Answering the question, "What do we want to be different?" doesn't mean that you should preordain the outcome. What it does mean is that you should have a clear idea, in general terms, of what you want to result from this retreat. "We're losing business to our competitors and I want to reverse that trend." "Our products are no longer on the cutting edge and I want us to get back in front." "Increased turnover is affecting our productivity and I want to know what we can do about it." "People are working harder than ever but we don't seem to be making much progress. I want to know why and what we can do about that." "We just merged with one of our former competitors and the marriage doesn't seem to be working. I want to fix that." "We're not getting the help and support we need from the board and I want to know how to engage them more productively."

Your Role and the Facilitator's Role

Regardless of your skill or experience in running meetings, we don't recommend that you lead your own retreat. Here's why:

- It's critical that the facilitator be neutral—and be perceived as neutral—with no personal stake in the outcome. You, by definition, have a big stake in the outcome.
- The facilitator must focus on how participants are working together to achieve their goals. You, in contrast, must be a fully engaged participant in achieving those goals. Playing both of these roles simultaneously is well nigh impossible.

So if not you, who? We recommend that you use an experienced facilitator, either someone from within your organization who is skilled at designing and leading retreats or an outside consultant, and that you work closely with the facilitator, starting as early in the process as possible. To ensure that the person you want is available, it's best to select the facilitator before you set the date for the retreat. The facilitator can make or break your event, so don't underestimate the importance of finding the right person.

Not everyone—and not every facilitator—has the experience and temperament to design and lead a retreat. Good retreat facilitators are able to

- Listen accurately to what others are saying, without injecting their own biases
- Be neutral (and be perceived as neutral) about the outcome of the discussions
- Suspend judgment about retreat participants
- Understand and help bring multiple perspectives to the surface
- Resist colluding with the group in avoiding thorny issues
- Urge participants whose viewpoints may not be popular to speak out, and encourage others to listen
- Help retreat participants recognize and deal with any behavior that might be hampering their work
- Deal skillfully with group members who might not want to accept the facilitator's guidance

- Empathize with others
- Analyze and summarize key issues
- Remain comfortable with ambiguous situations and circumstances they do not control
- Recognize and manage differences that may stem from the diversity (in culture, race, gender, age, sexual orientation, and so forth) of the participants
- Hear feedback from the participants without becoming defensive
- Adjust their approach, acknowledge missteps, and ask for help when they need it
- Provide candid feedback and coaching to you and to other senior executives

Once you have decided who will design and lead your retreat, you and that person must agree on what your and his or her respective roles will be.

You may have a sense of what you'd like the retreat to look like, and a good facilitator will listen carefully to your ideas. At the same time, an experienced retreat facilitator might have a better sense of what is likely to achieve the goals you have in mind.

And ideally, once the retreat begins you will "forget" that you are the boss and will behave like any other retreat participant—albeit an especially key one. This means letting the facilitator run the show. You will undermine the facilitator's credibility and effectiveness—as well as the likelihood of a successful retreat—if you compete with him or her for control of the agenda.

Most facilitators conduct interviews prior to the retreat to assess organizational issues. We urge you to take advantage of this opportunity to learn more about the impact of your leadership style by asking the facilitator to give you feedback—without identifying the individual source of any information, of course—from the interviews he or she conducts.

For more discussion on the importance of conducting participant interviews before the retreat is designed, see Chapter 2, "Pre-Retreat Interviews with Participants," pp. 33–38.

Prior to choosing the facilitator, make sure that you have confidence in his or her judgment, skills, and personal integrity. Then be prepared to allow him or her to work without undue interference from you.

This might sound easy, but it's not. You are the leader and you're used to taking the lead. But just as the wise patient selects his physician carefully, engages with her, and then generally follows her advice, the savvy executive trusts the judgment of the facilitator he chooses, expecting her to act professionally and competently and in the best interest of the organization.

Whom Should You Invite?

Sometimes there's no question about who will participate in the retreat. For example, a retreat might involve a relatively small and clearly defined work group—a team, a department, or a board. Often, however, you and other key people will have to determine who will be invited and who will not.

Size matters in retreats. Retreats should be limited to reasonably small groups if you want to accomplish serious work. If your goal is to make tough decisions, such as how to handle redundant functions after a merger, you will have to discuss highly sensitive information. Make the group too large, and there are bound to be people who don't normally have (and don't need to have) access to that information.

At the same time, inclusiveness is often important. The group can be larger if your retreat focuses on overarching cultural or teamwork issues. In addition, for some issues it can be invaluable to have the broader perspective that a larger group provides. For major change issues, the more people who participate in the decision making and planning, the more likely the initiative is to work.

We have seen successful retreats with as few as three participants and as many as a hundred, but be aware that if your group grows larger than about forty people, it will take longer to discuss every topic, and you won't be able to make many strategic decisions. Although excellent work can take place in breakout groups, large numbers make it difficult for everyone to hear all the comments and reach consensus.

It's important to communicate your criteria for whom you invite to the retreat, both to the people who will attend and to those who will not. Here's an example that shows why this matters:

> Mavis, the vice president of an insurance company, convened a retreat designed to improve communications and collaboration among senior managers. Mavis then decided that the retreat should be expanded to include the supervisors from one of the larger departments. She also invited a few—but only a few—members of the support staff who had requested professional development opportunities. Neither the retreat participants nor those who had been excluded understood the basis of her decisions. Retreat participants felt uncomfortable making recommendations for

change without consulting those who weren't in the room, and many who were excluded were resentful and resistant to implementing the ideas that emerged from the retreat.

There are several methods you can use to decide who will attend a specific retreat. The most common are described in the following sections.

Intact Work Group

This is the simplest way to choose retreat participants. A board, task force, department, or small organization has a retreat, and everyone is invited. Of course, it doesn't always work out that easily. If the department is large, you may still have to choose who will attend by applying additional criteria.

Intact Work Group with Invited Outsiders

In some cases an intact work group may want to involve selected outsiders (associates from elsewhere in the larger organization, for example) in its retreat. Take care not to expand the group too much, however, as too many outsiders can interfere with group cohesion.

Retreat Participants May Be . . .

- An intact work group
- All those with the same job title (such as all department heads)
- A representative cross section of the organization
- All those who have the capacity to help the organization make desired changes
- All those who want to come
- People who have successfully competed to attend
- People who want to shake up the status quo

People with the Same Titles

If the retreat will include people from many departments, a traditional way to select participants is simply by job title: all the vice presidents or department heads, for instance, or all the board committee chairs. This is a safe way to choose; no one can criticize you for playing favorites or leaving someone out. But it is common for peers to share many experiences, attitudes, and ways of seeing things, so this approach may not result in the breadth of perspectives that would be most useful for the group's discussions.

Cross Section Representatives

When an issue cuts broadly across the organization, the retreat attendees might be a cross section of people from the various functions and levels in the hierarchy. But how do you decide whom specifically to include? You might make this decision alone or with the advice of colleagues. Department heads may decide who will represent their departments, or employees themselves may choose their own representatives. Whatever method you employ, take care that staff do not perceive management bias in the selections.

People with the Right Stuff

This is a less common way to choose retreat participants, yet it can achieve powerful results. Here the CEO or a very senior leader asks, "Who are the people who can best help us get where we want to go?" She then invites the people most likely to have the expertise and experience necessary to address the issue most effectively.

One danger of selecting participants in this way is that there will always be people who weren't invited who feel that they should have been. Those who were not invited—and their supporters in the organization—may feel resentful and resist the decisions that come out of the retreat.

There is another danger as well: executives may believe that the people who have the right stuff are those who think as they do. They may thus inadvertently exclude divergent thinkers who could help move the organization forward.

People Who Accept an Open Offer

Sometimes everyone who wants to attend the retreat is welcomed. The assumption behind an open offer is that anyone who is willing to put the time and effort into the retreat is interested in the issues and committed to getting things done. One potential downside is that the group could become too large. (You can prevent this by limiting the number of slots.) Another possible pitfall is that the volunteers are likely to be employees with strong biases regarding the issues to be discussed, which could skew the results. Yet another concern is that some of the people you would most want to attend might choose not to take part.

People Who Compete Successfully

This is a variant on the open offer. People who want to come to the retreat compete for one of, say, twenty slots. All who are interested write their cases to the retreat convener, laying out why they should be included. They describe what they can contribute to the success of the event and what they would do to involve others who did not attend in the decisions that might be made.

This method produces highly motivated participants who feel it is a privilege to participate and who will work hard to make the retreat successful. The challenge is to make the offsite compelling enough that people will want to compete for a slot. Be aware that if your organization has a history of holding retreats that didn't meet people's expectations, potential participants are more likely to turn down an invitation to compete in your next retreat.

Revolutionaries Inside the Palace Walls

In his book *Leading the Revolution,* Gary Hamel (2000) wrote, "If senior management wants revolutionary strategies, it must learn to listen to revolutionary voices" (p. 250). It takes courage to invite nontraditional participants to a retreat. They tend to rock the boat (which is why you invite them, of course), and their selection can generate resentment among the loyal pillars of your organization's establishment.

Revolutionary thinkers can be a challenge to work with during the retreat. If they're not part of the usual group, they may not know the unspoken rules and rituals that guide communications. They ask questions that everyone else

Why You Might Want to Invite a Revolutionary or Two

An interactive communications company invited several young Web designers to a retreat we facilitated to help the company formulate a new marketing strategy. Eyes rolled when one young woman, Jody, suggested, "Why don't we just give away our work? Let's do it for free!" The initial reaction to Jody's suggestion was dismissal: "She can't be serious." Then someone said, "Wait a minute; let's look at this. It might not be so crazy after all." In the ensuing discussion, participants came up with several advantages of giving away some of their product. They saw how this might help the company attract potential customers, build goodwill, and sell other highly profitable services. The result was a bold new approach to marketing the company, and the giveaways led to an increase in purchases.

knows the answers to (or at least thinks they do). They come up with "weird" ideas. But by raising issues in new and challenging ways, they can stimulate creative thinking among all the participants.

Part-Time Participants

Occasionally we're asked whether some people can be invited for just part of the day or a portion of the retreat, to make the offsite more inclusive. This may sound like a good idea, but in our experience it usually does not work very well. The presence of part-time participants often diffuses the focus of the larger group and alters the dynamics of the interactions. Moreover, when some people arrive after the retreat has begun or leave before it ends, a sharp delineation becomes visible between the *ins* and the *outs* even though the intention may be just the opposite.

Retreat Logistics

You are attending a retreat in a windowless hotel ballroom that's been divided into smaller meeting rooms by sliding air walls through which you can hear applause from the group meeting next door. No daylight filters in. People are shifting uncomfortably in the narrow, armless chairs. You are sitting around a formal U-shaped table covered with white tablecloths. At 10:30 and 2:00, a waiter trundles the coffee cart in; lunch is set up buffet-style in a corner of the room promptly at noon. At 5:00 on the dot members of the hotel's banquet staff appear at the door, eager to begin breaking down the room for the next event. While the participants hurriedly gather up their belongings, the facilitator rushes to grab flip chart pages off the walls, and Post-it Notes float to the floor unnoticed. Your one-day retreat is over. (Not a pretty picture.)

For a retreat, far more than for a regular meeting, logistical details play a vital role in determining the event's success. We encourage you to work closely with the facilitator on your retreat's logistics. An apparently minor inconvenience—such as having a rich discussion interrupted by the arrival of the lunch service—can have a tremendous negative impact on the outcomes achieved at the retreat.

How Long Should a Retreat Last?

The length of a retreat will be constrained by several factors. They include the nature and complexity of the issues to be addressed, when and for how long key participants are available, and the budget for the event. There is also a practical upper limit to how long a retreat can continue to yield good results, after which the law of diminishing returns kicks in. Participating actively in a retreat requires effort, and people can give their full attention and energy for only so long before mental fatigue sets in and focus begins to blur.

But the key factor in determining length is the purpose, the answer to "What do you want to be different?" If the issues are so complex and important that it will take three days to address them adequately, don't schedule a one-day retreat because that's all the budget will allow or because busy employees can't get away for longer than a day. You may actually make things worse by raising

What Is a Two-Day Retreat?

What do we mean by a two-day retreat? Does it begin, say, mid-morning on Tuesday, after employees have traveled to the remote site, and end Wednesday right after lunch so employees can get home without getting stuck in rush hour traffic? No, that's actually a one-day overnight retreat when you add up the number of hours participants will actually be engaged in serious work. A two-day retreat allows participants two full working days to focus on the issues of concern. A two-and-a-half-day retreat adds an extra afternoon on the first day or a morning on the last day. See the accompanying table for some examples of formats.

Two-Day Offsite, Two Nights

Monday	Tuesday	Wednesday
Arrive p.m.		
	Begin retreat	Resume retreat
	Day One—full day	Day Two—full day
(Night One)	(Night Two)	
		End retreat, depart late afternoon or evening

Two-Day Offsite, Two Nights

Monday	Tuesday	Wednesday
Arrive a.m.		
Begin retreat	Resume retreat	Resume retreat
Day One—half day	Day Two—full day	Day Three—half day
(Night One)	(Night Two)	
		End retreat, depart mid-afternoon or evening

Two-and-a-Half-Day or Three-Day Offsite, Three Nights

Monday	Tuesday	Wednesday	Thursday
Arrive p.m.			
	Begin retreat	Resume retreat	Resume retreat
	Day One—full day	Day Two—full day	Day Three—half day or full day
(Night One)	(Night Two)	(Night Three)	
			End retreat, depart p.m.

Nearly Two-Day Offsite, One Night (for offsite very near home)

Monday	Tuesday
Arrive a.m.	
Begin retreat	Resume retreat
Day One—most of day	Day Two—most of day
(Night One)	
	End retreat, depart p.m.

expectations that cannot be met in the time allotted, like a surgeon opening a body for a procedure and not having the time to close it properly.

Ask your facilitator to guide you in what you can expect to accomplish in the time you have available. Be prepared to scale down your expectations if they're too ambitious or to lengthen the retreat (or to do some of both).

In our experience the most effective retreats are usually two- or two-and-a-half-day events. Retreats of this length allow participants time to create the climate of trust necessary to make genuine progress. They offer time to explore issues thoroughly and to build commitment to change. Yet they aren't so long that participants' energy flags and momentum dissipates.

Although there are many variations, the ideal two-day retreat begins in the evening before Day One. Participants arrive at a reasonable hour, enjoy an informal dinner, get to know each other if they're not already well acquainted, and have a good night's sleep before convening early the next morning. There might be a short program over dinner to provide a sense of what to expect and some ideas to think about. On Day One, they have a full day, including breaks, lunch, dinner, and downtime, and still have energy for Day Two, which might run through mid- or late afternoon, depending on the circumstances.

If the issues justify it, and if the organization can afford it, staying over a third night and having a half-day session on Day Three for action planning can be a very effective format. What goes on outside the formal sessions, particularly during and after dinner, nearly always reinforces and amplifies what takes place during those sessions. Issues are discussed, problems are solved, and personal relationships are formed and strengthened. Moreover, "sleeping on it" often produces breakthrough ideas. Participants have time to reflect, envision different possibilities, come up with additional questions, and rethink their positions on the issues. This time can help participants focus their enthusiasm and deal with their anxieties. We have seen people come in the second or third morning declaring, "We didn't aim high enough yesterday when we set our goals. Let's be more ambitious today."

If staying two nights is prohibitively expensive, consider convening your retreat close enough to the office that participants can arrive in the morning of the first working day and stay until late afternoon or early evening of the second day. In this case you would have the option of holding an after-dinner session on the first evening to make up for the loss of time that morning.

When Should You Schedule Your Retreat?

It's tempting to schedule a retreat over a weekend. People won't miss any of their regular work, and those who aren't included don't have to cover for the people who are away. The weekend option may be attractive to senior management but can present problems for employees who have family obligations or use their weekends to take care of their personal affairs. You might not hear it directly, but if you schedule a weekend retreat, there will likely be some grumbling in the halls. And resentful participants are less likely to be invested in the success of the offsite.

Some companies plan retreats over government holidays on which the company does not traditionally close, such as Veterans Day or Columbus Day. On those days the company's phone and e-mail traffic may be lighter because government agencies, many banks, and some other companies are closed.

Although convening a retreat during the workweek can make employees more enthusiastic about attending, they still may have scheduling problems. Moreover, they'll have to ensure that urgent matters are taken care of in their absence and be prepared to handle the extra work that will be waiting for them when they return to the office. There may be no perfect time for everyone, but it is helpful to consult with participants about when their workloads are heaviest before you set the dates.

> Be sure to confirm the availability of key participants and the facilitator before locking in dates with the retreat facility.

What Is the Ideal Length for a Retreat?

There's nothing sacred about a two-day retreat. A mini-retreat, involving a small number of people and a limited number of issues, can be successful in one day, without an overnight stay. And some highly successful retreats last longer than two or two and a half days.

And there are variations, such as a day-and-a-half retreat over a three-day stay at a resort, where meetings are interspersed with social activities and sports. (In such a setting, however, you and the facilitator have to work harder to ensure that participants are present and focused for the working sessions.)

In other words, be sensitive to people's needs, and give them plenty of time to make arrangements so they can attend. The longer in advance you can confirm dates for your retreat, the more likely you will be to have full attendance.

Even though everyone you invite is, by definition, important to the success of the retreat, some participants may be more critical than others. If so, be sure to gain a commitment from these key players before setting the dates. Who these key players are depends on the nature of the issues that will be addressed, but in nearly every case they include people who have the power to make decisions and commit resources. If decisions must be made, and you don't have the authority to make them, be sure that whoever does—the CEO, executive director, department head, board chair—agrees to take part and understands the importance of that commitment. Because senior executives' schedules are often filled many months in advance, the earlier you determine dates, the better.

There is no universal best season to schedule a retreat, but summer and the year-end holiday season are usually particularly bad times. Key participants might elect to skip a retreat that coincides with family trips or become resentful if vacations have to be cancelled or postponed. Even when everyone is able to participate, valuable momentum can be lost if some of the participants leave town shortly afterward. By the time everyone is back at the office, the retreat may be a dim memory. Also, it may be more difficult to cover retreat participants' work if a number of their colleagues are out of the office at the same time the offsite is taking place.

Many companies like to hold retreats in advance of their annual planning period. Because managers often have to find time for planning while still doing all their regular work, it's helpful to hold the retreat a month or two before the actual planning and budgeting work begins. This will allow participants to address the retreat outcomes in their thinking.

What if someone who has committed to the retreat well in advance finds at the last minute that he or she cannot make it? We use what we call the Aloha Rule. If the reason someone gives for skipping the retreat wouldn't cause that person to return early from a long-planned vacation to Hawaii, it isn't a valid reason.

But sometimes people who have agreed to participate really can't make it. Someone gets sick; family emergencies arise; unanticipated snowstorms strand people in faraway cities. If a participant suddenly has to cancel, the retreat can usually proceed as planned without serious consequences. If, however, the participant who must cancel is a key decision maker or has special skills or information critical to the success of the retreat, you have a dilemma.

How you deal with the situation depends on the circumstances. Will the retreat facility let you postpone? Can the other busy people who have planned to attend change their plans? Will the facilitator be available when you want to reschedule?

If not, consider whether it's worthwhile to proceed as planned even if a critical person cannot attend. There's no definitive answer because each situation is unique, but we offer these observations:

- The absence of a key player or several of the invited participants can hurt a retreat's chances of success.
- It is important not to allow individuals to be casual about their commitments to take part in the retreat. Hold their feet to the fire if their stated reasons for missing the retreat don't justify their absence.
- If the reason given is work related ("I have a big project to complete"), try to help the person overcome the problem. You might, for instance, ask his or her boss to extend the deadline, or arrange for someone who won't be at the retreat to take over the work.
- If key players cannot participate, try to obtain their commitment to support the outcomes even though they won't have contributed to them. Make sure that the facilitator takes the key players' absence into account in the design and facilitation of the offsite.
- Make a special effort immediately after the retreat to inform absentees—especially any key figures who couldn't attend—about what happened and why, what recommendations and decisions were made, and what the thinking behind them was.

Where Should You Hold Your Retreat?

Retreats work best in flexible, casual environments. The setting doesn't have to be fancy. In fact, if you hold a retreat in a posh resort, some participants will be more interested in finding time for a set of tennis or a round of golf than in attending to the business at hand. Instead, look for a place that encourages quiet reflection.

Many conference centers have sprung up around the United States and elsewhere in recent years. These large facilities are usually located outside city centers, often in parklike settings. They are set up specifically for handling group meetings, so they have flexible space and advanced audiovisual capabilities onsite. Their meeting rooms generally have fixed, soundproof walls, easily moveable tables, executive-type rolling chairs, and—importantly—windows!

Most conference centers provide meeting space, lodging, meals, continuously available snacks, and a broad array of AV equipment for a flat, per person price. Because conference centers specialize in group events, their staff are typically well trained, responsive to retreat participants' and facilitators' needs, and adept at making the unanticipated changes that offsites often require.

If a hotel is the only possibility for your retreat, we suggest avoiding the usual meeting rooms and ballrooms, which are often noisy and nearly always lack natural light from windows. For a small group you might book a large hospitality suite, where participants can relax in living room–style chairs and have access to a kitchen area where snacks and drinks are available all day. Also, keep in mind how much privacy from other groups you need. Meeting in a rented house or condo at a resort, for instance, will give your group more privacy than will meeting in a hotel or a large conference center that lacks private dining rooms and has a common area for snacks.

Sometimes the retreat site will be so attractive that participants will ask if they may bring their families, whom they'll expect to see at mealtimes and in the evenings. With rare exceptions family members are a distraction from the work of the retreat.

Some organizations hold retreats in religious retreat houses. Even though such facilities can be attractive and inexpensive, it's been our experience that not everyone feels at ease in a religious retreat house, even if its meeting facilities appear as secular as those in a hotel, and people might feel uncomfortable raising their objections.

Resorts in their off seasons are perfect for retreats: a (heated) beach house in winter, a ski resort in the late spring or early fall. They have beautiful natural

Help Us Spread the Word About Great Retreat Sites

Have you heard of a great place to hold a retreat? We'd love to know about it because clients often ask our advice. Please share the information with us at www.retreatsthatwork.com.

settings, they aren't crowded, they're much less expensive in the off season, and the participants will be less tempted to play instead of work. An inexpensive alternative can be the rustic lodges and cabins offered by many state, county, and municipal park systems. You might even consider holding the retreat in the living room of someone's vacation home if it's large enough. Although you'll have to bring in everything you need—flip charts and markers, coffee urns, meals, and snacks—the casual atmosphere is often just right to spark good dialogue.

No matter where you schedule the retreat, we suggest you look for a site that offers as many of the following amenities as possible:

- Soundproof rooms, so the facilitator and participants won't have to compete with a speaker on a microphone on the other side of a thin wall
- Hard-surfaced, easy-to-move tables that don't have to be covered by tablecloths
- Comfortable chairs—either padded, rolling executive-style chairs or comfy sofas and upholstered chairs
- Enough room in the main meeting space to allow participants to pull their chairs into a circle and to work away from the tables when required
- Space for breakout groups, either a main room that has movable chairs and is large enough for groups to move away from each other, or small rooms adjacent or very close to the main space
- Ample supplies of flip chart easels and pads, masking tape, and markers
- Space where people can congregate informally to talk or grounds where they can take walks
- Snacks and drinks available all day, rather than just at scheduled breaks

Sleeping Rooms and Meals

For overnight retreats, one question that will come up immediately is, "Will we have to share sleeping rooms?" Budget restraints often mean the answer is, "Yes, you will."

We find that most retreat participants prefer not to share rooms. But some facilities won't have enough space for everyone to have a private room, and in these cases we strongly suggest that roommates be assigned by some random process, especially if the offsite will last for only one night. When people are allowed to choose their roommates, some pairs will form immediately, and some individuals will be—and will feel—left out. Moreover, when close friends share rooms, they naturally compare notes on what's going on and what they think of other people. That kind of discussion does not help advance the teamwork that you need for a successful retreat.

To create an environment that is conducive to open and equal communication, don't set a double standard by giving senior executives single rooms while everyone else has to double up. If some single rooms are available, consider determining the occupants by lottery.

When the retreat location is within fifty miles of home, some participants may want to return home in the evenings. We discourage allowing people to go home unless remaining at the retreat site overnight would be a substantial hardship. People who return home will miss some of the downtime discussions that add to the richness of the retreat dialogue, and they often arrive late for the morning sessions.

It's a good idea for all participants (including you and other top executives) to take their meals together during the retreat. Mealtimes provide opportunities for people to talk over ideas informally.

Here are some points to keep in mind about meals:

It's sometimes fun for the participants themselves to prepare dinner, if the retreat facility has a kitchen you can use. Working together to plan, cook, and clean up can give people a great opportunity to practice their teamwork skills. At some retreats, meal preparation is actually part of the content. The facilitator may observe how the participants work together and give them feedback later, or dinner preparation may simply be a recreational activity.

- Lunch should be light (you don't want people falling asleep in the early afternoon) and reasonably quick.
- To make the most of participants' time in a one-day retreat, the facilitator might want to assign topics for lunchtime discussion.
- Find out in advance if anyone has food allergies or special requirements. Many retreat facilities offer buffets; this is perhaps the easiest way to handle meals and allows people to select what they eat. Or you might also provide participants with a menu to choose from in advance of the retreat.
- When participants order in advance, someone should keep a list of everyone's food orders, because people will forget what they requested. It's a good idea to order a couple of extra meals just in case there's a problem—a meal doesn't arrive, someone is given someone else's food, and so on.

- It's much better for meals to be served in a room separate from the room in which retreat sessions take place. People need a visual break, and it also will be distracting to the group if servers come in to set up while the retreat is in session. Weather permitting, it can be a particularly refreshing break to eat outdoors.

Sports and Recreation

Retreats are intense experiences. If your retreat will run two days or longer, at some point the facilitator will probably give participants a break long enough for them to visit the gym, get a massage, take a nap, or stroll around the grounds.

Once you announce the retreat location, many participants will look it up on the Web. If the facility offers tennis, golf, skiing, or other sports, or if there are shopping opportunities nearby, be sure to specify in your retreat invitation whether participants will have time to participate in these activities.

Notifying Participants

In addition to the initial memo you send notifying participants where and when the retreat will be held, you'll need to give them logistical information closer to the date. Make sure to include directions and route maps to the site, the amenities participants can expect, and how their families can contact them in an emergency. This is a good time to collect emergency contact information from the participants too, in case of illness or accident at the retreat.

Be clear about what to wear. "Jeans and sweats" is a lot easier for people to decode than "casual attire." Let people know when a gym or swimming pool is available so they can bring appropriate clothing. (This is the time to inform participants whether or not they'll have time for a game of tennis or golf.)

Provide a list of what people need to bring with them to the retreat sessions. If they will need pens and the retreat facility doesn't provide them, say so. (People assume—often correctly—that pens and note paper will be provided and show up at a retreat without something to write with or on.)

At large retreats for companies with offices across the country and at off-sites for boards of directors, you may have to arrange to pick people up at the nearest airport and transport them to the site. But most retreats take place within one to three hours' driving distance of the office. Because participants won't need cars once they arrive, you might want to encourage carpooling. Carpools have the added benefit of reducing the number of stragglers who arrive late. Some organizations rent buses to transport participants from the workplace and back.

Provide each driver with clear directions and maps. For drives of over an hour, you might give each carload an easy assignment to work on: for example, "Think of one thing you'd like to be different after the retreat."

The care with which you plan the details of the retreat will communicate volumes to people in your organization about its importance to you. We urge you to consult with your facilitator and be guided by his or her expertise before making important decisions about the retreat's length, venue, participants, or scope.

Logistics Checklist

☐ After selecting the facilitator, consult with him or her on the appropriate length for the retreat.

☐ Determine when the facilitator is available for your retreat.

☐ Check available dates with senior managers whose participation in the retreat is critical to its success.

☐ Select a retreat facility and determine dates when it is available. (Your facilitator may have suggestions for appropriate facilities.)

☐ Announce the retreat, and give participants two or three options for dates if possible. They should tell you which dates, if any, **do not** work.

☐ Notify participants of the dates you have chosen, and contract with the retreat facility for those dates.

☐ Make arrangements for the transportation, meals, lodging, and audiovisual support required.

☐ Provide participants with the information they need, including lodging arrangements, directions to the site, recreational options, the dress code, and how family members can get messages to them during the retreat.

☐ Ask invitees to confirm their participation, indicate any food preferences or limitations, and supply emergency contact information.

Chapter 16

Your Role at the Retreat

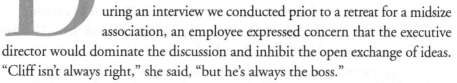

uring an interview we conducted prior to a retreat for a midsize association, an employee expressed concern that the executive director would dominate the discussion and inhibit the open exchange of ideas. "Cliff isn't always right," she said, "but he's always the boss."

This employee had put her finger on arguably the most single important factor in determining whether a retreat will succeed or fail: the role that the leaders play.

How you and other organization leaders behave before, during, and after the retreat is critical to its success.

Reaching an Understanding About Participants' Authority

An organization's leaders can undermine retreat participants' efforts either by ignoring or changing their recommendations or by denying them the resources required to implement the changes. They can delay the change process or punish people for their outspokenness. They can use their positions and status to dominate, thwart, manipulate, or hijack the discussions.

This is why it's important for you and the facilitator to reach a clear understanding prior to the retreat about the limits of participants' authority and to make these limits clear at or before the beginning of the retreat.

For an offsite to be successful, participants must believe that they can speak out honestly about their concerns without fear of retribution—and they must be right to believe that. They need an ironclad guarantee that there will be no repercussions if they express themselves candidly. If you do not have the power to make such a guarantee stick, it should come from the person who does. If you are unable or unwilling to make such a guarantee, participants won't open up and speak candidly. And if you (or your bosses) don't honor such a guarantee afterward, your organization could suffer immensely, both immediately and over the long term.

We encourage you and the other leaders present to assure participants that all of you are eager to listen and willing to consider the part you play both in moving your organization forward and in holding it back. And all of you must mean what you say.

The participants—consciously or not—will take their cue about what's important from the organization's leaders. Daniel Goleman, Richard Boyatzis, and Annie McKee (2001), in their article "Primal Leadership: The Hidden Driver of Great Performance," cite research that shows that a "leader's mood and behaviors drive the moods and behaviors of everyone else." This is an important principle of organizational life, and it particularly holds true at an offsite. The leader isn't behind closed doors or off on a trip. She's right there, across the room or in the next chair.

What Goleman, Boyatzis, and McKee call the "premier task" of a leader is "emotional leadership." This fosters "information sharing, trust, healthy risk-taking, and learning"—ideal conditions for a retreat. A low level of emotional

One CEO we know, Kathy, opened a retreat by issuing "Giraffe Awards" to recognize staff members who had "stuck their necks out" in the recent past. She praised them for taking risks and telling her things she might not have wanted to hear. This sent a clear signal to the other participants that Kathy wanted them to be candid at the retreat as well as in the office.

leadership, they say, produces "fear and anxiety"—precisely the feelings that will doom an offsite to failure. Even though a leader's emotional intelligence and its impact on an organization are rarely, if ever, discussed in the workplace, nothing could be more important to the success of a retreat.

We always assume that our clients hope that the retreat will stimulate positive change. For this reason, when we first talk with a new client we explore the role his or her behavior will play. If that client rejects a connection between his or her behavior and the success of the retreat, we are likely to recommend against holding an offsite, or we at least suggest considerably downscaling participants' expectations. But the vast majority of clients we have worked with do recognize the important role they play, and they welcome coaching on how best to contribute to the retreat's success.

Leadership Behavior During the Retreat

As a general rule, we offer the following guidelines for leaders at the retreat.

Be Aware of the Impact of Your Presence

Your opinions, expressions, body language—indeed, your very presence—carry a great deal of weight. We call this the Big Kahuna effect. If yours is a high-trust organization, you will have an easier time because you start out in an open and positive environment.

Mitigating the Big Kahuna Effect

When we worked with a large department of an international bank, the director, Judy, said she wanted feedback on what wasn't working well in the department. Judy repeatedly said that she welcomed comments, even critical ones, and assured participants that there would be no repercussions for speaking out. At a break a participant asked us to raise a particular issue that he felt strongly Judy should hear. We declined, explaining to the participant that if we, rather than a member of the group, brought up the issue we would be colluding in the myth that it was not safe to speak out. Later the participant did raise his concern himself, and Judy thanked him publicly for doing so.

If yours is a relatively low-trust organization, however, you will have to make a serious effort to convince participants that it is safe to speak candidly. This can be a real challenge, because you may have played a role, however unintentionally, in fostering the environment of distrust. One of the facilitator's jobs is to coach you in how best to encourage open participation. Take advantage of that assistance; it will be invaluable.

Don't Dominate the Discussions

Don't take over the proceedings, even if others defer to you (which they probably will, at least at first). It may be customary for you to take charge, but if you are an "air hog," serious discussion will be inhibited and differing viewpoints will be suppressed. Also, let participants know why you're holding back, so they won't attribute false motives to your actions.

How Leaders Can Help Ensure a Successful Retreat

- Be aware of the impact of your presence on participants' willingness to speak out.
- Don't dominate the discussions.
- Tell people what you think without inhibiting them from expressing ideas that differ from yours.
- Work with the entire group, not just a favored few.
- Provide realistic guidelines on the limits to participants' authority.
- Know when to hold back so ideas can emerge from the group.
- Be open with participants about what you have learned about yourself and what you're willing to change.
- Minimize the differences between you and the other participants.
- Be present, on time, and focused on the work of the retreat.
- Manage your emotions.
- Let the facilitator lead the retreat.
- Be open to trying new things.

Because most people find it difficult to change habitual behavior, it's helpful to agree in advance with the facilitator how and when he or she can tell you if you cross the line from participating to dominating.

Tell People What You Think—Carefully

At the same time, don't clam up and fail to express your opinions. You're not, as the saying goes, a potted plant. If you don't participate in the discussions, you will become a silent force in the room, and other participants will try to guess what your silence implies. Approval? Disapproval? Lack of interest? In any case, you certainly shouldn't hold back until, like a sleeping dragon, you suddenly awake and breathe fire on everyone in the room.

Rather you should feel as free as any other participant to express your opinion, although in most cases you should not be the first to do so. Be particularly sensitive to the words and body language you use when you speak. (This is true even during breaks and hanging-out time; your voice carries weight no matter when you use it.)

There are exceptions to the don't-speak-first rule. At a retreat we led for senior managers of a manufacturing company, we told the group what we learned from the interviews we conducted while planning the retreat. During those interviews managers had told us they were afraid to express their views freely because they were concerned that Lonnie, the CEO, would criticize or punish them.

When we asked whether our report accurately reflected the group's perspective, there was a profound silence in the room. After a while it was Lonnie himself who broke the silence. "That sounds right to me," he said, "and I want to change it." His comments made it safe for others to speak out and helped establish a tone of openness that encouraged participants to recommend workable strategies for improving the company's operations.

Work with the Entire Group

Don't raise your concerns privately with select participants. If there is an issue you need to raise, do it in front of the whole group. Retreats provide rare opportunities for everyone to speak candidly and openly. When you decline to raise issues publicly, you lose the opportunity to build the trust that a retreat can help foster. When you raise your concerns openly, however, you model ideal behavior.

Provide Realistic Guidelines About What Can Be Changed

There will be times when it is more productive for you to participate not as an equal but as the leader—when, for example, you have information people need to make realistic decisions and develop workable action plans. If participants are recommending an action that you know the board has already voted against, for example, tell them so. If you know that the company doesn't have the resources to pursue the particular course of action the group is recommending, say so and save everyone time. Such information will allow participants to alter their course. It's very frustrating for the group when a leader waits until the discussion is over and then says, "Sorry, but that won't fly."

Know When to Hold Back

On rare occasions you should refrain from participating at all in a discussion, especially if your involvement would inhibit participants from bringing a particularly thorny issue to the surface. You and the facilitator should put your heads together to decide what your participation in the various activities will be. Sometimes your role might be to listen intently but not to join in the conversation. At another time you might explain to participants why you are leaving the room temporarily.

Be Open About What You Have Learned About Yourself

If the facilitator gives you feedback on the impact of your behavior on others, tell the participants what you learned about yourself. If there are things you can do differently, say so. Also tell participants what they can do to help you make changes they and you would like to see. It's useful as well to tell people what you aren't willing or able to change and why. Understanding why certain things are the way they are can minimize grousing and wishful thinking. Your willingness to address the feedback you receive is critical for setting the tone of the retreat by showing participants that you value their candor.

Minimize the Differences

During the retreat, eliminate unnecessary symbols of your status that remind participants that you are the boss. If the whole group is supposed to eat lunch together, don't make an exception for yourself. If participants are expected to share rooms, make sure that you also have a roommate. If the dress code is casual, don't turn up in a business suit. If all the other participants have turned off their cell phones, turn yours off too. If all the others are on a first-name basis, you should be too—even if just for the period of the retreat.

We asked Marc, the commanding officer of a civilian-military unit, not to wear his uniform at the retreat, as he typically did at the office, but to come in casual civilian clothes like everyone else. We also suggested that he go by his first name rather than his military rank. Marc agreed, and also made a point of asking participants to drop the ingrained habit of responding to him with "Yes, sir," and "No, sir." Although that did not make his subordinates forget his status, by narrowing the gap between Marc and his staff, it fostered greater candor, openness, and trust.

Be Present

Woody Allen once famously observed that 80 percent of success is simply showing up. It's critical to the success of a retreat that the leaders be there—physically and mentally. A retreat shouldn't be an event for *others* to attend. If you and your peers don't make the commitment of time and energy to be present and engaged, the participants won't take the work seriously. As a result the retreat will, at best, yield no significant benefit; at worst, it could do a great deal of harm.

And you should be not only present but also *present*. Show up on time for retreat sessions and activities. Turn off your cell phone and pager (you might even want to make a public show of doing so), and make it clear to the folks who remain back at the office that you are not to be interrupted at the retreat for any reason short of a real emergency. And pay attention to what's going on in the room; don't read documents or make notes of things to do when you get back to the office.

The Importance of Being There

There's nothing deadlier than twenty people sitting around waiting for the boss to turn up. They won't want to start without you, and they're likely to interpret your absence or tardiness to mean that you don't consider the business of the retreat important.

Here's an example of what can happen when a leader does not make the retreat his first priority. For a large media company we led a yearlong series of offsites aimed at rethinking the way the company did business. As the culmination of the department heads' work, the company's executive committee had committed to come to the last afternoon of the final retreat to hear the managers' recommendations. As all the vice presidents were arriving, Rob, the CEO, called to say that he was held up in an important client meeting but that the retreat participants should give their reports without him.

It was extremely disheartening for the group. After they finished their presentation, we asked the managers to write down their reactions to what happened and post them anonymously on a wall. Several people wrote versions of, "If this is such important work, where's Rob?" When Rob finally made it to the retreat site, we asked him (with the group's permission) to read the comments that had been posted on the wall.

It was a tense moment as everyone watched Rob walk the length of the wall and read how people felt about his not showing up. He took a few moments to gather his thoughts, then said, "I'm so embarrassed. I've let you down, and that was never my intention. What can I do to make this right?" What ensued was possibly the first open conversation between the CEO and middle management that had ever taken place in that company.

Manage Your Emotions

Be careful not to let your emotions get the best of you during a retreat. No matter what you are feeling, you must control your behavior. It's very unsettling for participants to have the boss raise her voice or break into tears of defensiveness or frustration. That doesn't mean you should hide what you are feeling. If you are upset, angry, dissatisfied, or disappointed, say so. You're not a punching bag. Don't be afraid to speak your mind, but do so in a way that isn't accusatory or threatening. If the issue is too hot for you to talk about calmly, ask the facilitator to call a break. Then you'll have time to cool off and get coaching from the facilitator on how to raise your concerns.

Let the Facilitator Lead the Retreat

You did your homework and chose a facilitator you trust. Now let that person do the job. You may not understand why a facilitator is or isn't doing something at a given moment, but it's the facilitator's responsibility—not yours—to get you and the other retreat participants to the agreed-on destination.

That doesn't mean you should abdicate all responsibility for the retreat's success to the facilitator. On the contrary, you must communicate any concerns that arise so they can be dealt with on the spot. The most straightforward way to do that is to raise your concern in front of the group, just as any other participant might do. A skilled facilitator will know how to handle the interruption and will also be able to incorporate the group's perspective into deciding how to address your concern. For example, if you think the discussions have gone off track, the facilitator can solicit the group's input and help everyone decide what to do about the new issues being raised.

If you think that your concern is too sensitive to raise publicly (if, for example, you are concerned that an employee with whom you have had difficulty is trying to sabotage the retreat), then discuss the problem privately with the facilitator during a break. Avoid expressing your concerns angrily or covertly (through someone else, for instance, or by openly passing a note to the facilitator). Find a way to discuss differences that respects the facilitator's professionalism. Then take advantage of the facilitator's expertise to resolve these differences and move forward.

Be Open to Change

You should know that what happens at retreats is often hardest on the organization's leadership—on you and your peers. When you hear feedback from the facilitator, you may be surprised—perhaps unpleasantly—by how people have perceived your actions and how things are going in the organization. It takes self-discipline to listen intently and not become defensive.

When a client tells us that his goal for a retreat is to change others' behavior or attitudes, we ask, "Are you prepared to do the most changing? Because that's probably what will be called for."

A Common Post-Retreat Concern

In our many years of attending and leading retreats, we have observed an interesting and potentially unsettling phenomenon. Very often—so often that we warn our clients about it—within a month or so after a retreat, one or more of the participants quits the company or seeks a transfer to another department.

As part of a retreat we were conducting for the public relations department of a large broadcasting company, for instance, we asked participants to think about the direction they'd like to take in their careers and in their lives in general. Then we asked them to think about how the company could help them achieve their goals.

One of the participants, Allison, told the group that what she really wanted was to get married and have a child and that the long hours she put into her work were never going to permit her to do this. Over the course of the retreat, as the participants laid out ambitious plans for the department, Allison grew quieter. Three weeks after the retreat, Allison called Mary Margaret, the department head, to say she was leaving. She had decided she needed a less stressful and time-consuming job so that she could find what she really wanted from life. Although Mary Margaret was dismayed that Allison had decided to leave, she was not surprised, and she was also relieved. Allison had obviously been increasingly unhappy, and her dissatisfaction was contributing to a tense environment in the office.

A well-run retreat can do a great deal to clarify an organization's values, priorities, and future direction. Once these have been clarified, employees who were pulling in other directions may shift their efforts, or they may realize that their jobs (and perhaps the organization itself) do not match well with their values or aspirations. Discovering that their goals are fundamentally incompatible with those of the organization, they decide to look for other jobs. When this happens, it's usually for the best for everyone concerned and healthy for the organization itself.

Chapter 17

Keeping the Work of the Retreat Alive

W hile participants are deliberating at the offsite, their non-participating colleagues will be speculating about what surprises the retreat holds in store for *them*. They will be eager—even anxious—to know what happened (especially what *really* happened) at the offsite. If reliable, credible information is not shared with them very soon after the retreat, rumors will fill the information gap—and may be hard to dislodge with facts.

Thus it is critical that people who were not at the retreat be brought into the loop as quickly and completely as possible. Failure to carry out this crucial step may undo some or all of the hard work that was carried out at the retreat.

A common impulse at the end of a retreat is for everyone to agree not to say anything specific "until we work out the details." Another frequent decision is to make sure "we all say the same things." Both ideas sound good, but they inhibit immediate communication and undermine confidence and trust. The longer people go without hearing something specific, the more time they will have to speculate about why they aren't being told what happened. And the sooner everyone in the organization knows what actually took place, the sooner fears will be allayed and the collective energy of the whole can be brought to bear on implementing decisions for change.

Retreat participants, like witnesses at a crime scene, will recall events differently. We all remember best those things that affect us directly or provoke an emotional reaction. Our recollections of things we are less interested in are fuzzier. This phenomenon can influence and distort how participants remember what took place.

This is why you and the facilitator need to take time at the retreat to guide the group in a collective discussion of the context for the various recommendations and decisions. Otherwise, participants will tell their own versions of events, and the people back at the office will hear highly individualized (and sometimes contradictory) accounts.

Although you don't want participants to reveal any information that they agreed was confidential or to tout a "company line," you should encourage them to speak informally with their staffs the very first morning they are back in the office. Participants can certainly give their colleagues an idea of the broad outcomes: for instance, "We spent most of the day talking about strategies and budgets for next year. It looks like we're going to spend a lot more energy on developing our brand. The details aren't finished yet, but you should know that branding will be the general thrust when the report comes out." That's far better than, "As soon as we get the report back and the executive committee meets, then we can tell you what we talked about, but not before." A reluctance to speak can arouse suspicion that bad news is ahead. Hearing bad news is still better than speculating about it.

If anything unusual happened at the retreat, people will want to hear about that too: "After dinner we played charades until midnight, and you should have seen Jack, Essie, Kate, and Maurice hamming it up. I had no idea how well our board members could act!" Also be aware that any dramatic events that occurred—two executives getting into a shouting match, for example, or someone insulting the CEO—will immediately leak to everyone in the workplace in one form or another. If such an event has occurred, it's important that participants decide before they leave the retreat how to put this event in context for the people who weren't there. That way participants are prepared to respond immediately and effectively to nonparticipants' questions about the meaning of the occurrence.

Announcing the Retreat Outcomes

Even with the casual reporting back to colleagues that each participant will do, everyone in the organization needs a formal announcement of the retreat's outcomes. The guideline here is *overcommunicate!* Individuals process information differently, and if you use only one communication mechanism, some people won't fully grasp the message.

Here are some ways to get the word out quickly:

- Immediately send out an e-mail with an overview of the retreat proceedings and results.
- Post some of the key flip charts in convenient public locations where people can read them—in a common space such as a break room, for instance. One organization we worked with posted not only the charts from the retreat but also some blank flip chart sheets, with Post-it Notes and pens on a nearby table, so nonparticipants could add any comments they might have.
- If there is a written report, distribute it to those who weren't at the retreat as well as those who were. (That's one reason such reports should be written as soon after the retreat as possible.)

A written report that summarizes major issues, recommendations, conclusions, decisions, action assignments, and timetables is essential, but not sufficient. Plan to hold a meeting (or a series of meetings) with nonparticipating employees.

This meeting should be conducted in the spirit of the retreat itself. Instead of merely listening passively to oral reports, people who attend should be encouraged to ask questions and contribute ideas about implementation.

The meeting should not be announced as if it were an afterthought. It's a critical element in implementing decisions reached at the retreat, and it's best if it's scheduled even before the retreat takes place. You should encourage the widest possible attendance so that people who did not attend the retreat will still be able to participate in the process. Even though you may want to lead this meeting yourself, you need not be alone in presenting information and responding to questions; ideally, some of the retreat participants will share this task with you or even take the lead while you act as moderator, moving things along and fielding questions.

As work on action steps proceeds, everyone needs to be kept well informed of progress, delays, glitches, and alterations. It's a good idea to set up communication channels for passing along frequent updates, answering questions, and responding to rumors. E-mail can be a particularly effective means of accomplishing this.

Translating Decisions into Action

Once everyone has heard about the *what*—what occurred, what was discussed, what was recommended, what was agreed on—the next key step is involving employees who weren't at the retreat in the *how*—how the group will get things done and who is responsible for doing what and by when.

It's important to involve as many people as practical in the change process, of which the retreat was only one step. Employees who did not take part in the retreat should have the opportunity to participate in task forces or special work groups charged with implementing the changes agreed on at the retreat. But they shouldn't be expected merely to be good soldiers who salute and say, "Yes, ma'am!" Their views should be sought and considered as the change initiative takes shape.

The architectural plans for even the best-designed buildings are nearly always modified during construction. The same is true for the implementation phase of a change initiative. Plans may be drawn up at the retreat, but the structure has to be built in the real world. Modifications are inevitable and even desirable because it's important to take into account anything the retreat participants didn't foresee. (This doesn't mean, of course, that decisions made at the retreat should be revisited ad infinitum, just that you should expect and welcome modifications as the change initiative progresses.)

Once the implementation plan is underway, it's important to celebrate progress by acknowledging significant milestones. People involved in change initiatives tend to focus their attention on the road ahead, which may seem endless. It's important that they look back from time to time to appreciate how much distance they have already covered.

You might want to draw on the facilitator's expertise as you carry out your plan. Sometimes a little outside assistance can jump-start a stalled change initiative.

A high-tech company, for example, wanted to find a way to maintain the positive momentum growing out of its retreat. An external consultant helped the company set up a peer support network that fostered better information sharing and collaboration among the various department heads.

Similarly, a government agency established several task forces to work on specific aspects of the action plan that came out of the retreat we led. We remained involved with the process to help task force members sharpen their creative thinking skills, learn how to plan and conduct more effective meetings, and master various decision-making techniques.

Avoiding Post-Retreat Letdown

A successful retreat can be a peak experience for everyone involved. People come back to work excited about new initiatives, about the collegial spirit they have experienced, and about everything they have learned. Then they have to go right back to work on the same old stuff that was on their desks before they left.

When the bubble of the retreat environment bursts, participants may feel deflated. But you can take some steps to keep the retreat group engaged. For example:

> *Give participants mementos of the retreat.* A useful or decorative object sitting on someone's desk can serve as a reminder of the spirit of the retreat. It might be as simple as a portfolio distributed at the beginning of the retreat, printed with the organization's name and the retreat dates, for participants to use during the retreat, or a coffee mug with a theme imprinted on it, delivered a day or two later back at the office. Some groups have made a point of taking a group photo and having copies made for all the participants. Sometimes the mementos are more unusual. One group we facilitated in the Deep South had enjoyed an uproarious mid-retreat dinner at a catfish restaurant. When the participants returned to work, the CEO sent them all tacky stuffed-catfish plaques, which they proudly displayed on their office walls. (Don't, however, make this souvenir so valuable or desirable that nonparticipants will be jealous and see the object as yet another perk for the favored few or a

constant reminder that some people took part and they did not. Or give the same object to everyone, if practical, to remind the whole organization about the changes that are coming as a result of recommendations or decisions made at the retreat.)

Hold periodic post-retreat updates. Schedule regular times to meet with retreat participants (and others involved in implementation activities) to talk about the status of the change initiatives. The get-togethers can be weekly, biweekly, monthly, or quarterly, whatever makes sense for you, but get the dates on people's calendars right away. These meetings can be excellent forums for devising solutions to problems that arise in the implementation phases. And holding regular meetings doesn't preclude calling ad hoc sessions when necessary.

Convene mini-retreats. A half-day session with the retreat group can help keep the work moving forward. Each mini-session should focus tightly on one topic. The participants can mobilize to get some targeted work done and maintain the special relationships they formed.

Acknowledge accomplishments and celebrate reaching milestones. Look for ways to reward individuals and groups for the extra efforts they have made. Acknowledge progress often. Talk about large and small achievements in staff meetings and special *change champions* meetings. Send e-mails and personal notes to everyone who has made a special contribution to the change efforts. Help people see how far they have traveled as well as what remains to be done.

The Role of Senior Management

A retreat is over when it's over, but it will be judged a success only if it initiated a process that continues to unfold back at the office. For this forward momentum to continue, senior management must take the participants' recommendations and decisions seriously and be committed to implementing those they agreed to.

There are several ways you can personally champion change. You might, for instance, give staff members time to work on various retreat-related tasks.

You might decide to reduce or redistribute people's regular duties, provide funds for training and professional development, or offer rewards and recognition to staff members who contribute to achieving the goals agreed to at the retreat.

And you might look critically at your own management style and modify your behavior as necessary to foster desired change.

If change is difficult for staff members, it's much more difficult for executives. Executives typically (and usually correctly) credit their management styles for their ascension to the upper rungs of the organization ladder. So they're often reluctant or unwilling to modify their approaches. Or they may think they're unable to modify them.

But altering your management style to fit new demands doesn't mean becoming a different person, anymore than altering a jacket when you gain or lose weight makes it a different suit. It merely means accepting that you, like everyone else, could do some things better. If you alter elements of your management style to better fit the circumstances, you will encourage the changes that you want to see take place.

A retreat affords you a valuable opportunity to learn what you are doing right and what you could be doing better. Modifying behavior in response to feedback is the hallmark of a successful leader.

> The Center for Creative Leadership conducted a study of promising employees whose career paths flattened out or even took a nosedive (see McCall and Lombardo, 1983). The number one factor holding them back was inability or unwillingness to respond appropriately to the candid feedback they received.

Changing Cynicism to Support

One of the greatest impediments to making things better at work is cynicism—the belief that nothing will ever improve. "You can't change human nature," people might say.

Well, maybe you *can't* change human nature, but you *can* change human behavior, and that's what can make things better.

Brooks, for example, the newly appointed director of a large government bureau, was dissatisfied with the way her office operated. Staff took too long to respond to customers. New ideas weren't bubbling to the surface. Employees weren't motivated. Brooks recognized that this was the kind of bureau that gave bureaucracy a bad name. To remedy the situation, Brooks declared her commitment to change, introduced new concepts, held retreats to give employees a forum to decide how to make things better, and vowed to accept employee recommendations.

Some employees were enthusiastic about the possibilities, but most were indifferent ("We've seen this all before") or even hostile ("None of this will ever amount to anything"). "I don't trust this new boss," said one employee, "and I'm not going to get my hopes up only to be disappointed."

Brooks listened and took seriously what she was hearing. She realized that she would have to manage differently if her experiment were to succeed. She worked diligently to modify her management style. In time she overcame the resistance that accompanies any change initiative and won over the naysayers. In fact, by the time the bureau's new way of doing business was challenged a couple of years later by newcomers, some of the original critics who had opposed the changes most vocally had become their most ardent advocates.

The role of the leader in a change process is critical. If the leader's attitude is, "I can keep managing the old way; everyone else will have to change," the effort is almost certain to fail.

Change imposed from the top down rarely achieves the desired results in the long term. The cynics will dig in their collective heels and try to outdo each other in proving themselves right. But when leaders can see and hear—*really* see and hear—they can initiate and manage change efforts that transform their organizations.

Overcoming cynicism is not easy. It will require you to hear things that may be discomforting, embarrassing, even painful. You may have to reexamine and perhaps abandon some of the management principles you have successfully employed over the years in pursuit of the positions you have attained. You may have to change your style in light of new economic conditions, new attitudes among employees, new trends in society, or new goals and objectives.

When you ask for candor, you have to mean it. When you encourage subordinates to take risks, you must reward risk taking. When you demand honesty and loyalty from the staff, you also have to be honest with and show loyalty to the staff.

You won't transform cynicism to support for positive change overnight (and you may have to ask hard-core cynics who actively oppose or undermine the initiative to move on). If, however, you gain a reputation for listening to others, saying what you mean, and doing what you say you will do, things are likely to change for the better.

Making the Plan Stick

The most common reason a retreat fails to spark lasting change is that everyday events overtake good intentions. People start remembering the retreat as an occasion—something they experienced—rather than as a launching pad for their real work.

When they return from the retreat, participants must immediately make time to do the necessary follow-through. Not *find* time; *make* time. They have to make time in their schedules *regularly,* not just every now and then. That may mean giving up some other tasks or reordering some priorities.

Most important is the ongoing communication with everyone involved about where the organization is now headed and how it will get there. In our experience some of the most critical actions leaders must take are these:

> *Make the outcomes important.* People will not change unless they think it's really necessary and important to change. Make the reasons for change dramatic, compelling, and even urgent.

> *Design a clear and simple implementation plan.* The more complex the ideas that come out of the retreat, the harder they will be to remember—and the less likely they are to be put into practice. Make implementation strategies simple, clear, and explicit, and show people how these strategies apply as they set their everyday priorities and make decisions.

> *Demonstrate support and commitment among top management.* If a leader disparages any part of the plan, in public pronouncements or in private conversations with colleagues or outsiders, people will start perceiving the entire plan as full of holes. And if leaders don't keep their commitments, others will see such commitments as meaningless. Everyone will watch your behavior for clues to what's important. It's not only what you say but also—more important—what you do that matters.

Be unrelenting in pursuit of the goals. Do not accept excuses and delays. Be rigorous in demanding that people adhere to the new strategies and actions (with allowances, of course, for necessary modifications; wise leaders don't carve their plans in marble—and they know butter isn't a good medium either).

Keep everyone involved. Make it very clear that nothing will happen without everyone's best efforts. Create opportunities for people to advance the overall goals by getting involved and taking action at their own levels.

Remove obstacles. Remove barriers to organization success. Be willing to change systems and structures if necessary. Encourage risk taking in pursuit of the goals by tolerating errors along the way.

Report on progress frequently. People need a sense that their efforts are worthwhile. Hand out lots of praise and thanks for participation. If something derails, be up front about the problems, and engage with others in devising solutions.

Critical Leadership Actions for Retreat Follow-Up

- Make the outcomes important.

- Design a clear and simple implementation plan.

- Demonstrate total commitment among top management.

- Be unrelenting in pursuit of the goals.

- Keep everyone involved.

- Remove obstacles.

- Report on progress frequently.

Look Ahead, Plan Ahead

A retreat need not become an annual event, as predictable as a national holiday. That said, regular offsites can help an organization continue to evolve.

It's a good idea to build retreats into the annual budget, although not into the calendar. In other words, you'll want to have the resources available to convene a retreat when the time is right. But the right time will not necessarily be the same week every year. You don't want retreats to become routine and to take place whether they're needed or not.

Remember that holding a retreat will not guarantee an organization's success. Retreats are not cure-alls. A retreat should never be an end in itself.

Rather, a retreat is a tool. It's an event in the life of an organization that can refocus and reenergize people. It's a means to redefine an organization's future destination and delineate the route to reach it.

Make sure the retreat is genuinely supported by people above you in the chain of command, and hire a facilitator who will design and lead the appropriate retreat for your group's needs. In this way you will have prepared a strong and solid foundation for a retreat that works.

Chapter 18

Activities Indexes

Activities Index

Title	Purpose	Recommended for ...	Key Methodologies	Chapter
Alternative Futures	Explore impact of different levels of external change	Strategic planning	Storytelling; visual metaphor	9
Appreciation	Express appreciation to other participants	Culture change Team building Board	Whole group disclosure	14
Are We Dropping the Ball?	Determine if a group is living up to its potential	Culture change Team building Board	Structured analysis of a model; juggling as metaphor	11
Ask the Genie	Create goals	All retreats	Guided visualization; action planning	11
Bottom-Line Matrix	Determine which programs and services to continue, strengthen, or abandon	Strategic planning Board	Post-it Notes placed on a matrix according to group-developed criteria	13
Centers of Excellence	Determine which programs or services exemplify the organization or group at its best	All retreats	Visual metaphor	9
Change Conga	Make individual commitments	All retreats	Visual expression, movement, and rhythm	14
Closing Thoughts	Make individual commitments	All retreats	Individual reflection; whole group disclosure	14
Collective Quilt	Make individual commitments	All retreats	Visual expression	14
Conflicting Interests	Help participants learn how they manage conflict	Team building Board	Group-on-group observation during debrief of structured scenario	13
Considering Risk	Reduce risk	All retreats	Reflection and group discussion	12
Creative Limbering	Help participants flex creative thinking muscles	Creative thinking Strategic planning	Individual associations using trigger words	12

Activities Index (continued)

Title	Purpose	Recommended for . . .	Key Methodologies	Chapter
Criteria Evaluation Grid	Evaluate best actions to pursue	Strategic planning	Post-it Notes placed on a matrix according to group-developed criteria	8
Distinctive Competencies	Create succinct statement of organization's or group's uniqueness	All retreats	Role playing; individual and group writing of statement that could fit on the back of a business card	9
Expectations and Outcomes	Compare progress made at the retreat to expectations at outset	Culture change Team building Board	Individual letter writing	14
Expert Opinion	Help participants solve problems without usual constraints	All retreats	Individual reflection based on imagined "expert" advice	12
Exploring Strategic Direction	Establish the group's direction or vision	All retreats	Group collage made in silence to stimulate discussion of deeper meaning	9
Gains and Losses	Explore gains and losses associated with a change	All retreats	Individual four-quadrant diagrams	7
Gibberish Press Conference	Explore what's positive in an idea or option	All retreats	Improvisation	12
Glimpses into the Future	Explore trends that might affect the organization and strategies to be successful in any future	Strategic planning	Individual idea generation; group storytelling	9
Headline Buzz	Help participants solve problems without usual constraints	All retreats	Tabloid headlines as metaphor	12
How Conflict Affects Us	Determine the impact of conflict on the group's effectiveness	Culture change Team building Board	Individual reflection; group discussion	11
How Do I Contribute?	Help group members give one another feedback	Culture change Team building Board	Individual reflection on grid; anonymous structured feedback	11
How We Behave	Observe typical behavior	Culture change Team building Board	Role playing; improvisation	10

Title	Purpose	Recommended for . . .	Key Methodologies	Chapter
How We Communicate	Assess communication patterns	Culture change Team building Board	Structured information gathering	11
How Would I Use It?	Help participants flex creative thinking muscles	Creative thinking Strategic planning	Guided individual associations	12
I Want Those Resources!	Help participants learn how they interact and make decisions	Culture change Team building Board	Group-on-group observation during debrief of structured scenario	13
I'm Committing . . .	Make individual commitments	All retreats	Visual expression; photography	14
Impressions	Help participants solve problems without usual constraints	All retreats	Striking visual images as metaphor	12
Incident at Coyote Canyon	Help participants learn how they interact and make decisions	Culture change Team building Board	Group-on-group observation during debrief of structured scenario	11
Isolated Words	Help participants solve problems without usual constraints	All retreats	Changing word emphasis to change meaning	12
It's Important	Help participants determine which results are important to their team and which to the whole organization	Team building Board	Whole group four-quadrant diagram	13
It's Music to My Ears	Help participants solve problems without usual constraints	All retreats	Music as metaphor	12
Let's Take Our Chances	Choose among alternatives	All retreats	Dice roll or coin toss to spark group discussion	8
Letter to Myself	Make individual commitments	All retreats	Individual reflection; whole group disclosure	14
Metaphorical Management	Help participants learn how they are perceived by others	Team building Board	Visual metaphor; structured feedback	13
Multiple Perspectives	Assume someone else's perspective for additional ideas	All retreats	Individual reflection based on different people's wishes	12

Title	Purpose	Recommended for ...	Key Methodologies	Chapter
My Conflict Triggers	Help group members develop strategies for managing conflict more successfully	Culture change Team building Board	Structured reflection; pairs discussion and mutual coaching	11
Obstacle Busters I	Determine impediments to change	All retreats	Impediments written on paper and inserted in balloons to generate ideas to overcome obstacles	9
Obstacle Busters II	Determine which obstacles are in the group's power to remove	All retreats	Small and large group structured discussion	10
Obstacle Busters III	Anticipate obstacles	All retreats	Movement; physical metaphor	14
Our "Proverbial" Differentiation	Differentiate organization or group from others in its field	All retreats	Individual and group free association using the messages in proverbs	9
Our Stable of Clients or Resources	Rate programs, services, or clients	Strategic planning	Metaphorical categories to spark group discussion	8
Payoffs and Capabilities	Evaluate ideas	All retreats	Small group four-quadrant diagrams	12
Picturing Our Roles	Reach group agreement on individuals' roles	Team building Board	Visual representation of abstract concepts	11
Prioritizing Constituencies	Rank client or constituency relevance to the organization's mission	Strategic planning	Individual voting with color-coded dots that indicate relative importance	9
Purpose Check	Assess agreement on the group's purpose	All retreats	Individual reflection; group discussion	11
"Purposeful" Poetry	Determine group's purpose	All retreats	Group creation of limericks	11
Put on Your Thinking Cap	Evaluate ideas	All retreats	Color as metaphor for thinking styles	12
Rating Resources	Rate organizational competencies	Strategic planning	Individual and then group report card	8
Really Bad Ideas	Help participants generate innovative ideas	All retreats	Individual associations using reverse concepts	12

Title	Purpose	Recommended for . . .	Key Methodologies	Chapter
Reporters from Planet Arimira	Help participants solve problems without usual constraints	All retreats	Description of product, service, or process from perspective of someone from another planet	12
Resource/Impact Matrix	Determine which results the group will hold itself accountable for	Strategic planning	Small group four-quadrant diagrams	9
Reward Sonatas	Explore current and desired rewards	Culture change Team building Board	Groups form two improvisational "orchestras"	10
Sell Me Glamour	Decide how best to meet client needs	All retreats	Individual free association with Post-it Notes on what clients want to be "sold"	9
Show Me Our Future	Choose among options by looking at the best in each option	All retreats	Using props to create positive scenarios	8
Significant Stories	Identify defining events and their impact	Culture change Team building Board	Small and large group storytelling	10
Silent Dialogue	Explore reactions to sensitive issues	Culture change Team building Board	Group drawing in silence	10
Speed Feedback Rounds	Help group members give one another feedback	Culture change Team building Board	Structured feedback	11
Star Performers	Help participants change hindering characteristics	Culture change Team building Board	Structured reflection; whole group role playing	11
Taking Responsibility	Help group members assess their individual and collective roles in conflict situations	Culture change Team building Board	Individual reflection; group discussion	11
Targeting Results	Determine which results are key for success	Strategic planning	Group rank ordering of Post-it Notes in silence	9
The Messy Room	Assess potential reactions to change	All retreats	Whole group four-quadrant diagram	14

Activities Index (continued)

Title	Purpose	Recommended for ...	Key Methodologies	Chapter
The Road We've Traveled	Review progress made at the retreat	Culture change Team building Board	Visual metaphor	14
This Could Be Me	Help teams maximize individual contributions	Team building Board	Individual reflection; feedback	11
Timeline of Our History	Identify defining events and their impact	Culture change Team building Board	Timeline created from individual reflections	10
Top Priorities	Set priorities for action	All retreats	Whole group discussion	14
Trust Me	Help participants assess the trust in their group	Culture change Team building Board	Line-up continuum	13
Values Auction	Determine key values	All retreats	Competitive individual "bidding" for values	9
Values Vignettes	Explore current values and those the group aspires to	All retreats	Short skits with props	9
Vehicle for Change I	Assess how working relationships could be improved	Culture change Team building Board	Visual metaphor	11
Vehicle for Change II	Make group commitments to change	Culture change Team building Board	Visual metaphor	14
Villains in Charge	Help participants solve problems without usual constraints	All retreats	Guided individual associations	12
Visit Our Village	Observe group's own culture	Culture change Team building Board	Structured interviews using questions from "anthropologists"	10
We'll Keep . . .	Decide what elements of an organization's culture are worth keeping in the midst of change	All retreats	Creation of group metaphorical offering using props, including objects from nature	10

Title	Purpose	Recommended for ...	Key Methodologies	Chapter
What "Blocks" Cooperation	Help participants learn how differing goals hinder cooperation	Team building Board	Group-on-group observation during debrief of structured scenario	13
What Gets Rewarded Here?	Explore formal and informal rewards	Culture change Team building Board	Small group discussion	10
What I See for Me . . .	Make individual commitments	All retreats	Striking visual images as metaphor	14
Wide-Open Thinking	Help participants generate innovative ideas	All retreats	Individual associations using trigger words	12
Wouldn't It Be Great If . . .?	Create goals	Strategic planning Team building Board Creative thinking	Individual reflection; group categorization of goals	11
You Can Count on Me	Make individual commitments	All retreats	Peer support	14

Activities to Use in Any Retreat

Title	Purpose	Key Methodologies	Chapter
Ask the Genie	Create goals	Guided visualization; action planning	11
Centers of Excellence	Determine which programs or services exemplify the organization or group at its best	Visual metaphor	9
Change Conga	Make individual commitments	Visual expression, movement, and rhythm	14
Closing Thoughts	Make individual commitments	Individual reflection; whole group disclosure	14
Collective Quilt	Make individual commitments	Visual expression	14
Considering Risk	Reduce risk	Reflection; group discussion	12
Distinctive Competencies	Create succinct statement of organization's or group's uniqueness	Role playing; individual and group writing of statement that could fit on the back of a business card	9
Expert Opinion	Help participants solve problems without usual constraints	Individual reflection based on imagined "expert" advice	12
Exploring Strategic Direction	Establish the group's direction or vision	Group collage made in silence to stimulate discussion of deeper meaning	9
Gains and Losses	Explore gains and losses associated with a change	Individual four-quadrant diagrams	7
Gibberish Press Conference	Explore what's positive in an idea or option	Improvisation	12
Headline Buzz	Help participants solve problems without usual constraints	Tabloid headlines as metaphor	12
I'm Committing . . .	Make individual commitments	Visual expression; photography	14
Impressions	Help participants solve problems without usual constraints	Striking visual images as metaphor	12
Isolated Words	Help participants solve problems without usual constraints	Changing word emphasis to change meaning	12
It's Music to My Ears	Help participants solve problems without usual constraints	Music as metaphor	12

Activities to Use in Any Retreat (continued)

Title	Purpose	Key Methodologies	Chapter
Let's Take Our Chances	Choose among alternatives	Dice roll or coin toss to spark group discussion	8
Letter to Myself	Make individual commitments	Individual reflection; whole group disclosure	14
Multiple Perspectives	Assume someone else's perspective for additional ideas	Individual reflection based on different people's wishes	12
Obstacle Busters I	Determine impediments to change	Impediments written on paper and inserted in balloons to generate ideas to overcome obstacles	9
Obstacle Busters II	Determine which obstacles are in the group's power to remove	Small and large group structured discussion	10
Obstacle Busters III	Anticipate obstacles	Movement; physical metaphor	14
Our "Proverbial" Differentiation	Differentiate organization or group from others in its field	Individual and group free association using the messages in proverbs	9
Payoffs and Capabilities	Evaluate ideas	Small group four-quadrant diagrams	12
Purpose Check	Assess agreement on the group's purpose	Individual reflection; group discussion	11
"Purposeful" Poetry	Determine group's purpose	Group creation of limericks	11
Put on Your Thinking Cap	Evaluate ideas	Color as metaphor for thinking styles	12
Really Bad Ideas	Help participants generate innovative ideas	Individual associations using reverse concepts	12
Reporters from Planet Arimira	Help participants solve problems without usual constraints	Description of product, service, or process from perspective of someone from another planet	12
Sell Me Glamour	Decide how best to meet client needs	Individual free association with Post-it Notes on what clients want to be "sold"	9
Show Me Our Future	Choose among options by looking at the best in each option	Using props to create positive scenarios	8
The Messy Room	Assess potential reactions to change	Whole group four-quadrant diagram	14
Top Priorities	Set priorities for action	Whole group discussion	14
Values Auction	Determine key values	Competitive individual "bidding" for values	9

Activities to Use in Any Retreat (continued)

Title	Purpose	Key Methodologies	Chapter
Values Vignettes	Explore current values and those the group aspires to	Short skits with props	9
Villains in Charge	Help participants solve problems without usual constraints	Guided individual associations	12
We'll Keep . . .	Decide what elements of an organization's culture are worth keeping in the midst of change	Creation of group metaphorical offering using props, including objects from nature	10
What I See for Me . . .	Make individual commitments	Striking visual images as metaphor	14
Wide-Open Thinking	Help participants generate innovative ideas	Individual associations using trigger words	12
You Can Count on Me	Make individual commitments	Peer support	14

Activities for Culture Change, Team-Building, and Board Retreats

Title	Purpose	Key Methodologies	Chapter
Appreciation	Express appreciation to other participants	Whole group disclosure	14
Are We Dropping the Ball?	Determine if a group is living up to its potential	Structured analysis of a model; juggling as metaphor	11
Bottom-Line Matrix	Determine which programs and services to continue, strengthen, or abandon	Post-it Notes placed on a matrix according to group-developed criteria	13
Conflicting Interests	Help participants learn how they manage conflict	Group-on-group observation during debrief of structured scenario	13
Expectations and Outcomes	Compare progress made at the retreat to expectations at outset	Individual letter writing	14
How Conflict Affects Us	Determine the impact of conflict on the group's effectiveness	Individual reflection; group discussion	11
How Do I Contribute?	Help group members give one another feedback	Individual reflection on grid; anonymous structured feedback	11
How We Behave	Observe typical behavior	Role playing; improvisation	10
How We Communicate	Assess communication patterns	Structured information gathering	11
I Want Those Resources!	Help participants learn how they interact and make decisions	Group-on-group observation during debrief of structured scenario	13
Incident at Coyote Canyon	Help participants learn how they interact and make decisions	Group-on-group observation during debrief of structured scenario	11
It's Important	Help participants determine which results are important to their team and which to the whole organization	Whole group four-quadrant diagram	13
Metaphorical Management	Help participants learn how they are perceived by others	Visual metaphor; structured feedback	13
My Conflict Triggers	Help group members develop strategies for managing conflict more successfully	Structured reflection; pairs discussion/ mutual coaching	11
Picturing Our Roles	Reach group agreement on individuals' roles	Visual representation of abstract concepts	11

Activities for Culture Change,
Team-Building, and Board Retreats (continued)

Title	Purpose	Key Methodologies	Chapter
Reward Sonatas	Explore current and desired rewards	Groups form two improvisational "orchestras"	10
Significant Stories	Identify defining events and their impact	Small and large group storytelling	10
Silent Dialogue	Explore reactions to sensitive issues	Group drawing in silence	10
Speed Feedback Rounds	Help group members give one another feedback	Structured feedback	11
Star Performers	Help participants change hindering characteristics	Structured reflection; whole group role playing	11
Taking Responsibility	Help group members assess their individual and collective roles in conflict situations	Individual reflection; group discussion	11
The Road We've Traveled	Review progress made at the retreat	Visual metaphor	14
This Could Be Me	Help teams maximize individual contributions	Individual reflection; feedback	11
Timeline of Our History	Identify defining events and their impact	Timeline created from individual reflections	10
Trust Me	Help participants assess the trust in their group	Line-up continuum	13
Vehicle for Change I	Assess how working relationships could be improved	Visual metaphor	11
Vehicle for Change II	Make group commitments to change	Visual metaphor	14
Visit Our Village	Observe group's own culture	Structured interviews using questions from "anthropologists"	10
What "Blocks" Cooperation	Help participants learn how differing goals hinder cooperation	Group-on-group observation during debrief of structured scenario	13
What Gets Rewarded Here?	Explore formal and informal rewards	Small group discussion	10
Wouldn't It Be Great If . . .?	Create goals	Individual reflection; group categorization of goals	11

Activities for Building Cooperation and Dealing with Sensitive Issues

Title	Purpose	Recommended for ...	Key Methodologies	Chapter
Appreciation	Express appreciation to other participants	Culture change Team building Board	Whole group disclosure	14
Are We Dropping the Ball?	Determine if a group is living up to its potential	Culture change Team building Board	Structured analysis of a model; juggling as metaphor	11
Change Conga	Make individual commitments	All retreats	Visual expression, movement, and rhythm	14
Closing Thoughts	Make individual commitments	All retreats	Individual reflection and whole group disclosure	14
Collective Quilt	Make individual commitments	All retreats	Visual expression	14
Conflicting Interests	Help participants learn how they manage conflict	Team building Board	Group-on-group observation during debrief of structured scenario	13
Gains and Losses	Explore gains and losses associated with a change	All retreats	Individual four-quadrant diagrams	7
Gibberish Press Conference	Explore what's positive in an idea or option	All retreats	Improvisation	12
How Conflict Affects Us	Determine the impact of conflict on the group's effectiveness	Culture change Team building Board	Individual reflection; group discussion	11
How Do I Contribute?	Help group members give one another feedback	Culture change Team building Board	Individual reflection on grid; anonymous structured feedback	11
How We Behave	Observe typical behavior	Culture change Team building Board	Role playing; improvisation	10
How We Communicate	Assess communication patterns	Culture change Team building Board	Structured information gathering	11

Activities for Building Cooperation
and Dealing with Sensitive Issues (continued)

Title	Purpose	Recommended for . . .	Key Methodologies	Chapter
I Want Those Resources!	Help participants learn how they interact and make decisions	Culture change Team building Board	Group-on-group observation during debrief of structured scenario	13
I'm Committing . . .	Make individual commitments	All retreats	Visual expression; photography	14
Incident at Coyote Canyon	Help participants learn how they interact and make decisions	Culture change Team building Board	Group-on-group observation during debrief of structured scenario	11
It's Important	Help participants determine which results are important to their team and which to the whole organization	Team building Board	Whole group four-quadrant diagram	13
Metaphorical Management	Help participants learn how they are perceived by others	Team building Board	Visual metaphor; structured feedback	13
Multiple Perspectives	Assume someone else's perspective for additional ideas	All retreats	Individual reflection based on different people's wishes	12
My Conflict Triggers	Help group members develop strategies for managing conflict more successfully	Culture change Team building Board	Structured reflection; pairs discussion/mutual coaching	11
Obstacle Busters I	Determine impediments to change	All retreats	Impediments written on paper and inserted in balloons to generate ideas to overcome obstacles	9
Obstacle Busters II	Determine which obstacles are in the group's power to remove	All retreats	Small and large group structured discussion	10
Obstacle Busters III	Anticipate obstacles	All retreats	Movement; physical metaphor	14
Picturing Our Roles	Reach group agreement on individuals' roles	Team building Board	Visual representation of abstract concepts	11
Rating Resources	Rate organizational competencies	Strategic planning	Individual and then group report card	8

Activities for Building Cooperation
and Dealing with Sensitive Issues (continued)

Title	Purpose	Recommended for . . .	Key Methodologies	Chapter
Reporters from Planet Arimira	Help participants solve problems without usual constraints	All retreats	Description of product, service, or process from perspective of someone from another planet	12
Reward Sonatas	Explore current and desired rewards	Culture change Team building Board	Groups form two improvisational "orchestras"	10
Significant Stories	Identify defining events and their impact	Culture change Team building Board	Small and large group storytelling	10
Silent Dialogue	Explore reactions to sensitive issues	Culture change Team building Board	Group drawing in silence	10
Speed Feedback Rounds	Help group members give one another feedback	Culture change Team building Board	Structured feedback	11
Star Performers	Help participants change hindering characteristics	Culture change Team building Board	Structured reflection; whole group role playing	11
Taking Responsibility	Help group members assess their individual and collective roles in conflict situations	Culture change Team building Board	Individual reflection; group discussion	11
The Messy Room	Assess potential reactions to change	All retreats	Whole group four-quadrant diagram	14
The Road We've Traveled	Review progress made at the retreat	Culture change Team building Board	Visual metaphor	14
This Could Be Me	Help teams maximize individual contributions	Team building Board	Individual reflection; feedback	11
Timeline of Our History	Identify defining events and their impact	Culture change Team building Board	Timeline created from individual reflections	10

Activities for Building Cooperation
and Dealing with Sensitive Issues (continued)

Title	Purpose	Recommended for . . .	Key Methodologies	Chapter
Trust Me	Help participants assess the trust in their group	Culture change Team building Board	Line-up continuum	13
Values Auction	Determine key values	All retreats	Competitive individual "bidding" for values	9
Values Vignettes	Explore current values and those the group aspires to	All retreats	Short skits with props	9
Vehicle for Change I	Assess how working relationships could be improved	Culture change Team building Board	Visual metaphor	11
Vehicle for Change II	Make group commitments to change	Culture change Team building Board	Visual metaphor	14
Villains in Charge	Help participants solve problems without usual constraints	All retreats	Guided individual associations	12
Visit Our Village	Observe group's own culture	Culture change Team building Board	Structured interviews using questions from "anthropologists"	10
We'll Keep . . .	Decide what elements of an organization's culture are worth keeping in the midst of change	All retreats	Creation of group metaphorical offering using props, including objects from nature	10
What "Blocks" Cooperation	Help participants learn how differing goals hinder cooperation	Team building Board	Group-on-group observation during debrief of structured scenario	13
What Gets Rewarded Here?	Explore formal and informal rewards	Culture change Team building Board	Small group discussion	10
What I See for Me . . .	Make individual commitments	All retreats	Striking visual images as metaphor	14

Activities for Building Cooperation
and Dealing with Sensitive Issues (continued)

Title	Purpose	Recommended for . . .	Key Methodologies	Chapter
Wouldn't It Be Great If . . .?	Create goals	Create goals Team building Board Creative thinking	Individual reflection; group categorization of goals	11
You Can Count on Me	Make individual commitments	All retreats	Peer support	14

Activities for Idea Generation

Title	Purpose	Recommended for ...	Key Methodologies	Chapter
Alternative Futures	Explore impact of different levels of external change	Strategic planning	Storytelling; visual metaphor	9
Ask the Genie	Create goals	All retreats	Guided visualization; action planning	11
Centers of Excellence	Determine which programs or services exemplify the organization or group at its best	All retreats	Visual metaphor	9
Creative Limbering	Help participants flex creative thinking muscles	Creative thinking Strategic planning	Individual associations using trigger words	12
Distinctive Competencies	Create succinct statement of organization's or group's uniqueness	All retreats	Role playing; individual and group writing of statement that could fit on the back of a business card	9
Expert Opinion	Help participants solve problems without usual constraints	All retreats	Individual reflection based on imagined "expert" advice	12
Exploring Strategic Direction	Establish the group's direction or vision	All retreats	Group collage made in silence to stimulate discussion of deeper meaning	9
Gibberish Press Conference	Explore what's positive in an idea or option	All retreats	Improvisation	12
Glimpses into the Future	Explore trends that might affect the organization and strategies to be successful in any future	Strategic planning	Individual idea generation; group storytelling	9
Headline Buzz	Help participants solve problems without usual constraints	All retreats	Tabloid headlines as metaphor	12
How Would I Use It?	Help participants flex creative thinking muscles	Creative thinking Strategic planning	Guided individual associations	12
Impressions	Help participants solve problems without usual constraints	All retreats	Striking visual images as metaphor	12
Isolated Words	Help participants solve problems without usual constraints	All retreats	Changing word emphasis to change meaning	12

Activities for Idea Generation (continued)

Title	Purpose	Recommended for . . .	Key Methodologies	Chapter
It's Music to My Ears	Help participants solve problems without usual constraints	All retreats	Music as metaphor	12
Multiple Perspectives	Assume someone else's perspective for additional ideas	All retreats	Individual reflection based on different people's wishes	12
Obstacle Busters I	Determine impediments to change	All retreats	Impediments written on paper and inserted in balloons to generate ideas to overcome obstacles	9
Our "Proverbial" Differentiation	Differentiate organization or group from others in its field	All retreats	Individual and group free association using the messages in proverbs	9
Really Bad Ideas	Help participants generate innovative ideas	All retreats	Individual associations using reverse concepts	12
Reporters from Planet Arimira	Help participants solve problems without usual constraints	All retreats	Description of product, service, or process from perspective of someone from another planet	12
Sell Me Glamour	Decide how best to meet client needs	All retreats	Individual free association with Post-it Notes on what clients want to be "sold"	9
Villains in Charge	Help participants solve problems without usual constraints	All retreats	Guided individual associations	12
Wide-Open Thinking	Help participants generate innovative ideas	All retreats	Individual associations using trigger words	12
Wouldn't It Be Great If . . .?	Create goals	Strategic planning Team building Board Creative thinking	Individual reflection; group categorization of goals	11

Activities for Making Decisions, Planning, and Evaluating Ideas

Title	Purpose	Recommended for . . .	Key Methodologies	Chapter
Alternative Futures	Explore impact of different levels of external change	Strategic planning	Storytelling; visual metaphor	9
Ask the Genie	Create goals	All retreats	Guided visualization; action planning	11
Centers of Excellence	Determine which programs or services exemplify the organization or group at its best	All retreats	Visual metaphor	9
Bottom-Line Matrix	Determine which programs and services to continue, strengthen, or abandon	Strategic planning Board retreats	Post-it Notes placed on a matrix according to group-developed criteria	13
Considering Risk	Reduce risk	All retreats	Reflection; group discussion	12
Criteria Evaluation Grid	Evaluate best actions to pursue	Strategic planning	Post-it Notes placed on a matrix according to group-developed criteria	8
Distinctive Competencies	Create succinct statement of organization's or group's uniqueness	All retreats	Role playing; individual and group writing of statement that could fit on the back of a business card	9
Exploring Strategic Direction	Establish the group's direction or vision	All retreats	Group collage made in silence to stimulate discussion of deeper meaning	9
Glimpses into the Future	Explore trends that might affect the organization and strategies to be successful in any future	Strategic planning	Individual idea generation; group storytelling	9
Multiple Perspectives	Assume someone else's perspective for additional ideas	All retreats	Individual reflection based on different people's wishes	12
Obstacle Busters I	Determine impediments to change	All retreats	Impediments written on paper and inserted in balloons to generate ideas to overcome obstacles	9

Activities for Making Decisions, Planning, and Evaluating Ideas (continued)

Title	Purpose	Recommended for . . .	Key Methodologies	Chapter
Obstacle Busters II	Determine which obstacles are in the group's power to remove	All retreats	Small and large group structured discussion	10
Obstacle Busters III	Anticipate obstacles	All retreats	Movement; physical metaphor	14
Our "Proverbial" Differentiation	Differentiate organization or group from others in its field	All retreats	Individual and group free association using the messages in proverbs	9
Our Stable of Clients or Resources	Rate programs, services, or clients	Strategic planning	Metaphorical categories to spark group discussion	8
Payoffs and Capabilities	Evaluate ideas	All retreats	Small group four-quadrant diagrams	12
Prioritizing Constituencies	Rank client or constituency relevance to the organization's mission	Strategic planning	Individual voting with color-coded dots that indicate relative importance	9
Purpose Check	Assess agreement on the group's purpose	All retreats	Individual reflection and group discussion	11
"Purposeful" Poetry	Determine group's purpose	All retreats	Group creation of limericks	11
Put on Your Thinking Cap	Evaluate ideas	All retreats	Color as metaphor for thinking styles	12
Rating Resources	Rate organizational competencies	Strategic planning	Individual and then group report card	8
Resource/Impact Matrix	Determine which results the group will hold itself accountable for	Strategic planning	Small group four-quadrant diagrams	9
Sell Me Glamour	Decide how best to meet client needs	All retreats	Individual free association with Post-it Notes on what clients want to be "sold"	9
Show Me Our Future	Choose among options by looking at the best in each option	All retreats	Using props to create positive scenarios	8
Targeting Results	Determine which results are key for success	Strategic planning	Group rank ordering of Post-it Notes in silence	9

Activities for Making Decisions, Planning, and Evaluating Ideas (continued)

Title	Purpose	Recommended for . . .	Key Methodologies	Chapter
The Messy Room	Assess potential reactions to change	All retreats	Whole group four-quadrant diagram	14
Top Priorities	Set priorities for action	All retreats	Whole group discussion	14
Vehicle for Change II	Make group commitments to change	Culture change Team building Board	Visual metaphor	14

Afterword

We hope you found the stories and examples in this book—all of which came from our experience or that of friends and colleagues—interesting and useful.

In return we invite you, our readers, to share your stories with us—tales of triumphs, amusing anecdotes, interventions that fizzled—that we might include as lessons learned and illustrations in future publications and in our training programs in the art of designing and leading retreats.

We would also love to hear from you with questions, suggestions, and comments about this book or inquiries about our retreat facilitation training courses or the subject of retreats in general. And if you know of any great places to hold an offsite, let us know that as well.

You can communicate with us at the Retreats That Work Web site: www.retreatsthatwork.com

Whether you have something to contribute or are just interested in learning more about retreats that work, c'mon by.

Merianne, Sheila, and Jeff

Appendix

Checklists for the Client

1. *Is a Retreat Right for Your Organization?*

Nine Reasons to Hold a Retreat

☐ *To explore fundamental concerns.* Suppose turnover in your organization is exceptionally high or staff morale low. Or you have seen a significant drop-off in customers or increase in their complaints. A retreat can be the ideal forum to explore and address the underlying causes.

☐ *To harness the collective creativity of the group.* When it's important to generate ideas for new products, services, or work processes, typical brainstorming sessions often fail to produce significant results. Retreats, free of routine workplace demands, have fewer barriers to imagination and creative thinking. The offsite setting can help innovative solutions emerge.

☐ *To foster change.* A retreat can promote new approaches to strategic planning, product design, service delivery, or marketing. The open discussion that characterizes well-run retreats fosters understanding of and commitment to new directions.

☐ *To change perceptions, attitudes, and behavior.* In every organization, people make up stories to account for things they don't understand. These stories lead to attitudes and actions that can be harmful to the organization. A retreat can be a great setting for participants to raise concerns and ask questions. Participants can share information, clear up misunderstandings, discuss the impact of past decisions, and modify those decisions if priorities have changed or if the decisions failed to achieve their purpose.

☐ *To correct course when things are going wrong.* Executives can't turn organizations around by fiat. People will change only when they see that it's important to do so. Retreats provide a forum for discussions about the reasons for and the urgency of a desired change. When people play a role in deciding what could be improved, they are more committed to ensuring that the change effort succeeds.

☐ *To transform the organization's culture or improve relationships hindering its effectiveness.* Suppose members of a team or division are having difficulty communicating effectively with one another. Or two departments seem unable to work together. Or people are afraid to tell leaders what they think those leaders might not want to hear. Retreats can help people open up to one another and can create a climate of trust.

☐ *To create a collective vision for the organization.* Much of the tension that exists in organizations stems not from inherent personality conflicts but rather from individuals pursuing their own (and sometimes conflicting) visions of what is best for the organization. These visions often clash with one another because none of them necessarily represents the complete picture of an organization's circumstances. Retreats can foster alignment by helping participants understand and build commitment to the organization's overall priorities. This understanding and commitment can encourage individuals to hold themselves accountable for the organization's success, not just the success of their own work groups.

☐ *To accomplish something that cannot be done by the leader alone.* No matter how experienced and competent leaders are, they can't do everything on their own. Retreats provide an environment in which everyone can contribute knowledge, expertise, and skills to address issues that often plague and confound busy executives.

☐ *To make tough decisions.* Leaders often confront very tough decisions: Should they eliminate a signature product or service? Close down a particular operation? Reduce staff? Change the nature of a long-standing alliance? There will be greater commitment to the eventual course of action when many people from different levels in the organization have participated in deciding what to eliminate or change and how to go about doing so, rather than simply being told by the leaders what to do. At a well-led retreat, leaders receive the benefit not only of broad participation in idea generation but also of better decisions, because the group collectively will have a wider perspective and a greater number of ideas than the leader does alone.

Ten Reasons Not to Hold a Retreat

A retreat is not the best means of responding to every situation and addressing every concern you might have.

Don't convene a retreat if your intent is any of the following:

☐ *To improve morale through the retreat alone.* Although taking positive action based on the recommendations made at a retreat can increase participants' commitment to the organization, don't expect that simply holding a retreat will improve morale. In fact just the opposite can happen. A retreat can have a negative impact if the issues that come up aren't dealt with appropriately, if people feel that they are not heard and their concerns are not taken seriously, if conflict is not managed successfully, if trust is violated, or if participants feel the retreat was a waste of their time.

☐ *To use the retreat to reward people for their hard work.* Participants rarely see retreats as rewards for doing their jobs well. They're likely to have even more work waiting for them when they return from a retreat, juggling family needs can be difficult, and many would find time off with family and friends more rewarding than attending an offsite.

☐ *To discover and punish non-team players.* This is a terrible reason to have a retreat. If people sense that your purpose in bringing them together is to find out who is loyal and who is not, it will erode trust and do great—if not irreparable—harm to your organization's culture.

☐ *To advance a covert agenda.* If you try to pursue an agenda that is different from the retreat's stated purpose, you will undermine trust in yourself personally as well as in the organization. It is far better for you to tell participants that you have decided, for example, to cut a department's head count and to ask for their help in determining the best way to handle layoffs than for you to try to manipulate them during the retreat into endorsing your idea. When people figure out what you are up to (and they will!), it will foster resentment and engender much more resistance to your ideas than you would encounter if you had been truthful all along.

☐ *To control the conversation.* It is counterproductive for you to try to control what is said or who is authorized to say what. You must understand that just because something isn't said out loud doesn't mean that people aren't thinking it. Trying to direct what participants talk about deprives you of strategic information you need to make informed decisions. Putting everything out on the table and having a candid dialogue about participants' perceptions and misperceptions is better for you and for the organization as a whole than trying to stop people from saying what's on their minds.

☐ *To squelch conflict.* Some people relish conflict, but most dread it. Typically, the more people care about each other, the more averse they are to confronting conflict openly. But aiming to avoid conflict at all costs will practically guarantee that it will crop up in some form or another and that it won't be managed effectively. Successful retreats almost always involve surfacing and dealing with disagreements, disputes, or differences of opinion. If no conflict emerges, chances are participants aren't being honest with themselves or with others or that the retreat has focused on issues that aren't of great concern to them. Conflict is inevitable (and actually healthy) when people care about something. It's key not to ignore it or dismiss it. Instead, take advantage of your facilitator's expertise to find ways of managing conflict so that it can be explored openly.

☐ *To create a platform for your own ideas.* Retreats provide a valuable opportunity for leaders to hear from others. Don't squander it by doing too much of the talking yourself. It is best for you mostly to listen to what others have to say, and to repress your inclination to lead discussions, persuade others, and resolve disputes.

☐ *To disregard what participants recommend.* There is nothing more demoralizing to participants than being led to believe that they have a role in the decision-making process, only to learn that key decisions were preordained. Participants will naturally expect that you will take their advice into consideration before reaching a decision, and that if you don't accept their recommendations you will explain why. If you ask participants to rubber-stamp decisions that you (or others) have already made, or if after the retreat you announce and attribute to the participants decisions they didn't make or ideas they didn't generate, the effect is likely to be very destructive.

☐ *To defend your point of view, promote your position, or maintain the status quo.* Retreats are associated with change in most people's minds. If you want things to stay the same, have a meeting to encourage everyone to keep up the good work or throw a party to thank everybody for a job well done. Reserve retreats for times when you'd like things to be different. And remember, the first person who is likely to have to change is you. If you are not willing to explore more productive leadership practices, it's best not to have a retreat.

☐ *To merely keep up the tradition of having annual retreats.* Many leaders think that having a retreat with no other purpose than to bring everyone together on some regular basis is a good practice at best and harmless at worst. It is neither. A retreat is not a company picnic. Frivolous offsites give retreats a bad name. Do not plan a retreat unless you have a serious purpose in mind. Any other approach will communicate to participants that you don't value their time.

Also remember that a retreat is not a conference. A parade of presentations by in-house or outside experts can provide valuable information or training, but it doesn't constitute a retreat. It's certainly important that people be well informed, but a retreat should be about sparking change, not just absorbing or exchanging information.

This isn't to say that we're against an "annual" retreat if it serves a serious purpose. You might be able to take advantage of a tradition of holding regular retreats to accomplish some important things. However your organization's retreats may have been conducted in the past, you and the facilitator can structure the next one to address key issues that are of genuine concern to the participants.

2. Overall Retreat Logistics

☐ After selecting the facilitator, consult with him or her on the appropriate length for the retreat.

☐ Determine when the facilitator is available for your retreat.

☐ Check available dates with senior managers whose participation in the retreat is critical to its success.

☐ Select a retreat facility and determine dates when it is available for your group. (Your facilitator may have suggestions for appropriate facilities.)

☐ Announce the retreat and give participants two or three options for dates. They should tell you which dates, if any, *do not* work.

☐ Contract with the retreat facility for the dates you choose.

☐ Make arrangements for the transportation, meals, lodging, and audiovisual support required.

☐ Announce the dates of the retreat and provide participants with the information they need, including lodging arrangements; directions to the site; recreational options, if any; the dress code; and how family members can get messages to them during the retreat.

☐ Ask invitees to confirm their participation, indicate any food preferences or limitations, and supply emergency contact information.

3. *Assessing Facilitators*

When you check facilitators' references, find out as much as you can about their ability to:

☐ Listen accurately to what others are saying without injecting their own biases.

☐ Be neutral (and be perceived to be neutral) about the outcome of the discussions.

☐ Suspend judgment about retreat participants.

☐ Understand multiple perspectives, help bring them to the surface, and resist colluding with the group in avoiding thorny issues.

☐ Encourage participants whose viewpoints may not be popular to speak out, and urge others to listen.

☐ Help retreat participants recognize and deal with any behavior that might be hampering the group's work.

- [ ] Deal skillfully with the members of the group who might not want to accept a facilitator's guidance.

- [ ] Empathize with others.

- [ ] Analyze and summarize key issues.

- [ ] Remain comfortable with ambiguous situations and those they do not control.

- [ ] Recognize and manage differences that may stem from the diversity (in culture, race, gender, age, sexual orientation, and so forth) of the participants.

- [ ] Hear feedback from the participants without becoming defensive.

- [ ] Adjust their approach, acknowledge missteps, and ask for help when they need it.

- [ ] Provide candid feedback and coaching to you and to other senior executives.

4. Finding the Right Retreat Site

Look for a retreat site with these amenities:

- [ ] Soundproof rooms, so the facilitator and participants won't have to compete with a speaker with a microphone on the other side of a thin wall.

- [ ] Hard-surfaced, easy-to-move tables that don't have to be covered by tablecloths.

- [ ] Comfortable chairs—either padded, rolling executive-style chairs or comfy sofas and upholstered chairs.

- [ ] Enough room in the main meeting space to allow participants to circle their chairs and to work away from the tables when needed.

- [ ] Space for breakout groups: either a main room that has movable chairs and is large enough for groups to move away from each other, or small rooms adjacent or very close to the main space.

- [ ] Ample supplies of flip chart easels and pads, masking tape, and markers.

☐ Space where people can congregate informally to talk or grounds where they can walk.

☐ Snacks and drinks available all day, rather than just at scheduled breaks.

Checklists for the Facilitator

1. *Partnering Effectively with Your Client*

☐ Are you clear on exactly who your client is within the organization?

☐ Are the client's expectations of you clear? Do you know what specifically the client wants from you?

☐ Do you and the client agree on the outcomes for the retreat?

☐ Are you and the client in alignment about the balance between the business concerns and the interpersonal issues that will be addressed at the retreat?

☐ Will the client respect your need to protect the confidentiality of the people you interview?

☐ Do you and the client concur on whose desires and needs should be taken into account in planning the retreat?

☐ Does what the client wants or needs from a facilitator match your skills? Can you deliver the results the organization needs?

☐ Can you be open with this client? (Or do you feel the need to impress him or her or to hide your concerns?)

☐ Are you neutral about the culture (rather than being staked in particular outcomes)?

☐ Does your personality fit well with the client's? (Do you and the client like one another? Do you and the client trust one another? Are you and the client candid with one another? Do you want the client to succeed?)

☐ Do both you and the client feel free to walk away from this relationship if it's not productive? (Or are you financially overdependent on the client? Or is the client overdependent on your expertise and unwilling to do the hard work himself or herself?)

☐ Does the client seem to value your perspective and expertise?

☐ Does the client seem interested in his or her potential contribution to issues the organization is facing?

☐ Is the client willing to listen to your questions and concerns?

☐ Does the client have realistic expectations of you (and of the retreat) in terms of your ability to "fix" the organization?

☐ Do you and your client see one another as partners? (Or is there a hierarchical relationship?)

☐ Is the client willing and able to give you access to people (including key decision makers) and information so you can understand the full picture?

☐ Does the retreat seem more important to you (or to others in the organization) than it is to the client?

☐ Are the budget and the time allocated for the retreat sufficient for the agenda the client has in mind?

☐ Do you have enough access to the client to get your needs met and your questions answered?

☐ Is the client willing to take prudent risks for the good of the organization?

☐ Is the client willing to change?

☐ Is the client committed to implementing what is agreed to at the retreat?

2. Setting the Conditions for Design Success

Have you:

☐ Come to clear agreement with your client about mutual expectations?

☐ Interviewed participants and other relevant stakeholders in advance?

☐ Provided enough variety in the retreat activities?

☐ Taken the Big Kahuna effect into account?

☐ Included in your design opportunities for people to think before they speak?

☐ Allowed for spontaneous changes to the retreat plan?

☐ Built in unstructured time when you won't be facilitating the group?

☐ Devised activities that will compel participants to make hard choices?

☐ Left adequate time for action planning?

☐ Provided an appropriate close?

3. Matching the Retreat Design with Your Client's Expectations

Is your design:

☐ Suitable for the participants, taking into consideration their level of experience and expertise and their comfort level with certain types of activities?

☐ Focused sharply on delivering the expected outcomes?

☐ Likely to engage the participants, so they are strongly committed to the decisions they make?

☐ Attentive to using participants' time wisely?

☐ Adaptable enough to allow for changes if something unexpected happens, but still able to move the group toward the desired outcomes?

☐ Flexible enough to give participants time to discuss how decisions reached at the retreat will be implemented and integrated into the organization's work?

4. Structuring the Interview Questions

The success of the retreat will depend in large measure on your ability to ask questions that get to the heart of the issues. Here are some questions we often ask people before the retreat, which we recommend you modify to suit the needs of the organization you are working for.

☐ What do you think is most important to accomplish at this retreat?

☐ What might impede the group's ability to achieve that outcome?

☐ [*If this group has held retreats before.*] What did you find most helpful at the last retreat? Did you find anything troubling or frustrating about the last retreat and the actions that resulted from it?

- [ ] What words would you use to describe your experience at [your organization]?
- [ ] What do you think is going well at [your organization]? What do you like most about it?
- [ ] How would you describe relationships among the staff? Between staff and management? [Or between the staff and the board?]
- [ ] In every organization there is some conflict, disagreement, or difference of opinion. How is conflict or disagreement handled at [your organization]?
- [ ] If you had the power to change anything at [your organization], what would you change?
- [ ] Of the changes you said you'd like to see, are there any that you think would not be possible? Why not?
- [ ] How do you feel about taking part in this retreat?
- [ ] Do you have any concerns about what might take place?
- [ ] Is there anything else you think I should know, anything I haven't thought of asking, or anything you'd like to add to something you said before?

5. *The Facilitator's Toolkit*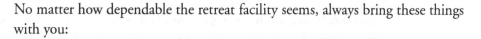

No matter how dependable the retreat facility seems, always bring these things with you:

- [ ] Several sets of fresh markers, in black, blue, green, and red.
- [ ] Two sizes of Post-it Notes, in multiple colors, one pad of each size for every participant, plus about 20 percent extra.
- [ ] Extra name tags for the participants in case someone loses his or her name tag or a participant you weren't expecting turns up.
- [ ] Several rolls of masking tape.
- [ ] Colored labeling dots (for "voting" on choices).
- [ ] Bell, chime, whistle, or whatever you like to use to indicate the beginning and ending of timed exercises.
- [ ] A timer (so you won't have to keep looking at your watch during timed exercises).

6. Inspecting the Meeting Room

☐ *Room arrangement.* Are the chairs and tables set up exactly as you planned? If not, move them now.

☐ *Room ambiance.* Is the temperature comfortable? If not, find out how it can be changed. Is the lighting appropriate? If not, what are your options for creating lighting that is more conducive to your work?

☐ *Your materials.* Is there a table for your notes and supplies? Has the facility provided the supplies you requested, such as pads of writing paper, markers, and masking tape?

☐ *Wall space.* Where will you post flip chart pages as they are filled? Is access to the walls blocked by tables, chairs, or lamps? Will you have to post charts on windows? Where will you put charts as the walls fill up?

☐ *Equipment supplied by the facility.* Do you have the right number of easels and pads of flip chart paper? Are the pads full, or do some only have a few sheets left? Is all the AV equipment you ordered in the room and set up properly? Does it work? (Don't take anyone's word for it; test it yourself.) Do you have extra bulbs for your projector?

☐ *Markers.* If you haven't brought boxes of new markers, have you tested every marker supplied by the facility and discarded those that are dried out?

☐ *Facilities.* Do you know where the bathrooms are? Where the snacks will be set up? Where (and when) lunch and dinner will be served?

☐ *Participant place setups.* Are the supplies—markers, writing pads, and pens or pencils—and handouts that participants need in place? Do you have extras in case they're required?

☐ *Outdoor space.* Do you have access to outdoor space? If so, how is it set up? How far is it from your meeting room? Will participants be able to use it for small group work without taking too much time moving back and forth?

Recommended Resources

Appreciative Inquiry

Cooperrider, D. L. (1995). Introduction to appreciative inquiry. In W. French & C. Bell (Eds.), *Organization development* (5th ed.). Upper Saddle River, NJ: Prentice Hall.

Cooperrider, D. L., Whitney, D. L., & Stavros, J. M. (2003). *Appreciative inquiry handbook: The first in a series of AI workbooks for leaders of change.* Bedford Heights, OH: Lakeshore Communications & San Francisco: Berrett-Koehler.

Hammond, S. A., & Royal, C. (Eds.). (1998). *Lessons from the field: Applying appreciative inquiry.* Plano, TX: Practical Press.

Watkins, J., & Mohr, B. (2001). *Appreciative inquiry: Change at the speed of imagination.* San Francisco: Pfeiffer.

Assessments

Amabile, T. M. (1995). *KEYS: Assessing the climate for creativity.* Greensboro, NC: Center for Creative Leadership.

Briggs, K. C., & Myers, I. B. (1998). *Myers-Briggs Type Indicator: Self-scorable Form M.* Palo Alto, CA: Consulting Psychologists Press.

Campbell, D. (2002). *Campbell Leadership Descriptor.* San Francisco: Pfeiffer.

Campbell, D. (2002). *Campbell Leadership Descriptor: Facilitator's guide.* San Francisco: Pfeiffer & Center for Creative Leadership.

Campbell, D. (2002). *Campbell Leadership Descriptor: Participant workbook.* San Francisco: Pfeiffer & Center for Creative Leadership.

Kirton, M. (1991). *Kirton Adaption-Innovation Inventory.* Berkhamsted, UK: Occupational Research Centre.

Kouzes, J. M., & Posner, B. Z. (2001). *The Leadership Practices Inventory.* San Francisco: Pfeiffer.

Porter, E. H. (1996). *The Strength Deployment Inventory.* Carlsbad, CA: Personal Strengths.

Thomas, K. W., & Kilmann, R. H. (2002). *Thomas-Kilmann Conflict Mode Instrument.* Palo Alto, CA: Consulting Psychologists Press.

Tosca, E. (1997). *Communication Skills Profile.* San Francisco: Pfeiffer.

Case Studies

Barbazette, J. (2004). *Instant case studies: How to design, adapt, and use case studies in training.* San Francisco: Pfeiffer.

Contracting with Your Client

Block, P. (2001). *The flawless consulting fieldbook & companion: A guide to understanding your expertise.* San Francisco: Pfeiffer.

Creative Thinking

De Bono, E. (1994). *De Bono's thinking course* (rev. ed.). New York: Facts on File.

Epstein, R. (2000). *The big book of creativity games: Quick, fun activities for jumpstarting innovation.* New York: McGraw-Hill.

Hall, D. (1996). *Jump start your brain.* New York: Warner Books.

Michalko, M. (1991). *Thinkertoys: A handbook of business creativity.* Berkeley, CA: Ten Speed Press.

Palus, C. C., & Horth, D. M. (2001). *Visual Explorer: Picturing approaches to complex challenges.* Greensboro, NC: Center for Creative Leadership.

VanGundy, A. B. (2005). *101 activities for teaching creativity and problem solving.* San Francisco: Pfeiffer.

Von Oech, R. (1986). *A kick in the seat of the pants.* New York: HarperCollins.

Von Oech, R. (1998). *A whack on the side of the head.* New York: Warner Books.

Diversity

Adler, N. J. (1997). *International dimensions of organizational behavior.* Cincinnati, OH: South-Western College Publishing.

Cross, E. Y., Katz, J. H., Miller, F. A., & Seashore, E. W. (Eds.). (1994). *The promise of diversity: Over 40 voices discuss strategies for eliminating discrimination in organizations.* Burr Ridge, IL: Irwin.

Esty, K., Griffin, R., & Hirsch, M. S. (1995). *Workplace diversity: A manager's guide to solving problems and turning diversity into a competitive advantage.* Holbrook, MA: Adams.

Gardenswartz, L., Rowe, A., Digh, P., & Bennett, M. F. (2003). *The global diversity desk reference: Managing an international workforce.* San Francisco: Pfeiffer.

Hofstede, G. (1997). *Cultures and organizations: Software of the mind.* New York: McGraw-Hill.

Thomas, R. R. (1996). *Redefining diversity.* New York: AMACOM.

Varner, I., & Beamer, L. (1995). *Intercultural communication in the global workplace.* Burr Ridge, IL: Irwin.

Dividing People into Groups

Pike, B., & Solem, L. (2000). *50 creative training openers and energizers: Innovative ways to start your training with a bang!* San Francisco: Pfeiffer & Minneapolis: Creative Training Techniques Press.

Ukens, L. L. (1997). *Getting together: Icebreakers and group energizers.* San Francisco: Pfeiffer.

Ukens, L. L. (2000). *Energize your audience! 75 quick activities that get them started . . . and keep them going.* San Francisco: Pfeiffer.

Facilitation

Bens, I. (2000). *Facilitating with ease! A step-by-step guidebook with customizable worksheets on CD-ROM.* San Francisco: Jossey-Bass.

Dick, B. (1987). *Helping groups be effective: Skills, processes and concepts for group facilitation.* Chapel Hill, Australia: Interchange.

Hogan, C. (2003). *Practical facilitation: A toolkit of techniques.* Sterling, VA: Kogan Page.

Hunter, D., Bailey, A., & Taylor, B. (1995). *The art of facilitation: How to create group synergy.* Tucson, AZ: Fisher Books.

Hunter, D., Bailey, A., & Taylor, B. (1995). *The zen of groups: The handbook for people meeting with a purpose.* Tucson, AZ: Fisher Books.

Kiser, A. G. (1998). *Masterful facilitation.* New York: AMACOM.

Rees, F. (1998). *The facilitator excellence handbook: Helping people work creatively and productively together.* San Francisco: Pfeiffer.

Schwarz, R. M. (1994). *The skilled facilitator: Practical wisdom for developing effective groups.* San Francisco: Jossey-Bass.

Flip Chart Preparation

Brandt, R. C. (1986). *Flip charts: How to draw them and how to use them.* San Francisco: Pfeiffer.

Rees, F. (1998). *The facilitator excellence handbook: Helping people work creatively and productively together.* San Francisco: Pfeiffer.

Silberman, M. L. (1999). *101 ways to make meetings active: Surefire ideas to engage your group.* San Francisco: Pfeiffer.

Westcott, J., & Landau, J. H. (1997). *A picture's worth 1,000 words: A workbook for visual communications.* San Francisco: Pfeiffer.

Specialized Retreat Formats

Brown, J. (2002). *The World Café: A resource guide for hosting conversations that matter.* Mill Valley, CA: Whole Systems Associates.

Discovery Learning. (n.d.). *Paper Planes, Inc.* Greensboro, NC: Author.

Oshry, B. (1996). *Seeing systems: Unlocking the mysteries of organizational life.* San Francisco: Berrett-Koehler.

Oshry, B. (1999). *Leading systems: Lessons from The Power Lab.* San Francisco: Berrett-Koehler.

Owen, H. (1997). *Expanding our now: The story of Open Space Technology.* San Francisco: Berrett-Koehler.

Owen, H. (1997). *Open Space Technology: A user's guide.* San Francisco: Berrett-Koehler.

Slater, R. (2000). *The GE Way fieldbook: Jack Welch's battle plan for corporate revolution.* New York: McGraw-Hill.

Weisbord, M. R., & Janoff, S. (1995). *Future Search: An action guide to finding common ground in organizations and communities.* San Francisco: Berrett-Koehler.

Strategy

Allison, M. J., & Kaye, J. (2005). *Strategic planning for nonprofit organizations: A practical guide and workbook.* Hoboken, NJ: Wiley.

Collins, J. (2001). *Good to great: Why some companies make the leap . . . and others don't.* New York: HarperBusiness.

Drucker, P. (1999). *Management challenges for the 21st century.* New York: HarperBusiness.

Hamel, G. (1996, July/August). Strategy as revolution. *Harvard Business Review.*

Hamel, G. (2000). *Leading the revolution.* Boston: Harvard Business School Press.

Kaufman, R., Oakley-Browne, H., Watkins, R., & Leigh, D. (2003). *Strategic planning for success: Aligning people, performance, and payoffs.* San Francisco: Pfeiffer.

Keen, P.G.W. (1997). *The process edge: Creating value where it counts.* Boston: Harvard Business School Press.

Nolan, T. M., Goodstein, L. D., & Pfeiffer, J. W. (1993). *Plan or die! 10 keys to organizational success.* San Francisco: Pfeiffer.

Porter, M. E. (1996, November/December). What is strategy? *Harvard Business Review,* pp. 68–69.

van der Heijden, K. (1996). *Scenarios: The art of strategic conversation.* Hoboken, NJ: Wiley.

Teamwork and Team Building

Biech, E. (Ed.). (2001). *The Pfeiffer book of successful team-building tools.* San Francisco: Pfeiffer.

Center for Creative Leadership. (n.d.). *EdgeWork.* Available at www.ccl.org.

Eggleton, C. H., & Rice, J. C. (1996). *The fieldbook of team interventions: Step-by-step guide to high performance teams.* Amherst, MA: HRD Press.

Gordon, J. (Ed.). (2003). *Pfeiffer's classic activities for building better teams.* San Francisco: Pfeiffer.

Gordon, J. (Ed.). (2004). *The Pfeiffer handbook of structured experiences: Learning activities for intact teams and workgroups.* San Francisco: Pfeiffer.

Gordon, J. (Ed.). (2004). *Pfeiffer's classic activities for interpersonal communication.* San Francisco: Pfeiffer.

Parker, G. (2002). *Team depot: A warehouse of over 585 tools to reassess, rejuvenate, and rehabilitate your team.* San Francisco: Pfeiffer.

Rees, F. (2005). *25 activities for developing team leaders.* San Francisco: Pfeiffer.

Senge, P. M., Roberts, C., Ross, R. B., Smith, B. J., & Kleiner, A. (1994). *The fifth discipline fieldbook.* New York: Doubleday Currency.

Sikes, S. (1995). *Feeding the zircon gorilla and other team building activities.* Tulsa, OK: Learning Unlimited.

Thiagarajan, S., & Parker, G. (1999). *Teamwork and teamplay: Games and activities for building and training teams.* San Francisco: Pfeiffer.

Ukens, L. L. (1997). *Working together: 55 team games.* San Francisco: Pfeiffer.

Weisbord, M. R. (1987). *Productive workplaces.* San Francisco: Jossey-Bass.

Varying Methodologies

Bowman, S. (1999). *Shake, rattle & roll: Using the ordinary to make your training extraordinary.* Glenbrook, NV: Bowperson.

Gesell, I. (1997). *Playing along: 37 group learning activities borrowed from improvisational theater.* Duluth, MN: Whole Person Associates.

Koppett, K. (2001). *Training to imagine: Practical improvisational theatre techniques to enhance creativity, teamwork, leadership, and learning.* Sterling, VA: Stylus.

VanGundy, A. B. (Ed.). (1998). *101 great games & activities.* San Francisco: Pfeiffer.

VanGundy, A. B. (2005). *101 activities for teaching creativity and problem solving.* San Francisco: Pfeiffer.

VanGundy, A. B., & Naiman, L. (2003). *Orchestrating collaboration at work: Using music, improv, storytelling, and other arts to improve teamwork.* San Francisco: Pfeiffer.

Wacker, M., & Silverman, L. (2003). *Stories trainers tell.* San Francisco: Pfeiffer.

References

Adler, N. J. (1997). *International dimensions of organizational behavior.* Cincinnati, OH: South-Western College Publishing.

Allison, M. J., & Kaye, J. (2005). *Strategic planning for nonprofit organizations: A practical guide and workbook.* Hoboken, NJ: Wiley.

Amabile, T. M. (1995). *KEYS: Assessing the climate for creativity.* Greensboro, NC: Center for Creative Leadership.

Amabile, T. M., Burnside, R. M., & Gryskiewicz, S. (1997). *User's manual for KEYS: Assessing the climate for creativity.* Greensboro, NC: Center for Creative Leadership.

Argyris, C. (1993). *Knowledge for action: A guide to overcoming barriers to organizational change.* San Francisco: Jossey-Bass.

Argyris, C., & Schön, D. A. (1974). *Theory in practice: Increasing professional effectiveness.* San Francisco: Jossey-Bass.

Barbazette, J. (2004). *Instant case studies: How to design, adapt, and use case studies in training.* San Francisco: Pfeiffer.

Bens, I. (2000). *Facilitating with ease! A step-by-step guidebook with customizable worksheets on CD-ROM.* San Francisco: Jossey-Bass.

Biech, E. (Ed.). (2001). *The Pfeiffer book of successful team-building tools.* San Francisco: Pfeiffer.

Block, P. (2001). *The flawless consulting fieldbook & companion: A guide to understanding your expertise.* San Francisco: Pfeiffer.

Bowman, S. (1999). *Shake, rattle & roll: Using the ordinary to make your training extraordinary.* Glenbrook, NV: Bowperson.

Brandt, R. C. (1986). *Flip charts: How to draw them and how to use them.* San Francisco: Pfeiffer.

Briggs, K. C., & Myers, I. B. (1998). *Myers-Briggs Type Indicator: Self-Scorable Form M.* Palo Alto, CA: Consulting Psychologists Press.

Brown, J. (2002). *The world café: A resource guide for hosting conversations that matter.* Mill Valley, CA: Whole Systems Associates.

Campbell, D. (2002a). *Campbell Leadership Descriptor.* San Francisco: Pfeiffer.

Campbell, D. (2002b). *Campbell Leadership Descriptor: Facilitator's guide.* San Francisco: Pfeiffer & Center for Creative Leadership.

Campbell, D. (2002c). *Campbell Leadership Descriptor: Participant workbook.* San Francisco: Pfeiffer & Center for Creative Leadership.

Cetti, C. E., & Craig, M. K. (2003). "Kaleidoscope: Team building through role expansion." In J. Gordon (Ed.), *Pfeiffer's classic activities for building better teams.* San Francisco: Pfeiffer.

Clarke, C. C., & Lipp, D. G. (1998). Conflict resolution for contrasting cultures. *Training & Development, 52*(12).

Collins, J. (2001). *Good to great: Why some companies make the leap . . . and others don't.* New York: HarperBusiness.

Consortium for Research on Emotional Intelligence in Organizations. (2005). *Emotional Competence Framework.* Retrieved January 2006 from http://www.eiconsortium.org

Cooperrider, D. L. (1995). Introduction to appreciative inquiry. In W. French & C. Bell (Eds.), *Organization development* (5th ed.). Upper Saddle River, NJ: Prentice Hall.

Cooperrider, D. L., Whitney, D. L., & Stavros, J. M. (2003). *Appreciative inquiry handbook: The first in a series of AI workbooks for leaders of change.* Bedford Heights, OH: Lakeshore Communications & San Francisco: Berrett-Koehler.

Cross, E. Y., Katz, J. H., Miller, F. A., & Seashore, E. W. (Eds.). (1994). *The promise of diversity: Over 40 voices discuss strategies for eliminating discrimination in organizations.* Burr Ridge, IL: Irwin.

Dana, D. (2003). "Retaliatory cycle: Introducing the elements of conflict." In J. Gordon (Ed.), *Pfeiffer's classic activities for managing conflict at work.* San Francisco: Pfeiffer.

Danko, D. P., & Cherry, R. (2003). "I hear that you . . . : Giving and receiving feedback." In J. Gordon (Ed.), *Pfeiffer's classic activities for building better teams.* San Francisco: Pfeiffer.

Day, L. B., & Blizzard, M. (2004). "Vacation schedule: Group problem solving." In J. Gordon (Ed.), *The Pfeiffer handbook of structured experiences: Learning activities for intact teams and workgroups.* San Francisco: Pfeiffer.

De Bono, E. (1994). *De Bono's thinking course* (rev. ed.). New York: Facts on File.

Dick, B. (1987). *Helping groups be effective: Skills, processes and concepts for group facilitation.* Chapel Hill, Australia: Interchange.

Drucker, P. (1999). *Management challenges for the 21st century.* New York: HarperBusiness.

Eggleton, C. H., & Rice, J. C. (1996). *The fieldbook of team interventions: Step-by-step guide to high performance teams.* Amherst, MA: HRD Press.

Epstein, R. (2000). *The big book of creativity games: Quick, fun activities for jumpstarting innovation.* New York: McGraw-Hill.

Garber, P. R. (2001). "TeamScores: Measuring and communicating performance." In E. Biech (Ed.), *The Pfeiffer book of successful team-building tools.* San Francisco: Pfeiffer.

Gardenswartz, L., Rowe, A., Digh, P., & Bennett, M. F. (2003). *The global diversity desk reference: Managing an international workforce.* San Francisco: Pfeiffer.

Gesell, I. (1997). *Playing along: 37 group learning activities borrowed from improvisational theater.* Duluth, MN: Whole Person Associates.

Goleman, D., Boyatzis, R., & McKee, A. (2001, December). Primal leadership: The hidden driver of great performance. *Harvard Business Review,* pp. 43–51.

Gordon, J. (Ed.). (2003a). *Pfeiffer's classic activities for building better teams.* San Francisco: Pfeiffer.

Gordon, J. (Ed.). (2003b). *Pfeiffer's classic activities for developing leaders.* San Francisco: Pfeiffer.

Gordon, J. (Ed.). (2003c). *Pfeiffer's classic activities for managing conflict at work.* San Francisco: Pfeiffer.

Gordon, J. (Ed.). (2004a). *Pfeiffer's classic activities for interpersonal communication.* San Francisco: Pfeiffer.

Gordon, J. (Ed.). (2004b). *The Pfeiffer handbook of structured experiences: Learning activities for intact teams and workgroups.* San Francisco: Pfeiffer.

Hale, J. (2002). *Performance-based evaluation: Tools and techniques to measure the impact of training.* San Francisco: Pfeiffer.

Hall, D. (1996). *Jump start your brain.* New York: Warner Books.

Hall, E. T. (1983). *The dance of life: The other dimension of time.* Garden City, NY: Anchor Press/Doubleday.

Hamel, G. (2000). *Leading the revolution.* Boston: Harvard Business School Press.

Hammond, S. A., & Royal, C. (Eds.). (1998). *Lessons from the field: Applying appreciative inquiry.* Plano, TX: Practical Press.

Ingvar, D. H. (1985). Memory of the future: An essay on the temporal organization of conscious awareness. *Human Neurobiology, 4,* 127–136.

Jones, J. E. (2004). "Role clarification: Developing a team norm." In J. Gordon (Ed.), *The Pfeiffer handbook of structured experiences: Learning activities for intact teams and work-groups*. San Francisco: Pfeiffer.

Kaufman, R., Oakley-Browne, H., Watkins, R., & Leigh, D. (2003). *Strategic planning for success: Aligning people, performance, and payoffs*. San Francisco: Pfeiffer.

Keen, P.G.W. (1997). *The process edge: Creating value where it counts*. Boston: Harvard Business School Press.

Kirton, M. (1991). *Kirton Adaption-Innovation Inventory*. Berkhamsted, UK: Occupational Research Centre.

Kiser, A. G. (1998). *Masterful facilitation*. New York: AMACOM.

Koppett, K. (2001). *Training to imagine: Practical improvisational theatre techniques to enhance creativity, teamwork, leadership, and learning*. Sterling, VA: Stylus.

Kouzes, J. M., & Posner, B. Z. (2001). *The leadership practices inventory*. San Francisco: Pfeiffer.

Maris, T. L. (2003). "Budget cutting: Conflict and consensus seeking." In J. Gordon (Ed.), *Pfeiffer's classic activities for managing conflict at work*. San Francisco: Pfeiffer.

Marshak, R. (1995, September 15–17). *The Introvert's Protection Act*. Lecture presented in the course "Organizational Dynamics," American University.

Maurer, R. (1996). *Beyond the wall of resistance*. Austin, TX: Bard Books.

McCall, M. W., & Lombardo, M. M. (1983). *Off the track: Why and how successful executives get derailed* (Technical Report No. 21). Greensboro, NC: Center for Creative Leadership.

Michalko, M. (1991). *Thinkertoys: A handbook of business creativity*. Berkeley, CA: Ten Speed Press.

Nevis, E. C. (1987). *Organization consulting: A gestalt approach*. Cleveland, OH: Gestalt Institute of Cleveland Press.

Nolan, T. M., Goodstein, L. D., & Pfeiffer, J. W. (1993). *Plan or die! 10 keys to organizational success*. San Francisco: Pfeiffer.

Oshry, B. (1996). *Seeing systems: Unlocking the mysteries of organizational life*. San Francisco: Berrett-Koehler.

Oshry, B. (1999). *Leading systems: Lessons from the power lab*. San Francisco: Berrett-Koehler.

Owen, H. (1997a). *Expanding our now: The story of open space technology*. San Francisco: Berrett-Koehler.

Owen, H. (1997b). *Open space technology: A user's guide*. San Francisco: Berrett-Koehler.

Palus, C. C., & Horth, D. M. (2001). *Visual explorer: Picturing approaches to complex challenges.* Greensboro, NC: Center for Creative Leadership.

Parker, G. (2002). *Team depot: A warehouse of over 585 tools to reassess, rejuvenate, and rehabilitate your team.* San Francisco: Pfeiffer.

Penderghast, T. F. (2003). "The genie's wish: Identifying and addressing team needs." In J. Gordon (Ed.), *Pfeiffer's classic activities for building better teams.* San Francisco: Pfeiffer.

Pike, B., & Solem, L. (2000). *50 creative training openers and energizers: Innovative ways to start your training with a bang!* San Francisco: Pfeiffer & Minneapolis: Creative Training Techniques Press.

Porter, E. H. (1996). *The Strength Deployment Inventory.* Carlsbad, CA: Personal Strengths.

Porter, M. E. (1996, November/December). What is strategy? *Harvard Business Review,* pp. 68–69.

Rees, F. (1998). *The facilitator excellence handbook: Helping people work creatively and productively together.* San Francisco: Pfeiffer.

Rees, F. (2005). *25 activities for developing team leaders.* San Francisco: Pfeiffer.

Richardson, T. (1997). "Transfer vehicle." In L. Solem & B. Pike, *50 creative training closers: Innovative ways to end your training with impact!* San Francisco: Pfeiffer.

Schwarz, R. M. (1994). *The skilled facilitator: Practical wisdom for developing effective groups.* San Francisco: Jossey-Bass.

Senge, P. M., Roberts, C., Ross, R. B., Smith, B. J., & Kleiner, A. (1994). *The fifth discipline fieldbook.* New York: Doubleday Currency.

Sikes, S. (1995). *Feeding the zircon gorilla and other team building activities.* Tulsa, OK: Learning Unlimited.

Silberman, M. L. (1999). *101 ways to make meetings active: Surefire ideas to engage your group.* San Francisco: Pfeiffer.

Slater, R. (2000). *The GE way fieldbook: Jack Welch's battle plan for corporate revolution.* New York: McGraw-Hill.

Solem, L., & Pike, B. (1997). *50 creative training closers: Innovative ways to end your training with impact!* San Francisco: Pfeiffer.

Thomas, K. W., & Kilmann, R. H. (2002). *Thomas-Kilmann Conflict Mode Instrument.* Palo Alto, CA: Consulting Psychologists Press.

Thiagarajan, S., & Parker, G. (1999). *Teamwork and teamplay: Games and activities for building and training teams.* San Francisco: Pfeiffer.

Tosca, E. (1997). *Communication Skills Profile*. San Francisco: Pfeiffer.

Ukens, L. L. (1997a). *Getting together: Icebreakers and group energizers*. San Francisco: Pfeiffer.

Ukens, L. L. (1997b). *Working together: 55 team games*. San Francisco: Pfeiffer.

Ukens, L. (2000). *Energize your audience! 75 quick activities that get them started . . . and keep them going*. San Francisco: Pfeiffer.

van der Heijden, K. (1996). *Scenarios: The art of strategic conversation*. Hoboken, NJ: Wiley.

VanGundy, A. (Ed.). (1998). *101 great games & activities*. San Francisco: Pfeiffer.

VanGundy, A. B. (2005). *101 activities for teaching creativity and problem solving*. San Francisco: Pfeiffer.

VanGundy, A. B., & Naiman, L. (2003). *Orchestrating collaboration at work: Using music, improv, storytelling, and other arts to improve teamwork*. San Francisco: Pfeiffer.

Varner, I., & Beamer, L. (1995). *Intercultural communication in the global workplace*. Burr Ridge, IL: Irwin.

Von Oech, R. (1986). *A kick in the seat of the pants*. New York: HarperCollins.

Von Oech, R. (1998). *A whack on the side of the head*. New York: Warner Books.

Wacker, M., & Silverman, L. (2003). *Stories trainers tell*. San Francisco: Pfeiffer.

Watkins, J., & Mohr, B. (2001). *Appreciative inquiry: Change at the speed of imagination*. San Francisco: Pfeiffer.

Weisbord, M. R. (1987). *Productive workplaces*. San Francisco: Jossey-Bass.

Weisbord, M. R., & Janoff, S. (1995). *Future search: An action guide to finding common ground in organizations and communities*. San Francisco: Berrett-Koehler.

Westcott, J., & Landau, J. H. (1997). *A picture's worth 1,000 words: A workbook for visual communications*. San Francisco: Pfeiffer.

Wood, C. (Ed.). (1991). *The complete rhyming dictionary*. New York: Bantam Doubleday Dell.

Young, S. D. (1991). *The new comprehensive American rhyming dictionary*. New York: Avon Books.

Index

A

Abandonment retreat: consensus on strategy in, 395; evaluating work processes in, 395; goal of, 394; guidelines, 394–396; obstacles to change in, 395–396; as precursor to other retreats, 394; suggested activities for, 397

Action plan: budget and resource implications of, 189–190; design, 84–85; format, 185–192; and group goals, 185–186; and implementation responsibility, 188–189; measures and observable results in, 186–187; "necessary and sufficient" test in, 188; nonparticipants and, 85; obstacles and resistance to, 191–192; setting targets and deadlines for, 191; time to prepare, 65, 190

Action steps: defined, 425; prioritizing, 178–179

Activity icons, explained, 2

Adler, N. J., 124

Administrator, retreat responsibilities of, 41–42

Allison, M., 194, 195, 375

Alport, G., 298

Amabile, T. M., 57

Analytic thinking, creativity and, 326–327

Appreciative inquiry (AI), 29–30

Argyris, C., 107, 250

B

Barbazette, J., 96

Beamer, L., 124

Behavioral assessment instruments, skillful use of 57–59

Benchmarking studies, 96–97

Bennett, M. F., 124

Bens, I., 113, 115, 162

Beyond the Wall of Resistance, 151–152

Biech, E., 281

Big Kahuna Effect, 63, 455

Blizzard, M., 386

Block, P., 21

Board retreats: and board-staff dynamics, 22, 373; corporate, 373–374; and mandated accountability, 373; suggested activities for, 374, 375–376. *See also* Nonprofit board retreats

Body language, 114

Bowman, S., 99

Boyatzis, R., 454

Brandt, R. C., 52, 134

Breaches of confidence, interventions dealing with, 158

Breakout groups: avoiding repetition in, 91; composition and size of, 90, 91–92; room arrangements for, 50

Briefing book, 66

Briggs, K. C., 58

Brown, J., 26, 27

Burnside, R. M., 57

C

Campbell, D., 57

Campbell Leadership Descriptor, 57

Case studies, usefulness of, 97

Center for Creative Leadership's Leading Creatively program, 347, 410

Centers of excellence, identifying, 216, 217

Cetti, C. E., 300, 301

Cherry, R., 305

Circus techniques, 102

Clarke, C. C., 128

Client: defined, 8; covert agenda of, 13–14; expectations of, 434; and facilitator selection, 435–436; facilitator's boss as, 17, 436; leadership style, feedback on, 436; opening remarks of, 115; partnering effectively with, 17–21; pre-retreat interview of, 37; ranking of, 204–206; as retreat convener and overseer, 40; as retreat facilitator, 435; and retreat goals and expectations, 434, 435; retreat planning input and decisions of, 39–40, 437–452

Closure. See Formal retreat closure

Co-facilitation, 41; benefits of, 47, 134; challenges in, 122–123; handling disagreements in, 123; internal-external partnerships in, 48–49; negotiations for, 47–48

Collaborative dialogue, retreat format for, 26–27

Collage activity, 100–101

Collins, J., 195, 198

Communication Skills Profile, 57

Communication, effective setups for, 50

Conflict. *See* Participant disagreement

Consensus: in abandonment retreat, 395; advantages and disadvantages of, 166–167; common misperceptions of, 163; and trust issues, 167; and unanimous consent, 167

Controversial issues, small-group activities for addressing, 261–265

Conversations. *See* Group discussions

Cooperrider, D. L., 29, 30

Corporate board retreats. *See* Board retreats

Craig, M. K., 300

Creative thinking skills: development, resources for, 326; types of thinking involved in, 326–328

Creativity retreat, 24, 325–367; adopting multiple perspectives in, 355–356; challenging assumptions in, 352–354; evaluating ideas in, 363–367; idea–generation technique used in, 334–338; mental limbering activities in, 329–332; minimizing groupthink in, 346–351; nonjudgmentalism in, 358–360; participants' fears in, 356; questioning technique in, 352; realistic risk assessment in, 360–362; thinking dimensions utilized in, 326–327; traditional brainstorming alternatives in, 333–342

Cross, E., 124

Cross-cultural differences, 123–132; areas of conflict in, 124–125; in communication styles, 125; in language/language use, 129; managing, 130–132; in perspectives and orientations, 125–129; physical manifestations of, 128, 130; seven-step model for dealing with, 128

Culture change retreat, 251–275; addressing sensitive issues in, 261–265; culture assessment activities in, 253–260; diagnostic activity in, 252, 253–254; and obstacles to change, 272–274; perceptions versus observations in, 270; performance rewards assessment in, 267–269; positive and supportive cultural focus in, 271; types of activities in, 251

D

Dana, D., 314

Dance of Life: The Other Dimension of Time, The, 126

Danko, D. P., 305

Day, L. B., 386

Decision making. *See* Group decision making

Dick, B., 138

Difficult situations, formula for intervening in, 137–138

Digh, P., 124

Diversity, types of, 123. *See also* Cross-cultural differences

Drawing, as individual or group activity, 100–101

Drucker, P., 195, 394

E

EdgeWork® (simulation), 28

Eggleton, C. H., 281, 297

Emotional leadership, concept of, 454–455

Emotional reactions, 8; facilitator responses to, 147–150

Energy check-in, 77

Energy voting, 179

Epstein, R., 100, 326

Executive authority, in group decision making, 164

Executive retreats, 22

F

Facilitator Excellence Handbook, The, 133, 134

Facilitator interventions: common language of, 159; describe-discuss-engage sequence in, 137–138; in difficult and/or unanticipated situations, 137–159; for disruptive participants, 142; for escalating disagreements, 156–158; for hostile participants, 145–146; inform-invite strategy in, 138; for keeping conversations on track, 139–140; nonjudgmentalism in, 138; questioning techniques in, 108–109; rules for 137–138; situation-specific strategies in, 139–159; for turf issues, 146

Facilitator role(s): as active contributor, 19–20; agreement on, 107, 436; dual, 41; post-retreat, 426–427; primary, 105; qualities required in, 435–436. *See also* Retreat facilitation

Facilitator: external, 49; group resistance to, 158–159; internal, 41; listening skills of, 108; mental preparation of, 54–55; neutrality of, 435; toolkit, 54

Feedback report, 80–83

Feedback, 78–83; client, 80, 436; and cultural sensitivity, 127; exercises, 305–309; organization and presentation of, 80–83; reasons for, 79; for senior executives, 275; tips for handling, 111

Fifth Discipline Fieldbook, 186

Fishbowl technique, 95

Fixed-format retreats: certification requirements for, 24; examples of, 25–32; pitfalls of, 31–32; versus tailor-made retreats, 24

Flip chart(s): information, in retreat report, 425, 426; "parking lot," 134; preparing and managing, 51; as record of retreat, 42; transcribing, 68–69

Flip Charts: How to Draw Them and How to Use Them, 134

Focus groups, information collection in, 35

Future Search® (large system intervention), 25, 29

G

Garber, P. R., 391

Gardenswartz, L., 124, 126, 128, 130, 131

General Electric's Work-Out™ program, 24, 31

Gesell, I., 98

Global Diversity Desk Reference, 124, 130

Goleman, D., 454

Good to Great, 198

Goodstein, L. D., 224, 225

Gripe session, retreat as, 149–150

Ground rules, 50; and emotional issues, 150; enforcement of, 137; establishment of, 73–74; executive compliance with, 143–144; setting, 73–74; suggested norms for, 74

Group assignment methods, 52–53

Group decision making, 161–192; and action options/planning, 183–192; categorizing and culling of information in, 178; by coin toss or dice roll, 167, 168; compromise in, 164, 166; by consensus, 163, 166–167; criteria evaluation in, 180–182; by default, 165; difficult choices in, 64; executive/consultative executive authority in, 164; and group's mandate, 83–84; and kinds of decisions, 169; limitations on, 84, 178; majority rule in, 164–165; methods and types of, 163–167; minority activist tactics in, 165–166; "moving right along" and, 165; poor, symptoms of, 162; prioritizing action steps in, 178–179; quality rating in, 175–177; and ranking by relative importance, 169–170; sensitive information and, 437; sequencing actions in, 183; unanimous consent in, 163, 167

Group discussions: avoidance of tough issues in, 142–143; as candid dialogue, 14; disruptions in, 142; facilitated, 90, 139–143; invented, 357; off-track, 139–140; open and explicit, 162; simultaneous, 90; whole group, 90

Gryskiewicz, S., 57

Guided visualization, 102–103

H

Hale, J., 228

Hall, D., 100, 213, 326

Hall, E., 126

Hamel, G., 195

Hammond, S. A., 30

Hedgehog Concept, 198

Helping Groups Be Effective: Skills, Process and Concepts for Group Facilitation, 138

Horth, D. M., 101

Humor, misuse of, 144–145

I

Icebreakers, avoidance of, 77

Icons, used in text, 2

Idea evaluation, 326–327

Individual check-in: abbreviated (30–Second Check–in) process of, 77; client modeling of, 75–76; and energy check-

in, 77; as icebreaker, 77–78; methods, 76; and self-introduction, 74–75

Informational reports, pre–retreat, 93

Informational sessions, 65

Inform-invite confrontation strategy, 138

Ingvar, D. H., 224

Innovation. *See* Creative thinking; Creativity retreat

Interdepartmental retreats, 22

Internal facilitator, 17; and content knowledge, 117; partnering with, 429

Interventions. *See* Facilitator interventions

Interviews, pre-retreat, 33–38; feedback on, 78; importance of, 62; sample questions for, 38; suggestions for conducting, 36–37; telephone, 35, 37

Introvert's Protection Act, 73, 76

J

Janoff, S., 25

Jones, J. E., 298

Judging, in creative thinking, 326–327

K

Katz, J. H., 124

Kaufman, R., 195

Kaye, J., 194, 195, 375

Keen, P.G.W., 208, 230

KEYS: Assessing the Climate for Creativity (assessment instrument), 57

Kilmann, R. H., 59

Kirton, M., 57

Kirton Adaptation-Innovation Inventory (KAI), 57

Kiser, A. G., 49, 105–106

Kleiner, A., 186, 220

Koppett, K., 98

Kouzes, J. M., 58

L

Landau, J. H., 52, 134

Large system interventions, 24, 25–26

Leaders. *See* Organization leaders

Leadership assessment instruments, recommendations for, 389

Leadership Practices Inventory (LPI), 58

Leading the Revolution, 440

Leisure activities, 451

Lipp, D. G., 128

Lombardo, M. M., 469

M

Majority rule: consensus and, 13; disadvantages of using, 164–165

Maris, T. L., 379

Markers, tips for provision of, 51

Marshak, R., 73

Masterful Facilitation, 105

Maurer, R., 151

MBTI behavioral assessment instrument, and team building, 58

McCall, M. W., 469

McKee, A., 454

Meals: planning for, 450–451; timing of, 50

Meeting room: pre-retreat inspection of, 55; setup, conversation-friendly, 50

Mentoring, 429

Metaphor: music as, 98; and 30–Second Check-In response, 77; types and uses of, 99–100

Michalko, M., 100, 326

Miller, F. A., 124

Minorities, teasing of, 144–145. *See also* Culture change retreat

Mission statements, and retreat planning, 197, 199

Mohr, B. J., 30

Morale improvement, 13

Music and rhythm, metaphorical possibilities of, 98

Myers, I. B., 58

Myers-Briggs Type Indicator®, 58

N

Naiman, L., 98, 101, 326

Nametags, recommendations for, 50–51, 52–53

Nevis, E. C., 117

Nolan, T. M., 195, 224, 225

Nonparticipants: and action planning, 85; implementation role of, 465, 466; sharing retreat information with, 45–46, 463–464

About the Authors

Merianne Liteman is president of Liteman Rosse, a consulting firm that specializes in offsite retreats and workshops on strategic planning, creative thinking, leadership development, and communication skills.

She has designed and conducted retreats and workshops in the United States and Latin America, Africa, Canada, and Europe. She speaks regularly at national and international conferences and has been published and profiled by national journals interested in organizational effectiveness issues. She conducts a retreat design and facilitation institute for internal facilitators and a regular leadership seminar for clients such as the U.S. Department of State and the World Bank. Her retreat clients include Mitsubishi Electric America; FannieMae; the Museum of Fine Arts, Boston; the International Monetary Fund; the Violence Prevention Network of Ghana; the U.S. Military Academy at West Point; the Red Cross of Mexico; the YMCA of Uruguay; and the U.S. Consumer Products Safety Commission.

Merianne has a master's degree in organization development from American University and has completed a postgraduate training program in facilitation at the same institution. She is a member of the NTL Institute for Applied Behavioral Science.

She is also the coauthor of the book *Retreats That Work: Designing and Conducting Effective Offsites for Groups and Organizations* (Pfeiffer, 2003), and the author of *Planning for Succession: A Toolkit for Board Members and Staff of Nonprofit Organizations* (IAAF, 2003).

Sheila Campbell is president of Wild Blue Yonder, a consulting firm centered around creative thinking, strategy, change, organization behavior, and corporate culture.

She designs and leads offsite retreats for numerous organizations in the United States, Canada, and the Far East. Her retreat clients include the Museum of Fine Arts, Boston; National Geographic Television; the Goodyear Tire and Rubber Co.; the U.S. Department of Energy; and Kodak. She also conducts a retreat design and facilitation institute for internal facilitators, as well as training sessions on creativity in the workplace, strategic thinking, and leadership skills for the World Bank. Other clients include the American Association of Advertising Agencies, FannieMae, OppenheimerFunds, AlliedSignal, and *Business Week* and *Barron's* magazines.

Sheila has taught both strategy and creativity in the MBA program at Johns Hopkins University and has served on the faculty of the University of Maryland and as director of the Mid-Atlantic Institute for Advanced Advertising Studies, cosponsored by the American Association of Advertising Agencies (AAAA). Also for AAAA, she conducts workshops in strategic planning and account management relationships for ad agency groups around the country.

She has a master's degree in organization development from American University and is the coauthor of the book *Retreats That Work: Designing and Conducting Effective Offsites for Groups and Organizations* (Pfeiffer, 2003).

Jeff Liteman is vice president of Liteman Rosse, a consulting firm that specializes in organization effectiveness, leadership development, strategic planning, creative thinking, and retreat design and facilitation.

He has consulted to organizations in the public, private, and nonprofit sectors and has developed and conducted workshops focusing on increasing creativity and improving communication to foster more productive and satisfying workplaces. His clients include WBEZ/Chicago Public Radio, the U.S. Army, National Defense University, the U.S. Department of Agriculture, FannieMae, the U.S. Consumer Product Safety Commission, the U.S. Military Academy at West Point, Mitsubishi Electric America, the Metropolitan Washington Airports Authority, and the Violence Prevention Network of Ghana. He also has consulted to the U.S. Department of State and regularly teaches leadership skills at the State Department's Foreign Service Institute.

A former member of the U.S. Foreign Service, he has been profiled by *Government Executive* magazine and published in several U.S. and foreign publications, including the *Washington Post,* the *Los Angeles Times,* the *Miami Herald,* and *Vital Speeches of the Day.*

Jeff received B.S. and M.A. degrees in psychology, sociology, and international relations from the University of Illinois, and a professional certificate in organization development from Georgetown University.

How to Use the CD-ROM

System Requirements

PC with Microsoft Windows 98SE or later
Mac with Apple OS version 8.6 or later

Using the CD With Windows

To view the items located on the CD, follow these steps:

1. Insert the CD into your computer's CD-ROM drive.

2. A window appears with the following options:

   Contents: Allows you to view the files included on the CD-ROM.

   Software: Allows you to install useful software from the CD-ROM.

   Links: Displays a hyperlinked page of Web sites.

   Author: Displays a page with information about the author(s).

   Contact Us: Displays a page with information on contacting the publisher or author.

   Help: Displays a page with information on using the CD.

   Exit: Closes the interface window.

If you do not have autorun enabled, or if the autorun window does not appear, follow these steps to access the CD:

1. Click Start -› Run.

2. In the dialog box that appears, type d:‹<\\><\\>›start.exe, where d is the letter of your CD-ROM drive. This brings up the autorun window described in the preceding set of steps.

3. Choose the desired option from the menu. (See Step 2 in the preceding list for a description of these options.)

In Case of Trouble

If you experience difficulty using the CD-ROM, please follow these steps:

1. Make sure your hardware and systems configurations conform to the systems requirements noted under "System Requirements" above.

2. Review the installation procedure for your type of hardware and operating system. It is possible to reinstall the software if necessary.

To speak with someone in Product Technical Support, call 800-762-2974 or 317-572-3994 Monday through Friday from 8:30 a.m. to 5:00 p.m. EST. You can also contact Product Technical Support and get support information through our Web site at www.wiley.com/techsupport.

Before calling or writing, please have the following information available:

- Type of computer and operating system.
- Any error messages displayed.
- Complete description of the problem.

It is best if you are sitting at your computer when making the call.

What will you find on pfeiffer.com?

- The best in workplace performance solutions for training and HR professionals

- Downloadable training tools, exercises, and content

- Web-exclusive offers

- Training tips, articles, and news

- Seamless on-line ordering

- Author guidelines, information on becoming a Pfeiffer Affiliate, and much more

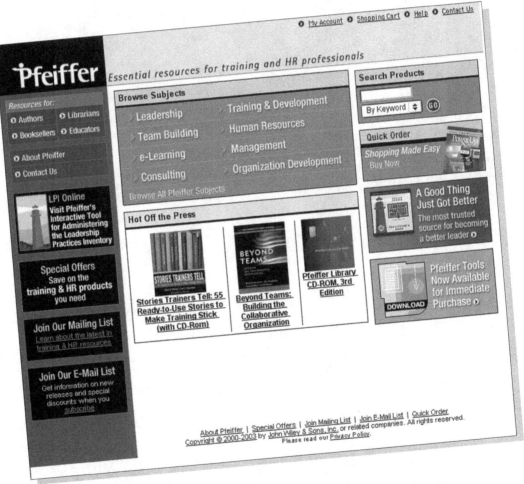

Discover more at www.pfeiffer.com